Theory of Culture

New Directions in Cultural Analysis
Edited by Robert Wuthnow

Theory of Culture

EDITED BY

Richard Münch
and Neil J. Smelser

UNIVERSITY OF CALIFORNIA PRESS

Berkeley / Los Angeles / Oxford

Dedicated, by his colleagues,
to the memory of Hans Haferkamp

University of California Press
Berkeley and Los Angeles, California

University of California Press, Ltd.
Oxford, England

© 1992 by
The Regents of the University of California

Library of Congress Cataloging-in-Publication Data

Theory of culture / edited by Richard Münch and Neil J. Smelser.
    p.   cm. — (New directions in cultural analysis : 2)
    Based on papers from a conference held July 23–25, 1988 in
Bremen, sponsored by the Theory Sections of the American
Sociological Association and the German Sociological Association.
    Includes bibliographical references and index.
    ISBN 0–520–07598–6 (cloth : alk. paper). — ISBN
0–520–07599–4 (paper : alk. paper)
    1. Culture—Congresses. 2. Cultural policy—Congresses.
3. Germany (West)—Cultural policy—Congresses. I. Münch,
Richard, 1945– . II. Smelser, Neil J. III. American
Sociological Association. Theory Section. IV. Deutsche
Gesellschaft für Soziologie. Sektion Soziologische Theorien.
V. Series.
HM101.T475   1992
306—dc20   91–37737
                                     CIP

Printed in the United States of America

9 8 7 6 5 4 3 2

The paper used in this publication meets the minimum requirements
of American National Standard for Information Sciences—
Permanence of Paper for Printed Library Materials, ANSI Z39.48–
1984. ⊚

Contents

Preface

Richard Münch and Neil J. Smelser

This volume is the intellectual product of a conference on the theory of culture held in Bremen on 23–25 July 1988. It was sponsored by the Theory Sections of the American Sociological Association and the German Sociological Association and made possible by a grant from the Volkswagen Foundation.

The Bremen conference was the third such event. An initial conference was held in Giessen in June 1984 and resulted in the publication of *The Micro-Macro Link* (Alexander, Giesen, Münch, and Smelser 1987). The second was held in Berkeley on 26–28 August 1986 and resulted in the publication of *Social Change and Modernity* (Haferkamp and Smelser 1991). Those primarily involved in planning the Bremen conference were Jeffrey Alexander, Bernard Giesen, Hans Haferkamp, Richard Münch, and Neil Smelser. Haferkamp and Smelser agreed to be the principal organizers for the conference. This arrangement was interrupted by Haferkamp's tragic death in a drowning accident in the summer of 1987. Münch subsequently took up the collaboration with Smelser. The choice of Bremen—Haferkamp's home institution—and the dedication of this volume reflect the collective appreciation of both the work and the person of Hans Haferkamp on the part of German and American social theorists.

When the planners of the Bremen conference met originally to plan its theme, there appeared almost a spontaneous consensus: it should be on the theory of culture. That consensus was based on an appreciation, reached more or less independently by each planner, that the sociology of culture is one of those intellectual areas that has experienced a striking revitalization in both Europe and America over the past fifteen years or so.

That this vitality continues to this moment and promises to endure makes publication of this volume timely. The origins of the revitalization of the sociology of culture are complex, and we do not intend to analyze that episode of recent intellectual history in this volume. We might mention, however, a few of the threads:

—The rise of "movements" of cultural analysis, especially deconstructionism and semiotics, that penetrated many of the disciplines of social-scientific and humanistic study.
—The premium placed on the analysis of "meaning" that accompanied the phenomenological impulse in the "microsociological revolution" of the 1960s and 1970s.
—The decline of the materialist impulse in general and the classical Marxian emphasis in particular, especially in contemporary European scholarship.
—The simultaneous resuscitation of Marxian scholars such as Gramsci (1971), who insisted on the independence of the cultural factor in the historical process.
—The work of such individuals as Clifford Geertz (1973), Raymond Williams (1958, 1965, 1977), and Pierre Bourdieu (1984, 1990), and groups of scholars they influenced.

Some of these threads find expression in the essays composing this volume. In chapter 6, for example, Wuthnow reviews the efforts of several neo-Marxist scholars who have attempted to reconcile the Marxist stress on "external" (that is, economic and social-structural) determinants of cultural life with the "autonomous" status of culture as revealed by the "inner logic" of its texts. In chapter 11, Alexander enters the polemic over the centrality of "meaning" as a defining characteristic of culture. At the same time, a number of long-standing issues in cultural analysis appear as well, for example, Kalberg's and Eder's examinations (from different standpoints) of the relevance of Weber's thesis on Protestantism and the work ethic in contemporary Western German society.

Consistent with the theme of *theory* of culture that framed the Bremen conference, almost half of this volume contains contributions that are essentially theoretical. These chapters constitute part one. Smelser's introductory chapter picks up the theme of cultural coherence and incoherence, reviews its status in anthropological and sociological writings, and offers a theoretical critique of and suggestions for reformulation. Chapters 2 and 3 offer discussions of classical issues in the social-scientific study of culture. Halton calls for a resuscitation of the biological linkages of culture, using the human dream as a peculiarly apt avenue of access to those linkages. Eisenstadt addresses the long-standing issue of the stabilizing and order-maintaining functions of culture (rooted especially in Durkheim's sociology of religion) and its changing and transformative functions (rooted especially in Weber's sociology of religion). Chapters 4 through 6 are expository and critical of historical figures and traditions of the analysis of culture. Schmid details the changing conceptions of culture in the work of Parsons and subjects these changes to a critical review. Weiss takes up the theme—derived mainly from the writings of Jacob Burckhardt—of how culture comes to be represented in its special carrying agents (charismatic figures, geniuses, political leaders) and how these leaders represent it. And Wuthnow subjects the works of Eagleton, Jameson, and Bakhtin—all neo-Marxist in orientation—to an analysis of how they deal with the enduring and controversial issues of materialism, domination, and the degree of independence and autonomy of culture in society.

Parts 2 to 4 examine the themes of culture's relations with the polity, the stratification system, and the economic order. These chapters are also theoretical in orientation, but for the most part they incorporate systematic empirical data. In chapter 7, Swanson, using aggregative/correlational techniques on a large sample of societies, takes as his major "dependent variable" the degree to which cultures envision a collective purpose for their societies and relates this purpose to a variety of social-structural features of those societies that are conducive or nonconducive to the presence of that vision. In chapter 8, Renate Mayntz presents an empirical analysis—based on interviews with legislators—of the kinds of norms that govern the public and private behavior of legislators in the Federal Republic of Germany and thus contributes to the ongoing dialogue about political culture.

Chapter 9, by Richard Münch, begins with the theoretical formulations of Parsons. Münch isolates several hypotheses from Parsons's theory of action and subjects them to an empirical examination in light of patterns of social inequality in the Federal Republic of Germany. The work of Featherstone, appearing in chapter 10, is a valuable assessment and extension of the German critical school and the British cultural studies traditions. It deals especially with the idea of the production and consumption of culture (the "culture industry") and presses the argument that the organization of cultural consumption lies in the dynamics of maintaining and striving for status.

Jeffrey Alexander's essay (chapter 11) comments on a number of recent formulations of culture, but his main empirical issue is the significance of the recent "computer revolution" in advanced industrial countries. Alexander is constrained to show the balance between the rational/magical and the apocalyptic themes that have arisen as the computer has established itself as a regular feature of organized life. The concluding chapters deal with a contemporary issue in West German society, namely the de-coupling of the work ethic from definitions of prestige and self-worth. Both Kalberg and Eder attack the problems of the apparent decline of work and the work ethic and the rise of leisure in the Federal Republic of Germany. They approach those phenomena, however, from different directions. Kalberg, in chapter 12, analyzes the de-coupling as an emerging result of the convergence of a diversity of economic, social, and political changes over the past century or more. In chapter 13, Eder, working more in the context of the neo-Marxian theory of crises of capitalism, treats the "de-coupling" as a kind of contradiction between the social-structural level (where work appears to be more central and essential) and the cultural level (where it appears to be decreasing). Eder's chapter is not so much an analysis of cultural change as it is an account of a crisis of class, especially the working class. Both Kalberg's and Eder's accounts of the culture of work in West Germany promise to be vastly complicated by the absorption of the East German labor force into the context of a unified Germany.

REFERENCES

Alexander, J., Giesen, B., Münch, R., and Smelser, N. J., eds. 1987. *The Micro-Macro Link*. Berkeley and Los Angeles: University of California Press.

Bourdieu, P. 1984. *Distinction*. Translated by Richard Nice. Cambridge: Harvard University Press.

———. 1990. *The Logic of Practice*. Stanford: Stanford University Press.

Geertz, C. 1973. *The Interpretation of Cultures: Selected Essays*. New York: Basic Books.

Gramsci, A. 1971. *Selections from the Prison Notebooks*. Edited and translated by Quintin Hoare and Geoffrey Nowell Smith. New York: International Publishers.

Haferkamp, H. and Smelser, N. J. 1991. *Social Change and Modernity*. Berkeley and Los Angeles: University of California Press.

Williams, R. 1958. *Culture and Society*. New York: Columbia University Press.

———. 1965. *The Long Revolution*. Harmondsworth: Penguin.

———. 1977. *Marxism and Literature*. New York: Oxford University Press.

PART ONE

Theory of Culture

1

Culture: Coherent or Incoherent

Neil J. Smelser

My objectives in this introductory chapter are the following:

—to examine some of the dimensions of the concept of culture, focusing on the issue of its degree of coherence or incoherence;

—to identify some methodological problems in the description and employment of the concept of culture, including a major methodological fallacy in the characterization of its coherence and incoherence;

—to review some imputed causes of cultural coherence;

—to suggest several resolutions of the problems revealed.

Major Dimensions of Cultural Analysis

Whatever the range of differences in the conceptualization of culture, the idea remains an essential one in the behavioral and social sciences. For decades it has been regarded as the central organizing base for social anthropology (sometimes, indeed, called *cultural anthropology*) and is one of the several major objects of study and tools for explanation in sociology and political science (Smelser 1968), as the terms *subculture, counterculture, organizational culture, civic culture,* and *political culture* indicate. Conspicuous exceptions to this generalization are sociobiology and its forebears, which tend to link culture to genetic or other biological factors, materialism in its Marxist and other guises, which tends to reduce culture to other forces, and rational-choice theory and its utilitarian forebears, which tend to freeze culture into simplified assumptions about tastes and preferences. These exceptions noted, the centrality of the concept must be affirmed.

Before the end of the nineteenth century, many social philosophers and historians tended to treat culture—it was not always called that—as a kind of idea, or spirit, or *Geist* that provided a basis for characterizing a society, denoting its advancement and distinctiveness, and capturing its integrity. Needless to say, such an approach almost dictated the corollary assumption that each civilization's culture possessed a coherent unity, or pattern, that encompassed its religious, philosophical, or aesthetic underpinnings. By further implication, the distinctive culture of society was something of an elitist conception, communicating that it was carried by the literate, urbane, self-conscious (and, by assumption, prestigious and powerful) classes in society; a society's culture was its "high" culture, only later to be distinguished from its "folk," or "popular," culture. This idea of culture continued to find expression in the twentieth century, for example in T. S. Eliot's ideas on culture and Christian civilization (1939, 1944).

The history of the idea of culture is multifaceted and includes a chapter on how its actual differentiation into "high" and "folk," or "culture" and "mass culture," was a part of the fabric of stratification and domination in various European societies.[1] A second theme, important for this essay, is the evolution of the term in anthropology in the late nineteenth century. Intellectual leaders in anthropology made the concept more inclusive than simply that of a coherent set of values and ideas. Tylor (1920), for example, expanded the notion to encompass "that complex whole which includes knowledge, belief, art, morals, law, custom, and any other capabilities and habits acquired by man as a member of society" (1). Lowie's definition was similar and excluded only "those numerous traits acquired otherwise, mainly by biological heredity" (1934, 3). Another feature of classical anthropological usage was that culture tended to be regarded as undifferentiated along class or other principles of social division; it was a concept that applied to whole societies. That formulation is perhaps understandable given that anthropology was then concentrating on simple, undifferentiated societies. It was certainly not consistent, however, with the growing differentiation and diversification of Western societies, which were then experiencing the decline of orthodox religions, cultural mixing through migration, and internal class divisions associated with urbanization and industrialization.

In any event, the intellectual development in classical anthropology toward a conceptualization of culture as inclusive and common—as contrasted with exclusive and carried by elite cultural agents—set the stage for two questions that have shaped (or perhaps beset) thinking and debates about culture by social scientists for a century. First, how unified or coherent are cultures? And second, to what degree does a society's population share, or have consensus of, values and other ingredients of culture? (The two questions, while interrelated, are distinguishable from one another. The first concerns the issue of the integrity or integration of elements; the second concerns their degree of sharedness. A given cultural system may be tightly organized and coherent and either shared or not shared. The same may be true of a cultural system that is vague and inchoate. The dimensions of coherence and consensus thus can be conceptualized as constituting marginals for a fourfold table, and there are feasible entries for all four cells.)

Anthropologists and others began early to disagree on the question of coherence. At one extreme was Tylor's characterization of culture as a thing of "shreds and patches," which suggested a miscellaneous congeries of religion, philosophy, technology, customs, and artifacts held together by no principle whatsoever. (In a way it seemed "natural" that Tylor, opting for such an inclusive definition of culture, would be pushed in the direction of regarding it as incoherent.) Another, more active, form of incoherence was found in Durkheim's work on *anomie* (1951 [1897]), conceived as a state of "normlessness," whereby society did not set any limits to the desires of individuals by providing any kind of systematic expectations to regulate them. Under anomic conditions there appeared to be no basis for cultural order, and, according to Durkheim, the results of anomie were likely to be social and individual pathology.

Another group of thinkers could be found at the "coherence" end of the spectrum. Evolutionists like Morgan (1963 [1877]) and Engels (1964)—who adapted his thought—found a definite principle of cultural unity in the ingredients of a culture at each of several developmental stages of civilization (savagery, barbarism, and so on). The principle, consistent with materialist principles, was that a given level of technology called for a certain kind of religion, family structure, stratification, and other customs and mores. Each stage and substage thus manifested a coherent cultural "package." In another formulation Durkheim (1956

[1925]) found a unified cultural principle in every civilization, perpetrated through its educational system: "[in] the cities of Greece and Rome, education trained the individual to subordinate himself blindly to the collectivity, to become the creature of society . . . [in] the Middle Ages education was above all Christian; in the Renaissance it assumes a more lay and literary character." Perhaps the most extreme formulation of cultural unity appeared in the work of Sorokin (1937), who grouped all the major facets of a culture under a single organizing principle. For example, in a "sensate" culture, which emphasizes the external senses as contrasted with the internal spirit, the principles of secularism, empiricism, science, philosophical realism, utilitarianism, and hedonism all fell together in one logico-meaningful whole.

Benedict (1934), often regarded above all as the advocate of a position of cultural integration, actually manifested an intermediate position on this question. On the one hand, she found any given culture to be "permeated by . . . one dominating idea" (3); examples were the Dionysian and the Apollonian. This integration was achieved through a complex process of selection and exclusion: "Gothic architecture, beginning in what was hardly more than a preference for attitude and light, became, by the operation of some canon of taste that developed within its technique, the unique and homogeneous art of the thirteenth century. It discarded elements that were incongruous, modified others to its purposes, and invented others that accorded with its taste" (47). At the same time, Benedict found extreme incoherence in some cultures: "Like certain individuals, certain social orders do not subordinate activities to a ruling motivation. They scatter. If at one moment they appear to be pursuing certain ends, at another they are off on some tangent apparently inconsistent with all that had gone before, which gives no clue to activity that will come after" (223). The contrast between coherent and incoherent was associated in Benedict's mind with the contrast between simple cultures, such as the Zuñi and Kwakiuitl, and modern Western cultures. In particular, she described "our own society" as "an extreme example of lack of integration" (229).

Such were some of the divergences in early twentieth-century anthropology on the issue of cultural coherence and incoherence. That issue survives today, although not always in the same terms. For example, in his discussion of "common sense," Geertz (1983) argued that one could not demonstrate that it was a culture by cataloging its content because it was not formally organized—it was "antiheap wisdom." He added, science, art, ideology, law, religion, technology, mathematics, even nowadays ethics and epistemology, seem genuine enough genres of cultural expression to ask . . . to what degree other peoples possess them, and to the degree that they do possess them what form they take, and given the form they take what light has that to shed on our own versions of them. But this is still not true of common sense. Common sense seems to us what is left over when all these more articulated sorts of symbol systems have exhausted their tasks, what remains of reason when its more sophisticated achievements are set aside (92).

In an even more recent formulation, Merelman (1984) regarded the degree of cultural coherence as *the* important element of American culture in explaining much about its class and political life. Modern American culture, he argued, is a "loosely bounded fabric", ill-organized, permeable, inconsistent, and tolerant of ambiguity. He regarded it as having arisen in part from the decline of three visions of American culture—puritan, democratic, and class-based—and from several distinctive historical experiences such as individualism, minimal age-grading, and immigration. The schools and the media are major agents in perpetrating loose-boundedness in culture. As his main thesis, Merelman argued that a loosely bounded culture obfuscates the stark division of labor, hierarchy, and fixity of the American social structure—in fact, a "gap between American social structure and American culture" (204). In addition, a loosely bounded culture made political mobilization for collective goals difficult and posed special difficulties for political regimes to legitimize themselves. In this formulation, the actual cultural content seems to take second place to its mode of organization as a determinant of sociopolitical life.

Two other theoretical issues, closely related to coherence, concern how perfectly cultures are realized or reproduced in the individual and in the social structure. With respect to the individual, some theorists regarded culture as manifesting itself in the individual in more or less complete form, mainly through the process of socialization. Durkheim (1956 [1925]) described the institutions of education and pedagogy as the main mechanisms involved in internalizing the ingredients of culture and in making conformity to them a matter of individual will. Freud (1930) formulated the process as the incorporation of the cultural prohibitions and renunciations of instinctual forces that culture had accumulated over the ages. Parsons (1955) treated socialization through the family as the main mechanism for internalizing and reproducing society's common culture.

These theorists, however, each added a qualification or twist to this more or less mechanical concept of the internalization of culture. Freud never regarded the victory of civilization (culture) as complete; he saw the erotic and aggressive side of humanity in constant struggle with and reassertion against culture. Durkheim, in his discussion of egoism (1951 [1897]), envisioned how the internalization of a coherent value and normative situation could produce conformity and freedom simultaneously. This internalization occurred in the culture of Protestantism and individualism, which, while itself coherent and passed from generation to generation, resulted in a most heterogeneous set of individual choices and styles traceable to a central cultural ingredient of individualism—freedom. Parsons regarded the process of socialization to values and norms as incomplete. This incomplete process could result in the phenomenon of deviance, when individuals take on behaviors and outlooks that are at odds with the dominant cultural orientations of society. At this point, however, the culture reasserts itself by bringing the deviant individuals "back into line" through processes of social control, such as resocialization, rehabilitation, and psychotherapy (Parsons 1951). One debate emerging from Parson's formulation was whether societal reaction to deviance was primarily a matter of reincorporation of deviants through social control or a matter of relegating them to a position "outside" the dominant culture, incorrigible or incapable of being reintegrated into society and thereby given a special "labeled" or "stigmatized" status in it (Becker 1963; Goffman 1963).

With respect to the institutionalization of culture into the social structure, we also witness a range of theoretical possibilities. At the one extreme we turn again to Durkheim (1950 [1895]) as a model. For him, "collective conscience" was a representation of all that was common in society. It stood above the individuals in society as a fact sui generis and constituted a set of organizing principles on the basis of it. The idea of collective conscience also carried the notion of consensus. People could not understand one another or communicate with one another if they did not have a common grasp of language, rules of interaction, and other cultural ingredients.

There is a tendency toward a "consensus" view of society in the Marxian tradition as well. In the high days of dominance of any kind of society—the most developed example was bourgeois society—there is a tendency for the dominant culture to become a common culture because the dominant classes can enforce it on the subordinate classes, as false consciousness, through the instruments of social control. (That solution was unstable, for, in Marx's theory of development, class and revolutionary consciousness on the part of the subordinated classes arose in the later stages of capitalist development.) The same theme of consensus is found in neo-Marxist critical sociologists (for example, Marcuse 1964 and Habermas 1975). Those theories stress the ability of the technical-administrative-state apparatus to lull the masses into a state of acceptance of postcapitalist values and expectations through the manipulation of the mass media and through the soporific powers of the welfare state.

At the other extreme are formulations that depict a very imperfect reproduction of any common culture in the social structure. This "no common consensus" variant is found in versions of "cultural pluralism," in which different cultural systems—organized along religious, political, ethnic, and linguistic lines—constitute the culture, bound together, perhaps, by only a consensus on procedural rules of the game regarding conflict management and conflict resolution. One "culture conflict" variant is found in the idea of countercultures, which defy the dominant cultures. Another variant is found in the Marxian tradition, which considers the true class consciousness as, in one sense, a revolutionary "counterculture" in relation to the culture of the dominant classes; this variant is closely related to those that regarded the subordinated as "making" their own culture, which is independent of and largely antagonistic to that of the ruling classes (for example, Thompson 1963).

So much for a number of selected formulations of culture during the past hundred years. These formulations themselves, ironically, manifest a high degree of both incoherence and lack of consensus on the status of those very issues in the subject—societies—under study.

Imputed Sources of Cultural Coherence

In a recent essay on the concept of social structure (Smelser 1988), I noted a fundamental distinction made by most theorists who have used the concept. That distinction is between:

1. The *designation* and empirical *description* of structures of (a) activities (commonly called *institutions*) that appear to be regularly and systematically related to one another and (b) the relations among collectivities (commonly groups, parties, or classes); this is social structure *proper*.

2. The *reasons, causes,* or *explanations* for these regularities; among the most common are ideas of survival or adaptive advantage provided by structure, meeting of functional requirements, economic domination, and the like; furthermore, these would constitute what we generally refer to as *theories* of social structure.

One conclusion I reached in the essay was that at the definitional and descriptive level most scholars revealed some consensus, despite serious methodological difficulties in measuring social structure. At the level of reasons, causes, and explanations, however, one could discover most of the major polemics in sociology—polemics that could be traced, moreover, to the major disputes over first premises and fundamental paradigms in the field.

A similar, but not identical, distinction can be made with respect to the issue of cultural coherence and incoherence. (The difference lies in the fact that the definition of culture is a subject of much uncertainty and ambiguity.) On the one hand, ethnographers and other empirical investigators have uncovered repeated patterns of beliefs, customs, values, and rituals that seem to persist over time. On the other, the *reasons adduced* for such patterning are multiple, and they are the subject for a great deal of theoretical difference and debate.

What follows is a sample of theoretical presuppositions about the reasons for a presumed cultural coherence that are found in the sociological and anthropological literature. These are not exhaustive, nor are all the subvarieties of each identified. This recitation, however, will cover a significant range of recent theorizing about culture.

AN EXPRESSION OF PSYCHOLOGICAL
CONDITIONS OR PROCESSES

Wuthnow (1987) described the emphasis on cultural coherence as an expression of psychological conditions or processes as the "subjective approach" to culture. Here I underscore not so much the contents, "ideas, moods, motivations and goals" (11), as the bases on which those contents are organized. One example of this approach is the "culture and personality" school that dominated post-World War II cultural anthropology. Its informing psychological perspective was the psychoanalytic. The integration of any particular cultural system (mythological or religious systems were commonly studied) was generally traced to some special feature of childhood socialization, some developmental trauma, or a "cultural neurosis." An instance is found in the work of Whiting and Child (1953), who attributed cross-cultural differences in popular explanations of disease to the relative severity of child discipline at various phases of psychosexual development. Malinowski's (1948) treatment of magic and, to a large extent, religion was psychologically—but not psychoanalytically—derived, for it treated beliefs and practices as addressing practical and existential uncertainties. The same might be said for Weber's (1968) comparative treatment of world religions as, in part, different resolutions of the uncertainties and anxieties associated with the universal "problem of theodicy."

A MODE OF SIMPLIFYING AND GIVING MEANING TO THE COMPLEXITY OF EXPERIENCE

The formulations of Geertz (1973) regard culture as simultaneously a product of and a guide to actors searching for organized categories and interpretations that provide a meaningful experiential link to their rounds of social life. As such, culture is both a simplifying and an ordering device. In a similar formulation, Berger and Luckmann (1967) found both cultural and social order arising from the processes of typification and reification that extend from situations of action and interaction—situations that are, without ordering, so uncertain and ambiguous that they could not be tolerated. The result of these processes is a system of patterned values, meanings, and beliefs that give cognitive structure to the world, provide a basis for coordinating and controlling human interactions, and constitute a link as the system is transmitted from one generation to the next. These formulations, like the psychoanalytic ones cited previously, are ultimately psychological, but rest more on cognitive, rather than motivational, bases.

A REFLECTION OF STRUCTURAL PRESSURE FOR CONSISTENCY

This emphasis is not unlike that just mentioned, but it contains elements of social-structural as well as cognitive consistency. An example is the phenomenon of the strain toward consistency among institutions and ideas in society, which is posited as a means of achieving cultural and social harmony among diverse and possibly contradictory sociocultural elements. Another example is found in Weber's (1968) notion of *elective affinity,* which is invoked to explain why certain groups (for example, peasants and merchants) are drawn to one or another religious belief. Finally, Parsons (1951) depicts ideology (an ingredient of culture) as a system of elaborated and rationalized statements (including empirical assertions) that attempt to make "compatible" those potential normative conflicts and discrepancies between expectations and reality that actors confront. The logic by which such cultural integration is achieved is variable; it may rest on a general sense of appropriateness, on distortion in the interests of minimizing contradiction or conflict, or on some special stylistic motif (Levine 1968).

A LOGICO-MEANINGFUL WORKING OUT
OF FIRST PREMISES

This line of analysis seeks to find consistency or coherence in logical or aesthetic tendencies in cultural organization. A prime example is the work of Sorokin, already mentioned, in which the first principles of the sensate mentality ramify and work themselves out in the realms of epistemology, philosophy, religion, the arts, and so on, and thus lend a consistent organization to sensate culture as a whole. A second example is the formulations of Kroeber (1944), who regarded cultural dynamics as involving first the selection of a few core cultural premises from the myriad of possibilities; second, the systematic differentiation, cultural specialization, cultural play, and elaboration of those premises; and, finally, the exhaustion and cultural decline of the premises.

The sociology-of-science approach of Kuhn (1962) bears a close formal relation to that of Kroeber; his notion of a scientific *paradigm* is that of cultural first principles, wherein permutations and combinations are gradually elaborated and played out through the work of "normal science." Scientific innovation—that is, the development of a new paradigm—arises as existing paradigms fail in their efforts to solve problems or exhaust their possibilities. Weber's theory of cultural rationalization is another example; in his sociology of music, Weber (1958b) tells the story of the development of first principles such as musical scale, harmony, and sequence into elaborated styles (baroque, Classical, and so on) as expressions of the possibilities of the basic parameters. The structuralism of Lévi-Strauss must also be placed in the tradition of assigning cultural coherence through the logico-meaningful working out of first principles; many of his analyses (1963) take the principle of "paired opposites"—a universal principle rooted in the nature of the mind (if not the brain)—and its cultural elaboration. This type of structuralism derived in part from the work of Durkheim (1951 [1913]) and Durkheim and Mauss (1963), who, however, tended to treat cultural categories as "projections" of social-structural realities.

In a general formulation of this principle, Benedict (1934) asserted that all the cultures she identified were "permeated . . . by one dominating idea." Parsons (1953) posited a "paramount value system" that characterizes the cultural system of any given society (for example, universalistic achievement in the United States) and works its way through a diversity of social and political systems, including stratification. In all these examples there does not appear to be any special basis for selecting the cultural first principles—though in some cases universal, existential features of the human condition are specified—but a logic of symbolic consistency governs the process by which cultural coherence develops. (These bases for coherence reviewed thus far all meld, but, viewed generally, they correspond to the tripartite specification of analytic levels depicted by Sorokin (1947) and Parsons and Shils (1951) among personality, society, and culture itself.

AN EXPRESSION OF DOMINATION

The main intellectual roots of this tradition of cultural analysis are found in the work of Karl Marx. In *The German Ideology*, he and Engels expressed the classic version:

The ideas of the ruling class are in every epoch the ruling ideas: i.e., the class which is the ruling material force of society, is at the same time its ruling intellectual force. The class which has the means of material production at its disposal has control at the same time over the means of mental production, so that thereby, generally speaking, the ideas of those who lack the means of mental production are subject to it. The ruling ideas are nothing more than the ideal expression of the dominant material relationships, the dominant material relationships grasped as ideas; hence of the relationships which make the one class the ruling one, therefore, the ideas of its dominance (1965, 62).

The twin themes of this formulation are cultural domination as such and, within that, the economic or class basis of domination. Examples of such domination, cited by Marxian analysts, are the imposition of salvationist religious ideas as soporific counters to workers' misery and the Malthusian theories of population and poverty as justifications for repressive poor laws (Engels 1987 [1845]). The meaning and coherence of these cultural ideas are made intelligible by their reference to the situation of class domination in classical capitalism.

Much of the history of one tradition of cultural analysis can be read as a working out of themes and variations on the notion of culture as an instrument of domination. In fact, a certain line of theory on culture in the past decades is a variation on the theme of class domination. This theoretical tradition is marked by efforts to retain the fundamental notion of domination or repression, but it rejects or alters other ingredients of the Marx-Engels formula, such as the idea of economic determination and the reduction of culture to material considerations. Without pretense of exhaustiveness, I close this section of the essay by noting some of the threads in this tradition.

The first is the explicit challenge to the emphasis on economic/class domination by those who still explicitly define themselves within the Marxist perspective. Gramsci's (1971) rejection of strict economic reductionism and assertion of the independence of superstructures, especially the political superstructure, is the most evident example. His notion of hegemony, with a cultural component, retains the idea of domination, however, and thus could be regarded (as he saw it) as faithful to the Marxist tradition. The formulations of both Marcuse (1964) and Habermas (1970, 1975) depart from the vision (early capitalist) of bourgeoisie cultural domination of the proletariat. For them both classes and class consciousness have become fragmented and diffused in late capitalism. For this phase Marcuse stressed a form of cultural domination through which the ruling classes imposed a false consciousness of consumerism on the masses, especially by employing technology and the media. Habermas also deemphasized traditional class domination and stressed, instead, the capacity of the state/ administrative apparatus in late capitalism to impose technical/rational ideologies on the masses and thus intrude on their culture and lifeworld. The formulations of Althusser (1970, 1971), while also critical of the determinative structure-superstructure relation, nevertheless retained the idea of a dominant class that reproduces itself, in large part through the control of ideology and culture. His concept of the ideological state apparatus as an instrument of reproducing the relations of production indicates the central role of culture in his formulations. Williams (1958) treated the idea of culture in transitional societies as "the product of the old leisured classes who seek now to defend it against new and destructive forces" (319). Despite these qualifications and reformulations, Abercrombie, Hill, and Turner (1980) argue that a key notion of a "dominant ideology" still survives, a notion that implies "benefit" for the dominant classes and quiescence of the subordinated classes as a result of concealing the major contradictions in society.

A second thread of culture-as-domination is found in analyses of the media as culture industry. The notion was developed in the early work of critical theory, especially in Adorno (1973), Horkheimer and Adorno (1972), and Lowenthal (1967), as one strand of the British school of "cultural studies" (see Featherstone in chapter 10 and Hall 1986), and in American studies on the media and advertising (for example, Gitlin 1983; Schudson 1984; Tuchman 1978, 1988). In this tradition, culture itself is regarded as an economic institution, with the processes of production, distribution, and consumption treated as a market, political, and class phenomenon. The culture industry thread can be regarded as a specialized strand of the Marxist/critical traditions, in which the particulars of a dominant economic class recede but the ideas of domination and hegemony persist.

Two figures in contemporary French sociology also retain the thread of domination in their sociologies of culture. Foucault's essays on punishment (1977) and sexuality (1981) are clearly studies of cultural domination, although he is vague about the precise agencies or apparatus that exercise power (and thus moves away from more specific theories of domination such as those of Marx or Habermas) and concentrates, rather, on the mechanisms and processes by which surveillance, discipline, and cultural repression are carried out. Bourdieu also takes the notion of hierarchy, class, and domination as his point of intellectual departure. He focuses, however, on how individuals and classes accumulate the "cultural capital"—language, education, cultivation, and so on—that constitutes a central mechanism in the reproduction of inequality and domination. This cultural capital is generated particularly in the educational system (Bourdieu 1974). The complex processes of socialization generate, for each relevant class in society, a distinctive *habitus,* or cultural outlook, that serves to shape their knowledge, aspirations, and attitudes toward society and their place in it (1977).

In the recent history of writings on culture, the various threads of culture-as-domination have been central. Interestingly, recent developments in this tradition have tended to diminish cultural *content*—and by direct implication, the degree of cultural coherence or incoherence—and to concentrate, instead, on *processes* and *mechanisms* by which culture is generated and used. In their review of the strands of analysis in the "dominant ideology thesis," for example, Abercrombie, Hill, and

Turner observe that "the precise content of [a dominant ideology] is not always carefully specified" (1980, 29). Similarly, for Bourdieu, the specific contents of a given *habitus* are less important than its significance and use as cultural capital in the domination process. In a recent study influenced by both Goffman and Foucault, de Certeau (1984) showed little interest in the content of culture but concentrated on the strategies and tactics of *using, making,* and *consuming* culture. Kertzer's (1988) study of ritual and symbolism in politics likewise concentrates on use rather than content:

How political ritual works; how ritual helps build political organizations; how ritual is employed to create political legitimacy; how ritual helps create political solidarity in the absence of political consensus; and how ritual molds people's understandings of the political universe . . . how political competitors struggle for power through ritual, how ritual is employed in both defusing and inciting political conflict, and how ritual serves revolution and revolutionary regimes (14).

Other recent formulations not associated with the culture-as-domination tradition also focus on the use and deployment of culture rather than on its content. For example, Swidler (1986) develops a notion of culture as a reservoir, or a tool kit of values, ideas, beliefs, symbols, and arguments, to be activated selectively according to the different interests of actors and according to different situations. Such a formulation virtually defies characterization according to specific content and even suggests that too much coherence of culture would likely constitute a liability from a strategic point of view.

As a conclusion to this selective survey, I would propose that the historical preoccupation with the degree of coherence and incoherence of culture has diminished as the motifs of domination, strategy, usage, politics, and practice have infused social-scientific thinking about culture.

A Positivist Fallacy in the Analysis of Cultural Coherence

The historical array of divergent opinions on cultural coherence and consensus should not conceal a certain thread of commonality that characterizes that array. Throughout, culture is treated as an object of study and its coherence or incoherence can be established empirically. The philosophical and methodological origins of this tendency are found in the tradition of sociological positivism, as voiced mainly in the traditions of Comte and Durkheim. This positivistic view carries with it the notion that culture, as an object, has distinctive characteristics that can be described, and a major task of the ethnographer is to describe them. Among those characteristics is the degree of coherence, integration, unity, structure, or system—whatever term is preferred—that a given culture, or culture in general, manifests. The question of coherence thus becomes a matter of empirical determination. Even the conclusion that culture is a thing of shreds and patches— that is, lacks coherence—is a descriptive empirical statement.

This view of cultural coherence, however, ignores the fact that cultural unity or disunity is in large part a function of *the vocabulary and the theoretical presuppositions of the investigator.* Much of what is thought to be empirical coherence or incoherence is, in fact, endowed or assigned. The conceptual framework of the investigator is thus a crucial "variable" in determining the degree and kind of coherence presented, and, as a result, these will vary with the framework employed. To acknowledge that, moreover, is to change the theoretical and methodological agenda for approaching the issues of cultural coherence and incoherence.

The phenomenon of "interpreter effect" can be appreciated vividly by considering a different but related subject: human dreams. Before the late nineteenth century the dominant explanations of dreams regarded them as the bizarre mental work of the night, gave them credence by referring to some supernatural or divine intervention, or dismissed them as some kind of distorted precipitate from the more conscious and rational psychic experiences of daily life (Freud 1953 [1900], 1–6). In all these explanations dreams certainly had meanings, but they were not thought to be very organized (coherent) productions. It was not until the great discoveries of Freud that dreams were given both a great measure of logical coherence and a closer link with the *general* processes of psychic life.

The coherence of dreams Freud "discovered" was not based on new empirical materials or crucial experiments. Freud linked the known and familiar subject with a new set of psychological principles: the ideas of instinct and their psychic representation in the human mind, the derived idea of the *wish* and its fulfillment, the idea of resistance of defense, and the idea of specific modes of distortion arising from defensive work (condensation, displacement, and other symbolic distortions). Further coherence was lent by the notion that certain symbols had universal psychological or anatomical significance (snake = penis, water = childbirth, oven = womb), which gave further meaning and organization to dreams. Freud employed precisely the same logic in his parallel interpretation of slips of the tongue and pen (1960 [1901]) and of jokes (1976 [1905]), and he gave both of these phenomena new meaning and organization as well. What was different about the psychoanalytic theory of dreams, slips, and jokes was a new way of looking at and explaining them. The same point applies to Schorske's (1980) effort to add coherence to Freud's own dreams by interpreting them according to Freud's career and to the circumstances of Viennese political life at the end of the nineteenth century. This observation about the nature of scientific discovery is not original. Toulmin (1967) showed that many such discoveries in the physical sciences have resulted from new ways of conceptualizing known experimental results or naturally observed regularities.

In returning to the arena of culture, we may note that Freud attempted to bring a similar kind of coherence into the world of collective productions as well. He regarded them (as he did dreams) as reflections of the dynamics of private neuroses and defenses; they were the "creation[s] of the popular mind in religion, myths and fairy tales as manifesting the same forces in mental life" (Freud 1959a [1907], 252). In one instance he referred to myths as "distorted vestiges of the wishful phantasies of whole nations" (1959b [1908], 152). And in a perhaps overzealous moment, he characterized mythology as "nothing but psychology projected into the external world" (1960 [1901], 258).

More specifically, Freud lent coherence to the content of totemic systems and symbols in primitive religions by treating them as derivatives of the culturally transmitted dread of incest in kinship groups (1953 [1913]). Another great, and competing, theory of primitive religions is found in Durkheim (1951 [1913]). In contrast to Freud, he found coherence in these religious systems by interpreting them as symbolic reflections of the *social structures* of the primitive societies that generated them. In a similar vein, Malinowski (1971 [1877]) regarded collective myths mainly in terms of their social significance: they express, enhance, and codify cultural beliefs; they safeguard and enforce morality; and they vouch for the efficiency of ritual and contain practical rules for the guidance of social behavior. But while the reasons for assigning coherence to cultural products differ greatly among the three theorists mentioned, their interpretations did not emerge from the discovery of any new material in the myths and religious systems they analyzed; most of their "data" were taken from secondary summaries produced by ethnographers and historians. The new "coherence" of culture was to be found in some view of human nature, social organization, or social control. Other interpretations generated within frameworks would portray different kinds and degrees of coherence or, perhaps, lack of coherence.

The tension between two methodological options reviewed—the empirical recording and description of cultural coherence versus a coherence derived from an imposed conceptual framework—has not been absent from theories of culture. Two of the great students of culture, Kroeber and Kluckhohn (1963), took an uneasy approach to the issue of whether cultural coherence is identifiable or whether it is the creative abstraction of an investigator. On the one hand, they defined culture as a kind of abstraction gleaned from a complicated array of empirical observations: "[Culture] is the name given to [the] abstracted, intercorrelated customs of a social group." That is to say, culture is an empirically derived construct. Furthermore, they insisted that the degree of integration of a culture should be considered an empirical variable to be investigated. With this definition Kroeber and Kluckhohn placed themselves in the positivist tradition.

They did not settle finally on this solution, however. Their ambivalence toward it appeared in the discussion of explicit versus implicit culture. The former consists of those patterns that were reportable and available to members of the culture and readily recordable on the basis of accounts given by those members. However, cultures manifest other patterns that must be teased out by anthropological investigators; these constitute implicit culture, which appears to demand a methodology different from that used in describing explicit culture:

When we turn to those unconscious (i.e., unverbalized) predispositions toward the definitions of the situation which members of a certain society traditionally exhibit, we have to deal with second-order analytic abstractions. The patterns of the implicit culture are not inductive, generalizing abstractions. . . . They are *thematic* elements which the investigator introduces to explain connections among the wide range of culture content that are not obvious from the world of observation. The patterns of the implicit culture start, of course, from a consideration of data, and they must be validated by a return to the data, but they undoubtedly rest upon systematic extrapolation. When describing implicit culture, the anthropologist cannot hope to become a relatively passive, objective instrument. His role is more active; he necessarily puts something into the data, whereas the trustworthiness of an anthropologist's portrayal of explicit culture depends on his receptivity, his completeness, his detachment, and upon the skill and care with which he makes his inductive generalizations. The validity of his conceptual model of the implicit culture stands or falls with the balance achieved between sensitivity, scientific imagination, and comparative freedom from preconception (1963, 334).

Kroeber and Kluckhohn seemed both to have and to eat their methodological cake—empiricism for explicit culture and investigator-generated "sensitivity and scientific imagination" for implicit culture. I find their dualistic solution methodologically unsatisfactory, largely because the description of "explicit culture" *also* involves an active investigator espousing explicit or implicit conceptual frameworks. Kroeber and Kluckhohn appeared to recognize this when they said that "[even] the culture trait is an abstraction. A trait is an 'ideal type' because no two pots are identical nor are two marriage ceremonies held in the same way" (334). The decision of what specific empirical items should be categorized as belonging to an ideal "trait" is in large part a function of an independent, framework-informed decision on the part of the investigator. For this reason both the distinction between explicit and implicit culture and the methodological distinction between the different understandings of the two tend to break down.

If this revision of the positivistic view of culture is correct, it also changes our approach to cultural coherence, leading us to treat it in large part as a product of how we as interpreters think about it. Such a conclusion may, moreover, appear to convey a somewhat pessimistic message to those with scientific aspirations about the study of culture. To regard cultural coherence as generated by its various students appears to lend a measure of arbitrariness to its study ("it all depends on how you look at it") and appears to undermine a scientific faith in the reality, observability, and measurability of the phenomena of culture. I do not share that pessimistic conclusion; at the end of the chapter, I will suggest a reformulation of the idea of culture that retains its place in social-scientific study. Before presenting that, however, I will note a few additional methodological problems in the use of culture as an explanatory category.

Several More Methodological Problems

As the idea of culture has evolved in the social and behavioral sciences, it has encountered a number of methodological problems that have limited its usefulness as a social-scientific concept. I list this interconnected set of problems in no particular order of gravity.

EVALUATIVE AND
IDEOLOGICAL CONNOTATIONS

Part of the problem of the concept's evaluative and ideological connotations and the accompanying difficulty in escaping them
derives from the fact that, historically, culture has meant something
higher on the part of those individuals, groups, or societies that possess
it (note the evaluative connotations of *cultured* and *uncultured*). In
addition, the concept itself has been used historically as a demeaning
and controlling ideology of stratification and class (Williams 1958).
This means that dialogues about culture tend to be about values and
preferences and that questions such as "Do African Americans have a
distinctive culture?" almost invariably become the stuff of ideological,
rather than intellectual or scientific, debates.

VAGUENESS

In their review several decades ago, Kroeber and Kluckhohn (1963) listed scores of identifiable, if somewhat overlapping meanings, and the parade of accumulation has continued at an unknown rate.
In the early pages of chapter 3, Eisenstadt traces various shifts in emphasis over time, and Wuthnow (1987, 6–7) elsewhere has noted some
difficulties, mainly in communication and replication, associated with
the proliferation of meanings. With respect to using the concept in
social-science analysis, the multiplicity of meanings makes it an entity
difficult to treat as a *variable,* either dependent or independent. Vagueness and multiple meanings means that a concept is, in fact, many
variables, not all of which are explicit.

INCLUSIVENESS

Historically, inclusiveness reflects the tendency in early
anthropology to embrace values, ideas, beliefs, customs, usages, institutions, technology, and material artifacts. This phenomenon of inclusiveness persists, as Mayntz indicates at the outset of chapter 8. From a
methodological point of view, it creates the same problems as vagueness: the difficulty of treating culture as an entity that can be explained
or can operate as an explanatory variable.

CIRCULARITY

The concept's tendency toward circularity follows in
large part from the two preceding characteristics. If the concept of

culture itself is so vague and inclusive, then including an empirical indicator within its scope of definition and meaning cannot be justified. Moreover, to say that some institution or item of behavior is "explained" by culture often amounts to little more than renaming it according to its cultural location or identity. These problems also frustrate the use of the concept in scientific explanations.

GLOBAL CHARACTER

Most concepts used in the behavioral and social sciences are at the individual, group, and social-relational (roles, institutions) levels of analysis and, as such, are identifiable *parts* of a larger unit of analysis: society. A typical explanation is the establishment of an association between two or more phenomena at one or more of these levels of analysis; for example, differential crime rates or political attitudes are found to be associated with group memberships or institutional location, and some causal—often psychological—mechanism linking the two is posited. Because the notion of culture is often conceptualized as a global, unitary characteristic *of* the society or a group, to link it causally with phenomena in individual, group, or institutional behavior poses difficulties in explaining *variations* in such behavior. This point is a variant on the general principle that it is methodologically difficult, perhaps impossible, to explain variations by reference to a constant. This observation is also related to the often-mentioned difficulty of extending the concept of culture—portrayed as relatively enduring—to processes of social change. Weber's (1958a, 1968) analysis of the transformative potential of certain types of religious belief is a noted exception to this complaint but does not diminish its force.

Some Corresponding Conceptual and Methodological Suggestions

While I was developing the observations in this chapter, a number of constructive suggestions came to mind, and I conclude with them. An immediate qualification is in order, however. There are evidently many avenues, styles, and emphases in investigating cultural phenomena: as a social-scientific concept and variable, as a literary or narrative text, as a philosophical system, and as a way to evaluate the high or low attainments of a civilization. All of these are legitimate enterprises in their own right, and all merit scholarly pursuit. Furthermore, they should be regarded as independent from one another in many respects and not as competitors in the same explanatory or methodological race. In venturing the following conceptual and methodological suggestions, I limit their intent to the first mode, namely culture as a social-scientific concept.

First, culture is in large part a construct about the society or group under study rather than a simple empirical attribute to be apprehended, recorded, and described. That means that the investigator, as well as the conceptual apparatus he or she brings to the study, must be considered as an active factor—a source of variation—in understanding what a culture is and what its characteristics are. To argue this is simply to assert that the process which necessarily occurs in investigating culture should be made explicit in the operation of apprehending it.

Second, the coherence and incoherence of a culture or some part of it also vary according to the framework that is used to describe it. To appreciate this point changes the investigator's scientific agenda. The salient question is *not* how coherent or incoherent is a culture; that repeats the positivist fallacy identified previously. The more appropriate question is how useful or powerful is it—from the standpoint of generating scientific explanations—to portray a culture as relatively coherent or incoherent. In short, a cultural description should be assessed primarily on its explanatory adequacy or its usefulness as an explanatory element rather than on its significance as an empirical description.

To thus conceptualize culture is to regard it as a heuristic device in scientific investigation. Its explanatory role is akin to the heuristic device of "rationality" or "rational choice" used by economists and others. (Note Eisenstadt's remark, in chapter 3, that rational-choice analysis treats "culture as the result of the aggregation of individual choices.") The idea of rational choice in economic and other analysis, is, indeed, an idea of culture, however thin that idea may be. Methodologically, moreover, the status of rational-choice constructs is that of an intervening explanatory variable. Its intervention is "between" certain changes in actors' environments (for example, price changes in products) and patterns of behavior that result from those changes. Changing the parameters of rational-choice constructs, that is, positing different preferences and rationalities, results in different ranges of prediction about the resultant behavior. More generally, other conceptions of culture—based on cultural constructs other than rational-choice models—can profitably serve as intervening devices in explanations of behavior and institutional structure.

Third, to argue that culture is a heuristic device does not imply that its conceptualization should be arbitrary or unconnected with empirical observation. There is every reason to believe that certain rules for the empirical description of culture can be developed and that the adequacy of posited descriptions can be assessed according to those rules. In that sense the concept of culture becomes similar to a hypothesis, that is, a statement that can be demonstrated to be more or less true (or adequate or inadequate) in light of its correspondence with empirical rules of verification (or description). Some depictions of culture will fare better than others in relation to these rules of description. Furthermore, empirical descriptions of cultures as coherent or as incoherent will also fare differently in relation to such rules. Given the rational-choice analysis, it is possible (and advisable) to rely on two separate modes of evaluating a given model. The first is its utility in accounting for market and other behavior when incorporated into a predictive statement; for example, an exclusively monetary definition of utility may not prove to be a valuable tool in predicting consumer behavior. The second is assessing the posited utility function by direct empirical evidence (for example, by interviews, laboratory investigations, and examination of document or rituals) of its existence and validity as a general psychological principle. Both its limitations as a heuristic device *and* its lack of presence or viability as a cultural/psychological principle may constitute occasions for revising it. The same general observations apply more generally to the use of culture as a variable in social-science explanation.

Fourth, the concept of culture should, as far as possible, be disaggregated into discrete parts (values, beliefs, ideologies, preferences) and, correspondingly, not be treated as a global entity. These parts should be represented, furthermore, as variables rather than as global attributes of a society or group. This strategy is aimed at overcoming the methodological difficulties occasioned by properties of vagueness, multiple meanings, and circular definition that the concept of culture has customarily carried.

Finally, and returning to the issue of coherence-incoherence, I suggest one approach above and beyond its empirically informed description and use as an intervening, explanatory concept. It seems that any systematic effort on the part of an investigator to depict a society's culture will inevitably yield a significant measure of incoherence—incompleteness, illogicality, contradiction—in his or her rendition. To choose only one example, it is likely that any culture will present a number of contradictory adages or sayings ("look before you leap" and "he who hesitates is lost") as part of its repertoire. Similar discrepancies will appear in a culture's moral system and ideologies. Such a depiction, however, is only the beginning of analysis. In addition to that representation of relative incoherence, it is necessary to identify the whole range of individual and social pressures and tendencies that *work to present the culture as more coherent or less coherent than it appears*. For example, just as individuals tend to develop personal "myths" about themselves that may downplay conflicts and contradictions in their personalities, so do individuals and groups tend to represent their culture as more coherent or consistent than it appears on the basis of a social-scientific investigator's depiction. Actors in society may tend to represent the culture as incoherent or contradictory as well; for example, opposition parties and revolutionary groups may be bent on discrediting the "integrative myths" advertised by those in power. By attending to these tendencies and their dynamics, the investigator moves beyond the issue of the empirical characterization of cultural coherence and incoherence and treats it as an integral part of the stakes of the game of social control, social conflict, and social change.

Note

1. See Raymond Williams's critique (1958, 297–312) of the concepts of mass civilization and mass democracy as instruments of domination.

References

Abercrombie, N., S. Hill, and B. S. Turner. 1980. *The Dominant Ideology Thesis*. London: George Allen and Unwin.

Adorno, T. 1973. *Philosophy of Modern Music*. Translated by Anne C. Mitchell and Wesley V. Blomster. London: Sheed and Ward.

Althusser, L. 1971. "Ideology and Ideological State Apparatuses." In *Lenin and Philosophy and Other Essays*, translated by Ben Brewster. London: New Left Books.

Althusser, L., and E. Balibar. 1970. *Reading Capital*. Translated by Ben Brewster. New York: Pantheon Books.

Becker, H. S. 1963. *Outsiders: Studies in the Sociology of Deviance*. Glencoe, Ill.: Free Press.

Benedict, R. 1934. *Patterns of Culture*. Boston: Houghton Mifflin.

Berger, P., and T. Luckmann. 1967. *The Social Construction of Reality: A Treatise in the Sociology of Knowledge*. Garden City, N.Y.: Doubleday.

Bourdieu, P. 1974. "The School as a Conservative Force: Scholastic and Cultural Inequalities." In *Contemporary Research in the Sociology of Education*, edited by John Eggleston. London: Methuen.

———. 1977. *Outline of a Theory of Practice*. Cambridge: Cambridge University Press.

———. 1984. *Distinction*. Translated by Richard Nice. Cambridge: Harvard University Press.

———. 1990. *The Logic of Practice*. Stanford: Stanford University Press.

de Certeau, M. 1984. *The Practice of Everyday Life*. Berkeley and Los Angeles: University of California Press.

Durkheim, E. 1950 [1895]. *The Rules of Sociological Method*. Glencoe, Ill.: Free Press.

———. 1951 [1897]. *Suicide*. Glencoe, Ill.: Free Press.

———. 1951 [1913]. *The Elementary Forms of Religious Life*. Glencoe, Ill.: Free Press.

———. 1956 [1925]. *Education and Sociology*. Glencoe, Ill.: Free Press.

Durkheim, E., and M. Mauss. 1963. *Primitive Classification*. Translated and edited with an introduction by Rodney Needham. Chicago: University of Chicago Press.

Eliot, T. S. 1939. *The Idea of a Christian Society*. London: Faber and Faber.

———. 1944. *Notes toward a Definition of Culture*. New York: Partisan Review.

Engels, F. 1964. *The Origin of the Family, Private Property, and the State*. New York: International Publishers.

———. 1987 [1845]. *The Condition of the Working Class in England*. Harmondsworth: Penguin.

Foucault, M. 1977. *The Birth of the Prison*. Translated by Alan Sheridan. New York: Pantheon.

———. 1981. *The History of Sexuality*. Translated by Robert Hurley. Harmondsworth: Penguin.

Freud, S. 1930. *Civilization and Its Discontents*. New York: J. Cape and H. Smith.

———. 1953 [1900]. *The Interpretation of Dreams*. In *The Standard Edition of the Complete Psychological Works of Sigmund Freud*, Vols. 9 and 10. London: Hogarth.

———. 1953 [1913]. *Totem and Taboo*. New York: Knopf.

———. 1959a [1907]. "Preface to Sandor Ferenczi's Psychoanalysis: Essays in the Field of Psychoanalysis." In *The Standard Edition of the Complete Psychological Works of Sigmund Freud*, Vol. 9, 252. London: Hogarth.

———. 1959b [1908]. "Creative Writers and Day-dreams." In *The Standard Edition of the Complete Psychological Works of Sigmund Freud*, Vol. 9, 141–154. London: Hogarth.

———. 1960 [1901]. *The Psychology of Everyday Life*. In *The Standard Edition of the Complete Psychological Works of Sigmund Freud*. London: Hogarth.

———. 1976 [1905]. *Jokes and Their Relation to the Unconsciousness.* New York: Penguin.

Geertz, C. 1973. *The Interpretation of Cultures: Selected Essays.* New York: Basic Books.

———. 1983. "Common Sense as a Cultural System." In *Local Knowledge,* 73–92. New York: Basic Books.

Gitlin, T. 1983. *Inside Prime Time.* New York: Pantheon.

Goffman, E. 1963. *Stigma: Notes on the Management of Spoiled Identity.* Englewood Cliffs, N.J.: Prentice-Hall.

Gramsci, A. 1971. *Selections from the Prison Notebooks.* Edited and translated by Quintin Hoare and Geoffrey Nowell Smith. New York: International Publishers.

Habermas, J. 1970. *Toward a Rational Society: Student Protest, Science and Politics.* Translated by Jeremy J. Shapiro. Boston: Beacon Press.

———. 1975. *Legitimation Crisis.* Boston: Beacon Press.

Hall, S. 1986. "Cultural Studies: Two Paradigms." In *Media, Culture, and Society: A Critical Reader,* edited by Richard Collins, James Curran, Nicols Garnham, Paddy Scannell, Philip Schlesinger, and Colin Sparks, 33–48. London: Sage Publications.

Horkheimer, M., and T. Adorno. 1972. *Dialectic of Enlightenment.* New York: Herder and Herder.

Kertzer, D. I. 1988. *Ritual, Politics and Power.* New Haven: Yale University Press.

Kroeber, A. L. 1944. *Configurations of Culture Growth.* Berkeley and Los Angeles: University of California Press.

Kroeber, A. L., and C. Kluckhohn. 1963. *Culture: A Critical Review of Concepts and Definitions.* New York: Random House.

Kuhn, T. 1962. *The Structure of Scientific Revolutions.* Chicago: University of Chicago Press.

Lévi-Strauss, C. 1963. *Structural Anthropology.* New York: Basic Books.

Levine, D. 1968. "Cultural Integration." In *International Encyclopaedia of the Social Sciences,* Vol. 7., edited by David Sills, 372–379. New York: Free Press.

Lowenthal, L. 1967. *Literature, Popular Culture, and Society.* Palo Alto, Calif.: Pacific Books.

Lowie, R. H. 1934. *An Introduction to Cultural Anthropology.* London: George G. Harrap.

Malinowski, B. 1948. *Magic, Science and Religion and Other Essays.* Boston: Beacon Press.

———. 1971 [1877]. *Myth of Primitive Psychology.* Westport, Conn.: World Publishing Co.

Marcuse, H. 1964. *One-Dimensional Man.* Boston: Beacon Press.

Marx, K., and Engels, F. 1965. *The German Ideology.* London: Lawrence and Wishart.

Merelman, R. M. 1984. *Making Something of Ourselves: On Culture and Politics in the United States.* Berkeley and Los Angeles: University of California Press.

Morgan, L. H. 1963 [1877]. *Ancient Society.* Cleveland and New York: World Publishing Co.

Parsons, T. 1951. *The Social System*. Glencoe, Ill.: Free Press.

———. 1953. "A Revised Analytic Approach to the Theory of Stratification." In *Essays in Sociological Theory*. Revised ed. Glencoe, Ill.: Free Press.

Parsons, T., and R. F. Bales et al. 1955. *Family, Socialization, and Interaction Process*. Glencoe, Ill.: Free Press.

Parsons, T., and E. A. Shils, eds. 1951. *Toward a General Theory of Action*. Cambridge: Harvard University Press.

Schorske, C. A. 1980. *Fin-de-siècle Vienna: Politics and Culture*. New York: Knopf.

Schudson, M. 1984. *Advertising: The Uneasy Persuasion*. New York: Basic Books.

Smelser, N. J. 1968. "The Optimum Scope of Sociology." In *A Design for Sociology: Scope, Objectives and Methods*. Philadelphia: American Academy of Political and Social Science.

———. 1988. "Social Structure." In *Handbook of Sociology*, edited by N. Smelser, 103–139. Newbury Park, Calif.: Sage Publications.

Sorokin, P. A. 1937. *Social and Cultural Dynamics*. New York: American Book Company.

———. 1947. *Society, Culture, and Personality: Their Structure and Dynamics, A System of General Sociology*. New York: Harper.

Swidler, A. 1986. "Culture in Action: Symbols and Strategies." *American Sociological Review* 51:273–288.

Thompson, E. P. 1963. *The Making of the English Working Class*. London: V. Gollancz.

Toulmin, S. 1967. *The Philosophy of Science: An Introduction*. London: Methuen.

Tuchman, G. 1978. *Making News: A Study in the Construction of Reality*. New York: Free Press.

———. 1988. "Mass Media Institutions." In *Handbook of Sociology*, edited by N. Smelser. Newbury Park, Calif.: Sage Publications.

Tylor, E. B. 1920. *Primitive Culture: Researches into the Development of Mythology, Philosophy, Religion, Languages, Art and Culture*. Boston: Estes and Lauriat.

Weber, M. 1958a. *The Protestant Ethic and the Spirit of Capitalism*. Translated by Talcott Parsons. New York: Scribners.

———. 1958b. *The Rational and Social Foundations of Music*. Translated and edited by Don Martindale, Johannes Riedel, and Gertrude Neuwirth. Carbondale: Southern Illinois University Press.

———. 1968. *Economy and Society*. Edited by Guenther Roth and Claus Wittich. New York: Bedminster Press.

Whiting, J. W. M., and I. L. Child. 1953. *Child Training and Personality*. New Haven: Yale University Press.

Williams, R. 1958. *Culture and Society*. New York: Columbia University Press.

Wuthnow, R. 1987. *Meaning and Moral Order: Explorations in Cultural Analysis*. Berkeley and Los Angeles: University of California Press.

2

The Cultic Roots of Culture

Eugene Halton

> *. . . man, proud man,*
> *Drest in a little brief authority,*
> *Most ignorant of what he's most assur'd,*
> *His glassy essence, like an angry ape,*
> *Plays such fantastic tricks before high heaven*
> *As makes the angels weep.*
> > —Shakespeare, *Measure for Measure,*
> > act 2, scene 2

> *"Sleep-pictures"*
> > —New word coined in sign language by
> > an ape to describe what it did at night.

> *A little knowledge is indeed a dangerous thing. No age*
> *proves it more than ours. Monkey chatter is at last the most*
> *disastrous of all things.*
> > —D. H. Lawrence, *Etruscan Places*

What is culture? The usual way of answering this question is to trace the modern history of the "culture concept" from E. B. Tylor to the present. Such a history can be quite revealing, because the culture concept itself is a cultural indicator of the major intellectual tendencies and battles over the past century. The joint statement in 1958 by A. L. Kroeber and Talcott Parsons on culture formalized a kind of a truce between structural functionalism and cultural anthropology, ratified by the two leading proponents of each camp (some may have regarded it as what in business is called a "hostile takeover attempt" of the culture concept by Parsons, although "corporate merger" might be a more apt expression).

The culture concept, now a hotly contested topic for sociologists (as perhaps signified by the theme of this book), remains a profound indicator of contemporary intellectual culture. Although academic sociology has finally seemed to acknowledge the importance of culture, as seen in the recent creation of cultural sociology sections of the German and American sociological associations in the past few years, this does not at all ensure that the concern with culture will animate new directions for theory. The very term *culture* is so indeterminate that it can easily be filled in with whatever preconceptions a theorist brings to it.

Indeed, the sociology of the new culture section in the American association suggests that the objectivist and positivist prejudices of mainstream American sociology are appropriating the "soft" concept of culture by making it "hard." A peculiar irony of this development is that the objectivists share a tendency with relativists to view culture in purely conventional terms. Hence the inner social aspects of culture—subjective meanings, aesthetic qualities of works of art or common experience, the "spontaneous combustion" of new ways of feeling, doing, and conceiving—are either proclaimed to be not sociological, reduced to external considerations, or are virtually ignored. The outer aspects, the externals of culture, such as reputations, "tool kit" strategies of action, social networks, and production standards, although admittedly social, are enlarged to cover the whole meaning of culture (for example, Becker 1982; Swidler 1986; Griswold 1987; Wuthnow 1987). The result is that culture legitimates new topics of study while simultaneously being tamed to meet the expectations of actually existing sociology: old wine comes out of new bottles, and we remain, to paraphrase Shakespeare, most ignorant of what we're most assur'd, our glassy social essence.

By beginning with a brief tour of the contemporary landscape of culture theory, I hope to show how current conceptions of meaning and culture tend toward extreme forms of abstraction and disembodiment, indicating an alienation from the original, earthy meaning of the word *culture*. I will then turn to the earlier meanings of the word and why the "cultic," the living impulse to meaning, was and remains essential to a conception of culture as semiosis or sign-action. Putting the "cult" back in culture requires a reconception of the relations between human biology and meaning, and I touch on this by looking at dreaming as a borderland between biology and culture, a thoroughly social, yet private, experience. Dreaming not only highlights the cultic roots of culture—the spontaneous impulse to meaning—but also illustrates one way in which the technics of the biosocial human body forms the primary source of culture. Sociologists have seldom considered dreaming itself, perhaps because it seems nonsocial. Yet I will attempt to show why dreaming, although private, is a thoroughly cultural, biological, communicative activity. The deepest implications of this chapter are that contemporary modern culture in general, and intellectual culture in particular, have unnecessarily narrowed our conceptions of meaning and culture and that by undertaking a broad historical reconstruction of human consciousness and communication—known in the German context as *philosophical anthropology*—we can see why culture seeps into our very biological constitution: *cultus,* the impulse to meaning.

A Report to the Academy

In Franz Kafka's "A Report to an Academy," an ape gives a lecture on his acquisition of symbolic consciousness. He describes his long months in a tiny iron cage on board the ship that brought him to occidental civilization and the unbearable loneliness that tortured him into a state of cultivation. Becoming communicative, as he put it, was his "only way out." He learned to become rational, to communicate, to drink schnapps and wine. He became socialized into a "cultural system," and, in ways quite consistent with what most contemporary theorists of culture believe, he became utterly estranged from his animal nature. Thus, when presented with a female ape mate, he could only see "the insane look of the bewildered half-broken animal in her eye," a dimwitted unconscious creature of nature, uncivilized, incapable of drinking wine, let alone schnapps.

I would like to propose Kafka's ape, this hairy biped virtually reduced to talking, as the ideal type of ethereal creature proposed by most contemporary theories of culture. This creature, regardless of whether one reads of him in structuralist, poststructuralist, or critical accounts, or in structural-functionalist and neofunctionalist ones, is a product of unfeeling systems; his or her actions thoroughly stamped with the impress of an inorganic, rational system.

The proponents of Kafka's ape usually assume that meaning is a systemic property, that signification forms a logical system, and that culture is a code for order. Even the antirationalist opposite proposed by some "postmodern" theorists, such as Jean Baudrillard, Jean-Francois Lyotard, and Jacques Derrida, remains tethered to the structuralist logic it acts out against and infected with the old Cartesian "ghost in the machine" dichotomy: the ethereal ape of deep structural code and poststructural fission, without presence; his or her body reduced to a text. When Lyotard proclaims his pseudorevolutionary postmodernism, "Let us wage a war on totality; let us be witnesses to the unpresentable; let us activate the differences and save the honor of the name," we see merely another avatar of what painter Ernst Fuchs has called *the invisible dictator,* a servant of the ghost in the machine mentality of modernity who happens to reside on the ethereal side of the dichotomy. If modernity is characterized as cultural nominalism (Rochberg-Halton 1986)—a dichotomous worldview that falsely divides thoughts from things, producing an ethereal conception of mind and a materialized conception of nature—then we can well understand why Lyotard suddenly waxes nostalgic to "save the honor," not of a flesh and blood creature but of "the name" itself in its abstract generality.

The same etherealizing and mechanizing tendencies reside on the other half of the great divide of cultural nominalism, for humanity incarnate is also the unacknowledged enemy of many current biologically based theories of culture, such as those of human ethology or sociobiology. The seeming antithesis to the ethereal ape of structuralism and poststructuralism, the so-called natural man of ethology and sociobiology, likewise shares a domination by the calculating character of modern rationality. Like Caliban of *The Tempest,* that nasty and brutish subhuman, the creature of ethology and sociobiology is all appetite and impulsive greed. Yet these Hobbesian "state of nature" emotions are themselves façades for a cunning, underlying, rational genetic choice theory. Indeed structuralism, poststructuralism, rational-choice theory, and the rational calculation imputed to the genes by sociobiology are only apparently opposed; inwardly they speak the same disembodied language. The incarnate human body, with its stored capacities of memory and tempered abilities to suffer experience and engender meaning, is epiphenomenal in the sociobiologists' accounts; all that truly matters is the ethereal rational self-interest and its total willy-nilly maximalization (Rochberg-Halton 1989a).

We see the same ethereal language, albeit in a different dialect, in those theories that view culture as "a system of symbols and meanings," as though system were the be-all and end-all of culture and human action. Such theories claim to do justice to the systematic nature of human signification, but in reality they grossly exaggerate those aspects of signification concerning conceptual systems—as though culture were a domain of knowledge instead of a way of living—while ignoring or distorting those aspects of signification that reside outside the boundaries of rationality and systems. These latter forms of significatory experience include dreaming, imaginative projection, lived and suffered experience and its contingencies—what Charles Peirce termed *iconic* (or *qualitative*) *signs* and *indexical signs* (signs of physicality or existence)—as well as *symbolic signs* that are conceived within a living context and a larger purport beyond the narrow confines of system and rationality.

In founding modern semiotics toward the end of the nineteenth century, Peirce proposed that signification occurs through three modalities of being. He demonstrated logically not only why signs can represent their objects qualitatively, existentially, and conventionally but also why all three modalities are inherently social (Rochberg-Halton 1986). His existential signs, or indexical signs, are therefore fundamentally unlike the positivist notion of semantic reference, with which they are sometimes confused. Similarly, iconic signs, in being wholly within semiosis, or sign-action, convey *essences,* or the qualities of their objects, within the social process of interpretation. Iconic signs may exist within social conventions, yet are not reducible to conventional signification. Both advocates and critics of *essentialism* tend to view essences as outside of the realm of signs, yet Peirce's concept of iconic signs undercuts both positions. Such nonconventional modalities of signification are fundamental to a vital culture and civilization, I claim, though they may fall outside the pale of conventionalist theories.

In the etherealized language of contemporary theory, the "natural" human of sociobiology and the "cultural" one of individualistic or systematic conceptualism are equally divested of organic nature and personhood. Even an ape can see that these creatures are simply lackeys of rationalism, ignorant of their "glassy essence."

Culture theory is facing the problem portrayed in the 1950s American science fiction movie, *The Invasion of the Body Snatchers*. In this movie the citizens of a small American city are secretly replaced gradually by alien replicas grown from pods that have fallen from outer space. When placed near a sleeping human body, the pods assume control by appropriating memory, personality characteristics, and a perfect physical resemblance; all they lack is human emotions. As the pod creature blooms in the night, the human creature withers, so that the next morning—presto!—a real vegetable substitute walks and talks in embodied form and the "system of symbols and meanings" is virtually unchanged: people still drink coffee and read the newspapers in the modern manner criticized by Camus, though fornication has become obsolete. But of course there is one major change in the culture of this town, for the system of symbols and meanings has taken on a distinctly alien life of its own, and the one passion left to the quasi-carnivorous vegetarians—if I may so describe creatures who absorb human flesh while remaining vegetables—is to transform all human life to their system of perfect, dispassionate being, to their rational system of symbols and meanings.

Now many valid interpretations of *The Invasion of the Body Snatchers* can be given. It could signify the paranoia of the McCarthy era in the 1950s. Or, in its remade version from the 1980s, it might signify the neo-1950s paranoia of the neo-McCarthyite neoconservatives. It could also be taken to signify the deadliness of "organization man," as a sort of collective synonym for Willy Loman of Arthur Miller's *Death of a Salesman*. We could also interpret this movie as a prophecy of the evisceration of the American city by the "alien" automobile and shopping mall, a process that began in earnest in the 1950s and continues unabated today, leaving in its wake "urbanoid tissue." For my purposes the movie is a popular narrative of mythic rationality: the progressive loss of natural human capacities resulting from the dictatorship of the megamachine of modernity. The cultural processes that effuse from the movie in phobic form are expressed in recent culture theories in intellectual form.

Culture theory, in its dominant contemporary manifestations, is to my poor ape eyes an old science fiction movie, practiced by would-be body snatchers: some claim to transform the body into a text or into communicative "talking heads"; still others seek to appropriate the human capacity to body forth meaning to the depersonalized system, for example, Niklas Luhmann's concept of *autopoeisis*. A considerable number of feminists have as their goal, not the reform of gender relations, but the eradication of gender: they take a neutered androgeny as an ideal instead of as a form of deprivation. Camus regretted modern man, reduced to a life of coffee drinking, newspaper reading, and fornicating. What would he say of our genderless, eviscerated, postmodern person, reduced to the status of a text? At least Camus's modern man could have a little coffee and sex now and then. Whether one regards gender as limited to conventional social roles or, as I believe, an aspect of one's identity with deep biosemiotic roots in the human body, femininity and masculinity ought to be celebrated as part of what it means to be human. The attempt to eradicate gender differences is based on the mistaken assumption that genderlessness is requisite for social equality. Those who would devalue gender are unwitting accomplices of the invisible dictator of modernity, the neutered ghost in the machine.

The body has recently emerged as a major theme in intellectual life, but it is for the most part a conceptualized and etherealized body modeled on the text: the gospel of postmodernism seems to proclaim that "the flesh was made word and dwells among us!" In other words, it is not so much "body language" that is now fashionable as the body as language. The rhetoric of the body, the conventionalization of the body, and the symbolism of gender differences can all be significant topics. But when we note how little is said about the organic, biological body in these discussions, we begin to suspect that the academic megamachine is continuing its work of rational etherealization. Such is perhaps more clearly the case in Paul Ricouer's and Jacques Derrida's calls to view human action and social life as texts or in Jürgen Habermas's theory of communicative action, which says much about rational talkers talking, but very little about actors acting: felt, perceptive, imaginative, bodily experience does not fit these theories (Rochberg-Halton 1989b).

Or consider the systems theorist Niklas Luhmann, who introduced the idea of *autopoeisis* to account for self-generating systems. Here we see another contemporary avatar of the megamachine. The abstract, lifeless "systems" theory, because it excludes the living humans who comprise the social "system" as significant, ignores those natural capacities of life for self-making and self-generation. *Autopoeisis* must ignore *poeisis,* the human ability to create meaning in uniquely realized acts and works that transcend mere system per se. Therefore Luhmann's theory can be seen as part of the age-old dream to give life to the machine, in this case the machinelike system. His concept of *autopoeisis* is like the robot, android, or other automaton fetishes of contemporary popular culture and movies, many of which involve (and even celebrate) a transformation of humans into automatons. Such sociological theories are not too distant from materialist artificial intelligence and "neural network" theories, which view human beings, to quote computer scientist Marvin Minsky, as highly systematic "meat machines." I take these intellectual and cultural phenomena as further signs of the capitulation of autonomous life to the automaton.

Hence the current interest in the body may have the further undoing of the body as its unacknowledged goal. Whether disembodied as conceptualism or reified as mechanistic system, we are still left with the ghost in the machine.

Contemporary culture theory is, for the most part, a form of sensory deprivation. Those who proclaim culture to be a "system of symbols and meanings" make an uncritical assumption that culture, symbols, and meanings neither touch nor are deeply touched by organic life. Indeed the ideologues of culture theory tend to regard any concern with the relations between culture and organic nature or evolution as a threat to the hegemony of the cultural system over meaning.

There are significant exceptions to this outlook, notably in the work of Clifford Geertz, Victor Turner, and Lewis Mumford (Rochberg-Halton 1989c, 1990). Geertz has written on the interaction of culture and biology in the emergence of human culture. As he says in his essay "The Growth of Culture and the Evolution of Mind": "Man's nervous system does not merely enable him to acquire culture, it positively demands that he do so if it is going to function at all. Rather than culture acting only to supplement, develop, and extend organically based capacities logically and genetically prior to it, it would seem to be ingredient to those capacities themselves. A cultureless human being would probably turn out to be not an intrinsically talented though unfulfilled ape, but a wholly mindless and consequently unworkable monstrosity" (1973:68). By implication one can also say that a natureless human being could not be considered "civilized," but a similarly unworkable monstrosity.

As the neurological disorder of autism reveals, it is possible to perform and remember complicated human tasks that are yet devoid of meaning. As cases of individuals who have suffered damage to the hippocampus reveal, it is possible to retain the heights of human consciousness, speech, and passion while trapped in a continual present, utterly devoid of the ability to remember anything since the time of the damage, to encode new information, or to project a course of action beyond the immediate situation. This misfortune tragically gives the lie to the avant-garde dream of erasing the past to achieve a "live" present: such a culture would truly be posthuman in the sense of being deprived of the means of human experience. Clearly human biology, as seen in the human brain and its meaning and memory capacities or in the vocal organs, is involved in a reciprocal relationship with culture.

Culture may be an objectified organ of meaning, but it remains potentially connected to the organic proclivities and limitations of human bodies through the tempering effects of experience. The plasticity of culture does not signify the poverty of underlying human instincts, as Arnold Gehlen thought, but the positive plasticity or vagueness of human instincts: culture does not free us (or deprive us) of biology but has coevolved as an intrinsic aspect of human biology.

To anyone who seriously considers how human culture came to be, Geertz's statement that culture is ingredient to organically based capacities challenges the so-called nature-culture dichotomy. Ironically though, Geertz's ideas on the interaction of culture and biology are rarely cited, whereas his more conceptualistic "cultural system" works are cited. Though Geertz is generally appreciative of the significance of organic human nature for culture, even he retains the reductionistic tendencies of the "cultural systematizers" to view meaning as limited to the mode of conventional signification.

Conventionalism, the view that all human meaning is based upon non-natural social conventions, holds a pervasive sway over contemporary life. The leading French schools of thought associated with structuralism and poststructuralism retain strong influences of Ferdinand de Saussure's conventionalist semiology, and even Pierre Bourdieu's attempt to develop a more experiential category of the *habitus* remains thoroughly conventionalist, viewing the habitus as a "system of dispositions."

This view is particularly clear in Bourdieu's discussions of aesthetic judgment in his book *Distinction,* in which he assumes the standard dichotomy between "essentialist" and conventionalist analysis and claims that essentialist analysis "must fail" because it ignores the fact that all intentions and judgments are products of social conventions. The term *essentialism* carries with it highly negative meanings in cultural studies today, and Bourdieu's criticism of essentialism represents the tendency to regard aesthetic qualities—the essential—as nonsocial. The producer's intention

is itself the product of the social norms and conventions which combine to define the always uncertain and historically changing frontier between simple technical objects and objets d'art. . . . But the apprehension and appreciation of the work also depend on the beholder's intention, which is itself a function of the conventional norms governing the relation to the work of art in a certain historical and social situation and also of the beholder's capacity to conform to those norms, i.e., his artistic training. To break out of this circle one only has to observe that the ideal of "pure" perception of a work of art qua work of art is the product of the enunciation and systematization of the principles of specifically aesthetic legitimacy which accompany the constituting of a relatively autonomous artistic field. The aesthetic mode of perception in the "pure" form which it has now assumed corresponds to a particular state of the mode of artistic production (Bourdieu 1984:29–30).

By claiming that all aesthetic experience is purely conventional and therefore social, Bourdieu is attacking the view that aesthetic judgment consists in an unmediated act of perception and that the work of art possesses inherent qualities unmediated by social signification. In the conventional view that Bourdieu takes, to be human is to be the enclosed product of those specific social norms in which one finds oneself. It is the same old world in which the social is limited to the conventional and modalities of nonconventional signification, such as iconic and indexical signs, are thereby falsely assumed to be nonsocial. It is a world in which the human creature, who, above all others *both is open to meaning and needs meaning,* is denied the social capacity to body forth genuinely new meaning not reducible to, though growing out of, prior social norms. Another route, which Bourdieu's conventionalism forbids him to take, is to view aesthetic experience as fully social, yet not necessarily conventional, so that conventions themselves are live processes of sign interpretation open to experience, growth, and cultivation or "minding." In such a view every sign can possess its own qualitative significance or essence qua communicative sign, as well as reflect social structures. Hence, from my perspective, aesthetic experience may be truly *formative* in giving birth to new "social norms." The ability to body forth new meaning, not reducible to prior conventions, has the added advantage of being able to explain how conventions developed in the first place, a question that conventionalism usually avoids.

Anthony Giddens and Jürgen Habermas have sought to reconstruct the basis of social theory, but both remain stalwarts of unreconstructed conventionalism at the heart of their theories of meaning. Giddens has sought to broaden the base of contemporary theory by using a French structuralist conception of structure and linking it with a theory of "agency" influenced by language analysis, ethnomethodology, and symbolic interactionism. His "structuration theory" can be seen as an attempt to deal with the old sociological problem (itself part of the older nominalist problem) of the relation of the individual with society, or "action" with "order," or subject with object. Yet even a reconstructed structuralism remains too narrow to encompass structure; while agency, even in a broad sense, remains too narrow to encompass subjectivity, and both are inadequate for the creation of a broader theory of meaning. French structuralism reifies structure, treating it as a deep code of "logical" differences divorced from human practices, habits, and memory. "Agency" does not go deeply enough into the personal or individual side of meaning, which includes the being acted upon or suffering of experience, the "patient" side of the agent-patient dialectic, let alone the inner dimensions of experience that do not fall under the rubric of agency.

Richard Rorty, who would seem to take a very different perspective, mistakenly called *neopragmatism*, remains within the conventionalist fold he seems to reject, viewing meaning as limited to arbitrary language games. Unlike the pragmatists, he denies that there are qualitative and existential modalities of signification not reducible to conventional signs alone (Rochberg-Halton 1992). Surely human languages involve conventions, but the full range of meaning or human communication—not to mention human social life—is simply not exhausted by conventional signification. As the neurologist Oliver Sacks put it:

Speech—natural speech—does *not* consist of words alone, nor . . . "propositions" alone. It consists of *utterance*—an uttering-forth of one's whole meaning with one's whole being—the understanding of which involves infinitely more than mere word-recognition. . . . For though the words, the verbal constructions *per se,* might convey nothing [to aphasics], spoken language is normally suffused with "tone," embedded in an expressiveness which transcends the verbal—and it is precisely this expressiveness, so deep, so various, so complex, so subtle, which is perfectly preserved in aphasia, though understanding is destroyed (Sacks 1987:81).

Given the undeniable facts of communication practices in humans and other species in which signification occurs through nonconventional modalities, why then does conventionalism hold such a power over the contemporary mind?

One way to answer this question is to view these theories as emanating from *cultural nominalism,* a term I use to characterize the modern epoch. Cultural nominalism denotes modernity as a culture rooted in the dichotomous principles of philosophical nominalism. I do not suggest that modernity was caused by nominalism, but that the philosophy that arose in opposition to scholastic realism was itself a symptom of the shift of epochs, one that put into philosophical form the underlying antipathies of the emergent ethos. Yet it should also not be forgotten that philosophy and theology had significant influences on the development of Western civilization in the Middle Ages.

Max Weber's patently false idea that modern capitalism should be viewed as a sixteenth-century product of the Protestant ethos ignores the clear emergence of capitalism out of medieval Catholic culture and the rising nominalism that gave birth to Protestant theology. Early nominalists, following the *via moderna* of William of Ockham, claimed that reality could be found only in knowledge of particulars, that general laws are fictions or conventions, and that conventions are simply names for particulars, hence nominal. Nominalism in effect created two worlds by driving a wedge between thought and things and then faced the problem of how to put them together, the problem of modern philosophy. What the scholastics might have accepted on faith or revelation becomes increasingly inexplicable in the nominalist ethos. Descartes, for example, assumed a dichotomy between thinking substance and extended substance, the ghost in the machine, and faced the problem of how we can have valid knowledge of objects if the only basis for knowledge is intuitive individual self-consciousness.

What is interesting about the nominalistic ethos is how it systematically undercuts *cultus*—the spontaneous impulse to meaning. The whole ideal of systematic, rational science modeled on the mechanical conception of the universe that one sees in Descartes and Hobbes, who both believed that life, as Hobbes put it, "is but a motion of Limbs," grows directly out of the spirit of nominalism. By the time of Calvin, who was educated in nominalist theology, "the impulse to meaning" becomes an intolerable threat to the great clockwork system of predestination and rational self-control. Hobbes, who also was taught nominalist theology, transformed the impulse to meaning into a mythic projection of individual competitive lust and aggression in the state of nature, which had to be repressed by a social contract—a non-natural artifice or convention. Bentham psychologized and nominalized it yet further into individual sensations of pleasure and pain. Even Freud, who is instrumental in the return of the cultic in twentieth-century culture, based his metapsychology in a Bentham-like underlying "pleasure principle" of the reflex-arc concept.

One cannot deny that much of meaning is conventional, though conventions themselves, it seems to me, are inherently purposive and subject to cultivation. Conventionalism is proposed as an antidote to reductionism, yet it radically reduces the realm of significance, meaning, and the social. That which is outside the system is regarded as meaningless until it is "systematized." The conventional view says that conventions or codes encompass culture. Hence a number of recent sociological studies take the position that art can be understood solely as social conventions, thereby denying aesthetic quality (Wolff 1981; Becker 1982; Bürger 1984; Griswold 1987). Similarly, attempts to discuss either the brute factuality or the esthetic or inherent meanings involved in human experience are frequently dismissed by cultural theorists as reductionistic or obsolete because these approaches fail to see that all meaning is conventional, that is, dependent on cultural belief systems or conventions. Hence the expressive outpouring of an artist is meaningful only insofar as it can be related to existing cultural values, beliefs, and constructions. The inner compelling expressiveness of a work of art is reduced to outer considerations.

One can view a late work by the sculptor Ivan Meštrović, *An Old Father in Despair at the Death of His Son* (figure 2.1), and, knowing that Meštrović's own son committed suicide, see the autobiographical source for the agonized figure. Clearly representational conventions are involved in the form of this sculpture. But one is still left finally with the sculpture itself, the powerful father's hands covering most of the face in grief. To say that the sculpture communicates the system of artistic representation or that it is an "aesthetic-practical" form of communication (Habermas) is to miss the point that this physical thing is a bodying forth of human feeling through the hands that shaped it, directly conveying the feeling of human grief through the hands covering the agonized face. It is not a "symbol" standing for something else; it is a living icon and secretion of human experience. It may involve conventions, but these are the vessel, the husk, that contains that actualized experience.

Most sociologies of art and culture do not consider that a work of art might be a spontaneous, meaning-generating gesture or sign not reducible to the conventions from which it grew. The organic, the inherent qualitative possibilities, the imaginative, the spontaneous, the contingent, the serendipitous—in short, the extrarational and nonsystematic—must be devalued or disregarded by the practitioners of conceptual *system*. The result is a systematic ethereal grid that treats only the externals of culture while denying its vital, extrarational, incarnate sources.

Culture as abstract, depersonalized system denies the living source of culture as *cultus*. In its reliance on culture as system, it raises system from a means of interpretation to a virtual end of cultural life. Hence culture theory itself is by and large part of a progressive externalization of meaning in cultural life generally: meaning as technique, meaning as prepackaged script, meaning as "the honor of the name."

Figure 2.1. Ivan Meštrović, *An Old Father in Despair at the Death of His Son*, 1961. Snite Museum of Art, University of Notre Dame.

The Culture and Manurance of Minds

When Francis Bacon in 1605 wrote of "the culture and manurance of minds," the literal sense of culture as tending and cultivating nature was still very much in the foreground, although the metaphoric extension of the term *to mind* was intended. The term *culture* traces back to the Latin *colere*, which meant variously to till, cultivate, dwell or inhabit, and which in turn traces back to the Indo-European root, *Kwel-, which meant to turn round a place, to wheel, to furrow. As Raymond Williams noted:

Some of these meanings eventually separated, though still with occasional over-lapping, in the derived nouns. Thus "inhabit" developed through *colonus*, Latin to *colony*. "Honour with worship" developed through *cultus*, Latin to *cult*. *Cultura* took on the main meaning of cultivation or tending, though with subsidiary medieval meanings of honour and worship. . . . *Culture* in all its early uses was a noun of process: the tending *of* something, basically crops or animals. . . . At various points in this development two crucial changes occurred: first, a degree of habituation to the metaphor, which made the sense of human tending direct; second, an extension of particular processes to a general process, which the word could abstractly carry (Williams 1976:77).

The term *culture,* according to Williams, was not significant as an independent noun before the eighteenth century and was not common before the nineteenth century. But even before the nineteenth century the term was already beset by the etherealizing tendencies of ethnocentric universalism, so that Johann Herder could state that "nothing is more indeterminate than this word, and nothing more deceptive than its application to all nations and periods." *Colonize* and *culture* are both derived from the same root, and Herder was well aware of how the Enlightenment dream of "universal reason" could also be used as an expression of European power. He complained of the treatment of human histories and diversities as mere manurance for European culture: "Men of all the quarters of the globe, who have perished over the ages, you have not lived solely to manure the earth with your ashes, so that at the end of time your posterity should be made happy by European culture. The very thought of a superior European culture is a blatant insult to the majesty of Nature" (1784–1791, cited in Williams 1976:79).

Cultural anthropology has in many ways taken Herder's words to heart, admitting—to use the title from one of Clifford Geertz's books—"the interpretation of cultures" in the plural as its central task. Yet in the long history and vicissitudes of the term *culture,* there has remained a broader sense of culture as meaning in general, which remains a central problematic of social theory even if it has lost its earthy origins. Cosmopolitans do not like the smell of Bacon's conception of "the culture and manurance of minds," preferring the intellectualistic "systems of symbols and meanings." Please do not misunderstand me, honored colleagues of the academy. I am not simply calling for an anti-intellectual, nostalgic return to farmer's wisdom, such as expressed in the following quotient: Die Quantität der Potate ist indirekt proportional zur Intelligenskapazität ihres Kultivators! (Or, as they say in the south, Der Dümmste Bauer hat die grösste' Kartoffel!).* I am simply saying that we must revitalize the concept of culture and free it from the abstractionist grip of our time: we must put the *cult* back in *culture*.

We have come a long way from the earthy conception of culture as a living process of furrowing and cultivating nature within and without, of the organic admixture of growth and decay that such a conception implies, of the springing forth of tendrils of belief needing active cultivation for survival. One of the glaring holes in most contemporary conceptions of culture is the lack of attention to the birth of meanings, a lack that applies equally to the term *conception*. In intellectual discourse, conception connotes, almost without exception, rational beliefs and not the gestation of something new, the birth of meaning. Likewise, *culture* now connotes systematized meaning for most culture theorists and has lost the fertile, seminal, and gestational meanings it once carried: "the culture and manurance of minds." Both the living source and the final aim of culture, I claim, is *cultus*. Yet it is precisely the cultic that is so frequently occulted by contemporary culture theory.

The word *cult*, despite its obvious relation to culture, seems worlds apart from its meaning in everyday language. Cults are usually associated with pathologically disturbed or ideologically brainwashed groups—satanists, the suicidal followers of Jim Jones at Jonestown, Moonies, and the lunatic fringe in general—but the term also applies to emerging religious sects, such as the early Christian cults. In the anthropological sense the word *cult* is strongly associated with ritual, as in the "cargo cults" that appeared in the South Pacific after World War II or the various rituals to Afro-Christian "saints" in the Umbanda cults of Brazil. The ethnographic record, Freud, and Durkheim have sensitized us to how certain objects become endowed with sacred or obsessional significance as fetishes—such as a wooden sculpture of a human form studded with nails by the Bakongo people of West Africa (figure 2.2). We see in these examples how deep human needs and desires seek objectified, and often fantastic or perverse, form.

One of the most insightful accounts of the cultic roots of culture is to be found in the work of Victor Turner. His masterful ethnography reveals the fundamental reality of the subjunctive mood in human affairs: the

---

*The size of the potato is indirectly proportional to the IQ of the farmer; or, the dumbest hick has the biggest spud.

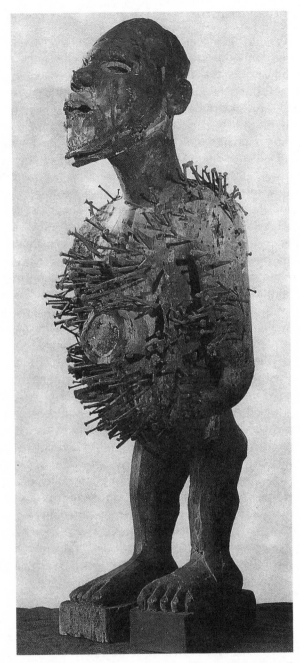

Figure 2.2. Large wooden figure studded with nails, Bakongo tribe, Angola, nineteenth century. The University Museum, University of Pennsylvania.

ritual process. In Turner's analyses of the *Isoma* and *Wubwang'u* rituals of the Ndembu of northwestern Zambia, one sees the fantastic interplay between human affliction and symbolic renewal, between human communities and a natural environment teeming with signification. The Ndembu are revealed to be a people with a deep appreciation of the complexity of existence and endowed with a sophisticated technics of meaning, a vast architectonic of felt, expressive forms through which they journey to those borderlands beyond human comprehensibility: death, the dead, the call of the mother-line, fecundity, transformation, the interstices of social structure. Systematizers who seek an airtight scheme with absolute closure will not find it in Turner's work. His theories are open-ended, ever acknowledging the greater richness and potentiality and not-yet-decipherable and perhaps not systematizable richness inherent in experience and culture. He continually directs our gaze instead to those social "openings" through which the ferment of culture erupts. Cultures are not simply inert structures or bloodless "systems," but form a "processual" dialectic between structure and liminality.

In his well-known essay, "Betwixt and Between: The Liminal Period in Rites of Passage" (1967:93–111), Turner attempted to grasp that virtually ungraspable mercurial element in human affairs in which normal social structure and mores of conduct are temporarily eclipsed. Liminality was that which dismembered structure in order to transform, renew, and re-member it. Turner went on to show, in this essay and in other works, how liminality provides a time of visceral or meditative (or both together) reflection, a time of reflective speculation: "Liminality here breaks, as it were, the cake of custom and enfranchises speculation. . . . Liminality is the realm of primitive hypothesis, where there is a certain freedom to juggle with the factors of existence. As in the works of Rabelais, there is a promiscuous intermingling and juxtaposing of the categories of event, experience, and knowledge, with a pedagogic intention" (1967:106). Turner notes, however, that the liberty of liminality is ritually limited in tribal societies and must give way to traditional custom and law.

In Turner's works, one continually confronts the drama and mystery of life itself in its humanly perceivable forms. The live human creature, not the dead abstract system, is the source of what he termed *processual anthropology*. Throughout *The Ritual Process,* he engages Claude Lévi-Strauss in a dialectical contrast, posing his processual anthropology against Lévi-Strauss's structuralism, while yet drawing from Lévi-Strauss's analyses that which he finds useful. In Turner, one sees that meaning is much more than a "logical structure," because it involves powerful emotions not reducible to logic, a purposiveness not reducible to binary oppositions, "a material integument shaped by . . . life experience." In short, a processual approach views structure as a slow process, sometimes very slow indeed. Or as Turner puts it, "Structure is always ancillary to, dependent on, secreted from process" (1985:190).

Turner is very much concerned with systemic or structural questions, but he continually reminds us of the human face behind the social roles, status hierarchies, and social structures. That human face may be painted with the red and white clays of *Wubwang'u,* or it may be adorned with the phantasms of carnival, or it may be soberly dressed in ritual poverty, but Turner's theories, and the body of his work itself, never let us forget those deep human needs for fantastic symboling to express the fullness of being.

Central to Turner's processual anthropology and comparative symbology is the ritual symbol, which he considered the "core" unit of analysis. The symbol is the "blaze"—the mark or path—that directs us from the unknown to the known, both in the Ndembu sense of *ku-jikijila* (to blaze a trail by cutting marks or breaking or bending branches on trees) and in C. G. Jung's sense. Key to the indigenous hermeneutic of the Ndembu is the term *ku-solola*—"to make visible," or "to reveal"—which is the chief aim of Ndembu ritual, just as its equivalent concept of *aletheia* is for Hans-Georg Gadamer's hermeneutic. These Ndembu terms derive from the vocabulary of hunting cults and reveal their high ritual value. The idea of making a blaze or path through the forest also draws attention to the significance of trees for the Ndembu, not only as providing the texture of the physical environment, but also as sources of spiritual power. The associations of substances derived from trees with properties of blood and milk, or of toughness with health and fruitfulness with fertility, which Turner discusses in his description of the *Isoma* ritual, also reveal why he chose Baudelaire's phrase "the forest of symbols," as the title for one of his books. In his ground-breaking discussions of color symbolism in Ndembu ritual, Turner shows how the social system of classification comes into play, but he roots the social meanings of red, white, and black symbols to the experiential level of bodily fluids and substances of blood, milk and sperm, and feces.

At the time of his death Turner was fully engaged in the struggle to achieve a new synthesis—a theoretical rite of passage to a broadened vision of anthropology and social theory. A number of social theorists have been claiming to be transforming social theory—I am thinking here of Habermas, Luhmann, Giddens, and others—but for the most part they have been replaying tired variations on old themes without ever questioning the premises of modern social theory. But in Turner's synthesis of social dramas, liminality, communitas, Deweyan and Diltheyan understandings of "experience," and neurobiological semiotics, perhaps we see the unexpected outline of a new understanding of the human creature: one which reconnects biological life and meaning, which embraces the "subjunctive" as no less fundamental a reality of human existence than the "indicative," which views the realm of the fantastic as a precious resource for continued human development rather than as a vestige of an archaic and obsolete past.

Turner is regarded as an anthropologist in the Anglo-American sense, but his late work, like that of Lewis Mumford, reveals him to be a philosophical anthropologist in the German sense as well. Turner and Mumford are no throwbacks to biological reductionism. Quite the contrary: both are master interpreters of meaning, both are original contributors to the semiotic turn of the social sciences, both are exponents of a dramaturgical understanding of human action. Yet both felt compelled, *in the name of human meaning,* to delve into the biological sources of signification. The liminal processes revealed in lucid detail by Turner and the broad historical account of human development and sociocultural transformation given by Mumford complement each other and illustrate how both authors share a deep appreciation of the cultic roots of culture. Their work shows the way toward undoing the etherealizing spectre that haunts the contemporary study of meaning and culture as well as its mechanico-materialist opposite in human ethology and sociobiology. At the heart of Turner's and Mumford's work is ever the incandescent human form.

To those who can no longer live within the frame of mythic rationality and its cultural nominalism, the artificial split between a mechanical nature devoid of generality and a culture reduced to human conventions devoid of tempered experience and organic roots seems a quaint relic from the bifurcated world of cultural nominalism, mythic modernity. This peculiar mindset took the rationalization of culture, the technicalization of society, and the mechanization of the universe to be a troubling, yet logical, development in occidental culture: *Disenchantment* is the name and cost of freedom.

Is *rationalization* ultimately the proper term for Weber's project? Or does *rational maximization* better capture the processes that Weber thought he saw inherent in religion and in the peculiar developments of the Occident?

Rationalization ought to describe the normal growth and context of rationality in human life, the place of rational capacities as organs of a mind deeper and broader than rationality alone. The human mind, in both its individual and collective manifestations, reveals the extrarational capacities of memory and invention, interpretative "sensing" and organic balancing, rich emotional communication—not at all limited to what words alone can say—and an obsessive need for the semblance of meaning.

The fullness of the human body also reveals dark, destructive impulses potentially active in all of the human capacities, impulses generated no doubt from our own animal depths but by no means excluded from our rational heights: for every Caliban there is also one of Kafka's devitalized rational apes. The rationalist too frequently places the blame for human evil and folly on the irrational, ignoring the great tendencies of decontextualized rationality toward self-destruction. "The devil made me do it" alibi only works when one fully acknowledges the ever-present devil within: criticism must always invoke self-criticism. There is in pure rationality a profound aptitude for cold-blooded murderousness and its seeming opposite: *Weltschmaltz,* the self-beautifying lie of sentimentalism. Albert Speer said that Hitler in his more manic moods and rages would discuss plans he did not necessarily mean to carry out. But when he was calm, cool, and collected—"rational"—his inner circle knew he fully intended to carry out his calculations, no matter how extreme. In Speer's account one sees what is perhaps the twentieth century's most notable "achievement": rational madness.

Though mythic rationality saw the many distortions that entered into modern life through capitalism, rationalism, technicalism, and individualism, it never questioned whether the mechanization of nature in the seventeenth century might also be part of this distorting process. Because virtually all of social theory has grown out of the same processes of cultural nominalism, theorists tend to accept uncritically the reified split between thought and things, between culture and nature. Culture can then be assumed to be free from nature or to seek as its goal to escape from nature through the perfection of rationality. In both cases the underlying task is to etherealize the human creature, to divest it of its organic, cultic, biosemiotic roots. Yet all the inner autonomous forms of culture, all the outer technical codes and know-how, and all the rational justifications for progressive, modernized, "communicative" culture remain insufficient for a truly vital culture when disconnected from the tissues of life, from human bodies and their social relations.

The cultic is the springing forth of the impulse to meaning, which culminates in belief. As such the cultic is no throwback to "vitalism" but involves the deepest emotional, preconscious, and even instinctive capacities of the human body for semiosis. Although most theories of culture tend to view meaning as conventional knowledge or system, I am proposing that the essence of meaning resides in bodied sign-practices that circumscribe mere knowledge. Conventions of language, gesture, image, and artifact should be viewed as the means toward incarnate sign-practices, not as the structural or systemic foundations or ends of meaning. The very attempts to ground meaning in a theory of pure conventionalism are signs of the evisceration of meaning, the hollowing out of living human experience to the external technique or the idolatry of the "code."

By "incarnate sign-practices" I mean that culture is a process of semiosis, or sign-action, intrinsically involving the capacities of the human body for memory, communication, and imaginative projection, and is not completely separable from those capacities. Social structure, in this perspective, cannot be severed from the living inferential metaboly of human experience through systematic or structuralist abstraction, but it needs to be conceived in some relation to lived human experience and its requirements, limitations, and possibilities. Human life, in its organic fullness, remains the yardstick for social theory and cultural meaning, and neither the abstractionist distortions and perversions of the life-concept through biological reductionism nor the equally abstractionist repression of the life-concept through cultural reductionism will suffice any longer.

Dreams as Organs of Meaning

Let us turn to the social fact of dreaming, a nightly experience shared by all human beings, as an unexpected way to explore the cultic roots of culture. To most social theorists, dreams emanate from a twilight zone of questionable value: dreams are "imaginary" and therefore unimportant aspects of modern life. The task of modern social theory, after all, is to wake humanity from its dream and bring it to self-consciousness. Yet dreams, I claim, cannot be wished away from our evolutionary past, from our sociocultural present, or from our potential futures. There is good reason to suspect that dreaming was a significant component of the experiential world of the protohumans: the fantastic image-making process, autonomously produced by the psyche, a private, though social, self-dialogue of the organism, its "language" fashioned from the forms of experience. Dreaming may very well have helped to "image" us into humanity. And we may yet remain creatures of the dream.

Sociologists might take the view that dreaming is nonsocial and therefore unsuitable for sociological analysis, except perhaps as dreams are somehow recorded and become social "texts." This sociological view remains insufficiently social, however, in not acknowledging how actual dreaming itself, like speaking, is both a social trait of all humans and consists of narrativelike structures and a "language" of images incorporated from cultural experience. Whereas speech communicates publicly shared meanings, dreams can incorporate private meanings that transcend local culture. For this reason it is important to view dreams as private, yet thoroughly social, experiences. Dreams are self-communications, feelings that have already been elaborated into communicative, imagistic signs. Dreams may be indicators not only of individual development but also of formative experiences in the inner growth of the person and the origins of human symbolic activity.

In attempting to fathom the vanished past from visible remains, we tend to ignore the most perfect archaeological artifact of human evolution: the living human body. Although archaeologists have become quite sophisticated in using medical and physical evidence from ancient corpses, they have not been as willing to use the living human body today as evidence for prior likely evolutionary developments. Yet *archaeoneurology* remains an area of potentially great significance, not only for an understanding of how humans became human, but also for understanding contemporary human nature and signification.

Though I am not familiar with earlier uses of the term *archaeo-neurology*, the idea was familiar to Sigmund Freud, the neurologist and archaeologist of the psyche and amateur archaeologist of ancient civilizations. If anti-Semitism had not barred Freud from an academic career, he might have become a noted archaeologist instead of the founder of psychoanalysis. Yet Freud's investigations of the unconscious show that he remained a psychic archaeologist, attempting to show how the dreams of his turn-of-the-century patients revealed both a personal history and a biological drama as old as the human race. In *The Interpreta-*

tion of Dreams, Freud uses a stratigraphic method of symbol interpretation in which the contents of dreams are shown to reveal underlying
sexual and familial themes, such as the Oedipal myth, and these themes
are ultimately rooted in Freud's nineteenth-century neurological understanding of the reflex-arc concept. The layers of the unconscious are like
the layers of time embedded in an archaeological site: each level a
farther step into the past, until one arrives at the mechanical model of
the reflex arc as explanation.

Freud's archaeoneurology is a curious blend of literary interpretation
and scientistic mechanism. Freud posits a divided psyche, which is a
classic example of cultural nominalism: there is the subject whose question is "How do I know?" and the object whose question is "How does
it work?" The first Freud called *das Ich,* the I or ego, the second he called
das Es, the it or id. The id is the realm of mechanical force, the ego is the
realm of symbolic purpose. One might also read the id as Thomas
Hobbes's "state of nature" and the ego as a kind of "social contract."
Symbolic representation is achieved through the successful resolution of
the Oedipal conflict, in which the metaphoric Oedipus in us all comes
to harness the inner "natural" urges to murder and to commit incest by
identifying symbolically with the same sex parent and thereby "having"
or relating symbolically, rather than genitally, to the opposite sex parent.
One establishes an inner triadic, psychic family representation, which
serves to mediate the subject to the object, the unconscious.

One of Freud's positive achievements was to show the power of the
human family in the psyche. Just as Feuerbach had unmasked the "holy
family" as standing for the earthly family and Marx had unmasked the
earthly family to reveal the bourgeois family, Freud attempted to show
that the earthly family was itself a surface manifestation of deeper and
darker forces of the unconscious. Yet his choice of the Oedipus myth
and his own myth of a "primal horde," which had collectively killed the
primal father and then banded together to form a social contract against
further killings, have come to look much more, with the passage of time
and the accumulation of archaeological evidence, like the fin-de-siècle
fictions they were, when all of Europe, and Vienna in particular, banded
together to kill off the past. Freud's "primal horde," perhaps more than
his other images, reveals the workings of a mythic nominalism, of a
world of convention banded together for its own protection and set
utterly apart from its own ground of development: competitive struggle
for individual survival is natural, relationship or mutual aid is not and
must therefore be invented.

One sees in Freud's psychoanalytic theories the deep imprint of Hobbes and other English thinkers admired by Freud, such as John Stuart Mill, transposed to the "innerness" of German/Austrian thought. Freud helped to open up the floodgates of the unconscious in the face of twentieth-century rationalism, yet his view of the workings of the psyche is itself another manifestation of that rationalism: it is tethered to an outmoded mechanical model of biology and to a conception of human communities and communication as epiphenomenal aspects of consciousness, superimposed on the underlying reality of the id.

Freud's junior colleague, C. G. Jung, broke with him because of Freud's rationalism. Jung increasingly appreciated the purposeful role of nonrational symbols and the limited place of rationality in the purposeful activities of the psyche. One might say that whereas Freud's unconscious becomes darker the farther one penetrates into the unconscious, Jung's unconscious becomes increasingly luminous, perhaps too much so. One moves from the darkness of the personal unconscious to the archetypal figures of the collective unconscious. Jung believed that the deepest processes of the unconscious were collective, purposive symbols: literally personalities. The images of the trickster and the hero were not solely the products of legends and myths, but were realities embodied within the psyche. These personalities were related through narrative inner transformations that could be observed in dreams, in artistic activities, and, Jung believed, in the symbolism of myths and religions.

In many ways Jung comes closer to the idea of archaeoneurology, but he remained, as did Freud, bound by an overly inner view of the human psyche and too ready to deprive experience of its own formative influence in the generation and meaning of symbols. Freud and Jung opened new dimensions for the human sciences, but their theories give short shrift to the thoroughly social nature of dreaming and psychic life in general. Freud's metapsychological foundations are rooted in the nominalistic individualism of Hobbes, with symbolic consciousness the inner psychic equivalent of Hobbes's social contract, erected over the "Warre of Each against all" of the state of nature, or, in Freud's term, the *id*. Jung's concept of the archetypal unconscious is more social than Freud's, but it still is based on a Kantian-like structuralism that does not explain how archetypal structures came about or how human experience and culture may transcend archetypal imperatives both individually and institutionally. Sociologists may see in Durkheim's theory of *conscience collective* a more socially based understanding of dreams. In his late work Durkheim attempted to show how the faculties of knowing are social, as opposed to the individual faculty theory of knowledge deriving from Kant. Yet Durkheim, too, remained tethered to the legacy of Kantian structuralism, in believing that: (1) a fundamental duality between individual consciousness and collective consciousness exists; (2) collective representations ultimately represent one fundamental, underlying, unchanging entity: society; and (3) collective representations are essentially conventional. These beliefs reveal why Durkheim remains inadequate to understand the social reality of dreaming. As opposed to Durkheim's claims: (1) individual consciousness is a social precipitate continuous with the collective biosocial heritage rather than dualistically opposed to it; (2) that which collective representations signify may emerge, grow, die, and undergo genuine transformation in time; and, finally, (3) as dream-symbols make abundantly clear, collective representations are not limited to purely conventional signification, but they draw from other modalities of signification, such as iconic and indexical signs.

The evolution of humans is marked by various anatomical changes, such as the development of the upright stance, the radical enlargement of the cranium and specifically the forebrain, and the creation of a vocal cavity with lowered larynx and subtle tongue and lip movements capable of producing an enormous variety of utterances. Speech is clearly one achievement of this process that uniquely identifies us as humans. But so too, for that matter, is artistic expression. Both are sign-practices dependent on the achievement of symbolic representation, and both reveal how to be human is to be a living, feeling, communicative symbol. Now a symbol, in the Peircean view I have adopted, is a social fact: a triadic relation whose meaning "depends either upon a convention, a habit, or a natural disposition of its interpretant or of the field of its interpretant" (Peirce 1958:8.335). In the case of the symbolic sign, as distinguished from iconic or indexical signs, the process of interpretation comes to the foreground, and, from a cultural perspective, this is to say that to be human is to be an interpreter. The very achievement of symbolic signification stands upon the vast capacities for pre- and protosymbolic communication developed by our forerunners and tempered into our physical organisms. And dreams may very well have provided the inner drama necessary to provoke us into interpretation by presenting images of a phantasmagoric "here and now," which break into the habits of everyday life.

The neurophysiology of dreaming suggests that dreaming is the inner life of humanity in a virtually purified state: the inner conversation of brain and mind. Brain "speaks" its ancient voices of phylogenetic experience through neurotransmitters that either emanate from the old "reptilian" brain and flow upward to the cortex, where visual, associative, and motor areas are excited (Hobson 1987:338–340), or, in the view of other researchers, through a reciprocal activation of the "old" brain centers with the "new," upper ones. In this process ancient neurophysical impulses become transformed into acts and associated meanings expressed in the images—whether visual or not—themselves. Iconic signification, which is to say the inherent presence or the communicative character of the sign itself, is the predominant language of this inner world, the meeting place of brain and mind. Yet, in contemporary humans, those icons of dreams are themselves frequently shaped from the reservoir of cultural experience and symbolic signification. The resources of mind and memory, incorporating both collective cultural experience, such as language, and personal experience play an active role in either consummating or frustrating the neurochemical dance.

Dreaming is the cultic ground of mind, a communicative activity between the most sensitive archive of the enregistered experience of life on the earth, the brain, and the most plastic medium for the discovery and practice of meaning, the mind or culture. Most explanations of dreaming have tended to view it as ultimately passive, as a compensatory mechanism for daytime existence. In the Freudian view dreaming is the way that repressed wishes of the unconscious can be actively disguised through symbolism, thereby "venting" their energies in a way that will not undo consciousness. In many recent neurophysiological views, dreaming allows the recharging of the brain's neurochemical batteries. If human bodies were simply machines, these theories would perhaps be adequate. But it is important to realize that just as the mind is formative, generating new ideas collectively and individually, the brain, as the chief organ of mind, may also be formative or active.

One wonders what the neurophysiologists' answers to other human activities might be: Why do we make music, images, and dance? Why does belief play such a central role in human affairs? Why can dreams wreak such havoc upon habituated experience and memory through fantastic associations or inversions? Why are all humans compelled to participate in these strange cults of the night? Why are such bizarre antics—the nightly Mad Hatter's party of REM sleep to which all are invited whether we remember it or not—absolutely necessary to our ability to function in the day world? When we begin to ask questions such as these, it becomes possible to turn the dream question around. In other words, only by exploring that strange culture within us in its own terms, taking the "native's" point of view toward our inner life, can we begin to understand the alien within and our glassy essence.

Perhaps dreaming itself is the purpose of dreaming, the end for which the neurophysiology is the means. As Milan Kundera writes in *The Unbearable Lightness of Being,* "Dreaming is not merely an act of communication (or coded communication, if you like); it is also an aesthetic activity, a game of the imagination, a game that is a value in itself. Our dreams prove that to imagine—to dream about things that have not happened—is among mankind's deepest needs." This interpretation may strike the reductionists among neurophysiologists and social theorists as too fantastic, but perhaps the fantastic is an inbuilt aspect of evolutionary reality, difficult though it may be to understand in our utilitarian age.

Although it is frequently acknowledged that the unconscious is the source of creativity, it may be that dreaming, the night music of the soul, may also help generate new neural pathways. In other words, dream images may function as prospective symbols for mind, just as REM neural activity may function as neural network-making for brain: perhaps the two work in psychophysical relation, as might be indicated by the large proportion of time devoted to REM sleep in fetuses and infants, when the brain itself is rapidly growing.

Lewis Mumford proposes that man's inner world "must often have been far more threatening and far less comprehensible than his outer world, as indeed it still is; and his first task was not to shape tools for controlling the environment, but to shape instruments even more powerful and compelling in order to control himself, above all, his unconscious. The invention and perfection of these instruments—rituals, symbols, words, images, standard modes of behavior (mores)—was, I hope to establish, the principal occupation of early man, more necessary to survival than tool-making, and far more essential to his later development" (Mumford 1967:51).

Although humanity has become increasingly conscious of itself, it has never stopped dreaming. Nor have its dreams become any less wondrous and terrifying. Communicative signs, not utilitarian tools, were the first human technics, created out of the human body itself, which was then and remains today the most sophisticated human achievement.

If we consider then the influence of dreaming as creating a movement toward interpretative order, we can see how that process could lead to an excess of order. When stretched beyond organic limits, such as life-purposes, local habitat, and local social organization, the tendency toward interpretation could take on a life of its own. Archaeological evidence suggests that proto- and early humans lived for the most part in environments that could localize and thereby neutralize the tendency to overreach for order or system. If we think of early cities and emergent civilizations as going beyond the earlier environmental resources and limits, we can suggest that the "megamachine"—reified, centralized order—was a product of that time, as Mumford claims, but that it was also a latent possibility already built into the human creature as a negative consequence of the dream-induced body technics.

Biological evolution and cultural development are not simply a progressive casting off of shackles and a movement toward a greater and ultimately unrestrained freedom, but they involve trade-offs of one kind of limitation for another. The achievement of human symbolic consciousness may have cost us a somewhat diminished perceptual or emotional life: who is to say that the forms of feeling produced by Neanderthal burial rituals, and the dawning significance of death and mortality for Homo erectus and even earlier creatures, may not have more to do with the real essence of human symbolic consciousness than a modern rationalist treatise on culture produced by a human product of that consciousness? On the other hand, the Mozart and the Verdi *Requiem* provide ample evidence that the achievement of symbolic consciousness also enlarges and enhances perceptive and emotional capacities. There may have been a trade-off of emotive brain power in the overall reduction of brain size from earlier humans, such as Neanderthal, to Homo sapiens sapiens, but the subtilizing of brain through the enlargement of the forebrain may have provided compensation. One is reminded of Herman Melville's dictum: "Why then do you try to 'enlarge' your mind? Subtilize it."

Mumford and only a very few other social theorists point to the unusual fact that our big brains seem possessed of excess energies and that this characteristic may explain a number of peculiar features of human existence. But there is an even more fundamental question that seems to me ignored, even though it goes to the crux of the evolutionary debate dating back to Darwin and Wallace: How did our big brains come about? It is not simply that we had big brains which we then had to control, but also that we evolved big brains, presumably through an evolutionary increase of brain use and adaptiveness. What was it that made big brains adaptive? Increasingly complex social organization?

Increasingly complex dreaming? Or both? Did the human brain evolve in the context of an evolving mind? Did mind, and not simply chance variation or adaptiveness, need more brains? Did the emergent symbolic consciousness need more forebrain and therefore "select" for the growth of this region?

Is it possible that the idea of the megamachine goes back much farther again, back to the emergence of Homo sapiens sapiens? If protohumans evolved the tools of ritual, speech, artistic expression, and mores of conduct as means of controlling the inner anxieties, anxieties related to our big brains, perhaps the tendency to automatonlike order was also embedded in the central nervous system. Hence we would be creatures biologically impelled toward autonomy and meaning, as Mumford says, yet also biologically constructed to take the quest for meaning too far, thereby substituting order for meaning. The acquisition of meaning and autonomy may have been achieved at the cost of repetition compulsions or even the removal of biological inhibitions against overcentralization. Though cultural reductionists claim that human culture helped free us entirely from instincts, this view overlooks the possibility that human instincts continue to operate in vague and suggestive, yet vitally important, ways. Largely liberated from the genius of instinctive determination, we may be creatures neurologically constituted to walk the knife-edge between autonomy and the automaton, our task being, not to escape biology, but to make human autonomy instinctive.

Or let me express this view in another way. Perhaps the symbol itself, as the medium of human consciousness, is so constituted, both in its freedom grounded in human conventions and in its mysterious relations to the central nervous system, that it *needs* to be connected to perceptive and critical—that is, lived—experience. Contrary to celebrated views of the symbol (or *sign* in Saussure's terminology) as completely "unmotivated" or arbitrary, I claim the symbol is that sign most dependent on vital and critical experience for its continued development.

We live in signs and they live through us, in a reciprocal process of cultivation that I have elsewhere termed *critical animism*. If most tribal peoples have traditionally lived in a world of personified forces—or animism—and if this general outlook was evicted by the modern "enlightened" view of critical rationality and its "disenchanted" worldview, then I am proposing a new form of re-enchantment, or marriage, of these opposites. Critical animism suggests that rational sign-practices, though necessary to contemporary complex culture and human freedom, do not exhaust the "critical" and that the human impulse to meaning springs from extrarational and acritical sources of bodily social intelligence.

The evolution of protohumans, though marked by the greater reliance on symbolic intelligence, did not necessarily mean the complete loss of instinctive intelligence as some theorists, such as Gehlen, have implied. On the contrary, one key aspect of the emerging symbolic intelligence "in the dreamtime long ago" may very well have been an instinctive, yet highly plastic or generalized, ability to listen to and learn from the rich instinctual intelligence of the surrounding environment. The close observation of birds, not only as prey but also as sources of delight, could also help to inform one of an approaching cold spell or severe winter.

A better example might be the empathic relations to animals and natural phenomena shared by many tribal peoples. One frequently sees an identification with an animal or plant related to the practices of a people, such as the cult of the whale for fishing peoples, and a choice of an object that somehow symbolizes a central belief of a people, such as the white *mudyi* tree as a symbol of the milk of the matrilineally rooted Ndembu of Africa. There exists then a range from a practical, informing relationship to nature, or a fantastic elaboration of that relationship, to a purely symbolic relationship to the environment that either may be unrelated to the surrounding instinctual intelligence or that might even function as a kind of veil to obscure the informing properties of the environment. These relationships were crucial to the emergence of humankind: the deeply felt relationship to the organic, variegated biosphere, which was manifest in those natural signs or instincts of other species, and the corresponding pull away from the certainties of instinctual intelligence toward belief, toward humanly produced symbols that created a new order of reality, and in doing so, both amplified and layered over the voices of nature.

Through mimesis, emerging humankind could become a plant or bird or reindeer, and thereby attune itself to the cycles of nature through the perceptions of these beings. A mimetic understanding also involves the generalizing of nature into symbolic form. A man dressed as a raven or bear at the head of a Kwakiutl fishing boat and the lion-headed human figurine found in Germany that dates back thirty-two thousand years (a very early find possibly suggesting interaction between Neanderthals and anatomically modern humans) signify the sym-

bolic incorporation of animal qualities into human activities and provoke human reflection, through what William James called the "law of
dissociation," on the meaning of human activities.

Dreaming is central to mimesis, and dreaming itself may be seen as
an in-built form of "recombinant mimetics"—with all the power and
danger of recombinant genetics—in which fantastic juxtapositions of
neural pathways and cultural images and associations take place. Dreaming is perhaps the primal "rite of passage," through cult, to culture.

In examining the brain-mind dialogue of dreaming we see a domain
that bridges nature and culture, which may have been essential to the
emergence of human symbolic culture and may remain essential to its
continued development. In that sense dreaming opens an unexpected
window onto the cultic roots of culture: the spontaneous springing
forth of belief. And if Mumford is correct that dreaming may have
impelled us toward a technics of symbolism both to control the anxieties produced by the inner world and to be animated by its image-
making powers, then perhaps we can better understand the cultic origins of culture through examining the ritual symbol itself and the drama
of communication that emerged from it. I cannot undertake that analysis here. But in indicating the line we big-brained apes must have followed in entering and establishing the human world, one conceivable
consequence has, I hope, become somewhat clearer. The impulse to
meaning is both original to our nature and ineradicable.

Modern deratiocination, falsely termed *rationalization* by Max Weber, is that decontextualized form of rationality whose continued and
unlimited growth involves the progressive elimination of the impulse to
meaning. Its logical terminus is a closed rational system *and* stochastic
indeterminacy. This is what Jürgen Habermas euphemistically calls "a
progressive unfettering of the rationality potential inherent in communicative action" (1987 [1981]:191). Contrary to Habermas's unshakable
Enlightenment optimism, the unfettering of the limits of rationality led
to Kundera's "unbearable lightness of being," which no new and improved "communicative" rationality is sufficient to correct. Dressed in
our little, brief "rationalization," we become most ignorant of what we
are most assured, our extrarational impulse to meaning, and cultural life
withers as do rationalistic theories of culture.

We are left, it seems to me, with centering our investigation of the
roots of culture in the most sophisticated technics the world has yet
known: those of the human body. Through human memory we have a
profound connection to the past: to historical, prehistorical, and even

transhuman memory as the incorporation of organic experience. Living human memory, which is something quite different from mere nostalgia, makes it possible for collective and personal past experience to infuse its wisdom into the present and so generate new prospects for future conduct. No computer memory chip can help a computer to *feel* a novel situation, as human memory can, or to generate a truly novel interpretation. The generalization of human memory in myths, rituals, traditions and writing vastly broadened the spatiotemporal environment and human power. But power is double edged, and as Milan Kundera has said, "The struggle of man against power is the struggle of memory against forgetting."

The origins of culture are to be found in those communicative practices through which emergent humanity literally bodied itself forth, creating a forebrain with language, speech, and personality capacities, creating a tongue, larynx, and throat capable of articulate speech, creating forms of expression, rituals of affliction and celebration, dramas of mythic, social, and personal communication, and stable institutions such as agriculture, villages, and later, cities, which have endured from Neolithic times to the present. The very expression "the culture and manurance of minds" may reflect the invention of manuring and its connection, through agriculture, to the development of permanent villages and protocities in the Neolithic Age. In other words, the very concept of culture may be an achievement and legacy of the Neolithic Age. Contemporary culture and culture theory seem intent on etherealizing these achievements out of existence and may very well succeed.

No age proves more than ours what a dangerous thing a little knowledge can be. Overweening knowledge and technique have characterized the modern age, producing great and terrible ideas and powers. The modern age created new possibilities for autonomy and human freedom, ideals which more often than not turned into their opposites, but which yet might remain compelling. Yet the foundation of this nominalistic epoch has been a ghost in the machine worldview, which has increasingly displaced and devalued organic human purpose and the impulse to meaning.

Modern nominalistic culture may be characterized as seeking to escape its organic roots through spectral theories of mind and mechanistic theories of matter. The chief task of a theory of culture today is to rediscover those extrarational, incarnate sources of meaning that the cult of modernity has now reduced to insignificance and to create a new outlook that can encompass humanity incarnate. This task is not a retreat into "irrationalism" or biological reductionism but is a frank recognition that the beliefs of modern progress and modern rationality were built on false nominalistic premises: the reified view of nature as a mechanical system and the etherealized view of culture or mind as subjectivistic and set apart from nature. Human reason, in all its fullness, is in living continuity with the cultic roots of culture and is much more than merely rational. The cultic roots of culture, expressed in mother-infant bonding and those playful, dreamlike, inquisitive, and ritualistic forms of conduct, gradually impelled our protohuman ancestors to humanity and, whether we like it or not, remain deeply embedded sources of human cultures and conduct.

References

Becker, H. S. 1982. *Art Worlds*. Berkeley and Los Angeles: University of California Press.

Bourdieu, P. 1984. *Distinction: A Social Critique of the Judgement of Taste*. Translated by Richard Nice. Cambridge: Harvard University Press.

Bürger, P. 1984. *Theory of the Avant-Garde*. Translated from the German by Michael Shaw. Minneapolis: University of Minnesota Press.

Geertz, C. 1973. *The Interpretation of Cultures*. New York: Basic Books.

———. 1983. *Local Knowledge*. New York: Basic Books.

Griswold, W. 1987. "The Fabrication of Meaning." *American Journal of Sociology* 92 (5): 1077–1118.

Habermas, J. 1987 [1981]. *The Theory of Communicative Action*. Vol. 2, *Lifeworld and System: A Critique of Functionalist Reason,* translated by Thomas McCarthy. Boston: Beacon Press.

Hobson, J. A. 1987. "Dreaming." In *Encyclopedia of Neuroscience*. Boston: Birkhäuser.

Kroeber. A. L., and T. Parsons. 1958. "The Concepts of Culture and of Social System." *American Sociological Review* 23: 582–583.

Lyotard, J. F. 1984 [1979]. *The Postmodern Condition*. Minneapolis: University of Minnesota Press.

Mumford, L. 1967. *The Myth of the Machine*. Vol. 1, *Technics and Human Development*. New York: Harcourt Brace Jovanovich.

———. 1970. *The Myth of the Machine*. Vol. 2, *The Pentagon of Power*. New York: Harcourt Brace Jovanovich.

Peirce, C. S. 1958. *The Collected Papers of Charles Sanders Peirce*. Vol. 8. Cambridge: Harvard University Press.

Rochberg-Halton, E. 1986. *Meaning and Modernity*. Chicago: University of Chicago Press.

————. 1989a. "On the Life-Concept in Social Theory." *Comparative Social Research* 11 (1): 319–343.

————. 1989b. "Jürgen Habermas's Theory of Communicative Ethe-realization." *Symbolic Interaction* 12 (2): 343–363.

————. 1989c. "Nachwort" (Afterword). In *Das Ritual: Struktur und Anti-Struktur,* German translation of Victor Turner's *The Ritual Process,* translated by Sylvia Schomberg-Scherff, 198–213. Frankfurt: Campus Verlag.

————. 1990. "The Transformation of Social Theory." In *Lewis Mumford: Public Intellectual,* edited by Thomas and Agatha Hughes. New York: Oxford University Press.

————. 1992. "Habermas and Rorty: Between Scylla and Charybdis." *Symbolic Interaction.* In press.

Sacks, O. 1987. *The Man Who Mistook His Wife for a Hat.* New York: Harper Perennial.

Swidler, A. 1986. "Culture in Action: Symbols and Strategies." *American Sociological Review* 51: 273–286.

Turner, V. 1967. *The Forest of Symbols.* Ithaca, N.Y.: Cornell University Press.

————. 1969. *The Ritual Process.* Chicago: Aldine.

————. 1985. *On the Edge of the Bush: Anthropology as Experience.* Edited by Edith Turner. Tucson: University of Arizona Press.

Williams, R. 1976. *Keywords.* New York: Oxford University Press.

Wolff, J. 1981. *The Social Production of Art.* New York: St. Martin's Press.

Wuthnow, R. 1987. *Meaning and Moral Order.* Berkeley and Los Angeles: University of California Press.

3

The Order-maintaining and Order-transforming Dimensions of Culture

S. N. Eisenstadt

The Problem: Its Background and Development in Contemporary Sociological Analysis

One of the central problems in the sociological analysis of culture, and especially of the relations between culture and social structure, has been that of the order-maintaining versus the order-transforming functions of culture. One line of analysis, coming from Marx and Durkheim (and, in a modified form, from Parsons), tends to regard culture (especially religion or ideology) mainly as a reflection of society or as its major legitimizing or consensus-creating mechanism. The second line, epitomized in Weber's analysis of the world religions, especially of the Protestant ethic, stressed the order-transforming, innovative dimensions of religion, of culture.

These different visions of the place of culture in the construction of social order are closely related to the problem of the degree to which social structure determines culture or vice-versa. They are closely related to the extent of mutual determination of culture, social structure, and social behavior; or, as Renato Rosaldo has put it, the degree to which culture is a cybernetic feedback-control mechanism controlling behavior and social structure, or whether there exists a possibility of choice and inventiveness by various social actors in the use of cultural resources.

These problems have been at the center of many theoretical discussions and controversies in the social sciences, especially since the mid-

1960s, and have developed in close conjunction with criticism of the structural-functional approach. These discussions have touched on many of the substantive problems of the social sciences: the nature of modern society or societies; the vision of humanity and history; the different modes of analysis and explanation in the social sciences; the place of the social sciences in the modern and postmodern intellectual traditions; and the boundaries of different scholarly disciplines (Eisenstadt and Curelaru 1976, 1977). In conjunction with these controversies, there have been far-reaching shifts in the definition of the major concepts of social science analysis, in the relations between the major explanatory models employed in the social sciences, and in the consequent directions of research.

The major shift in the basic concepts of social science analysis, concepts that include culture as well as religion, knowledge, social structure, and social behavior, was in their conceptualization as distinct and "real" ontological entities and not (as in earlier periods of sociological and anthropological analysis) as analytical constructs referring to different aspects or dimensions of human action and social interaction, that is, as constitutive of each other and of patterns of social interaction. Concomitantly, there developed a shift of emphasis with respect to several dimensions of culture and of social structure, especially away from the structural-functional emphasis on values and norms. One view—explicit among the structuralists and implicit among some of the ethnomethodologists—regarded culture as containing the programmatic codes of human behavior and espoused (to use Geertz's felicitous, if ironical, expression) the view of man as cerebral savage (for example, Lévi-Strauss 1983). According to this view, culture is fully structured or programmed according to clear principles and is embedded in the nature of the human mind, which, through a series of codes, regulates human behavior. By contrast, the symbolic anthropologists, such as Clifford Geertz, Victor Turner, and David M. Schneider and to some extent the symbolic interactionists in sociology, shifted from values and norms to a conception of culture as a set of expressive symbols of ethos—a worldview constructed through active human interaction (Geertz 1973, 1983; Turner 1974, 1947, 1968; Schneider 1973, 1980, 1977). As R. Peterson has stated:

The focus on drama, myth, code, and people's plan indicates a shift in the image of culture. . . . It was once seen as a map for behavior. In this view, people use culture the way scientists use paradigms to organize and normalize their activity. Like scientific paradigms, elements of culture are used, modified, or discarded depending on their usefulness in organizing reality as equivalent to the term ideology, but without the latter's pejorative connotations. Sociologists now recognize that people continuously choose among a wide range of definitions of situations or fabricate new ones to fit their needs (Peterson 1979).

Yet another development involved an individualist (or rational-choice) mode of analysis, which regarded culture as the result of the aggregation of individual preferences, reflecting differences of power or patterns of individual choices (Hirshfeld, Atran, and Yengoyan 1982). Parallel shifts in the concept of social structure have also evolved since the mid-sixties. The concept has become firmer in new definitions that view social structure and institutions—especially the "state"—as "real" and "autonomous" agents or actors (for instance, Skocpol 1979; Wolff 1950, 1957; Blau 1964, 1965; Boudon 1981; Merton 1963).

In another development closely related to the rational-choice approach, social structure was viewed as networks or organizations arising from the aggregation of interactions, with almost no autonomous characteristics except for some emergent qualities often described as "primitive effects." This network approach tended to neglect or downplay the tradition of structural analysis represented in the works of Simmel, Merton, Blau, and Boudon, which have stressed the formal characteristics and emergent properties of social structure (Blau 1964; Boudon 1981; Merton 1963).

Finally, these shifts were accompanied by a preference for exclusive deterministic, reductionist, idealist, or materialist interpretations of social action and culture creativity. They were also connected with a growing dissociation between studies of culture and of social structure.

These shifts and the studies they generated sharpened and diversified the definitions of culture and articulated the problems of positioning it in the construction of social order. At the same time they continuously oscillated in their view of the relationship between culture and social structure in any given society as either static and homogeneous or as entirely open, malleable, and continuously changing.

The first view, typical of some structuralists and extreme Marxists, depicts cultural orientations or rules—whether they are, as among the structuralists, reflections of some basic rules of the human mind or, as among the Marxists, reflections of social forces—as relatively uniform and homogeneous within the society and as relatively static with little change throughout the histories of the societies or civilizations in which they are institutionalized. Such a picture leaves little room (beyond the initial institutionalization of the different cultural visions) for reconstruction and change in the relations between culture and social structure. Nor does it allow for, or explain, various aspects of praxis and the construction of changing mentalities that have been analyzed in recent anthropological, historical, and sociological literature. Finally, it does not explain the development of strategies of choice, maximization, and possible innovation as depicted in individualistic approaches.

In the second view, culture is regarded as an aggregate result of patterns of behavior, structure, or power or—as Ann Swidler has explained it—as a tool kit of different strategies of action that can be activated in different situations according to the "material" and "ideal" interests of different social actors (Swidler 1986). This view implies that culture is merely a mirror or aggregate of continuously changing rational or expressive choices made by individuals and groups without any autonomy of their own.

Toward the Reintegration of Studies of Culture and Social Structure: Comparative Analysis of Liminality and Heterodoxies

It is not surprising that many scholars from different schools soon recognized the need to reconnect the many different strains of research and analysis. This chapter attempts to contribute to such a reconstruction and to reintegrate the studies of culture and social structure. In so doing, I hope to shed new light on the place of culture in the construction of social order in general and on the order-maintaining and order-transforming functions of culture in particular. The contribution will be made on the basis of comparative studies of liminal situations and of heterodoxies in different civilizations.[1]

Our analysis begins with the recognition of the ubiquity of *liminality* in human societies. By this term I mean seemingly unstructured situations, "in between" more structured ones, and symbols of antistructure and communitas. Such situations and symbols can indeed, in different connotations, be found in all human societies, as can the unruly behavior that is often connected with them. The ubiquity of such situations is not given in some "natural," spontaneous tendencies, in an outburst against the discontents of civilization. Rather, these symbols, situations, and patterns of behavior are culturally and socially constructed, and the behavior that develops within them is also so constructed; even if it often seems spontaneous and "natural," it is a socially and culturally regulated spontaneity and definition of natural behavior. This is similar to the situation with respect to the "biological" crises of life—birth, adolescence, death, and so on—which, while rooted in clearly biological givens of human existence, are at the same time socially and culturally channeled (Homans 1962).

The central focus of the symbols found in such liminal situations is a very strong ambivalence to social and cultural order. This ambivalence and the strong emphasis on antistructure or communitas, which are built into many of these situations, are as much culturally constructed as the social structural and cultural order against which rebel the patterns of behavior that develop in these situations.

Such ambivalence to social order is rooted in several basic characteristics of human existence, indeed in some aspects of human biological nature. Among these are the relatively open biological program that characterizes the human species (Meyer 1984); the consciousness of such openness; a basic existential uncertainty or anxiety, most closely related to the consciousness of death, of human finality, and in attempts to overcome it (Dobzhansky 1973; Bloch and Parry 1982); and the capacity to imagine various possibilities beyond what is given here and there (Sartre 1956).

All societies construct such a social and cultural order, designed in part to overcome the uncertainties and anxieties implied in these existential givens. They do so by constructing symbolic boundaries of personal and collective identity (Durkheim [1912] 1954), by defining membership in different collectivities in terms of universal biological *primordial* categories such as age, generation, sex, and territorial attachment, by "answering" certain perennial problems of death and immortality in religious belief systems, and by distinguishing between the given, mundane world and another world beyond it and between the profane and the sacred.

Ironically, however, the very construction of such boundaries and of their institutional derivatives adds another element or component of uncertainty to the human situation, which exacerbates the original uncertainties and generates a strong ambivalence to social order. This element is the consciousness of the arbitrariness of any cultural construction: the consciousness that any given order is only one of several, perhaps many, possible alternatives, including the possibility of living beyond any social order whatsoever. In other words, the very construction of any social order, while a manifestation of human creativity, necessarily imposes severe limitations on such creativity and gives rise to an awareness of such limitations.

The awareness of such arbitrariness and limitation and the attempt to convince members of the society that social order, in general, and the specific social order in which they live, in particular, are the "correct" ones are portrayed in the myths and symbols promulgated in all societies through various ritual and communicative situations. These myths and symbols, the closely related "folktales," depict the combination of the attraction of the world outside the boundaries of social order and of the fear of stepping outside such boundaries. They stress the purity of the world inside, the pollution of the world outside (Douglas 1966), and the need to remain within such boundaries. They are not, however, able to eliminate the awareness of various possibilities that exist beyond these boundaries and hence the certain arbitrariness of any such boundaries, of any instituted social order.

The Roots of the Consciousness of the Arbitrariness of Social and Cultural Order: The Constructive and Destructive Dimensions of Charismatic Predispositions

The consciousness of the arbitrariness of any social and cultural order is exacerbated by the exigencies of reproducing social order through social institutions. It is important here to recognize the fact that constitutes the cornerstone of modern sociological analysis; namely, the inadequacy of the organization of social division of labor to explain the construction and maintenance of social order. The founding fathers of sociology, while recognizing the importance of the various mechanisms of social division of labor, emphasized that the social division of labor, in general, and the market mechanisms analyzed in great detail by economists, in particular, would not suffice to explain the construction of social order (Eisenstadt 1981).

The conditions necessary for sustaining social order are several: the construction of trust and solidarity, stressed above all by Durkheim and to some degree by Tonnies (Durkheim 1964a, 1964b; Tonnies 1957);

the regulation of power and the overcoming of the feelings of exploita-
tion, stressed above all by Marx and Weber (Marx 1965); and the
provision of meaning and of legitimation to the different social activities, emphasized above all by Weber (1952, 1958, 1951).

The founding fathers stressed, moreover, that the very construction
of any concrete social division of labor generates uncertainties with
respect to each of these conditions. Because of these uncertainties no
concrete social division of labor can be maintained without attending to
these dimensions. They emphasized accordingly that the construction
and maintenance of social order depends upon the development of
some patterned combination of the division of labor, the regulation of
power, and the construction of trust, meaning, and legitimation.

But the development of such a combination is not given. There are
inevitable uncertainties, unanticipated crises, and struggles reflecting
the tension between different dimensions of social order. These exacer-
bate the consciousness of the arbitrariness of any social order and the
concomitant ambivalence toward it.

The consciousness of the arbitrariness of any cultural and social order, the fact that such consciousness exacerbates the uncertainties and
anxiety rooted in the consciousness of the openness of biological program, of awareness of death and in the capacity of imagination and the
concomitant ambivalence to the social order, constitutes one of the
most important manifestations of the problems inherent in the process
of "routinization" of charisma. Above all, such consciousness constitutes a manifestation of the problem inherent in the limitations on
human creativity that any institutionalization of a charismatic vision
entails (Weber 1968). The essence of the charismatic dimension in
human life is the attempt to contact the very essence of being, to go to
the very roots of existence, of the cosmic, cultural, and social order, to
what is seen as sacred and fundamental.

This charismatic dimension focuses, in the cultural and social realms,
on the construction of cultural and social order in terms of some combination between primordial and transcendental symbols in terms of relation to some conception of the sacred. This charismatic dimension is
manifest in the construction of the boundaries of personal and collective
identity, of societal centers, and of major symbols of prestige. Such a
construction is indeed one of the fullest manifestations of human creativity. At the same time, however, the very institutionalization of such a
charismatic dimension generates very severe limitations on such creativ-

ity, and, in connection with the tendencies analyzed above, it also generates consciousness of such limitations.

The basic root of the limitations on human activity lies primarily in the fact that the process of the institutionalization of any concrete social setting entails a certain closure in the selection from a variety of potential or imagined possibilities. Second, the roots of such limitations lie in the routinization of the creative act, which is inherent in any such institutionalization, and in the close relation between such closure and the elements of power and domination that any such institutionalization entails.

Indeed, the restrictions and exclusions entailed by the institutionalization of any charismatic vision become necessarily closely associated with, although not necessarily identical to, the maintenance of the distribution of power and wealth, the control over resources, and the limitation of the scope of participation of various groups in the central arenas of a society and their access to meaningful participation in the social and cultural order. Such limitations on human creativity are also inherent in the ways in which the basic conditions of social order—the construction of trust (solidarity), meaning, power, and social division of labor—are related to one another in the process of concrete institution building. The crucial tension or contradiction is between the conditions that generate the construction of trust between different members of a group or society and those that ensure the availability of resources and institutional entrepreneurs in the formation of broader institutional complexes and their legitimation.

The conditions that make for maintenance of trust are best met in relatively limited ranges of social activities or interaction, such as in family or kinship groups in which social interaction is regulated according to primordial and particularistic criteria. Such limited ranges of interaction seem to constitute the necessary minimal conditions for the initial development of such trust, even if they may not be enough to guarantee its continuity. At the same time, however, these very conditions are inimical to the development of those resources and activities needed for broader institutional creativity and for the construction of broader institutional complexes based on more variegated orientations. The very conditions that generate resources for broader complex institution building also tend to undermine the simple, or "primitive," settings of potential trust as they exist within the family and kinship groups or in small communities.

The possibility of such institutionalization is above all dependent on the effective extension of the range of symbolism of trust beyond the narrow minimal scope of primordial units. Such extension is found, for example, in the depiction of rulers as "fathers" of their countries or in the infusion and legitimation of economic activities with some transcendental meaning. But any such extension necessarily heightens the combination of such extended trust and the distribution of power. Indeed, any construction of concrete social order necessarily institutionalizes some limitations on potential or imagined activities and exclusions of some sectors from full participation in it.

Such exclusions and limitations are, as we have seen, legitimized in various ritual and communicative situations, but the very attempts at such legitimations tend only to underlie and sharpen the awareness of arbitrariness and ambivalence toward the constructed social order. Accordingly, such situations may bring out strong antinomian orientations and many destructive tendencies. Such tendencies are not primitive, or "animal," reactions to the restriction of social and cultural life, but, paradoxically, they constitute the reverse and complementary side of the creative process of construction of order: the constructive aspect of the charismatic dimension of human activities (Weber 1968). They are as inherent in the very nature of the charismatic predisposition or fervor in the very attempt to come into contact with the essence of being, to go to the roots of existence, of cosmic, social, and cultural order, as are constructive tendencies.

The attempt to reestablish direct contact with these roots of cosmic and sociopolitical order may also contain a strong predisposition to sacrilege and to the denial of the validity of the sacred, and it may breed opposition both to more attenuated and formalized forms of this order and to the sacred itself. Similarly, on the personal level, it is in its charismatic roots that the human personality can attain its fullest creative power and internal responsibility, but these roots may also represent the epitome of the darkest recesses and excesses of the human soul, its utter depravity and irresponsibility, and its more intensive antinomian tendencies.

Thus, the very process of the construction of social and cultural order generates tendencies toward its destruction. The destructive aspects of charisma often involve the denial not only of the concrete restrictions inherent in institutionalization but also of the very fact of institutionalization and the social restrictions it entails. But even the seemingly total negation of the social order, the potentially destructive behavior related to it, and the attempts to overcome them are elements of the construction of cultural and social order.

Hence, however destructive and seemingly spontaneous are many of the manifestations of such ambivalence to social order, most are structured around several basic orientations and themes, particularly around major themes of protest that develop in all human societies in various culturally and socially structured situations, among them various liminal situations.

Liminal Situations and Orientations of Protest

This ubiquity of both the constructive and destructive aspects of the charismatic dimension of human activity, of the attempt to reestablish contact with the roots of the social and cultural order, and the manifestation of these aspects in liminal situations, indicates that the order-maintaining and order-transforming dimensions of culture are but two sides of the construction of social order.

Orientations and symbols of protest contain two basic components, out of which the more concrete themes of protest develop. The first is the attempt to overcome the predicaments and limitations of human existence in general and of death in particular. The second is the attempt to overcome the tension and predicaments inherent in the institutionalization of the social order: the tension between equality and hierarchy; the tensions among the social division of labor and the regulation of power, construction of trust, and provision of meaning; and the tension between the quest for meaningful participation in central symbolic and institutional arenas by various groups in the society and the limitation on the access to these arenas, which exists in every society. Out of the combination and development of these two basic components there develop four concrete themes of protest found in all societies.

1. The search to overcome the tension between the complexity and fragmentation of human relations inherent in any institutional division of labor and the possibility of some total, unconditional, unmediated participation in social and cultural orders.
2. The search to overcome the tensions inherent in the temporal dimension of the human and social condition, especially the

search for immortality; the tension between the deferment of gratification in the present and the possibility of its attainment in the future; and the tension between an emphasis on productivity and labor and the distribution and the accompanying stress of visions of unlimited goods. These tensions are often played out in various myths of the relations between Time of Origin and Time of End: *Uhrzeit* and *Endzeit* (Van der Lieuw 1957).

3. The quest to suspend the tension in the model of the ideal society; the principles of distributive justice upheld within it on the one hand and the reality of institutional life on the other.

4. The quest to suspend the tension between the personal and the autonomous self and the social role, that is, the possibility of finding full expression of the internal self in social and cultural life as opposed to the retreat from it.

These themes focus on specific aspects of the institutional order: on the construction of boundaries between the personality and the collectivity; on symbols of authority; on symbols of stratification that express hierarchy and the structural aspects of division of labor and distribution of resources; and on the family as the primary locus of authority, socialization, and restriction imposed on an individual's impulses and activities and as the locus in which those restrictions are closely related to the basic primordial data of human experience, especially to differences in age and sex. Focusing these themes of protest generates the themes of communitas, of antistructure, which constitute, in every society, part of the map of such antinomian symbols.

These orientations of protest are not marginal to the central symbols of a tradition of a society, erupting only in periods of social disorganization and change. They contain the elements of potential dissent and heterodoxy as inherent and continuous components of every social order.

Such potentialities of dissent and heterodoxy become manifest in a great variety of more fully articulated counter and secondary orientations (see, in greater detail, Eisenstadt 1976). First, they become articulated in the development of some ideals and orientations found in almost any great tradition, and while antithetical to some of the predominant basic premises of the tradition, they are nonetheless derived from its basic respective parameters. Each set of ideals and orientations points in a seemingly opposite direction, although they may reinforce one another. The interrelations between the Brahman ideal and the renouncer in Indian civilization, between the active church engaged in the world and the

monastic ideal in Western Christianity, and between the power orientation and the monastic ideal in the Eastern church illustrate contradictory
orientations within a single tradition.

These potentially antinomian tendencies often become connected
with the exaltation of those dimensions of human existence that are not
institutionalized in the tradition, for example, expressions of sub-
jectivism and privatization and an emphasis on the symbols of primordial attachment. The individuals or group that brings forward such
sentiments may claim that it is only within its own confines that the
pure, pristine, or primordial qualities emphasized in the ideals of the
center can be fully realized. Similarly the ideals of equality and communal solidarity may be emphasized instead of those of hierarchy, power,
and unequal distribution of wealth, which are seen as being upheld in
the center.

Second, such potentialities of dissent become articulated as the "double," "contradiction," or "other side" of a society's institutional image
(Decoufle 1968).

Third, the potentialities produce images of the pristine ideals of the
existing society, uncontaminated by its concrete "profane" institutionalization.

Fourth, they project images of a social and cultural order totally different from the existing one or uncontaminated by any institutionalization.

These various orientations and themes of protest, these "heterodox,"
antinomian, and potentially rebellious orientations, are articulated by
different groups or individuals in a great variety of social situations. The
various double images of the society are articulated and played out in
most of the major ritual and communicative situations in which the
models of social order are promulgated (Eisenstadt 1963).

These themes and the consciousness of the arbitrariness of such order
are first most fully and paradoxically promulgated in the rituals of the
center, such as coronation and national thanksgiving, attesting to the
fact that the consciousness of such arbitrariness is never fully obliterated
but is transposed to a more sophisticated, reflexive level of symbolism
and consciousness. These themes are also played out in fully structural
liminal situations—the various collective *rites de passage* such as first-
fruit ceremonies and collective rituals of initiation—in which the space
between the strict boundaries of various institutional arenas is symbolically constructed.

Third, these themes are articulated in special rituals of rebellion, in
which the existing power, hierarchy, and often sexual relations are mo-

mentarily, symbolically, and ritually reversed, but in which the potential antinomian tendencies are checked or regulated by full legitimation and institutionalization of the rituals.

Fourth, they are played out in a great variety of more loosely structured situations, such as for instance those of pilgrimage and play (Bruner et al. 1976; Turner 1973).

These varied images and themes may also become "stored" as it were in some arenas, institutions, or among social groups such as Buddhist monks. These groups may serve as the carriers of the symbolic attributes of membership in a collectivity and as its primordial, preinstitutional symbols (a good illustration is found in Mus 1967, 1968). These themes and images may also become defined as *esoteric* in both private and public life and as *private* and *personal* and opposed to the public sphere (Eisenstadt 1974; Eisenstadt and Roniger 1984). Alternatively, they may be witnessed in eruptions of chiliastic, millenarian, messianic outbursts or more organized movements of heterodoxy or protest.

In most of these situations some liminal space is created in which different orientations and themes of protest are played out, aiming, in one way or another, at the reconstruction of the relations between trust, power, social division of labor, and broader meaning and at reconstituting, reaffirming, or changing the boundaries of personal and collective identity: the symbols of the center and the delineation of pure, as opposed to dangerous, space. However, the ways in which these different types of liminality develop, and their specific location and impact, vary greatly in differing societies.

Protest and Liminal Situations in Tribal Societies and Axial Civilizations

The structuring of the symbolism of protest and of liminality and liminal situations is influenced by the different configurations of the major components of the construction of social order.

The social division of labor—the division of social roles in society— appears to play a very important role in shaping liminal situations. In less differentiated societies, many liminal situations are more structured and more fully ritualized. Accordingly, different themes of liminality, protest, and antistructure are more fully articulated and, in fact, highly regulated. Max Gluckman's classical analysis of rituals of rebellion

(1963) portrays exactly this type of situation, in which protest, liminality, and antistructure are very closely interrelated, fully structured, and placed in the center of the society. This distinctive feature also seems to minimize the disruptive potentialities of these activities and their potential for "change" and "real rebellion." However, as Beidelman's critique of Gluckman has shown (1966), the conflicts and ambivalences articulated in rituals of rebellion originate not only in tensions inherent in social organization but also in the nature of the symbolic construction of social and cultural life, which shapes and provides an overall meaning to the social order and of symbols of collective identity.

The structure and symbols of collective identity and of the center, their symbols and ideology, as they articulate the relations between trust, power, and social division of labor, and their broader meaning, are of crucial importance in the structuring of different types of liminal situations and their symbolism.

Even within societies with similar levels of social differentiation there develop different types of center and of liminal situations. A great variety of centers and concomitant different types of liminal situations can be identified in various African societies. Thus, the case of the Desanett, analyzed by Uri Almagor, points to contrasts between their situation and that of the Zulu described by Gluckman (Almagor 1985).

Almagor's analysis indicates that, even in such relatively undifferentiated societies, a multiplicity of liminal situations develop, many of which constitute the nuclei of an extension of trust and which may also be starting points for social change. This change may not be at the center of a society; it may occur in the restructuring of the symbolic boundaries of collectivities by creating nuclei of new tribal segments, thus pointing to the importance of such situations in analyzing different modes of change and changes in different components of the social order.

The variability of centers in societies is seen in the great premodern civilizations, especially in the so-called Axial Age civilizations (Eisenstadt 1982), those which crystallized out of the revolutions or transformations connected with what Karl Jaspers designated as the Axial Age in the first millennium before the Christian era—namely ancient Israel, later on Christianity in its great variety, ancient Greece, partially Iran during the development of Zoroastrianism, China during the early Imperial period, Hinduism and Buddhism, and, much later, beyond the Axial Age proper (Jaspers 1949; Voegelin 1954–1974). Common to all was the development of the conception of a basic tension between the transcendental and the mundane orders.

The institutionalization of such a conception of tension was not simply an intellectual exercise. It connoted a far-reaching change in humanity's active orientation to the world—a change with basic institutional implications—and it generated the symbolic, intellectual, and institutional possibilities for the development of sects and heterodoxies as potential agents of civilizational change.

On the symbolic level, the conception of a chasm between the transcendental and the mundane orders created a problem of how to overcome this chasm, how to bridge the transcendental and the mundane orders. This gave rise—to use Weber's terminology—to the problem of salvation, usually phrased in terms of the reconstruction of human behavior and personality given a higher moral or metaphysical order. As a result, as Gananath Obeysekere has explained, rebirth eschatology becomes ethicized (1983). But every attempt at such a reconstruction was torn by internal tensions. These tensions and their institutional repercussions ushered a new social and civilizational dynamic into history.

At the institutional level, the development of the conception of a chasm gave rise, in all these civilizations, to attempts to reconstruct the mundane world according to the transcendental principles. The mundane order was perceived as incomplete, inferior, and often in need of being reconstructed according to the precepts of the higher ethical or metaphysical order. This perception, and the attempts to reconstruct the mundane order, gave rise to far-reaching, concrete institutional implications. Among the most important of these implications was the construction of distinct civilizational frameworks and the development of the concept of the accountability of rulers.

Some collectivities and institutional arenas were singled out as the most appropriate carriers of the attributes required to reconnect the transcendental and the mundane. As a result, new types of collectivities were created or seemingly natural and "primordial" groups were endowed with special meaning couched in terms of the perception of this tension and its resolution. The most important innovation was the appearance of "cultural" and "religious" collectivities as distinct from ethnic or political ones. These collectivities tended to become imbued with a strong ideological dimension and to become a focus of ideological struggle with a strong insistence on their own exclusiveness and closure and on the distinction between inner and outer social and cultural space defined by them. This tendency became connected with attempts to structure the different cultural, political, and ethnic collectivities in some hierarchical order, and the very construction of such an order usually became a focus of ideological and political conflict.

Closely related to this mode of structuring special civilizational frameworks was a restructuring of the relations between the political and the higher, transcendental order. The political order as the central locus of the mundane order has usually been, in these civilizations, conceived as lower than the transcendental. It had to be restructured according to the precepts of the latter; i.e., according to the perception of how best to overcome the tension between the transcendental and the mundane order and how to implement the transcendental vision. The rulers were usually held responsible for organizing the political order according to such transcendental orientations.

At the same time the nature of the rulers was greatly transformed. The king-god, the embodiment of the cosmic and the earthly order alike, disappeared, and in its place appeared a secular ruler—sometimes with sacral attributes—in principle accountable to some higher order. There emerged the concept of the accountability of the rulers and the community to a higher authority, God, divine law, and the like. The possibility emerged of calling a ruler to judgment, presumably before the representatives of such higher authority. The first, most dramatic appearance of this conception appeared in ancient Israel, in the priestly and prophetic pronouncements. A different conception, that of accountability to the community and its laws, appeared in ancient Greece. In varying forms such conceptions of accountability appeared in all Axial civilizations (Eisenstadt 1981). The development of different concepts of accountability of rulers—and the continuous struggle between the rulers and the different groups that espoused such concepts and among the latter—generated a new political and cultural dynamic and intensified awareness of the arbitrariness of social order.

In connection with these specific symbolic and institutional characteristics of the Axial Age civilizations, far-reaching changes in the map of liminal situations and symbols and of movements and symbolism of protest have also taken place. While many of the liminal situations—especially different types of rituals of rebellion—have persisted, many new types, beyond those found in tribal societies, have developed, and at the same time the structure and the symbols of "older" situations have greatly changed.

First, in these civilizations the central, fully structured, and regulated rituals tend to become increasingly limited to fully elaborated rituals of the center, with the periphery playing a much more passive role, mainly as spectators or, at most, as rather passive recipients of the regnant vision. In these rituals the antistructural and the protest components and the symbols have been on the whole weakened and minimized, although there may develop a strong articulation of the ambivalences toward the arbitrariness of the cultural order combined with a strong, "orthodox" emphasis on the danger of diverting from it.

Second, there tend to develop within these societies and civilizations relatively autonomous spheres of behavior (currently denoted as *popular culture*) with different degrees of connection to central rituals. These include local festivals and leisure activities, as well as more elaborate carnivals, in which many of the ambivalences of protest are played out. These situations may become connected in different ways to more official regional rituals linking the center and the periphery, combining different mixtures of antinomianism and an acceptance of the hegemonic order (one classic analysis is Granet 1932, 1950; see also Wolf 1974).

Third, there develop an entirely new type of liminality and protest—fully fledged heterodoxies, sects, and sectarianism, a phenomenon closely related to the basic characteristics of the Axial civilizations (Eisenstadt 1982). Closely connected with the development of heterodoxy and sectarianism is the appearance of carriers of the "pristine" religious vision, the holy men of antiquity, such as Indian or Buddhist renouncers, Christian monks, and religious virtuosi (Silber 1981).

The Variability of Protest and of Liminal Situations in Axial Civilizations

These various types of liminal situations and protest can be found in all the Axial Age civilizations. There exist, however, far-reaching differences in the exact structure and symbolism of these liminal situations, in their organizational and symbolic maps, in their connection to movements of protest, and in their impact on the macrosocial order in general and processess of change in particular (Eisenstadt 1973). These differences are related to the combination of the mode of social division of labor and the structure of power, together with the basic cultural orientations, especially the nature of the concepts of salvation, that are predominant in them.

The greatest differences are those among the monotheistic civilizations, with their strong orientation to the reconstruction of the mundane order, and the otherworldly Asian civilizations, especially the Hindu and the Buddhist ones with their rejection of the world. There is also a significant difference between all these civilizations and the Chinese Confucian one, with its very strong affirmation of the mundane (especially political) order as the only arena of "salvation,"—the reconstruction of the mundane world according to the transcendental vision.

In the otherworldly civilizations, such as Buddhist (and, in a different mode, also Hindu), the major orientations of protest and the major impact of liminal situations are not, as in the monotheistic civilizations, on the reconstruction of the political centers of the respective societies. These centers are often seen as irrelevant to the major concept of salvation, and hence their reconstruction does not play a major role in these orientations and the movements of protest in these civilizations.

This does not mean that the Buddhist and Hindu sects did not have immense impacts on the dynamics of their respective civilizations. They extended the scope of the different national and political communities and imbued them with new symbolic dimensions (Tambiah 1976; Bechert 1966–1968; Sarkisyanz 1965; Reynolds 1977; Keyes 1977).[2] They also changed some of the bases and criteria of participation in the civilizational communities, as was the case in Jainism, in the Bhakti movement, and, above all, in Buddhism when an entirely new civilizational framework was reconstructed. Buddhism also introduced new elements into the political scene, particularly the unique way in which the Sangha, usually politically a very compliant group, could in some cases, as Paul Mus has shown, become a sort of moral conscience of the community, calling the rulers to some accountability.

This impact is different from that of the struggles between the reigning orthodoxies and heterodoxies in monotheistic civilizations (Eisenstadt 1982), most of which aim at the reconstruction of the mundane world, especially of the political centers.

But even in the monotheistic civilizations such impact may be limited by the strength of the center, by its distance from the centers of Christianity, by the position of the Church vis-à-vis the state, and by the degree of monopolization of sacred symbols by the rulers. In this connection it is fruitful to compare these developments with Eastern Christianity in general and the Byzantine and Russian empires in particular (Kaplan 1985; Eisenstadt 1973, 1982b). All these cases revealed variations in types of liminal situations and movements of protest and in the degree of their impact on the institutional arenas (Smelser 1963).

The full impact of the different symbols and movements of liminality and protest on the symbols of the center, as derived from the combination of this and otherworldly orientations, can be found in western Europe, in the transition of modernity, in the Great Revolutions (Eisenstadt 1978; Heyd 1985), and to some degree in the Jewish case in the Sabbatean movement. (The classical analysis on this movement is found in Scholem 1941, 1973.) In all these cases many of the symbols of protest, which were promulgated by the major movements of protest, such as demands for full participation of all members of the community in the political process and full equality and full accountability of rulers, were incorporated in the new revolutionary and postrevolutionary centers.

At the same time, however, this strong impact of these movements on the center should not obliterate the importance of the other types of liminal situations and of popular culture that tend to develop in such societies and that become even more pronounced—and transformed—with the development of modernity.

From the standpoint of the conceptions of salvation, the accountability of rulers, and the characteristics of liminal and sectarian activities, the legalistic Confucian Empire constitutes an interesting case between this-worldly and otherworldly civilizations. In many ways, this empire came closer to the monotheistic than to the otherworldly Axial Age civilizations, and yet it is also significantly different from the former (Fairbanks 1967; Fingarette 1972; Metzger 1977; Schwartz 1975).

Powerful heterodoxies, utopian visions, movements of protest, and orientations of protest and liminal situations did develop in China, especially among the neo-Confucians from the Sung period onward. These visions were also oriented—as was the case in other Axial civilizations—against specific aspects of the institutionalization of the major metaphysical and ethical messages and visions. And yet in China, unlike in the monotheistic civilizations in which the political arena also constituted an important focus of the soteriological quest, orientations and movements of protest did not lead to far-reaching institutional reconstruction of the political centers of the society.

Confucian thinkers of different generations, and especially neo-Confucians dating back to the Sung period, were concerned with the imperfection of the political system, of the emperor, of the examination system, and of the bureaucracy and attempted to find some fulfillment beyond them. But, given their basic adherence to the identification of the center, in the broad sense and especially in the political arena as the major arena of implementation of the Confucian vision, they did not go beyond the suggestion of reforms to any concrete reconstruction of the political premises of the center itself. The orientations of protest of the Confucian intellectuals mainly concerned the direction of cultural, and to some extent educational, activities, greater moral sensibility and responsibility, and, to a much lesser extent, the direction of the political arena.

The strong emphasis on individual responsibility and the moral cultivation of the individual, which was highly developed especially among the neo-Confucians and which entailed a strong orientation of protest and liminal connotation, was oriented either toward perfecting the philosophical premises of their respective systems or toward the development of private intellectual or even mystical religious tendencies and reflexivity. These could become connected with otherworldly tendencies but mostly on the private level.

Culture and Social Structure in the Order-maintaining and Order-transforming Dimensions of Culture

The discussion brings us back to the general problem of the relations between culture and social structure, the possible ways of analyzing them as constituents of one another and of social and cultural order, and the order-maintaining versus the order-transforming dimensions of culture.

In principle, the order-maintaining and the order-transforming aspects of culture are but two sides of the same coin. There is no basic contradiction between the two; they are part and parcel of the symbolic dimensions in the construction of social order.

No social order or pattern of social interaction can be constituted without the symbolic dimension of human activity, especially of some basic cultural and ontological visions. It is such visions that constitute the starting point for articulating the premises and institutional contours of any patterns of social interaction and especially of institutional and macrosocietal formations. Such a construction of social order, of the interweaving of social and cultural dimensions, is effected by processes of intensive social interaction and conflict among different elites and influentials and among them and broader groups and strata.

Such processes are effected by coalitions and countercoalitions of different social actors. These actors who promulgate such different ontological visions activate various processes of control—among them the various ritual and communicative structures analyzed above—and these very processes give rise to orientations and movements of protest, to the structuring of liminal situations, some of which may become harbingers of social change.

Such developments are not accidental or external to the realm of culture. They are given in the basic fact of the inherent interweaving of culture and of social structure as two constitutive elements of the construction of social order. It is because the symbolic components are inherent in the construction and maintenance of social order that they also bear the seeds of social transformation.

Such seeds of transformation are indeed common to all societies. Yet the ways in which they grow—the concrete constellations of different liminal situations, of different orientations and movements of protest, and their impact on societies within which they develop—greatly vary among different societies, giving rise to different patterns of social and cultural dynamics.

Notes

1. This analysis is based on a seminar on Comparative Liminality and Dynamics of Civilizations conducted by the late Victor Turner and the author in Jerusalem in 1982–1983 within the framework of the program on Sociological Analysis of Comparative Civilizations at the Department of Sociology and Social Anthropology and the Truman Research Institute of the Hebrew University in Jerusalem. On this program see S. N. Eisenstadt, "Sociological Approach to Comparative Civilizations." The Development and Directions of a Research Program, Jerusalem, The Hebrew University, 1986. The papers of the seminar on Comparative Liminality were published in *Religion* 15 (July 1985).
2. On some aspects of the dynamics of Buddhist civilization, from the standpoint of our analysis, see S. J. Tambiah (1976).

References

Almagor, U. 1985. "Long Time and Short Time Ritual and Non-Ritual Liminality in an East African Age-System." *Religion* 15 (July): 219–235.

Bechert, H. 1966–1968. *Buddhismus, Staat und Gesellschaft in der Länder des Theravada Buddhismus*. 4 Vols. Frankfurt am Main: Alfred Metzner.

Beidelman, O. 1966. "The Swazi Royal Ritual." *Africa* 36: 373–405.

Blau, Peter M. 1964. *Exchange and Power in Social Life*. New York: John Wiley.

———. 1965. "Justice and Social Exchange." *Social Inquiry* 34: 193–206.

Bloch M., and J. Parry, eds. 1982. *Death and the Regeneration of Life*. Cambridge: Cambridge University Press.

Boudon, Raymond. 1981. *The Logic of Social Action*. London: Routledge and Kegan Paul.

Bruner, J. S., A. Jolly, and K. Sylva, eds. 1976. *Play, Its Role in Development and Evolution*, 119–156, 174–222. Harmondsworth: Penguin.

Decoufle, A. 1968. *Sociologie des Revolutions*. Paris: Presses universitaires de France.

Dobzhansky, T. 1973. *Genetic Diversity and Human Equality*, chap. 3. New York: Basic Books.

Douglas, M. 1966. *Purity and Danger*. London: Routledge and Kegan Paul.

Durkheim, E. [1912] 1954. *The Elementary Forms of the Religious Life*. New York: Macmillan.

———. 1964a. *The Division of Labor in Society*. New York: Free Press.

———. 1964b. *The Rules of Sociological Method*. New York: Free Press.

Eisenstadt, S. N. 1963. "Communication and Reference Group Behavior." In *Essays in Comparative Institutions*. New York: John Wiley.

———. 1973. "Religious Organizations and Political Process in Centralized Empires." In *Tradition, Change and Modernity*. [1976]. New York: John Wiley.

———. 1974. "Friendship and the Structure of Trust and Solidarity in Society." In *The Compact Selected Dimensions of Friendship*, edited by E. Leyton, 138–146. St. John's: Memorial University of New Foundland.

———. 1976. *Tradition, Change and Modernity*. New York: John Wiley.

———. 1978. *Revolutions and the Transformation of Societies*. New York: Free Press.

———. 1981a. "The Schools of Sociology." *American Behavioral Scientist* 24(3): 329–344.

———. 1981b. "Cultural Traditions and Political Dynamics." *The British Journal of Sociology* 32 (June): 155–181.

———. 1982a. "Heterodoxies, Sectarianism and Dynamics of Civilization." *Diogenes* 120: 5–26.

———. 1982b. "The Axial Age: The Emergence of Transcendental Visions and the Rise of Clerics." *Archives Européennes de Sociologie* (European Journal of Sociology) 23: 294–314.

Eisenstadt, S. N., and M. Curelaru. 1976. *The Form of Sociology, Paradigms and Crises*. New York: John Wiley.

———. 1977. *Macro Sociology, Theory Analysis and Comparative Studies*. The Hague: Mouton.

Eisenstadt S. N., and L. Roniger. 1984. *Patrons and Friends*. Cambridge: Cambridge University Press.

Fairbanks, J. K., ed. 1967. *Chinese Thought and Institutions*. Chicago: University of Chicago Press.

Fingarette, H. 1972. *The Secular as the Sacred*. New York: Harper and Row.

Geertz, C. 1973. *The Interpretation of Culture*. New York: Basic Books.

———. 1983. *Social Knowledge*. New York: Basic Books.

Gluckman, M. 1963. *Order and Rebellion in African Tribal Society*. London: Cohen & West.

Granet, M. 1932. *Festivals and Songs in Ancient China*. London: Routledge.

———. 1950. *La Pensée Chinoise*. Paris: Micel.

Heyd, M. 1985. "The Reaction to Enthusiasm in the Seventeenth Century." *Religion* 15: 279–291.

Hirshfeld, L. A., S. Atran, and A. Yengoyan. 1982. "Theories of Knowledge and Culture." In *Social Science Information* 21 (1): 161–198.

Homans, G. C. 1962. "Anxiety and Ritual—The Theories of Malinowski and Radcliffe Brown." In *Sentiments and Activities*, 192–202. New York: Free Press.

Jaspers, K. 1949. *Vom Urspruch und Ziel der Geschichte*. Zurich: Artemis.

Kaplan, S. 1985. "The Ethiopian Holy Man as Outsider and Angel." *Religion* 15: 235–251.

Keyes, C. F. 1977. "Millennialism, Theravada Buddhism and Thai Society." *Journal of Asian Studies* 36(4): 297–327.

Lévi-Strauss, C. 1983. *Structural Anthropology*. New York: Basic Books.

Marx, K. 1965. *Selected Writings in Sociology and Social Philosophy*. New York: McGraw-Hill.

Merton, R. K. 1963. *Social Theory and Social Structure*. New York: Free Press.

Metzger, T. 1977. *Escape from Predicament: Neo-Confucianism and China's Evolving Political Culture*. New York: Columbia University Press.

Meyer, E. 1984. "Behavior Programs and Evolutionary Strategies." *American Scientist* 62 (November–December): 651.

Mus, P. 1967. "La Sociologie de George Gurevitch et l'Asie." *Cahiers Internationaux de Sociologie* 43: 1–21.

———. 1968. "Traditions asiennes et bouddhisme moderne." *Eranos Yahrbuch* 32: 161–275.

Obeysekere, G. 1983. "The Rebirth Eschatology and Its Transformations: A Contribution to the Sociology of Early Buddhism." In *Karma and Rebirth in Classical Indian Tradition*, edited by W. D. O'Flaherty, 137–165. Berkeley and Los Angeles: University of California Press.

Peterson, R. 1979. "Revitalizing the Culture Concept." *Annual Review of Sociology* 5: 137–166.

Reynolds, F. 1977. "Civic Religion and National Community in Thailand." *Journal of Asian Studies* 36 (4): 267–282.

Sarkisyanz, E. 1965. *The Buddhist Background of the Burmese Revolution*. The Hague: M. Nijhoff.

Sartre, J. P. 1956. *L'Imagination*. Paris: Presses universitaires de France.

Schneider, D. M. 1973. *Class Differences and Sex Roles in American Kinship and Family Structure*. Englewood Cliffs, N.J.: Prentice-Hall.

————, ed. 1977. *Symbolic Anthropology*. New York: Columbia University Press.

————. 1980. *American Kinship*. Chicago: University of Chicago Press.

Scholem, G. 1941. *Major Trends in Jewish Mysticism*. New York: Schocken Books.

————. 1973. *Shabetai Zwi, The Mystical Messiah*. Princeton: Princeton University Press.

Schwartz, B. 1975. "Transcendence in Ancient China." *Daedalus* (Spring): 57–63.

Silber, I. F. 1981. "Dissent through Holiness, The Case of the Radical Renouncer, in Theravada Buddhist Countries." *Numen* 28 (2): 164–193.

Skocpol, T. 1979. *States and Social Revolutions*. Cambridge: Cambridge University Press.

Smelser, N. 1963. *Theory of Collective Behavior*. Chaps. 8 and 9. New York: Free Press.

Swidler, A., 1986. "Culture in Action: Symbols and Strategies." *American Sociological Review* 51 (April): 273–288.

Tambiah, S. J. 1976. *World Conqueror and World Renouncer*. Cambridge: Cambridge University Press.

Tonnies, F. 1957. *Gemeinschaft und Gesellschaft* (Community and society). East Lansing: Michigan University Press.

Turner, V. W. 1947. *The Forest of Symbols*. Ithaca: Cornell University Press.

————. 1968. *The Drums of Affliction*. Oxford: Clarendon Press.

————. 1973. "The Center Out There, Pilgrim's Goal." *History of Religions* 12: 191–230.

————. 1974. *Dramas, Fields and Metaphores*. Ithaca: Cornell University Press.

Van der Lieuw, G. 1957. "Primordial Time and Final Time." In *Man and Time, Papers for the Eranos Yearbooks,* edited by J. Campbell, 324–353. New York: Bollinger Foundation.

Voegelin, E. 1954–1974. *Order and Periphery*. Vols. 1–4. Baton Rouge: University of Louisiana Press.

Weber, M. 1951. *The Religion of China*. Translated and edited by H. H. Gerth. New York: Free Press.

————. 1952. *Ancient Judaism*. Translated and edited by H. H. Gerth and D. Martindale. New York: Free Press.

————. 1958. *The Religion of India*. Translated and edited by H. H. Gerth and D. Martindale. New York: Free Press.

————. 1968. *On Charisma and Institution Building. Selected pages edited by S. N. Eisenstadt*. Introduction by S. N. Eisenstadt, ix–lv. Chicago: University of Chicago Press.

Wolf, A. S., ed. 1974. *Religion and Ritual in Chinese Society*. Stanford: Stanford University Press.

Wolff, K. H. 1950, 1957. *The Sociology of George Simmel*. Glencoe, Ill.: Free Press.

4

The Concept of Culture and Its Place within a Theory of Social Action
A Critique of Talcott Parsons's Theory of Culture

Michael Schmid

Explaining the concept of culture is usually held to be a difficult task; there is, however, general agreement that a satisfactory definition is likely to be attainable only within the framework of an elaborated theory of social action. In this regard, it may be worth looking at Talcott Parsons's attempt to locate "culture" systematically within his theory of social systems. Closer examination will show that the various proposals he makes reveal not only empirical deficiencies but also a number of faults characteristic of his own theorizing, which can be corrected only by revising his theory's metatheoretical basis. In order to discuss the virtues and limitations of Parsons's concept of culture, I propose first to review his most important thoughts on culture; second, I shall evaluate his conceptualization critically; and third, I shall use my criticism as a starting point for suggesting some ways in which an improved version of a theory of culture might be worked out.

Parsons's Theory of Culture

During the last four decades of his life, Parsons constantly modified his theory of culture. This development cannot be reviewed in all detail here; I shall restrict myself to differentiating between three distinct phases of his conceptualization.

CULTURE AND SYMBOLISM

Within the so-called action frame of reference of Parsons's first and admirable sketch of a theory of the "structure of social action," the concept of *culture* did not play a central role (Parsons 1968 [1937]). Only later, evidently under the influence of Morris and Mead, did he turn his attention to culture, incorporating it into a theory of symbolization (Parsons 1951, 1953, 1964; Parsons and Shils 1951). This theory served to reconcile his analysis of the equilibrium of social systems with the fact that actors can interconnect their actions only by externalizing their mental states (for instance, their motivation to act in a certain way or their emotionality and need-dispositions) with the help of symbols in order to grant their coactors the opportunity to do the same. Symbols both express and communicate what other actors may expect in a given action situation and encourage or stimulate them to express their own attitudes in a situation (Parsons 1953:36 and elsewhere). Such symbolizations can serve to render less uncertain the inevitable "contingency" of mutual gratification and can increase the possibility that projected actions will be undertaken mutually (Parsons 1951:26–45, 36–43, 1953:42, 44, and elsewhere).

Insofar as symbols allow for such an externalized and interactive coordination of different actions, the single intentional act may be described as "having a meaning" (Parsons 1951:5–6, 10, 1953:31). But in order that such acts may be understood (that is, mutually interpreted by the participants of a social interaction as a relation or interconnection between an actor and his situation) and used to establish a mutually adopted orientation of actions, some necessary conditions must be met. Expressive symbols must "materialize" themselves as external signs; only as signs are the meaningfully intentional acts of an individual actor at the disposal of his fellow actors (Parsons 1951:10, 1953:33–39). But signs are not understood by themselves, even in this externalized form: they can only be interpreted unambiguously through the help of a set of quite conventional rules of appropriateness (Parsons 1951:11, 16, 1953:38, 1972:256; Sheldon 1951:32 and elsewhere). Only under this condition do they have a "common meaning" (Parsons 1953:36); only then do they serve to construct a "shared order of symbolic meaning" (Parsons 1951:11, 1961:980); and only then can they be used as a reliable means of communication (Parsons and Shils 1951:16; Parsons 1951:36–37, 1953:38–39, 1964:21). In this context, "symbolic generalization" seems to be the most important process by which symbols can be generated and transformed transindividually, transsituationally, and transgenerationally; this in turn permits them to be learned and internalized within social interaction (Parsons 1951:11, 15–18, 209–226, 1953:42–44, 1959:617; Parsons and Shils 1951:106, 126, 130, 161, and elsewhere).

On the basis of this symbolic generalization, a kind of common "symbolic significance" (Parsons 1953:31, 38, and elsewhere) is established by which specific "objects" are constituted as a "reality sui generis" (Parsons 1953:44) and to which all the actors in a given action situation can refer. These objects can be connected with an individual's actions if the "common meanings," through which the intended action performances are constructed (Parsons 1953:44–45), form either an "ordered pattern of value orientations" (Parsons 1951:37, 1953:42) or a "normative pattern structure of values"(Parsons 1951:37), which in turn supplies the selective standards for one's cognitive, cathectic, and evaluative decision dilemmata (which are described by the famous "pattern variables"). In other words, these symbolically ordered standards that help to determine individual decisions in the form of cognitive, evaluative, and value related "cultural orientations" are used by the actor to plan all kinds of instrumental, expressive, or moral courses of action. Actors can thus order their cognitions, motivations, and need-dispositions and use this order to adapt to a given situation (Parsons 1951:3–23, 45–51, 58–67, 101–112, 1953:45–53, 58–62; Parsons and Shils 1951:78–79, 183–189, 203–233).

If several actors can perform this process mutually and in a stable (that is, institutionalized) form, they are likely to succeed in coordinating their collective actions. The coordination of mutual action orientations, which is at the basis of any social interaction, is thus the result of an ordered symbolic commonality, which Parsons regularly calls a *cultural pattern* (Parsons 1951:48) or a *common culture* (Parsons 1964:22, 1977:168; Parsons and Shils 1951:105). Such a pattern or culture is considered ordered (and thus legitimate) if it reveals "pattern consistency" (Parsons 1951:15) and "symmetry" (Parsons 1951:87) or "meaning congruence" and "logical consistency" (Parsons 1961:963).

If these various definitional elements are taken together, the following concept of culture emerges (Parsons and Shils 1951:160–189): Culture is understood as an ordered symbolic system (Parsons 1977:168), that is, a symbolically mediated pattern of values or standards of appropriateness that permits the construction of a set of action-guiding, normative, conventional rules through which significant cultural objects are generated and used. If a symbolic system has validity for all of the participating actors, it is able "to give order to action" (Sheldon 1951:40). At least for the early Parsons this common order embraces not only the system of standards, regulating the use of symbols, but also the symbolically signified objects themselves, allowing differentiation between the principles of symbolic order and their actional products (Parsons 1951:4, 120–121, 418–429; Kroeber and Parsons 1958:583).

This definition of culture involves a number of explicit or tacit assumptions. First, it becomes clear that "society" exists only in the projections of its members, that is, in their action orientations and expectations (or in those symbolically regulated factors that contribute to forming those orientations and expectations) (Parsons 1953:52–53). Culture thus becomes the "pure and free creation of mind" (Sheldon 1951:39). Parsons's definition also implies that the actors depend on the use of shared symbols in order to coordinate, in an ordered and stable way, their motivations, cognitions, and need-dispositions, and, consequently, their attitudes concerning their social and nonsocial actional situations. Finally, contrary to any theoretical expectation, actors may succeed in stabilizing those "doubly contingent" social relations (Parsons 1951:10, 36; Parsons and Shils 1951:190–230) that they must establish in order to obtain their mutual gratification. Parsons's theory repeatedly shows that the establishment of such stable social relations is the result of individual learning processes, interactive socialization and control, and collective decision making (Parsons 1951:34–36, 52–53, 207, 211, 226–243, 1953:42–44, 1964:4–10, 36–37, 49–50, 75–76, 79–80, 88–89, 105–106, 212–217, 234–235, 263–266, and elsewhere; Parsons and Shils 1951:123–131, 304–318, and elsewhere; Parsons and Bales 1955:353–394).

CULTURE AS A SYSTEM
WITH ITS OWN LOGIC

My reconstruction so far has shown that Parsons evidently succeeded in formulating a viable action-theoretical definition of culture. According to this definition, culture finds its objective reality in the interactively established and coordinated subjective representations of actors and in their action orientations and their ability to deal systematically with those sets of rules that help them construct and use these orientations (Parsons and Shils 1951:159 and elsewhere). But as actors mutually constructing a cultural reality have recourse to intersubjective symbols that are incorporated in physical entities and whose function is dependent on an externalization of subjective meaning (Parsons 1953:52; Parsons and Shils 1951:160–162 and elsewhere), a notion of *culture* is introduced that slightly changes the definitions. In this modified definition of culture, Parsons stresses that the sphere of culture has a logic of its own. Culture as a *system* possesses its own standards of logical consistency and semantic congruence and is provided with a framework of order that is not immediately connected with the motives and the orientational problems of the culture-using actors. Culture (its constitutive logic and its products) thus cannot be reduced to the motives of actors simply because it is only effective as an internalized outline that helps them choose between different possible orientations and attitudes (Parsons 1951:14–15). Nor can culture, by virtue of its own particular logic, be reduced to those very social relations that actors try to stabilize by symbolically reconciling their individual action orientations (Parsons 1951:51–58 and elsewhere). As a logical consequence of this reasoning, culture cannot and must not be placed on the same conceptual level as those actions and actional relations that are initially constructed by means of these symbolic presuppositions of culture; as an ordered "set of norms for action" and as a "set of symbols of communication" (Parsons and Shils 1951:106), culture has to be kept analytically distinct from the social and the mental realms.

This analytical distinction, which was supported by Kroeber (Kroeber and Parsons 1958) and which even in his later work Parsons believed to be indispensable (Parsons 1972:253), became significant when Parsons began to consider culture as a part of a more comprehensive "action system." This theoretical move had already been prepared for, by the original conceptualization of culture, inasmuch as Parsons had always believed that culture would be unable to fulfill its action-guiding functions unless it could be regarded as a *system;* culture, that is, should not be conceived of as a random list of principles or as a series of unconnected artifacts (Parsons 1953:38). This central theoretical conviction was now embedded in a more comprehensive thesis: every individual act and set of connected actions should be analyzed as a "system," or an ordered set of differentiated elements. To promote such an analysis, Parsons initially differentiated between three (and later four) subsystems of a "general action system" (Parsons and Shils 1951:3–27; Parsons 1959, 1961a,

1977, 1978; Ackermann and Parsons 1966; and elsewhere). Within the systematics of this general action system, the actor and his mental system (his *consciousness* and its *operation*, terms no longer used by Parsons) were dealt with as a "personal system" (Parsons and Shils 1951:110–158; Parsons 1959) with its own dynamic and structure, the main outline of which Parsons borrowed from the theories of Freud and Olds and from culture and personality research (Parsons 1951:14–15, 239n.). Similarly, the "social system," as the second subsystem of the general action system, followed its own logic of normatively regulated self-stabilization on the basis of mutual gratification exchange (Parsons 1951; Parsons and Shils 1951:23–26, 190–233). In a later phase of the development of his theory, Parsons additionally accepted a proposal by the Lidz brothers (Parsons 1977:5, 106, 126) to consider a "behavioral system" that would serve as a specialized subsystem of the general action system. Its function was to contact, or to "intersect," with its (nonsocial) environment; it was designed to replace the original definition of that subsystem as *organic*.[1] Finally, a *cultural subsystem* was distinguished as a system of wholly abstract and symbolically mediated entities, for the analysis of which Parsons needed to refine his existing model only slightly (Parsons and Shils 1951:161, 369).

Parsons emphasized the analytical differentiation between the cultural system and its neighboring systems for several reasons. First, he required an independent cultural system as a hierarchically superordinated control system. According to the cybernetic guidelines of that phase of theoretical development, the latter should be able, as a low-energy system of high (semantic and symbolic) information, to control and regulate the other subsystems of the more comprehensive action system; these in turn were regarded as systems with downgrading information and upgrading energetic levels (Parsons 1977:49–50, 236, 1978:327, 362–367, 374–381, 388). Second, by introducing an analytically independent culture system, it was possible for the L-component, which fulfills the function of pattern maintenance within the AGIL-schematization of the general action system and thus assumes the role of an ultimate guarantor of order, to be given an easy and plausible action-theoretical interpretation (Parsons 1961a:37–41, 1969:439–472). Finally, a cultural system so defined could easily be connected with the theoretical idea, originally developed in collaboration with Smelser, that the sub- or partial systems of any more comprehensive system (including the general action system itself) should be able to enter into relations of exchange for mutual stabilization or equilibration (Parsons and Smelser 1956; Parsons 1961a:60–66, 1969:352–396).

CULTURE AS CODE

All of the preceding definitional elements of culture were retained during the third phase of conceptualization, but they underwent a more comprehensive theoretical interpretation in light of biological genetics and Chomsky's theory of generative grammar. As before, *culture* is taken to mean "symbolic formulations" of cognitive, cathectic, and expressive orientations and a "system of ordered"—symbolically mediated, as it were—"selective standards," and, as before, the concept of *culture* is connected with the theoretical idea of a symbolic, hierarchical control of those subsystems that are situated below the L-component of the general action system. But Parsons's concept of culture now additionally contains the thesis that the culture-constitutive set of standards should be understood as a *code;* such a code has a dispositional character and realizes itself in the construction or generation of concrete symbolic acts. This code is explicitly analogous to the principles of generative grammar, which serve to formulate individual messages or utterances, or to the genetic code, which determines the generation of species and within which variations are established (Parsons 1977:113, 131, 281, 1978:220–221, 1982; Parsons and Platt 1973:220n.40). This is well on the way to being a generative (or structuralist) linguistic model of "culture as language" (Parsons 1977:235), whose most general explanatory principle is located in a "culturally structured 'symbolic code' " (Parsons 1977:330).

The advantages of this further conceptual modification of Parsons's theory are easily summarized. Drawing on the now well-grounded identification of language and medium, Parsons interprets all forms of personal interaction and intersystemic exchange as based on a languagelike code; this interpretation, by implication, enables him to understand the connections and interchanges within and between independently differentiated systems and subsystems as the products of a number of *Sondersprachen* (Jensen 1980:12) or as forms of "communication" (Parsons 1969:352–396, 405–429, 433–438, 457, 1977:204–228, 1978:394–395). At the same time, Parsons's theory of the mutual interpenetration of divergent systems and subsystems takes on a new shape. The interpenetration of systems[2] is no longer represented by the idea of an overlapping or intersecting membership of parts or elements of different systems, and thus by implication as a relationship between a system and its parts, but is now conceptualized as a form of symbolic mediation (Parsons 1977:200 and elsewhere). Finally, Parsons has an empirically reliable explanation for the relative longevity of the cultural system compared with the transitory nature of the singular acts that it helps to generate; for it is obvious that the control system of culture, if understood as a code, can change only partially and as the result of an increased input of energy, which, for Parsons, means *charismatic energy* (Parsons 1961a:78–79), as even the construction of precisely those actions that might eventually change the cultural code necessarily presupposes such a code (Parsons 1961a:61–62, 72, 73–74).

A Critique of Parsons's Theory of Culture

It can hardly be denied that Parsons tried hard to find an appropriate place for the concept of culture within a general theory of individual and social action, and that his ideas were developed in close contact with modern linguistics and semantics. This attempt is in line with his general strategy of integrating diverse and apparently divergent theoretical traditions within a common frame of reference. In light of such attempts at theoretical integration, it is advisable to modify somewhat the symbolic interactionists' widespread objection that Parsons's theory deals exclusively with structural factors and neglects their symbolic mediation (cf. Blumer 1969:15–21, 85–89, 1975:62–65; Parsons 1974; Marrione 1975). But even given this modification, there remains in his integrational theorizing[3] a number of somewhat questionable implications that fail to stand up to closer scrutiny.

TERMINOLOGY PROBLEMS

There are, first, some purely terminological problems. Parsons nowhere accounts for the fact that he introduces his cultural system through terminology and concepts that should under no conditions be persistently equated with one another and thus conflated. For example, Parsons uses the concept of *meaning* partially in the sense of *reference*, thus expressing in a usual way that certain signs have the task or function of referring to an extrasymbolic *Gegenstand* (or *object*) (Parsons 1953:34); in discussing some basic ideas of Max Weber, he understands the concept of *meaning* as *relevance* in the sense that an object might be *bedeutsam* (*meaningful*) for an actor and his aims insofar as such an actor has a "problem of meaning" (a *Sinnproblem* according to Weber) (Parsons 1951:164–167, 1986:93–94), which in turn implies that it might be appropriate to differentiate between *empirical* and *nonempirical meanings* or *aims* (Parsons 1951:328–329, 332–334, 359–379, 1986:87–109). It is obvious that these two "meanings of meaning" should not have been confused and that by implication these *Sinnprobleme* are elements of the cultural system only as they are symbolically formulated. Thus they have, if one likes, only a kind of derivative cultural status, and we require an additional argument why such *Sinnprobleme* should be so dominant in the definition of the cultural system. I do not overlook the fact that Parsons is here examining a problem posed by Max Weber, and that Weber might have some quite acceptable reasons for emphasizing the *Kulturbedeutung* of *Sinnfragen* or that, as Parsons has expressed it himself, "die affektive Anpassung an eine emotional aufwühlende Situation" (the affective adjustment to an emotionally stirring situation) could be a problem worth avoiding (Parsons 1986:94). But it is puzzling that Parsons, as late as his *Human Condition* (1978:352–433), should lend such weight to the problem of meaning in his theorizing on actors' orientations and situational definitions. Parsons's assumption is questionable because he clings to the idea that such problems of meaning demand religious (Parsons 1951:163–167, 367–368, 1972:258–259, and elsewhere), or, as he calls it in his later work, *telic*, answers (Parsons 1978:381–392). He is ultimately adhering to a Durkheimian thesis that cannot be derived without additional qualifications from his conceptual definition of the cultural system and that can be contested empirically.

A similar objection can be raised to Parsons's constant identification of culture with values, values with norms, and meanings with values (1968:75–77, 1951:213–215, 263–264, 1972:236–237, and elsewhere). Without wishing to be pedantic, I feel it necessary to point out that a number of normally discrete ideas have been yoked together in Parsons's definition of the cultural system as a "normative pattern-structure of values" (Parsons 1951:37), or in the statement that "culture provides the standards (value orientations) that are applied in evaluative processes" (1953:16), or in the conceptualization of culture as "the organization of the values, norms, and symbols" (Parsons and Shils 1951:55). The original definition of culture as an exclusively symbolically organized system of abstract *Sinnzusammenhänge* (Parsons 1951:11, 237, 1953, 1961:963) quite evidently does not justify limiting the definition of culture to an ordered set of values, even if these values are the ultimate instances that have to be appealed to in order to resolve provisionally those decisional dilemmata that are a logical consequence of the voluntaristic character of human action (cf. Alexander 1978; Procter 1978). Culture actually includes everything that is symbolically accessible to actors, and values quite obviously do not exhaust the set of culturally encoded *Sinnzusammenhänge*. Parsons, indeed, is well aware that this is the case (1972:258–262); nevertheless, we repeatedly encounter these quite misleading summaries and easy definitions, and even the most benevolent reader can only conclude that Parsons intends to confine culture to standards and values (1951:237; Parsons and Shils 1951:159–160, 170–172). It should be obvious that this limited understanding of culture cannot be accepted on the basis of Parsons's formal definitions.

In addition, the internal differentiation of the cultural system (and, consequently, the development of an acceptable theory of action) is poorly served by the lack of a firm distinction between norms and values.[4] The concept of *value* denotes a "desired state of affairs" (as Parsons knows [1969:441]), while the concept of *norms* can indicate "demands" or "expectations"; if conceptualized in this way, *value* and *norm* obviously refer to two completely different phenomena that can vary independently of each other. The empirical relation between them cannot be examined scientifically if both concepts are constantly conflated, as occurs, for example, whenever the assumption is made that a certain state is desired if it is normatively expected or that the formulation of a norm is identical with the achieving of a desirable state.[5] Unfortunately, this danger of conflation has not been exposed even by some of the most prominent interpreters of Parsons's work (cf. Alexander 1982:65–69, 73–74, 76–79; Münch 1982:68–69; an exception can be found in Saurwein 1988:21).

Similar objections can be raised to the equating of *meaning* with *values*. It may be uncontestable that "questions concerning the meaning" (or relevance) of a phenomenon (in the sense of *Sinnfragen*) can sometimes amount to "questions concerning ultimate values" ("Fragen nach den 'letzten Werten,'" as Schluchter [1980:131] formulates it). It is, however, somewhat rash to conclude that such a thesis will hold for all questions of relevance, for it is conceivable that people might wish to solve problems (or to answer questions) of meaning that have nothing to do with ultimate values (or *letzten Stellungnahmen* in a Weberian sense) or that they may believe in the validity of these ultimate values without thus invoking problems of meaning or *Sinnfragen*. Thus, to clarify such impermeable relations between values and meanings, it may be advisable to eschew purely terminological questions when proposing hypotheses about their factual status.

In order to clear away such conceptual discrepancies and inconsistencies, I propose the use of the word *cultural* (or *culture*) solely to denote the fact that a certain object is available in a symbolic form, that is, only when actors necessarily orient themselves toward these objects by means of symbolic operations. This definition implies a twofold conclusion that is crucial to my understanding of the theoretical problem. The existence of nonsymbolic cultural objects[6] need not be postulated; nor does the proposed definition of *culture* imply any a priori stipulation concerning the specific (empirical) character of those cultural objects. The important thing is for actors only to be able to communicate with each other by having at their disposition an intersubjectively shared and normatively regulated set of symbolic operations that allows the construction of informative propositions, which in turn can be kept open to collective (critical or confirmative) argumentation and use. It is exclusively the dispositional character of symbols that grants them (and the rules of symbolic operations) their "objectivity," which is irreducible to the mental preconditions of their subjective use.[7]

CULTURE AND SOCIAL INTEGRATION

Parsons is customarily regarded as a theoretician of social integration (see Demerath and Peterson 1967; Gouldner 1971). This is correct insofar as he (like Durkheim) reconstructs the dynamics of all (not just social) system processes by presupposing a state of perfect system integration in order to identify a set of mechanisms that necessarily produce this very state of integration. It is this mode of reasoning that defines his *functionalism* (Parsons 1951:480–490, 1977:234).

This kind of explanatory logic, the merits of which need not be discussed in the present context (see Schmid 1989:130–164), also determines Parsons's conceptualization of culture. Like all systems, the cultural system is analyzed on the assumption that the conditions of its internal integration are fulfilled, that is, that culture can be regarded as a logically and semantically consistent system. The most important consequence of this functionalistic analysis is clear. For Parsons, every ordered communication between actors depends on a logically consistent use of symbols; this in turn seems to be possible only so long as the actors can refer to a commonly shared system of rules or, in one of Parsons's formulations, to a "shared cultural tradition" (1951:12); as this common culture is in turn an inevitable precondition of any successful mutual adaption of action orientations, social integration will result if and only if the necessary preconditions are realized. Taking these considerations to their logical conclusion, we may infer that social order and solidarity will immediately occur if the rules of symbolic usage are consistently formulated and shared by all actors. Conversely, as Parsons cannot conceive of these rules and standards—the cultural code, in short—functioning without being consistent and mutually shared, we may further conclude that the very existence of a common code is sufficient to evoke such actions that eventually lead to mutually integrated social relations (cf. Parsons 1953). In any case, the commonality of consistent collective symbols suffices to ensure *societal solidarity* (to put it in Durkheimian terms).

However, this assumption is open to criticism in several ways. Parsons seems to be defending the position that the ordered, integrative functioning of culture can only be assumed if all actors have free and equal access to their cultural tradition. But in a society that exhibits a high degree of division of labor and that secures its continuity by anonymous exchanges of goods and achievements rather than exclusively by a common culture, at least two problems arise that Parsons does not consider. First, he seems unable to imagine a society that is integrated, not on the basis of a common moral or value system, but largely by means of the external control of such externalities as are unacceptable to the controllers. The decisive theoretical point is that we might (under conditions requiring further clarification, of course) expect the perfect integration of a society even if there is no complete consensus on those externalities that have to be controlled and excluded. On the other hand, Parsons's position seems to imply that there will be no integration if the actors, in order to assimilate their actions to their social or nonsocial situations, activate quite divergent parts of their cultural tradition. That is to say, Parsons seems unable to imagine the empirical possibility of conflict-free social relations where actors are orienting themselves, not to a common culture, but to quite different, and possibly contradictory, parts of it (cf. Lechner 1985).

These considerations are closely related to another point. Parsons obviously presupposes that the commonality of cultural symbols implies that the cultural system contains no contradictory elements, neither in the sense that the rules constituting the cultural code may be formulated inconsistently nor in the other sense that it is possible to construct incompatible, ambivalent, and contradictory cultural objects (or propositions referring to these objects). Parsons seems, that is, to exclude the possibility that divergent cultural interpretations may arise from one and the same set of symbols or codes. It would surely be unfair to imply that Parsons's idea of a unified cultural system entails the conclusion that every empirical (or contingently factual) cultural system must be logically consistent and without incongruencies of meaning. Otherwise his repeated theoretical treatment of control mechanisms (1951:31–32, 207, 234–235) and integrative communication (1961a: 68–69, 74–76) would be quite superfluous. Nevertheless, his functional analysis constantly presupposes that these standards of logical consistency and semantic congruency might serve as a "theoretical point of reference," including the assumption that a system of social relations can indeed be regarded as stable and integrated only if the corresponding actors have recourse to a commonly binding cultural tradition. But, quite contrary to this assumption, it is empirically incontestable that under certain conditions it may well be possible to detect socially stable relations between actors without reference to a unified and commonly accepted cultural system. That is to say, actors may be able to exchange gratifications fairly and to the satisfaction of each without the exchange being mediated and supported by an unambiguous, nondivergent system of symbols (cf. Archer 1988:185–226).[8] This conclusion suggests that Parsons's thesis is definitely in need of serious qualification.

That Parsons's hypothesis of the necessary accord between cultural consistency and social integration might be untenable can also be shown by the aid of an argument found in the writings of Luhmann and Bauman (Luhmann 1971:48–50, 84–86, 100, 1986a:176; Bauman 1973:170–178). These authors assert that it is erroneous to identify the unity of a symbolic code with the factual guarantee of social consensus; the logical consistency of a code does not rule out saying "no," thereby negating the normative demands or value convictions of other actors by proposing a new regulation of social relations or even by initiating conflict. It is even possible to strengthen this argument: without a unified consensual code, actors would be unable to negate at all, and, without recourse to a consensual cultural tradition, they might never have a forum for their deviant opinions and proposals. But that would mean that actors are never able to circumvent the uncertainty of their social relations, a fact that Parsons quite correctly took as a starting point for his whole theoretical program. Consequently it is difficult to believe that the "double contingency" of these relations can ever be neutralized by the fact that actors speak the same language. Of course actors may minimize that double contingency to a certain degree by finding a common set of normative ideas to define their mutual rights and duties, even if such a means of stabilizing their mutual social relations cannot answer all the questions that may arise, as the "dilemma of altruism" clearly shows (cf. Spencer 1875:234, 1894:253–256, 260–265; Ullmann-Margalit 1977:48). But such a commonality of normative duties does not logically derive from the acceptance of a common symbolic code, which can only serve as a medium of communication, and which, as such, can guide action but not determine it (Luhmann 1986a:176); Parsons seems to be suggesting as much when he calls himself a "cultural determinist" (1977a:234). This argument remains true notwithstanding Kluckhohn's correct observation that actors without a consistent normative orientation "feel uncomfortably adrift in a capricious, chaotic world" (1951:399). In short, the logical consistency of a normative code must not be identified with the existence of a socially integrative consensus; to believe the contrary would be to commit a "fallacy of normative determinism" (Blake and Davis 1968:470–472).

The deficiency of Parsons's argument centers on one misleading deduction: from the fact that a symbolically meaningful code is grounded on a set of normative regulations that actors have to accept to communicate without friction and constant misunderstanding, he draws the logically untenable conclusion that actors cannot accept motivations and interests that are not normatively legitimized and supported (1951:327, 1953:39, 1961:980). "Parsons has turned Hobbes's error on its head, arguing that if actors engage in normative, noninstrumental action their activities must be complementary" (Alexander 1983:222, 1984:291). In Luhmann's words (1988:135), Parsons constantly confuses a symbolic "code" with the "programme," which may or may not be formulated by the help of this code.

Parsons's misleading theory of the allegedly integrative function of cultural codes helps to explain the relative one-sidedness of his theory of understanding. This theory seems to presuppose that it would suffice to interpret the actions and utterances of alter ego if ego recognizes that alter ego, in order to make his or her own intentions plausible or understandable, uses the same symbols and accepts the same set of rules for their use as ego does (Parsons 1953:61), and that this recognition in turn would be enough to guarantee the appropriateness of the mutual reactions and interactions of ego and alter ego (1953:38). But such a thesis is clearly open to criticism on several points. First, understanding the intentions of another actor can serve at most as one necessary condition for the successful mutual assimilation of interests and gratification exchanges (Luchmann 1986a:176). Second, Parsons's theory of intentional understanding, perhaps inspired by Weber's theory of motivational understanding, is much too simple to account for the actual variety of understanding processes. Parsons does not seem to see that intentions constitute only one field of understanding among others, and problems of theory may arise that his somewhat restricted theory is not equipped to handle.[9] Nor has he kept pace with recent hermeneutic theories of understanding, which vigorously question whether a commonality of meaning between actors trying to understand the utterances of their fellow actors can realistically be presupposed at all (see Gadamer 1965). As Parsons constantly ignores such objections and qualifications, for reasons about which I can only speculate, they cannot, of course, persuade him to modify his thesis of the integrative function of a language code; consequently, even in his later work he retains the idea that a mutually understandable language should be regarded as the primary normative and constitutive element of an analytically distinct cultural system (1972:254, 1977:169, and 1961:971–976, where language is believed to be the "groundwork of culture"). We would be well advised to compensate for these deficiencies by seeking a much more elaborated theory of understanding.[10]

There is one very general consequence to be drawn from Parsons's repeated, yet quite misleading, equation of cultural consistency with social integration: we need to take as seriously as possible the analytical autonomy of the cultural system from its neighboring systems (something Parsons frequently emphasized) and to deduce from this autonomous status of culture (as a purely symbolic system) that the cultural and the social systems not only are mutually irreducible systems but also reveal factual relations and connections that are much more complicated and complex than Parsons's theory admits. Parsons's assumption of an integrated synchronization of culture and social systems can thus be reduced to a somewhat improbable limiting case of a much more comprehensive theory.[11]

CULTURE AS AN ENERGETIC SUBSYSTEM

Although the theory of Talcott Parsons emphatically recommends the analytical separation of the cultural from the other subsystems of the general action system, he seems compelled in certain decisive passages to revoke his own hallowed theoretical standpoint. The reason for this revocation seems to be his belated insight that the cultural system cannot be regarded as a valid subsystem unless it is taken to be an acting system itself—a theoretical position that Parsons originally did not defend at all (1951:66, 1961:964, 1967:194, 1978:367n.).[12] It is certainly true that this revision of his theoretical conception does not mean that Parsons wholly intends to discard the structural component of the cultural system (1961:964), that is, the symbolically codified generative formalism that serves to construct cultural objects. On the other hand, he wants to do justice to his insight that "the important patterns of culture . . . could not be created and/or maintained as available recourses for action unless there were processes of action primarily oriented to their creation and/or maintenance. These processes may be part of a 'society,' just as the life of an individual as personality may be; but analytically, the subsystem of action focused in this way should be distinguished from the social system as focused on interaction relationships" (1961:964). Thus the maintenance of a religious actional orientation by a church may be considered an interpenetration of the cultural and the social system, "but a church as such would be regarded as a collectivity with cultural primacy, i.e., as first a cultural 'system of action,' and second, a social system" (1961:964).

I am inclined to share Larry Brownstein's opinion that this passage is somewhat "obscure" (Brownstein 1982:108). It evidently says that the original distinction between the cultural and the social spheres should be maintained by continuously defining the cultural system through its symbolic and generative formalisms; as such, this cannot be regarded as an acting entity in any technical sense of Parsons's action terminology. But Parsons also tries to convince his readers that the cultural system does act by ensuring that those cultural objects that actors require for their orientation are actually constructed and maintained; he is thus suggesting that the original analytical distinction between culture and the social system can be blurred. But in view of Parsons's statements on cultural institutions (1951:52–53) and his conception of culture as a set of *Idealfaktoren* (1972:265), such an argument is quite inconclusive and in need of commentary. As I see it, the inconclusiveness of Parsons's theoretical position derives from the fact that he is combining two quite divergent lines of argument: on the one hand, Parsons intends to develop a valid analytical instrument that, with the help of the concept of a system, allows for the conceptualization of relations between analytically distinct theoretical elements of a general action scheme. On the other hand, such a system-theoretical explication of the concept of action should also be able to answer the question of how actions are "energized" and by what "forces" they are driven; without a valid answer to this question, there can be no hope of developing a genuinely *dynamic theory* of individual and collective action. Originally Parsons had found quite an acceptable solution to this problem in his theory of motivation, which was located exclusively within the framework of the personal and the social subsystems of the general action system. But these two lines of theoretical argument are rendered incompatible and even contradictory as soon as Parsons begins to strengthen his thesis that an appropriate conception of action depends on the presupposition that *all* subsystems of the general system should be able to *act* in a technical sense of the word (Brownstein 1982:74–114). For under no circumstances is it admissible to conceptualize the cultural system as an "energetic system," one which, in Parsons's theoretical strategy, would be a "motivational system." That is, the thesis that culture as a system of abstract symbolic entities and rules can energetically force actors to act in a certain way can hardly be regarded a fruitful contribution to the development of an acceptable theory of action.[13] As Parsons evidently reserves the status of an energetic system for the personal and the social subsystems (of the general action scheme), I shall not try to defend his tendency to darken this essential theoretical assumption by taking back his analytical distinction between the cultural and the social systems. I would rather concede the irreparable logical deficiency of Parsons's theoretical construction of the general action system than relinquish the analytical gains that result from recognizing the analytical self-sufficiency of the cultural system.[14]

There was a logical outcome to Parsons's tendency (culminating in Parsons and Platt 1973) to act against his original insights by interpreting the cultural system as an energetic, or acting, system. He tends to negate his initial theoretical position that the cultural system as such, that is, as a symbolically ordered system, obviously cannot of itself enter into active communication or exchange relationships with the other subsystems of the general action system. It also makes little sense for Parsons, in the same context, to assume that there might be "interchanges" between the different subsystems of the cultural system itself

(Parsons and Platt 1973:65), a slip that has been openly and rightly criticized by Jeffrey Alexander (1983:170–174, 176–183). Difficulties in understanding such a theoretical position are caused not only by the topology of the AGIL-schema, which does not allow the L-component to make representable connections with its neighboring systems, but also, and even more importantly, with itself;[15] problems also arise when the cultural system, understood as a symbolically structured system, is taken to be an active one capable of entering into real interactions and interchanges with the other subsystems. It is hard to see how these interactions or interchanges can be understood in anything but a meta-phorical sense (Alexander 1983:173–177). But Parsons evidently can-not, of course, accept such objections. By dropping the thesis that the cultural system could be regarded as an energetically acting system, his theoretical construction of a cybernetic control hierarchy would break down, along with the associated idea that the cultural system can ac-tively steer the hierarchically subordinated neighboring systems; this would rob Parsons's theory of social order of an essential theoretical support.

Parsons's argument is persuasive only when he deals with cultural symbols and their codificational rules as resources, and thus as restric-tions on action orientation that constrain an actor's scope for decision making (1951:33, 35–36, 1961:964, and elsewhere). Such a thesis is not dependent on the dubious idea that the cultural system has an energetic potential of its own. Unfortunately Parsons cannot accept such a restricted understanding of culture.

Thus Parsons's theory of culture can be regarded as a fruitful attempt to support a thesis that he had already formulated decades before, to the effect that "culture . . . is on the one hand the product of, and on the other hand a determinant of, systems of social interaction" (1951:87). As I have attempted to demonstrate, however, Parsons's solution has been reached only at the cost of theoretical and empirical validity.

Heuristic Prospects for the Development of a Valid Theory of Culture

To conclude this chapter, I should like to offer some heuristic reflections on how a convincing theory of culture might be shaped—one that retains the acceptable parts of Parsons's theory yet avoids its deficiencies. It is most profitable to proceed roughly along the following lines.

CULTURE AND CONTRADICTION

It is crucial that the terminology used to describe culture and locate it within the framework of a general theory of social action neither implies nor excludes specific empirical assumptions about the content of a possible cultural order. At the same time, it would be unwise to speak of a culture only if the cultural "symbolic-meaning complex" (Parsons 1955:396) exclusively comprehends logically consistent and semantically meaningful rules and cultural objects. If we did, we would sacrifice the chance to investigate those cases where the cultural system is clearly not logically and consistently ordered but is still used by the actors as a basis for organizing their mutual actions. That implies that cultural-theoretical analysis should concentrate on investigating quite different internal orders of symbolically formulated propositions and should accept the fact that meaning congruence, symmetries, relations of logical consistency, and unambiguously derivative relations between propositions can only be ideal or limiting cases and empirical exceptions. The individual theoretician should, of course, feel free to examine the presuppositions and consequences of cultural consistencies and logically ordered symbolic systems rather than their inconsistencies and weaknesses; indeed Parsons's continuous interest in the development of "rational" kinds of action orientation has doubtlessly contributed to this "positive" tendency (Parsons 1951:499–503, 1972a, 1977:35–36, 71–74, and elsewhere). But such a one-sided interest cannot serve as the basis of a really comprehensive and integrated theory of cultural systems. It should not (as Parsons's theoretical functionalism inevitably tends to do) regard cultural inconsistencies, incongruencies, contradictions, and imbalances as necessary deficiencies and insufficiencies. Rather, it should analyze the precise content of such propositional incompatibilities with a view to understanding how these incompatibilities are reflected in the situational logic[16] of the actors concerned and as special restrictions and problems that they must confront. Closer examination of these restrictions and problems shows that the formation of a self-sufficient cultural (or, more precisely, social) subsystem dedicated to securing and maintaining the logical consistency of the cultural tradition (including the subsystem's own tradition) constitutes only one of the many ways of dealing with cultural contradiction. It should be clear that the specific conditions necessary for this or any other process of cultural problem solving to take place cannot in practice be isolated by exclusive reliance on Parsons's AGIL-architecture.

CULTURE AND SOCIAL SYSTEM

The foregoing has, of course, introduced another potentially fruitful heuristic approach that is likely to trouble only those who still find virtue in Parsons's conflation of culture and social system, and that is the strict separation of these two areas. If no analytical distinction between these concepts is made, then there is potential for a number of errors, all of them detrimental to a fruitful analysis of cultural systems. I would therefore maintain, along with Margret Archer, that by refusing to draw a precise line between these two fields, one is obliged either to take a reductionist approach to the analysis of culture or to favor a theory of the mutual constitution of cultural entities and social actions. Neither line of argument is without pitfalls.

If one accepts a reductionist program, there are two directions one can take. One procedure involves showing why and how the cultural system can totally control actions and action relations. Empirically, however, such cultural determination of actions is not universally observable.[17] The other procedure, which may be regarded as a Marxian version of cultural reductionism, has to explain how different forms of social relations between actors can help determine modes of cultural orientation. But even such an inverse reductionist thesis encounters the empirical objection that no cultural system—that is, its content and its operative rules—can be determined by the sociostructural organization of specific action relations.[18] Dogmatic rejection of such empirical observations means failing to explore the much more complicated relations and connections that actually obtain between culture and social systems. The same is true of the assumption that cultural traditions and social actions are mutually constitutive, which would mean that cultural entities are "real" only insofar as they find their expression in the practical actions of actors and, conversely, that these actions cannot be realized without recourse to cultural factors (see Bauman 1973; Giddens 1979; and, with grave qualifications, Tenbruck 1986). This assumption is flawed simply because, expressed more precisely in the form of a biconditional, it comes dangerously close to being an empty tautology (for culture); furthermore, to consider it seriously is to render impossible any independent analysis of cultural propositions and social relations.

One can, however, avoid having to choose between these empirically and theoretically untenable theses by distinguishing between culture and social relations. This distinction is legitimate if one accepts that the cultural system represents exclusively "propositional systems" or (because propositions can be formulated only by means of symbols and corresponding operative rules) wholly "symbolic systems" (Hornung 1988:295); "social systems" instead have to be regarded as "systems of action," which are not based on a kind of propositional order but on *Handelnsordnungen* in von Hayek's sense (see Hayek 1969: 161–198). Such ordered connections between different actions cannot arise without actors using information that symbolically encodes the preconditions and expected results of their action situation, even if it often contradicts their beliefs and can occur independently of their available knowledge (see Wippler 1978; Boudon 1982). But neither the existence of such actional connections nor the specific forms they take can be identified with the fact that the actors really use certain kinds of codes or with the assumption that these codes are logically consistent.

I would uphold the present thesis against both Luhmann and Parsons. The approach I have outlined clarifies that Luhmann, in defining social relations as communicational processes, thereby seems to defend a kind of questionable reductionism (Luhmann 1984, 1986, 1986a, and elsewhere).[19] At the same time, the argument against the conflation of culture and social structure helps to explain why Parsons's assumption that unified and common symbolic rules are sufficient to guarantee social integration should constitute only one of several theoretical possibilities. This can be simply illustrated by constructing a cross table that, accepting the distinction between cultural and social systems, uses two specific dichotomies, "logical consistency" and "logical inconsistency" (of culture) versus "integration" and "nonintegration" (of social relations), to describe the set of logically possible relations between the two systems (Alexander 1984). The resulting matrix clearly shows not only the case argued by Parsons but also three additional states, the preconditions for which unfortunately cannot be derived from Parsons's general theoretical apparatus. But the ability to perform such derivations should, in my view, be one of the indispensable prerequisites of an integral, sociologically relevant theory of culture formation.

CULTURE AND THE ANALYSIS
OF CULTURE CHANGE

I attempt to show, in conclusion, that the deficiencies of Parsons's theory of culture are not traceable simply to the particular intransigence of its object. On the contrary, Parsons successfully incorporated the most important and relevant theoretical discussions of his time into his theoretical scheme, thereby promoting profound understanding of the function of cultural systems. Nevertheless, in the course of establishing his theoretical program, he became too frequently involved in hypotheses and assumptions concerning the specific attributes of cultural and social systems and their mutual relations; closer examination has proved many of these assumptions to be empirically and theoretically untenable. The reasons for these deviations are, I believe, found in Parsons's functionalism,[20] that is, his inclination to analyze any kind of system (both its internal structure and its external relations) by hypothesizing a state of (perfect) system integration and asking under what conditions and with what mechanisms certain processes can be detected and described that produce such states of integration. The basic flaw of this analytical technique is not, as has been repeatedly supposed and exposed, that it has set up system integration as a kind of "theoretical fetish" responsible for Parsons's reckless theoretical presuppositions concerning the factual and desirable degree of integration of (empirical) systems (see Lockwood 1976). The opposite seems to be true. A much more serious criticism is that Parsons, because of his unshakable functionalistic approach, did not stop trying to carry out systems analysis as a form of equilibrium analysis; indeed, the state of systems analysis in his time and his own training as an economist prevented him from doing so.[21] One immediate and logical result of this constraint was his entrapment by quite specific methodological consequences and preconditions, which did not allow him to develop his theories beyond a certain point (Schmid 1989:115–197).

Parsons's wholly inadequate theory of cultural change reflects this entrapment only too clearly.[22] To meet the challenge of such a theoretical program, he really elaborated only his theory of internalization (Parsons and Bales 1955), which helped to explain how cultural patterns can be incorporated and fixed within the personal system. His cultural theory has to some extent also been influenced by his theory of social control (1951), which specifies the conditions under which we can expect deviant beliefs and motivations to be invalidated by the help of accepted cultural standards. In some passages, too, a rough model can be glimpsed of a functionally specialized cultural subsystem that establishes and maintains the use and function of logically consistent cultural patterns (Parsons 1961, 1978:133–153, 154–164; Parsons and Platt 1973). As a logical consequence of this line of reasoning, culture has to be taken as an institutionalized guarantor of a shared tradition. But not very much is actually learned about the nature of the processes that generate this unified cultural tradition or about their chances of success. These lacunae can be filled to some extent by recourse to Parsons's self-regulation hypothesis (1951:350, 482–483, 1953:43, 1959:634, and elsewhere). This hypothesis, which was intended to solve the general theoretical problem of how any system behaves whenever it is under reproductive pressure, implies that a system will constantly strive to restabilize itself by regaining its original state. But this hypothesis is vaguely formulated and largely ignores or leaves quite open the conditions required for the successful re-equilibration of a disturbed system. It also leaves unclear whether anything more than sheer chaos can result from the breakdown of regulative structures, which have to restore system equilibrium. In Parsons's philosophy of science there are also indications that he conceives of the reconstruction of symbolic systems as an "accumulation" and "integration" of divergent themes and theories (1959:703–709, 1961:984–988). But, even in this case, Parsons tends to overlook the fact that the connection between theoretical accumulation and conceptual integration is only one of several strategies of cultural change; he is unable to specify the conditions under which actors are likely to unify divergent theories and propositions instead of modifying or even relinquishing them.[23]

These points of criticism suggest inescapably that Parsons does not have an elaborated theory of cultural change, although his earlier work correctly stated that culture should be understood as both product and determinant of human social interaction (1951:87). But neither his preferred analytical instrument of functional equilibrium analysis nor his conceptualization of culture as an ultimate instance of action control allows him to see that an acceptable theoretical analysis of cultural change and, more generally, of any structural change demands a totally different theoretical starting point (see Schmid 1989:19–81, 115–197).

Parsons saw that, in any of their action situations, actors encounter cultural objects (among other things). However, his Durkheimian perspective led him to forget that such objects involve both restrictions and opportunities and that the two generate quite divergent consequences depending on whether the cultural system contains contradictions. If Parsons had been able to accept this idea, he might have noticed that the various discrete logical properties of actors' theories or beliefs create entirely different kinds of situational logic (see Archer 1988:145, 154, and elsewhere), thus giving rise to heterogeneous problems that actors try to solve in divergent ways and (a fact critical to the development of a valid theory) with no prospect of lasting integrative success. This situation implies, among other things, that even solutions that are collectively acceptable and are regarded as part of a common tradition will inevitably lead to further problems. These problems, by changing the empirical and logical conditions that the actors have to meet, will destabilize their common action situation anew; and because the actors can never be sure that the new questions can be given traditional answers, the development of their culture will find no natural resting point. It is precisely the constant recursive process of disequilibration that is the most essential condition continuing the cultural process.[24] In consequence of such a manifest insight, Parsons would certainly not have been able to miss the point that this kind of irresistible cultural dynamic involves not only accumulative or integrative changes but also "cultural revolutions" (as Parsons [1977:301] recognizes), abrupt losses of traditions, breakdown of regulative structures, and all other kinds of discontinuous transformation.[25]

I do not wish to adhere dogmatically to the view that these shortcomings are a logical implication of Parsons's conceptual apparatus.[26] However, I do think that the theoretical and empirical deficiencies of Parsons's views discussed so far can be summarized by the fact that the functional logic that he favors—a logic of equilibrium analysis which, contrary to his belief, is not a necessary prerequisite for dealing with his main theoretical problem, the establishment of social order—is fundamentally and logically ill-equipped to deal with the morphogenesis of cultural and other kinds of systems. Functional analysis cannot come to terms with the active and formative meaning of cultural contradictions in explaining the transformation of cultural systems because it allows for no reconstruction of the reproductive and selective system processes as disequilibrium and fundamentally discontinuous phase transition processes (see Freber and Schmid 1986; Tiryakian 1985; Schmid 1989:145–153, among others). Such a mode of theoretical analysis requires the logic of equilibrium analysis to be rejected or at least modified; there is no place for the guiding metatheoretical idea, or *Leitmotiv*, that systems and their dynamics can be stable or integrated under all possible boundary conditions and parameters; likewise absent is the logical consequence of this: that it is inadvisable to persist in analyzing cultural (and other) systems by unshakably adhering to contrary metatheoretical presuppositions, no matter what the circumstances.[27]

Conclusion

My reconstruction of Parsons's theory of the cultural system has necessarily involved criticizing it. I conclude that we should not accept all its implications without considerable modifications. Such a conclusion is justified by recent empirical and theoretical findings that show Parsons's theoretical analysis of the cultural system and its constitutive processes is not universally valid. It is important, however, to recall that Parsons once showed—in *The Structure of Social Action,* which I regard as his classic contribution to the theory of sociology—that even such a highly rated theory as the utilitarian theory of action is merely a specific instance of a much more general and comprehensive theoretical model.[28] Let us hope that Parsons could have reconciled himself to the fact that his own theories would suffer the same fate.

Notes

1. For further details of this modification see Brownstein (1982:75–82).
2. For further details of the theory of interpenetrative systems, see Luhmann 1977, 1978, 1984:286–345; Jensen 1978.
3. There are somewhat divergent judgments on the metatheoretical status of this integrative strategy: Brownstein (1982:68) tends to believe that Parsons's endeavor can best be described as a form of obsessive eclecticism, while Alexander (1983:45, 74, 129, 154, 183, and elsewhere) characterizes them mildly as "ecumenicism" and more forcefully as "imperialistic ambitions" or "accumulationism." For a more comprehensive discussion of Parsons's metatheoretical ideas, see Schmid (1989:19–115).
4. This confusion can already be observed in Parsons's first major theoretical treatise of 1937 (1968:75–77).
5. I discuss this conflation at some length in Schmid (1972:177–180). For a typical example of this conflation, see Parsons (1969:8), where, at the same time, he defines *values* by the help of *norms* and defends a "distinction between value and differentiated norm" on the basis of the belief that norms can be regarded as situational specifications of the "common societal value system" (1969:9).

6. Whether there is a "nonlinguistic subsystem of human culture" (Bauman 1973:88–91) depends entirely on whether the nonlinguistic part of culture can be symbolically formulated (see Leach 1978:62–63), whereas it is not decisive whether this symbolization takes place on a conscious or a nonconscious level.

7. For this theory of an objective use of symbols, see Popper (1972:106–152, 153–190, 1984:11–40) and Schneider (1973:137–139).

8. Alexander takes this case to be a "logical illusion" and "sociologically unfounded" and believes that if cooperation between actors actually takes place, a "cultural commonality" will tend to build up (1984:311–314). In my view this position is incorrect. First, Alexander certainly cannot mean that the factual coexistence of cooperation and a contradictory cultural system is logically excluded; he believes rather, as his example shows, that such coexistence is unstable to a large degree, which is quite a different notion. Furthermore, and in true Parsonsian tradition, Alexander's understanding of culture is evidently restricted to values (and norms), which suggests a belief that cooperation without a common set of values simply does not exist. But both theses are contradicted by recent theoretical (and empirical) considerations of the condition of "egoistic cooperation" (see Axelrod 1984; Kliemt 1985, 1986; Voss 1985). The forms of cooperation described by these authors remain stable as long as the participant actors do not lose interest in the returns they get from cooperation; they are certainly not in need of a cultural commonality of values to maintain this interest. But, of course, if they actually lose their interest in mutual cooperation, such (nonexistent) common cultural values cannot serve to sustain cooperation. However, an interest guided form of cooperation is neither logically impossible nor empirically improbable.

I assume that Alexander's assumptions are based on a conflation of (normative) integration (by the help of a set of common values) and stability of a relation in the sense that no actor has good reason to relinquish his participation. These two theses are quite independent of each other, but can be unified: for example, membership of a normatively integrated social relation may (under quite debatable circumstances) be accepted as one reason not to leave it.

9. Such additional fields of understanding are enumerated by Simmel and Sombart, who differentiate between *Sachverstehen* (objective understanding), *Gefühlsverstehen* (emotional understanding), *Stilverstehen* (stylistic understanding), and so on (Simmel 1984:61–83; Sombart 1929:208–226).

10. Such an elaborated theory has been developed, among others, by Gadamer (1965) and Popper (1969, 1972:162–180) and even more radically by Luhmann (1984:191–241).

11. Space does not permit detailed discussion of this theory here. For further clarification I draw the reader's attention to M. Archer's important study (1988) and to an interesting article by P. Drechsel (1984), especially to the extensive literature cited there; I limit myself to an outline of such a theory in the section on heuristic prospects for the development of a valid theory of culture in this chapter.

12. Brownstein (1982:64–65) has convincingly shown that Parsons's idea of an acting cultural system does not follow necessarily from the basic assumption of the AGIL-schematization.

13. It would be interesting to know whether Parsons has adopted Simmel's theory of the cultural system, which implies this very idea that cultural entities can have a dynamic of their own. See my critical discussion of this theory in Schmid (1987:256–259).

14. This involves the view that the de-coupling of different system levels is, in the last analysis, a product of the actors themselves (or, to express it in Parsons's terminology, of the social system); see Giesen and Schmid (1989).

15. Some of Parsons's commentators have been led by this fact into somewhat daring and overcomplex modifications of the AGIL-schema (for example, Gould 1976); Brownstein (1982:29–30) quite correctly regards this as theoretically and empirically indefensible.

16. For the importance of this "logic of the situation," see Popper (1961: 147–152, 1969); for a more critical explanation of individual and/or social action, see Schmid (1985).

17. Parsons's own theory of culture has been interpreted as representing such a form of reductionism; see Archer (1988:30–38).

18. To exclude a strict determination of culture by some sort of *Produktionsverhältnisse* does not, of course, imply that there are no restrictions resulting from how actors organize their social relations (see Douglas 1970; Swanson 1968, among others). Reductionist determinism has been conclusively criticized by Alexander (1982a).

19. I have criticized Luhmann's position in Schmid (1987a:40–43).

20. Refering to Parsons's "functionalism," I do not pretend that he really believed any system to be in the state of a perfect reproductive equilibrium, but that he can be considered a "methodological functionalist" insofar as he saw the necessity to analyze systems as "boundary maintaining systems" (see Lackey 1987:42). For a more general statement concerning functional analysis see Davis (1959).

21. The state of systems analysis in Parsons's time is well documented by Buckley (1968); for Parsons's original qualifications as an economic theorist, see Camic (1987).

22. For a negative appraisal of Parsons's commitment to developing such a theory of culture change, see Savage (1981:204).

23. That it is possible to theorize on this issue is exemplified by Archer (1988:158–171, 183–184, 199–201, 207–208).

24. For such a model of change, see Popper (1972:180–183), Schmid (1987), Mayntz and Nedelmann (1987), and others.

25. For such a model of "revolutionary" changes in cultural traditions see especially Popper (1966).

26. Thus Parsons (1972a:10) speaks of a "sprunghafte Entwicklung des (gesellschaftlichen) Anpassungsvermögens," and he is well aware that there are breakdowns in cultural traditions; see his conception of a seed society (1977a).

27. For the possibilities of such a modified theoretical program, see Prigogine (1976), Boulding (1978), Jantsch (1979), Martens (1985), D'Avis (1984), Valjavec (1985), Bühl (1988), Gleick (1988), and many others.

28. Worthy of consideration are the objections of Camic (1979), which suggest that Parsons improperly included in his critique of the utilitarian per-

spective some of its original representatives, such as David Hume, and was thus led to an inappropriate judgment of that tradition. I would like to counter this view with the thesis that a utilitarian explanation of purely economic actions, as Parsons showed, frequently ignores the fundamentally normative character of orders of action; there are, of course, exceptions to this thesis, such as the theories of Friedrich von Hayek.

References

Ackermann, C., and T. Parsons. 1966. "The Concept of 'Social System' as Theoretical Instrument." In *Concepts, Theory and Explanation in the Behavioral Sciences,* edited by C. J. DiRenzo, 24–40. New York: Random House.

Alexander, J. 1978. "Formal and Substantiative Voluntarism in the Work of Talcott Parsons: A Theoretical and Ideological Reinterpretation." *American Sociological Review* 43 (1):177–198.

———. 1982. *Theoretical Logic in Sociology.* Vol. 1, *Positivism, Presuppositions, and Current Controversies.* London: Routledge and Kegan Paul.

———. 1982a. *Theoretical Logic in Sociology.* Vol. 2, *Antinomies of Classical Thought: Marx and Durkheim.* London: Routledge and Kegan Paul.

———. 1983. *Theoretical Logic in Sociology.* Vol. 4, *The Modern Reconstruction of Classical Thought: Talcott Parsons.* London: Routledge and Kegan Paul.

———. 1984. "Three Models of Culture and Society Relations: Toward an Analysis of Watergate." In *Sociological Theory,* edited by R. Collins, 290–314. San Francisco: Jossey-Bass.

Archer, M. S. 1988. *Culture and Agency. The Place of Culture in Social Theory.* Cambridge: Cambridge University Press.

Axelrod, R. 1984. *The Evolution of Cooperation.* New York: Basic Books.

Bauman, Z. 1973. *Culture as Praxis.* London: Routledge and Kegan Paul.

Blake, J., and K. Davis. 1968. "On Norms and Values." In *Theory in Anthropology,* edited by R. A. Manners and D. Kaplan, 464–472. Chicago: Aldine.

Blumer, H. 1969. *Symbolic Interactionism: Perspective and Method.* Englewood Cliffs, N.J.: Prentice-Hall.

———. 1975. "Comments on Turner's 'Parsons as a Symbolic Interactionist.'" *Sociological Inquiry* 45 (1):59–62.

Boudon, R. 1982. *Unintended Consequences of Social Action.* New York: St. Martin's Press.

Boulding, K. 1978. *Ecodynamics: A New Theory of Social Evolution.* Beverly Hills: Sage Publications.

Brownstein, L. 1982. *Talcott Parsons' General Action Scheme: An Investigation of Fundamental Principles.* Cambridge, Mass.: Schenkman.

Buckley, W., ed. 1968. *Modern Systems Research for the Behavioral Scientist.* Chicago: Aldine.

Bühl, W. L. 1988. "Die dunkle Seite der Soziologie. Zum Problem gesellschaftlicher Fluktuationen." *Soziale Welt* 39 (1):18–46.

Camic, C. 1979. "The Utilitarians Revisited." *American Journal of Sociology* 85 (3):516–550.

———. 1987. "The Making of a Method: A Historical Reinterpretation of the Early Parsons." *American Sociological Review* 52 (3):421–439.

Davis, K. 1959. "The Myth of Functional Analysis." *American Sociological Review* 24 (4):757–772.

D'Avis, W. 1984. *Neue Einheit der Wissenschaften. Methodologische Konvergenzen zwischen Natur- und Sozialwissenschaften.* Frankfurt: Campus Verlag.

Demerath, N. J., and R. A. Peterson, eds. 1967. *System, Change, and Conflict.* New York and London: The Free Press and Collier Macmillan.

Douglas, M. 1970. *Natural Symbols: Explorations in Cosmology.* Harmondsworth: Penguin.

Drechsel, P. 1984. "Vorschläge zur Konstruktion einer 'Kulturtheorie,' und was man unter einer 'Kulturinterpretation' verstehen könnte." In *Ethnologie als Sozialwissenschaft,* edited by E. W. Müller et al., 44–84. Sonderheft 26 der Kölner Zeitschrift für Soziologie und Sozialpsychologie. Opladen: Westdeutscher Verlag.

Freber, J., and M. Schmid. 1986. *Instabilität und Dynamik. Zur Anwendung der Katastrophentheorie in der Soziologie.* Forschungsberichte der Universität der Bundeswehr. München/Neubiberg.

Gadamer, H. G. 1965. *Wahrheit und Methode.* Tübingen: J. C. B. Mohr (Paul Siebeck).

Giddens, A. 1979. *Central Problems in Social Theory. Action, Structure and Contradiction in Social Analysis.* London: Macmillan.

Giesen, B., and M. Schmid. 1989. "Symbolic, Institutional, and Social-Structural Differentiation. A Selection-Theoretical Perspective." In *Social Structure and Culture,* edited by H. Haferkamp, 67–85. Berlin: Walter De Gruyter.

Gleick, J. 1988. *Chaos. Die Ordnung des Universums. Vorstoß in Grenzbereiche der modernen Physik.* München: Droemer Knaur.

Gould, M. 1976. "Systems Analysis, Macrosociology, and the Generalized Media of Social Action." In *Explorations in General Theory in Social Science,* edited by J. J. Loubser et al., 493–506. New York and London: The Free Press and Collier Macmillan.

Gouldner, A. W. 1971. *The Coming Crisis of Western Sociology.* London: Heineman.

Hayek, F. V. 1969. *Freiburger Studien. Gesammelte Aufsätze.* Tübingen: J. C. B. Mohr (Paul Siebeck).

Hornung, B. R. 1988. *Grundlagen einer problemfunktionalistischen Systemtheorie gesellschaftlicher Entwicklung. Sozialwissenschaftliche Theorienkonstruktion mit qualitativen, computergestützten Verfahren.* Frankfurt: Peter Lang Verlag.

Jantsch, E. 1979. *Die Selbstorganisation des Universums. Vom Urknall zum menschlichen Geist.* München: Hanser Verlag.

Jensen, S. 1978. "Interpenetration. Zum Verhältnis personaler und sozialer Systeme." *Zeitschrift für Soziologie* 7 (2):116–129.

———, ed. 1980. "Einleitung." In *Zur Theorie der sozialen Interaktionsmedien*, by Talcott Parsons, 7–55. Opladen: Westdeutscher Verlag.

Kliemt, H. 1985. *Moralische Institutionen. Empirische Theorien ihrer Evolution.* Freiburg: Alber Verlag.

———. 1986. *Antagonistische Kooperation. Elementare spieltheoretische Modelle spontaner Organisationsentstehung.* Freiburg: Alber Verlag.

Kluckhohn, C. 1951. "Values and Value-Orientations in the Theory of Action. An Exploration in Definition and Classification." In *Toward a General Theory of Action. Theoretical Foundations in the Social Sciences,* edited by T. Parsons and E. Shils, 388–439. New York: Harper & Row.

Kroeber, A. L., and T. Parsons. 1958. "The Concept of Culture and of Social System." *American Sociological Review* 23 (October):582–583.

Lackey, P. N. 1987. *Invitation to Talcott Parsons' Theory.* Houston: Cap and Gown Press.

Leach, E. 1978. *Kultur und Kommunikation. Zur Logik symbolischer Zusammenhänge.* Frankfurt: Suhrkamp Verlag.

Lechner, F. 1985. "Parsons' Action Theory and the Common Culture Thesis." *Theory, Culture and Society* 2:71–83.

Lockwood, D. 1976. "Social Integration and System Integration." In *Social Change: Explorations, Diagnosis and Conjectures,* edited by G. K. Zollschan and W. Hirsch, 379–383. New York: Schenkman.

Luhmann, N. 1971. "Sinn als Grundbegriff der Soziologie." In *Theorie der Gesellschaft oder Sozialtechnologie. Was leistet die Systemforschung?,* by J. Habermas and N. Luhmann, 25–100. Frankfurt: Suhrkamp Verlag.

———. 1977. "Interpenetration. Zum Verhältnis personaler und sozialer Systeme." *Zeitschrift für Soziologie* 6 (1):62–76.

———. 1978. "Interpenetration bei Parsons." *Zeitschrift für Soziologie* 7 (3):299–302.

———. 1984. *Soziale Systeme. Grundriß einer allgemeinen Theorie.* Frankfurt: Suhrkamp Verlag.

———. 1986. *Ökologische Kommunikation. Kann die moderne Gesellschaft sich auf ökologische Gefährdungen einstellen?* Opladen: Westdeutscher Verlag.

———. 1986a. "The Autopoiesis of Social Systems." In *Sociocybernetic Paradoxes: Observation, Control and Evolution of Self-Steering Systems,* edited by F. Geyer and J. van der Zouwen, 172–192. Beverly Hills: Sage Publications.

———. 1988. "Warum AGIL?" *Kölner Zeitschrift für Soziologie und Sozialpsychologie* 40 (2):127–139.

Marrione, T. J. 1975. "Symbolic Interactionism and Social Action Theory." *Sociology and Social Research* 59 (3):201–218.

Martens, B. 1985. *Differentialgleichungen, Katastrophen und dynamische Systeme in den Sozialwissenschaften.* München: Profil Verlag.

Mayntz, R., and B. Nedelmann. 1987. "Eigendynamische soziale Prozesse. Anmerkungen zu einem analytischen Paradigma." *Kölner Zeitschrift für Soziologie und Sozialpsychologie* 39 (4):648–668.

Münch, R. 1982. *Theorie des Handelns. Zur Rekonstruktion der Beiträge von*

Talcott Parsons, Emile Durkheim und Max Weber. Frankfurt: Suhrkamp Verlag.

Parsons, T. 1951. *The Social System.* New York and London: The Free Press and Collier Macmillan.

———. 1953. "The Theory of Symbolism in Relation to Action." In *Working Papers in the Theory of Action,* edited by T. Parsons, R. F. Bales, and E. Shils, 31–62. New York and London: The Free Press and Collier Macmillan.

———. 1955. "A Note on Some Biological Analogies." In T. Parsons and R. F. Bales, *Family, Socialization and Interaction,* 395–399. New York and London: The Free Press and Collier Macmillan.

———. 1959. "An Approach to Psychological Theory in Terms of the Theory of Action." In *Psychology. A Study of Science.* Vol. 3, edited by S. Koch, 612–711. New York: McGraw-Hill.

———. 1961. "Introduction to Part IV: Culture and the Social System." In *Theories of Society,* edited by T. Parsons et al., 963–993. New York and London: The Free Press and Collier Macmillan.

———. 1961a. "An Outline of the Social System." In *Theories of Society,* edited by T. Parsons et al., 30–79. New York and London: The Free Press and Collier Macmillan.

———. 1964. *Social Structure and Personality.* New York: The Free Press.

———. 1967. *Sociological Theory and Modern Sociology.* New York: The Free Press.

———. 1968 [1937]. *The Structure of Social Action.* Vol. 2. New York and London: The Free Press and Collier Macmillan.

———. 1969. *Politics and Social Structure.* New York and London: The Free Press and Collier Macmillan.

———. 1972. "Culture and Social System Revisited." *Social Science Quarterly* 53:253–266.

———. 1972a. *Das System moderner Gesellschaften.* München: Juventa Verlag.

———. 1975. "Comment on 'Parsons as a Symbolic Interactionist.' " *Sociological Inquiry* 45 (1):62–65.

———. 1977. *Social Systems and the Evolution of Action Theory.* New York and London: The Free Press and Collier Macmillan.

———. 1977a. *The Evolution of Societies.* Englewood Cliffs, N.J.: Prentice-Hall.

———. 1978. *Action Theory and the Human Condition.* New York and London: The Free Press and Collier Macmillan.

———. 1982. "Action, Symbols and Cybernetic Control." In *Structural Sociology,* edited by I. Rossi, 49–65. New York: Columbia University Press.

———. 1986. *Aktor, Situation und normative Muster. Ein Essay zur Theorie sozialen Handelns.* Herausgegeben und übersetzt von Harald Wenzel. Frankfurt: Suhrkamp Verlag.

Parsons, T., and R. F. Bales. 1955. *Family, Socialization and Interaction.* New York and London: The Free Press and Collier Macmillan.

Parsons, T., R. F. Bales, and E. A. Shils. 1953. "Phase Movements in Relation to Motivation, Symbolic Formation, and Role Structure." In *Working*

Papers in the Theory of Action, edited by T. Parsons et al., 163–269. New York and London: The Free Press and Collier Macmillan.

Parsons T., and G. Platt. 1973. *The American University.* Cambridge: Harvard University Press.

Parsons, T., and E. Shils, eds. 1951. *Toward a General Theory of Action: Theoretical Foundations in the Social Sciences.* New York: Harper & Row.

Parsons, T., and N. Smelser. 1956. *Economy and Society.* London: Routledge and Kegan Paul.

Popper, K. R. 1961. *The Poverty of Historicism.* London: Routledge and Kegan Paul.

———. 1966. *Logik der Forschung.* Tübingen: J. B. C. Mohr (Paul Siebeck).

———. 1969. "La rationalité et le princip de rationalité." In *Les fondements philosophiques des systèmes économiques,* edited by E. M. Claassen, 144–147. Paris: Payot.

———. 1972. *Objective Knowledge: An Evolutionary Approach.* Oxford: Clarendon Press.

———. 1984. *Auf der Suche nach einer besseren Welt. Vorträge und Aufsätze aus dreißig Jahren.* München: Piper Verlag.

Prigogine, I. 1976. "L'ordre par fluctuation et le système social." *Rheinisch-Westfälische Akademie der Wissenschaft. Vorträge Nr. 260.* Opladen: Westdeutscher Verlag.

Procter, I. 1978. "Parsons's Early Voluntarism." *Sociological Inquiry* 48 (1):37–48.

Saurwein, K.-H. 1988. *Ökonomie und soziologische Theorienkonstruktion. Zur Bedeutung ökonomischer Theorieelemente in der Sozialtheorie Talcott Parsons.* Opladen: Westdeutscher Verlag.

Savage, S. P. 1981. *The Theories of Talcott Parsons: The Social Relations of Action.* London: Macmillan.

Schluchter, W. 1980. "Gesellschaft und Kultur. Überlegungen zu einer Theorie institutioneller Differenzierung." In *Verhalten, Handeln und System. Talcott Parsons' Beitrag zur Entwicklung der Sozialwissenschaften,* edited by W. Schluchter, 106–149. Frankfurt: Suhrkamp Verlag.

Schmid, M. 1972. *Leerformeln und Ideologiekritik.* Tübingen: J. C. B. Mohr (Paul Siebeck).

———. 1985. "Die Idee rationalen Handelns und ihr Verhältnis zur Sozialwissenschaft. Bemerkungen zu Karl Poppers Philosophie der Sozialwissenschaften." In *Karl Popper: Philosophie und Wissenschaft,* edited by F. Wallner, 88–107. Wien: Wilhelm Braunmüller Verlag.

———. 1987. "Georg Simmel. Die Dynamik des Lebens." In *Grundprobleme großer Philosophen. Philosophie der Neuzeit 4,* edited by J. Speck, 216–264. Göttingen: Vandenhoeck & Ruprecht.

———. 1987a. "Autopoiesis und soziales System. Eine Standortbestimmung." In *Sinn, Kommunikation und soziale Differenzierung. Beiträge zu Luhmanns Theorie sozialer System,* edited by H. Haferkamp and M. Schmid, 25–50. Frankfurt: Suhrkamp Verlag.

———. 1989. *Sozialtheorie und soziales System. Versuche über Talcott Parsons.* Forschungsberichte der Universität der Bundeswehr. München/Neubiberg.

Schneider, L. 1973. "The Idea of Culture in the Social Sciences: Critical and Supplementary Observations." In *The Idea of Culture in the Social Sciences,* edited by L. Schneider and C. M. Bonjean, 118–143. Cambridge: Cambridge University Press.

Sheldon, R. C. 1951. "Some Observations on Theory in the Social Sciences." In *Toward A General Theory of Action,* edited by T. Parsons and E. A. Shils, 30–44. New York: Harper & Row.

Simmel, G. [1918] 1984. "Vom Wesen des historischen Verstehens." In G. Simmel, *Das Individuum und die Freiheit: Essais,* 61–83. Berlin: Wagenbach.

Sombart, W. 1929. "Sinnverstehen, Sachverstehen, Seelenverstehen." In *Verhandlungen des 6. Deutschen Soziologentags,* 208–226. Tübingen: J. C. B. Mohr.

Spencer, H. 1875. *Einleitung in das Studium der Soziologie.* Stuttgart: F. A. Brockhaus.

———. 1894. *Die Principien der Ethik. Bd. 1.* Stuttgart: E. Schweiterbart'hsche Verlagshandlung (E. Nägele).

Swanson, G. 1968. *The Birth of Gods. The Origin of Primitive Beliefs.* East Lansing: Michigan University Press.

Tenbruck, F. H. 1986. *Geschichte und Gesellschaft.* Berlin: Duncker & Humblot.

Tiryakian, E. 1985. "On the Significance of De-Differentiation." In *Macro-Sociological Theory. Perspectives on Sociological Theory,* edited by S. N. Eisenstadt and H. J. Helle, 118–134. Beverly Hills: Sage Publications.

Ullmann-Margalit, E. 1977. *The Emergence of Norms.* Oxford: Clarendon Press.

Valjavec, F. 1985. *Identité sociale et évolution.* Frankfurt: Peter Lang Verlag.

Voss, T. 1985. *Rationale Akteure und soziale Institutionen. Beitrag zu einer endogenen Theorie sozialen Tauschs.* München: Oldenbourg Verlag.

Wippler, R. 1978. "Nicht-intendierte soziale Folgen individueller Handlungen." *Soziale Welt* 29 (2):155–179.

5

Representative Culture
and Cultural Representation
Johannes Weiss

The ideas I present here arise from a lengthier investigation into the sociology of representation. For this reason they are somewhat tersely formulated and in any case represent provisional working hypotheses. I have two aims: to take a fresh analytical look at a part of the social landscape that has been undeservedly neglected by sociology, for all its fundamental importance of well-nigh universal presence,[1] and to demonstrate, or at least test, the empirical utility of the concept of representation in several different areas.[2]

In what follows I address the role of representation in the realm of culture. That I have singled out here an important aspect of "culture" is not as obvious as in the case of law or religion, to say nothing of politics. Nonetheless, my investigations to date have only served to convince me that this cluster of concerns is of the greatest sociological relevance. As Abbé Sieyès, the theorist of representative democracy and the father of the representative constitution of 1791, states: "In every walk of social life everything is founded on representation. It is met with everywhere in both the private and the public orders; it is as much the mother of the manufacturing and trading industries as of advances in the liberal arts and in statecraft; it would not be too much to say that it is integrally bound up with the essence of social life."[3]

The concept of representation (at least in the sense I am using it) has not yet been used systematically in the sociological theory of culture. The reason (apart from the general neglect of this concept in sociology) may be connected with the fact that the notion of cultural representation, even more than the idea of a *representative culture,* flies in the face of certain fundamental intellectual preconceptions of sociology, for the most part unconsciously held.

I may be treading on thin ice—for my comments may be criticized for taking a point of view supposedly downright unsociological—but at least I shall be doing so with open eyes. To make matters worse, I shall begin with an author, who, for all his distinction in his own subject and fame with the educated public at large, has not exactly set sparks flying or won any disciples in sociology itself. I am referring to Jacob Burckhardt; not so much the Jacob Burckhardt of the investigations into cultural history, but rather the one of the *Weltgeschichtliche Betrachtungen.* Clearly the only practical justification for proceeding in this fashion must be the extent to which it helps to disengage the sociological imagination from any possible tendencies to parthenogenetic torpor!

Before getting into our subject, though, I must first say a few words on what I mean by *representation* and *representative.* The word *representative* has three principal meanings in the English language:[4]

1. an agent or spokesperson who acts on behalf of somebody else,
2. a person who symbolizes the identity or qualities of a class of persons, and
3. a person who shares some of the characteristics of a class of persons.

I restrict myself to the first two meanings. In German these meanings have come to be denoted by different words: in the first case, when we mean an agent or spokesperson acting on behalf of somebody else, we use the expression *Stellvertretung;* in the second case, we use the expression *Repräsentation.* I point this out because I envision a certain relationship between these two distinct things; in particular, there exists a historical sequence between representation in the sense of *Stellvertretung* and representation in the sense of *Repräsentation.* For this reason, the title of my paper could doubtless be more adequately rendered in German, "Repräsentative Kultur und kulturelle Stellvertretung" or even "Von der repräsentativen Kultur zur kulturellen Stellvertretung." These titles would hopefully have a certain provocative effect to the extent that they exclude some other title such as "Von der repräsentativen zur authentischen Kultur."

II

One of the chapters of Burckhardt's *Weltgeschichtliche Betrachtungen* is headed "The Individual and the Universal (Historical Greatness)." It is not necessary here to spend much time on the general intellectual background against which Burckhardt's reflections were elaborated, which would mean, among other things, going into their ambivalent relationship to Hegel's philosophy of history (cf. Löwith 1984: 9) or assigning their place in the development of his thought as a whole.

According to Burckhardt, "uniqueness" and "irreplaceability" are the qualities normally associated with the idea of the "great individual." He writes, "He alone can be considered unique and irreplaceable who possesses an abnormal degree of intellectual and moral force, whose energies are focused on a universal goal, i.e., one that concerns whole peoples or whole cultures, even mankind in its entirety" (1982: 379). Greatness in Burckhardt's sense is also found when modalities of experience, judgment, and action that concern at once the whole of society and society as a whole culminate in certain individuals and indeed *only* in certain individuals, so that they alone are in a position to transform these modalities (380). The key and, one might say, dialectical point is that those universal goals that are most binding and paradigmatic—the very ones involving the modalities of experience, judgment, and action that are valid for whole societies or even for the whole of humanity—can only be brought into existence, receive fitting embodiment, and be transformed at the hands of outstanding individuals. It is by virtue of this idea that such individuals are designated representatives of the universal, in a double sense.

First, they embody and give expression to the universal in their work and person and do it in a characteristically well-rounded and impressive fashion. By doing so—and here we encounter the second sense of representation—they open for the rest of humanity opportunities to gain experience or to act that otherwise simply would not exist. Burckhardt notes that, particularly because of the great "writers and artists," people are able to "multiply their inmost being and powers" (383). Individuals endowed with exceptional creative gifts engage in activities that the rest of humankind can draw on to achieve a significant extension of their own existential possibilities. By the same token, humankind will not be able to evade the consequences of these widened possibilities. Great individuals are irreplaceable because they alone are able to discharge certain necessary or, at any rate, important functions for all the others, that is, they act as their representatives.

Depending on just how improbable fundamental innovations are in the different cultural areas, the need for great representatives will vary. In any event, for Burckhardt it is an incontestable fact that "art, poetry and philosophy and indeed all the great achievements of the human spirit are sustained by their great representatives and that if there ever does come about a general raising of standards it is solely due to these few" (380). He points out that among many peoples of the world artists and poets were revered as virtual gods because they "are able to exteriorise what is internal and express it in such a way that as an expression of what is internal it has the force of a revelation" (383). For this reason, past ages have considered their poets to be the "mouthpiece" for their "deepest longings and awareness" (384).

A comparable importance does not attach to those whom he refers to as the "mere inventors and discoverers in professional disciplines." That is because their achievements would usually have been duplicated sooner or later by others and because such achievements do not attain the highest degree of universality, whose goal is the "world in its entirety." The great exception for Burckhardt is Christopher Columbus. Though it is correct to regard Columbus as replaceable, nonetheless his discovery—which was so fraught with consequences—has come to be tied once and for all to his person and to the quite exceptional energy with which he went about his purpose. Burckhardt notes, "The proof of the global nature of the earth is a precondition for all later thought; and to the extent that all later thought has been liberated by this preconception, so it reflects back inevitably upon Columbus" (381).

A similar achievement of momentous importance and universal validity in terms of later consequences is the attachment of the basic laws of nature to the natural sciences. Burckhardt writes, "All subsequent thought owes its liberation to Copernicus' expulsion of the earth from the centre of the world to the minor orbit in one particular solar system" (382). But for Burckhardt the cultural import of the historical sciences (in the widest sense) and their representatives is, by contrast, restricted and likely to remain so for the time being because they have not come up with any comparable discoveries.

One particular group of the great representatives, the actual group of historical individuals in the narrow sense, is made up of the founding figures and renewers in the world religions, the protagonists of religious, political, and social movements and revolutions and then, too, the founders of state. The fact that some of them assume an ideal or at least idealized form and, indeed, may even be no more than mythical figures is for Burckhardt the strongest proof of the need for great representatives on the part of peoples. Through them the *idées directrices* of the religious or political spheres and movements, with their claim to universal validity and their ability to confer unity, are defined, actualized, and authenticated in a quite singular way, not in the least bit a symbolical remove but in fact perfectly concrete. "They subsume states, religions, cultures and crisis" (392). Their individual will stands for a *volonté générale,* which, depending on the exact circumstances, can be interpreted "as the will of God, as the will of a nation or collectivity, or as the will of the age" (401).

This summary should be enough to make Burckhardt's views on great individuals clear. One of the irritating aspects of his thinking on the matter is his almost pedantic insistence on demarcating the "great representatives" of the highest rank from those to whom he is only willing to attribute "relative greatness" (382) or who—especially in art—only count as "masters" of the second or third degree (384). This extreme fixation on "genuine" or "real" greatness may even make us suspect ideological motives behind these reflections as a whole. However, it would be wrong to dismiss even Burckhardt's extremely controversial closing remarks on the impossibility of great individuals emerging from the context of contemporary culture. Burckhardt saw the present as characterized by a "universal guarantee of mediocrity," an "antipathy against achievements of genius," and an all-consuming interest in the "exploitability of the given" (404). Such tendencies and, above all, the "prevailing passion of our day, the desire of the masses for a better life" were incapable of being "concentrated into one genuinely great figure."

III

I would not dare to suggest that the excerpts just presented from Burckhardt's *Weltgeschichtliche Betrachtungen* constitute a sociological analysis. In fact it would be much more plausible—and certainly more in line with Burckhardt's intentions—to perceive in these reflections not merely a definitely antisocial undercurrent of feeling but also an antisociological one. Nonetheless, these reflections on the role of great representatives point to a problem that sociology, and particularly the sociological theory of culture, will avoid at its own peril. After all, it often happens that exciting developments in sociology crystallize around problematical phenomena that are allegedly external to, or even set over, society.

Thus it seems both appropriate and necessary that sociology should take Burckhardt's theme and treat it in line with its own specific modalities. Perhaps the following statement will command at least provisional assent: It is not only the production and transformation but also the maintenance and provision of the "objective culture" of a society that is in need of both institutional or material "symbolization" and the concrete representation by individuals of the complex of interpretations and evaluations that lay claim to objective validity and binding force. Of course the representation by individuals also has a symbolic dimension related to the function of giving expression or actualization. Still, the decisive difference is that an individual capable of action (a natural person) stands for and embodies central and fundamental cultural ideas and values, and, what is more, in so doing stands proxy or deputizes for the many others who do not have the necessary abilities but who are still integrally affected by the meaning and the practical consequences of these cultural ideals.

This is all the more true when what is involved is, not the preservation, further development, or paradigmatic depiction of value ascriptions, modes of living, and traditional interpretations of the world, but rather their invention and implementation in novel, possibly even revolutionary, forms—that is, we are dealing with processes in which fundamental cultural innovation takes place. Burckhardt, to be sure, also treats such processes for the most part. Perhaps understandably, sociology has clearly found it difficult to recognize and accept that outstanding individuals can play irreplaceable and decisive roles in such processes. In contrast to such a personalizing standpoint, the explanatory task of sociology—in the commonly expressed opinion, in any event—consists precisely in demonstrating the decisive importance of social structures and structural conflicts—at least in the final analysis—and the essential irrelevance or replaceability of such actors. In this fashion, sociologists hope to discharge the professional mandate of "explaining the social through the social." Yet one of our classical thinkers has not adhered to this *opinio communis;* instead he has propounded a theory of cultural innovation that assigns to exceptional individuals an integral and quite indispensable function. I am referring to Max Weber and his notion of *charisma.* Although this notion is so frequently cited in the literature, it has usually been received with mixed feelings, and on only rare occasions has it been subjected to a systematic analysis. To what extent—*even* here—Burckhardt's direct influence on Weber may be assumed will be left open.[5] It will suffice to remark that Weber treats the role and function of charismatic personalities only from the standpoint of leadership and rule and not from that of representative action (at least not in the sense used here).[6] Therefore, his analyses are incapable of advancing us further into our particular enquiry and need not detain us.

Only one classical figure, though admittedly not one of the first importance, has turned up ideas that fit well with my theme. I am referring to Theodor Geiger and, in particular, to his book *Aufgaben und Stellung der Intelligenz in der Gesellschaft,* which was first published in 1949. Geiger begins his investigations by making a number of distinctions about the concept of culture. He takes what he terms the *substantial* concept of culture (he opposes it to the *dynamic* concept, which relates to culture in what he terms an *intellectual social process*) and differentiates between representative culture and anonymous culture. What entitles both cases to be considered substantial is that culture here is conceived of as the "store of such cultural values as may have been acquired," which approximately corresponds to what Georg Simmel called *objective culture*. Geiger terms *representative* that branch of substantial culture in which the identity and the image that whole societies (or at least their ruling classes) and even whole ages form of themselves is expressed, manifested, and kept alive. In traditional societies the representative culture is primarily religious in form. For Geiger a profane representative culture first became a possibility in the Italian Renaissance.

I turn now to the cultural strata that function as the social carriers of representative culture. Geiger singles out two as being of decisive importance. The first is the *Intelligenzija*, not to be confused with the large and amorphous group of intellectuals, which constitutes the circle of what he calls "creators of resources of representative culture." It is in the nature of things that such individuals comprise only a "vanishingly small part of the population" (1987: 12). The second is the cultural stratum of the "educated"—likewise a small group—whose members possess an "immediate relationship" to the resources of representative culture. They are responsible for conferring a second meaning on this concept of representative culture; their immediate relationship to objective culture imposes on them the task of "representing culture inside society and society itself as a culture unit" (7).

In contemporary Western society, Geiger asserts, as a consequence of the progressive "democratization of education," on the one hand, and the splitting off of education from utilitarian training, on the other, this stratum has been deprived of its functional justification and raison d'être. He states, "The educated caste of earlier times is losing its representative status" (9). The closely related question, whether this does not mean that the time of "representative culture" itself is also over, is not taken up by Geiger, and he certainly provides no answer to it. Similarly, the present and future situation of the *Intelligenzija* is left undiscussed. And the same applies to the question of why this cultural stratum does not play a representative role alongside (or as a consequence of) its creative one.

This loss of representative status in turn is intimately connected with the fact that Geiger does not address the double meaning of representation contained in the notion of "representative culture." This double meaning—*allegedly* contradictory in its very nature—resides in the fact that it is precisely the exceptional and outstanding individuals (or else a relatively small collection of such persons) who are responsible for creating and underwriting cultural contents possessing general validity and binding force. They are able to do so by virtue of the exceptional and nongeneralizable qualifications they bring to bear; so that what we find that is truly representative in a culture—that which concerns *everybody* as a whole—is in fact only able to be instigated and kept alive by the very few, who nonetheless function as representatives for all.

It may be objected to that for Geiger, the sociologist, the Burckhardtian problem loses much of its force—if indeed it is not revealed as a pseudoproblem—by virtue of the fact that in place of these exceptional, irreplaceable individuals he substituted a whole social group, the *Intelligenzija*. My impression, though, is that the problem is by no means laid to rest by its socialization here. Indeed other sociological theorists (and their dependents) of the *Intelligenzija* provenance were well aware that this was so. One very general definition stemming from Leszek Kolakowski (1969: 159) even has it that intellectuals are those "whose profession [it] is to create and to communicate cultural values." This definition, however, requires a coda, which runs as follows: this they do "in such a way as to typically claim that in so doing they are really acting in place of and on behalf of society, the people or at least the underprivileged class[es]." A qualification of this kind is needed to do justice to the intellectuals' own understanding of their social role along with the justifications they usually offer in defense of it, at least in modern Western society. Elsewhere (Weiss 1987) I have characterized the historical breeding ground and the ultimate demise of this self-explanatory syndrome—namely the intellectual as cultural advocate of the oppressed masses—using a particularly important and instructive example, the Communist movement (from Marx to Sartre and Gramsci).

Such a claim to cultural representation on the part of the intellectuals has today lost virtually all of its former plausibility, especially even in the landscape of socialist parties and movements. E. P. Thompson (1987: 8) sharply attacked what he calls the "theory of substitution";[7] similarly—indeed above all—there is Pierre Bourdieu, who has castigated the Marxian "demand for unconditional delegation" as a particularly objectionable form of "expropriation" of the people by those who dispose of the "cultural capital" (cf. Bourdieu 1975).

When intellectuals conceive of and justify themselves as representatives or delegates of the people in cultural matters, they naturally do not mean to imply that they have been formally appointed or elected. Rather, they derive their legitimation directly and expressly from an alleged capability to discern what is true and right (or even good), that is, they base it on cognitive or normative states of affairs in the broadest sense. The decline of the intellectuals (certainly in the West, but presumably in socialist states as well) is therefore closely bound with the declining plausibility of this very claim on their part to possess a universally valid, objectively based fund of knowledge to which the broad masses (so far) have no access. These modern Western intellectuals can only exist in a historical situation where the traditional representative culture is progressively losing its binding force, but the idea of a representative culture *as such,* that is, the idea of a universally valid cognitive and normative order (or *Weltanschauung*), is not itself under attack. In point of fact, the representative role of such intellectuals can only be legitimized by the belief in the attainability of a new cultural order (which can also be the "good old," or natural, order); what is impossible is for legitimation to be purchased solely by an attack on the status quo, no matter how radical or devastating.

IV

Now I wish to define a little more rigorously a distinction already mentioned, the concept of representation by individuals. This concept has two possible meanings:

1. The realization and embodiment of universal ideas and ideals of a religious, aesthetic, and political kind, or even of suitably idealized communities. This actualization and embodiment is achieved by exceptional personalities. Hence, in this case, what is represented is itself an idea of a hypostatization but not a subject capable of acting.

2. The vicarious actions undertaken by individual, exceptional persons either for, on behalf of, or acting as proxy for the other members of the group in question or society (or even the whole human race). In this case, a person stands in for others, and so what is represented certainly is a subject capable of action.

Perhaps it would be more useful and appropriate to speak of symbolic or ritual representation in the first sense and of social representation in the second sense. In the concept of representative culture the different strands of meaning of representation are woven together. In this sense, Burckhardt too is talking about representative culture, although he does not actually use the term. For there can be no doubt that the function of the great representatives lies, not so much in social as in symbolic or ritual representation, that is, in the actualization and embodiment of ideas or ideal communities. To this extent they represent something that in principle also transcends the bounds of their exceptional personality and *for this reason* can lay claim to universal recognition and binding force.

At the same time, though, what emerges from Burckhardt's strong emphasis on the individuality of his great representatives is that he is really describing a state of incipient dissolution of representative culture (in terms of the transcendental nature of the meanings represented), or at least that these reflections indicate his own experience of a progressive dissolution of representative culture.[8]

In the title of this chapter, I have attempted to express the difference between *this* situation, which even Burckhardt perceived as belonging to the past, and the present situation. Admittedly with a certain amount of license, even if only to emphasize the contrast more starkly, I draw on the conceptual duality of *representative culture* and *cultural representation*. I suspect that by drawing on this duality it is possible to designate the starting and (provisional) finishing point of a multistage development that is in reality very complex. This development consists then in the fact that the representative culture undergoes progressive disintegration and is replaced by a culture of representation. What is mainly involved is a change in the type of relationship between the objective culture, or *society,* and its exceptional creators and bearers.

The starting point of this development is defined by the fact that the extraordinary cultural achievements of certain individuals in no sense can be attributed to any individual or subjective factors about them, but rather that they flow exclusively from their specific participation in the objective and universally binding contents of the culture. Their representative function thus consists solely in the actualization, personification, and appropriation of preexistent truths, not in the fulfillment of a mandate conferred on them by "normal" people or society at large.

In contrast to this (admittedly largely hypothetical) starting point, Burckhardt goes on to describe, as has already been remarked, a state of affairs characterized by a peculiar dialectic between universality and individuality, objectivity and subjectivity. "Great individuals" create or transform the culture of whole societies (in fact, even humanity in its entirety) in such a way that they, by virtue of being distinct personages in all their singularity and irreplaceability, indeed *cannot* withdraw into or vanish behind their tasks. Their insights, discoveries, and inventions, binding and fraught with consequences for all, remain inseparably connected with their persons and names: Columbus, Luther, Galilei, Descartes, Copernicus, Newton, Kant, Marx, to name only some of the more outstanding. However, in our present context of concern this means that the representative function does not merely possess a symbolic or ritual significance; on the contrary, it also (and indeed principally) possesses a social or intersubjective significance. The great individuals can be considered as representative in the sense that in their actions they function as proxies for all humans; that this is so can be recognized by the fact that everybody from now on has to live with the consequences of their world-transforming actions.

At the second stage of the development, Burckhardt clings *as a matter of principle* to the notion of a universal and (in this sense) representative culture. This notion also applies, at least programmatically, to the phase where *the intellectuals as a group* advance to become the social carriers of culture (particularly cultural innovation or transformation). The rise of what Karl Mannheim referred to as "free-floating" intellectuals is closely connected to the process of social differentiation, where even culture becomes relegated to a separate, relatively autonomous sphere of society. Their specific importance—and this means too the specific importance of the intellectuals—is seen as residing in their mission to create a new, all-embracing body of meanings and values by going beyond the "disintegration of society" (Marx 1962: 504) and subsuming it into a higher synthesis or unity. The idea that "the ruling thoughts are always the thoughts of those that rule" could only be formulated precisely because there no longer existed a representative culture in the traditional sense. At the same time, though, this formulation of Marx derives its underlying logic from the intention of taking the old, still class-oriented forms of the "cultural superstructure" and replacing them with a truly universal cultural form owing allegiance only to the (*one single*) truth or reason (that is, for Marx and many others, the *one single* science).

I will not go into the details of this viewpiont and the various modifications it has taken. In any case, the logical consequence of it was that the few who believed themselves in possession of the requisite insights and competence came to regard themselves in a highly novel and quite explicit fashion as representatives and delegates of the people. This self-image as representatives of the people (but not their leaders or their advisors) reflects their vision of themselves as the *metteurs en scène* and articulators (even if only in a vicarious, anticipatory fashion) of the very same clarificational and revaluational process that by right was, and should be, the people's own affair. Thus, the representative role of the intellectuals should—unlike that of Burckhardt's great individuals—only be temporary. The ideas and evaluations of the new cultural order should differ from all preceding orders because they not only apply for everyone, but they also should—in principle at least—readily command rational assent from everyone, especially through the cogency of their reasons. Corresponding to this notion was the demand that the procedure, with whose help the new ideas and values of the intellectuals were obtained and propagated, had to be egalitarian and nonviolent; that is, the debate carried on by the intellectuals had to be both a paradigm for and a forerunner of the coming cultural democratization en masse.

Now a new cultural order that is in this sense "authentic" and based on universal and egalitarian participation has certainly *not* emerged in place of the representative culture of earlier times. In recent years demands have been raised, with ever-increasing vehemence, for a radical democratization of culture, for a culture for all, for culture as a basic right, or socioculture, which indicates that so far this anticipation has not been fulfilled. What has happened instead is that cultural life in Western society—to the extent that it displays any innovative and creative tendencies at all, as opposed to being merely conservative and backward-looking (the stuff of museums)—now manifests a new form of cultural representation. This manifestation cannot be explained by any failure on the part of the intellectuals, for example, or by people showing that they have not yet come of age culturally or proved incapable of full cultural autonomy. Rather the idea of a new and comprehensive cultural synthesis, of a new and unified *Weltbild,* has turned out to be untenable. Both the removal of the cultural sphere from the other subsystems of the social order, and (more important) the *internal* differentiation of this sphere have progressed even further and have certainly not been subsumed in some higher-level unity. We have witnessed the formation of that particular kind of pluralism or polytheism in the social "value hierarchies," which find expression in the insight "that something can be holy not only despite not being beautiful, but *because and only if* it is not beautiful . . . and that something can be beautiful not only despite not being good, but by participating in and being what is not good about it . . . (and) something can be true, despite not being and through not being beautiful and holy and good" (Weber 1968: 603). The intellectuals have certainly played a key role in the emergence of this polytheism, despite their universal, holistically minded intentions. But in so doing, they have unwittingly eroded their own position—whether real or merely claimed—as general representatives. But at the same time, new—though indeed much more modest—functions have also come to devolve on them: because the far-reaching autonomization affecting the cultural order and its individual provinces of meaning, with the progressive detachment of the latter from the lives, experiences, and the working world of most people, has created a great need for specialists and experts to work at defining and solving particular specialized and expert problems in the interests of social progress. Moreover, because the general opinion is that these are important problems and even approach existential significance—key problems of principle affecting our personal lives—they cannot be regarded as simply a further case of the progressive division of labor. Rather they present a form of job division that possesses representative character: for the cultural experts are in the position of deciding and doing things that people actually should decide and do for themselves (if only they could); moreover, these are things that are or claim to be of specific importance for the meaning and future fate of people's lives. I have contrasted representative culture and cultural representation and have attempted to place them within a developmental process. The following remarks, in similar provisional fashion, are addressed to the present situation. I will discuss several ways in which cultural representation is manifested and some problems that arise in connection with this manifestation.

V

Daniel Bell (1976: 16) has pointed out—although he is certainly not the first to do so—that the axial principle of modern culture or modernity is actually the "self": "The fundamental assumption of modernity, the thread that has run through Western civilization since the sixteenth century, is that the social unit of society is not the group, the guild, the tribe, or the city, but the person. The Western ideal was the autonomous man who, in becoming self-determining, would have freedom." Bell's thesis is that a "hypertrophic individualism" has emerged from the universalization and generalization of the search for self-realization and self-fulfillment, and this he sees as the decisive cause of the crisis of modernity he has diagnosed. For Bell, the axial principle of any democratic political order is that those ruled should give their assent to their government. Together with the idea of freedom, this principle is based on the modern axial structure of "representation or participation." Bell does not address the idea that the self is of fundamental significance to the political sphere too. But from the standpoint of this idea it must be said that the two processes he mentions—participation and representation—are by no means equivalent, in neither a substantial nor a functional sense. From this standpoint it would appear that representation can be no more than a perhaps inevitable, but still rather poor, substitute for participation.[9]

In the controversies over democracy, top priority, particularly since the Enlightenment (for example, Rousseau's writings and the Federalist Papers), has been given to clarifying the circumstances under which a representative system founded on the delegation of participatory and decision-making rights is permissible. The issue is particularly clear when political participation is held to be the inalienable right of autonomous individuals. For this same political individualism and liberalism that declares the *res publica* to be the inalienable affair of each and every subject in practice leads *inevitably* to the establishment of parliamentary structures. That such an inevitable link existed did not escape the attention of the conservative critics of modern democracy; it led them to reject both individualism and the representative system as the outgrowth of "mechanistic" ways of thinking.[10] On the other hand, the more recent critique of "the politics of representation" emanating from the new social movements of the day is typically modulated by core democratic ideas and action patterns, and it is, at least in part, quite radical.[11] The ideas and action patterns have clearly not yet passed the empirical litmus test; rather we too often find confirmation of the old insight (Griffith 1968: 463) that the alternative to representation is not active participation, that is, acting oneself, but is nonrepresentation or nonself-action.

Representation in political affairs must appear in a dubious light—or may even appear to be quite inadmissable—to the extent that under the basic pretext of modern individualism it elevates political programs to the rank of moral and/or religious imperatives or even replaces them entirely. What was novel and modern about Protestant theology was mainly its insistence that there was, at least in principle, no barrier between the individual believer and his God that might require intercessional and representative offices to be performed by third parties.[12] Similarly, modern ethical and moral systems, clearly influenced by this theological conviction, are characterized by the basic assumption that any attempt to delegate responsibility and blame would be nonsensical. Moreover, attempts were quite frequently made in the past, and continue to be made, to radically reformulate this basic assumption. At least in the postconventional stage of morality—in the sense distinguished by Kohlberg and Habermas—it now seems that reflection and discourse on moral norms must be also practiced by the individual subject's own person. This would mean that a "proxy" or "advocatory" ethic is acceptable only as an interim solution pending a suitable opportunity or in the case of minors or incompetents who cannot be held to blame.[13]

This conviction inevitably had a strong influence on the practice of law in modern times and particularly on criminal law—at least for as long as it permitted itself to be guided by the regulative ideas of individual responsibility and capacity for remorse (and also, incidentally, the related idea of atonement). On the other hand, in a legal system (in contradistinction to moral and religious systems) it is impossible to do without norms that are positivistic and formalistic in nature and that are established in advance. Thus a postconventional stage of legal development cannot be envisaged without resorting to unrealistic presuppositions. This and the related fact that only those with the appropriate expertise are able to act successfully within the legal system have been jointly responsible for heading off a radical, broadbased critique of legal representation that would certainly have focused on the status and function of trial lawyers.[14]

This is not the place to discuss these important and extremely complex problems or to inquire into the likely long-term consequences of the radical detheologization of morality and demoralization of law. Rather, the question to be raised here is how the tension-laden nexus between individuality, participation, and representation finds present expression in the field of culture (conceived in the narrow sense of the word).

It is only natural that attempts to replace the principle of representation with the principles of autonomy and participation (or, for that matter, authenticity [cf. Ferrara 1985]) should encounter great difficulty when the activities in question depend on a formidable amount of expertise and the knowledge in question—even in its most general premises and implications—is inaccessible to the nonexpert. In the culture of modern societies, though, this point applies above all to the *scientific* and *artistic* fields. Still, for all the similarities, there also exist significant differences between the two fields.

The development of modern science was closely bound up with the idea that this type of knowledge would lead not only to general validities but also to insights into nature that were universally accessible and verifiable, meaning that it would put an end to the unequal, hierarchical distribution of culturally prized knowledge and deprive the tutelage of the many by the few of its cognitive underpinnings. This expectation has not been fulfilled. In line with implications of its own logic, this form of knowledge has given rise instead to such a refined level of differentiation, specialization, and abstraction that the obtained scientific findings—though admittedly in principle universal and open to all—are de facto only accessible to a small coterie of experts who draw on them as they see fit. This situation, along with the fact that the technological outlets of such knowledge have increasingly infiltrated the daily lives of people, has been responsible for a progressive loss of cognitive competence and cognitive self-determination in modern society. The sheer scope and complexity of the skills, data, and know-how required in various disciplines go well beyond the cognitive and technological competence of most people.

This inevitable consequence of the domination of modern culture by science, rationalization, and differentiation was already noticed by—to take only two examples—Weber (at the end of his treatise "Über einige Kategorien der verstehenden Soziologie") and Simmel (in his comments on the "Tragedy of Culture"). A contemporary author, Stanley Diamond, has formulated this insight as follows: "In the way he relates to his social environment and the level of scientific and technological knowledge attained, the average primitive literally possesses a much more comprehensive education than most civilized individuals. He can respond to the cultural opportunities open to him in a much more comprehensive and immediate fashion; and this he does not as a consumer or vicariously, but as an actively engaged, authentic person" (1974: 143).

It follows from this—admittedly only relative—"experiential deprivation" that, in many matters of the gravest importance, members of modern society are in the position of having to depend on "secondhand experience" (cf. Gehlen 1964), that is to say, on "delegating experience" to "experienced functionaries" (Blumenberg 1986: 224). The onward march of specialization in knowledge has, as Arnold Gehlen (1963: 17) saw, made the separation between specialist and layperson irreversible: "The result is that one acquiesces without much ado in relinquishing any claim to competence, responsibility and at all being in the know as soon as one leaves one's own speciality; i.e., the individual learns to delegate his judgement." Hence it is not surprising that this delegation of judgment has been institutionalized in the role of the experts wielding their expertise. This role is defined by the expectation that the expert should, in Friedhelm Neidhardt's (1986: 3) formulation, "be able to express dauntingly matters in the kind of language consumers and normal citizens use when making judgements—and what's more, that he should even make *their* judgements for them."

All this flies in the face of the *idées directrices* of modernity, as has already been pointed out. And it is this, rather than simply the operation of certain dysfunctional effects, that explains the principal criticism that is brought again and again against the modern "expertocracy" and its reduction of the average person to a state of tutelary bondage to a combined front of scientifically and technologically versed experts (cf. Illich et al. 1979). Still it is not realistic to solve the problem by simply doing away with the experts, as certain critics have occasionally demanded; however the dubious knowledge is looked at, it clearly is *only* to be had from experts. Likewise it is clear that any attempt to set up "counterexperts" (Hartmann and Hartmann 1982)—while it might be effective at ending power monopoly abuses sometimes committed by unscrupulous experts—holds little promise of solving the main problem, unless of course the experts and the counterexperts were to neutralize each other so that neither could act effectively.

That it would be unwise to overdramatize the situation at least in the case of science is suggested by a single factor: that the experts themselves depend on scientific insights whose very validity, scope, and utility depend, at least in the long run, on rational scrutiny and evaluation; nor can they escape this fate. Science cannot renounce the idea of the universality of the truths of nature it reveals and the idea that these must stand up to intersubjective scrutiny. Indeed it is precisely this idea that scientific knowledge is universally binding and fraught with consequences for humankind that makes it necessary to encourage an ethic of responsibility for the whole of humanity and also gives some grounds for optimism. What exactly this encouragement would involve cannot detain us further here. May it suffice to reproduce the words of the astronaut, Russell Schweickhart, "Are you separated out to be touched by God, to have some special experience that others cannot have? And you know the answer to that is no . . . you look down and see the surface of that globe that you've lived on all this time, and you know all those people down there, and they are like you, they are you, and somehow you represent them. You are up here as the sensing element, that point out on the end, and that's a humbling feeling. It's a feeling that says you have a responsibility. It's not for yourself" (Keeley 1989: 144).

The situation in the contemporary arts is far more complicated and difficult. The more recent history of the arts has been accompanied by a vociferous critique of their contents that charges that the authority of the works of art, their ability to communicate, and their dependability as a source of value judgments are all steadily declining. The insight that modern poetry has moved from general intelligibility and general significance to mere mannerist, individual, and interesting effects was charged by such an early figure as Friedrich Schlegel ("Über das Studium der griechischen Poesie"). In regard to music and the fine arts, by the beginning of this century (at the latest) such charges had come to be commonplace in critical and public debate.[15]

The situation in the arts is much more difficult to assess than that in science because in the former it was necessary to go so far to abandon the regulative idea of a common (or, in principle, generalizable) frame of reference of binding force. In contrast, neither religion nor science (nor any other lifesphere or perceptual or experiential tradition laying a claim to self-evident validity and/or exemplary status) can pretend to offer such a frame of reference in the first place. As a result, attempts to delegate judgment in artistic matters are bound to be much more a matter of course than in science but are not the less risky and controversial for all that. To an extent wholly unknown in earlier times, artists today are called upon to explain, justify, and comment on their works, that is, they are expected not only to produce them but also to play a large role in orchestrating an appropriate reception for them. In addition, a need has developed for a steadily growing number of experts— mainly drawn from media—whose job it is to identify, interpret, and criticize the contemporary arts. These experts are clearly as indispensable as their competence is disputed. It has become difficult to believe that there can exist neither any generally valid, binding knowledge concerning the significance and cultural relevance of the contemporary arts, nor, by implication, is there any need for a corps of experts to interpret it. Paradoxically enough, this is precisely the reason why the widespread doubts about the competence of the art experts have had little overt effect in provoking a resolute attempt at curtailing their interpretive and communicative mandate. This paradox may in turn be connected with the evident fact that, despite all rhetorical assertions to the contrary, the contemporary arts have little to do with truth and reality, at least in the "old European" sense of these concepts, and certainly nothing to do with the "full weight of life" encountered on the personal or social levels (cf. Enzensberger 1988: 95). Indeed many of the leading lights of postmodernism have recently tried to interpret this very fact as one of the great advantages of the contemporary arts, to be welcomed as an expression of final emancipation from all extraneous bonds.[16]

A separate important and complex problem can only be briefly addressed here, and it concerns the role the mass media play in connection with cultural representation in contemporary society. Evidently it was the development of the mass media—first the printed word then, above all, radio and television—that was responsible for the fact that a cultural division of labor could ever be practiced at all as a form of cultural representation, or—which in the end boils down to the same thing— that it could ever be interpreted as such and so have the stamp of social legitimation placed on it. In highly differentiated mass society, the power wielded by the media alone is sufficient to create and maintain the pretense that, between those responsible for the production of cultural objects and/or pronouncing authoritatively on their meaning and merits on the one hand and the great mass of laypeople on the other, there really does exist a social, if not indeed a communicative, tie predicated on the understanding that these selfsame cultural experts represent all the nonexperts (with all that this implies for their public prominence and answerability to criticism). And to the extent that this is true, the mass media can be said to provide the technological and institutional infrastructure for the phenomenon of cultural representation.

Nonetheless, in recent times we find that the critique of the "expertocracy" has increasingly joined forces with the critique of the "mediocracy" to charge that the sound and the visual media in particular are used to sharply bring out the questionable side of cultural representation—and not merely as its star witness or shining instantiation. The critical voices point particularly to the extremely onesided, barely interactional or communicative character of the cultural representatives. At the same time the media promote (or demand), especially for pluralistic societies, that the cultural experts should suitably orchestrate and dramatize the manner in which they present themselves; even though such theatricalization will, at least in the long run, prove destructive if (and to the extent that) it should ever succeed in undermining trust in the competence of the experts and the necessity for their existence. It does seem that the criticism leveled against the mediocracy is not so much directed against the right to represent as such (or against the failure of those represented to issue an express mandate to that effect); rather criticism focuses on the manner in which the experts hosted by the media play their roles. However, it can hardly escape notice—and to a certain extent is probably also inevitable—that the medium most dependent on theatrical orchestration, namely television, is much more given to encourage narcissism, triviality, and an emphasis on dramatic effects than to treat seriously the materials presented. Nevertheless, just such a tendency would appear to be more inherently likely, for very much the same reasons as already given, in several areas of cultural life (the arts, politics, and religion) than in others (for example, science). To the extent, though, that it succeeds in gaining ground, we will be faced not only with a progressive loss of authentic experience and a confusion of mediated with actual experience but also with the disintegration of our ability to tell the real and the necessary apart from the bogus and the irrelevant. If this ever happens, the dream of cultural representation will have succeeded in destroying its own indispensable presuppositions. One thing is clear: as a staged happening, as a show put on for the entertainment and idle distraction of a society of onlookers, cultural representation can have no long-term future. For in a state of cultural entropy, where both everything and nothing is real and important, it will soon lose all significance, even of the most dubious, far-fetched, or contrived kind.

Notes

1. For some general considerations see Weiss (1984).
2. A first effort in this direction is Weiss (1987).
3. Quoted from Hofmann (1974: 408).
4. Adopted, with minor modifications, from Birch (1971: 15).
5. For a scanty reference to these affinities see Bendix (1965); Bendix, too, is disinclined to speculate on Burckhardt's possible influence on Weber.
6. In Weber's (1965: 847) view, charismatic leadership and representation exclude each other principally.
7. "The party, sect, or theorist, who disclose class-consciousness, not as it is, but as it ought to be."
8. Admittedly Burckhardt did not see a sign of cultural decay in the existence of great individuals; but there can be no doubt that he did see the intellectuals, with their proclivity for ahistorical rationalism and their "advocatory" claim, asserted in the cultural and political arenas. He (1974: 215) spoke of Robespierre as being "a terrible man who was a mere dallier for all his legal logic, though he tried to prevail here whatever the cost"; this is reminiscent of Hegel's (1961: 59) disparaging remark on the "lawyers, ideologists and men of principle" who thoroughly deserved being banished by Napoleon.
9. It is necessary to keep in mind (Burckhardt 1939: 68) that as far back as the beginning of occidental democracy (the *polis* of the Greeks) "mere delegation by representation" did not measure up to the Greek idea of democracy.
10. Thus J. von Eichendorff (n.d., 780) notes about F. Schlegel's political views, "Opposing the dead rule of mechanical equilibrium in the representation state (*Vertretungsstaat*) he, on historical and religious foundations, raised the Christian state, depending on faith and love."
11. See for example Simone de Beauvoir (Schwarzer 1983: 103).
12. "Whoever teaches [the gospel] shall and must submit his teachings to the judgement of his hearers. . . . Thus here again it is evident that a Christian not only has the right and the power to teach the word of God but he is obliged to do so under pain of his soul and the grace of God" (Luther 1983: 11, 13).
13. Recent discussions (cf. Brumlik 1986) about "advocatory ethics" (the legitimacy and necessity of representation of proxy action or decision making in *moralibus*) mainly refer to questions of environment, biotechnology, and euthanasia. These discussions are particularly difficult because they cling to the idea of a universalistic moral but reject the assumption of practical reasoning a priori. Things become even more, not less, complicated if (as in Benhabib 1986) the reference to the "generalized other" is completed by taking into account the perspectives and claims of the "concrete other(s)."
14. For a rather radical, as well as inoperative, contemporary criticism of the trial lawyer, see Illich et al. (1977).
15. "The artist, having withdrawn inwardly from society, is only searching for the appreciation of art dealers, critics, director's museums, exhibitors, and

collectors" (Gehlen 1986: 230). On the problematic influence of experts in this field, see also Janssen (1982) and, with regard to contemporary music, Dahlhaus (1987).

16. Thus Lyotard (1979: 8) advances the "variety of inventors" against the "one-dimensionality of the experts"; his expectation is that the universal "participation in an aesthetic community, which has always been promised" is now coming into being.

References

Bell, D. 1976. *The Cultural Contradictions of Capitalism*. New York: Basic Books.

Bendix, R. 1965. "Max Weber and Jacob Burckhardt." *American Sociological Review* 30: 176–184.

Benhabib, S. 1986. "The Generalized and the Concrete Other. The Kohlberg-Gilligan Controversy and Feminist Theory." *Praxis International* 5: 402–424.

Birch, A. H. 1971. *Representation*. London: Pall Mall Press.

Blumenberg, H. 1986. *Die Lesbarkeit der Welt*. Frankfurt: Suhrkamp.

Bourdieu, P. 1975. *Sozialer Raum und "Klassen." Leçons sur le leçon*. Frankfurt: Suhrkamp.

Brumlik, M. 1986. "Über die Ansprüche Ungeborener und Unmündiger. Wie advokatorisch ist die diskursive Ethik?" In *Moralität und Sittlichkeit. Das Problem Hegels und die Diskursethik*, edited by W. Kuhlmann. Frankfurt: Suhrkamp.

Burckhardt, J. 1939. *Griechische Kulturgeschichte*. Vol. 1. Stuttgart: Kröner.

———. 1974. *Vorlesungen über die Geschichte des Revolutionszeitalters. Rekonstruktion des gesprochenen Wortlauts von Ernst Ziegler*. Basel/Stuttgart: Schwabe.

———. 1982. *Über das Studium der Geschichte. Der Text der "Weltgeschichtlichen Betrachtungen" nach den Handschriften*, edited by P. Ganz. München: C. H. Beck.

Dahlhaus, C. 1987. Das "Verstehen" von Musik und die Herrschaft der Experten. In *Epochenschwelle und Epochenbewußtsein (Poetik und Hermeneutik 7)*, edited by R. Herzog and R. Koselleck. München: Fink.

Diamond, S. 1974. *In Search of the Primitive. A Critique of Civilization*. New Brunswick, N.J.: Transaction Book.

Eichendorff, J. von. n.d. *Werke*. Vol. 3. München: Winkler.

Enzensberger, H. M. 1988. Rezensenten-Dämmerung. In *Wo wir stehen. Dreißig Beiträge zur Kultur der Moderne*, edited by M. Meyer, 89–95. München: Piper.

Ferrara, A. 1985. "Dall' autonomia all' autenticità. Riflessioni sulle origini del mutamento culturale tra modernità classica e modernità contemporanea." *La Critica Sociologia* 75: 51–93.

Gehlen, A. 1963. *Über kulturelle Kristallisation.* In *Studien zur Anthropologie und Soziologie.* Neuwied/Berlin: Luchterhand.

———. 1964. *Die Seele im technischen Zeitalter. Sozialpsychologische Probleme der industriellen Gesellschaft.* Hamburg: Rowohlt.

———. 1986. *Zeit-Bilder.* 2d ed. Frankfurt: V. Klostermann.

Geiger, T. [1949] 1987. *Aufgaben und Stellung der Intelligenz in der Gesellschaft.* Stuttgart: Enke.

Griffith, A. P. 1968. "Auf welche Weise kann eine Person eine andere repräsentieren?" In *Zur Theorie und Geschichte der Repräsentation und der Repräsentativverfassung,* edited by H. Rausch, 443–469. Darmstadt: Wissenschaftliche Buchgesellschaft.

Hartmann, H., and M. Hartmann. 1982. "Vom Elend der Experten— Zwischen Akademisierung und Professionalisierung." *Kölner Zeitschrift für Soziologie und Sozialpsychologie* 34: 193–223.

Hegel, G. W. F. 1961. *Vorlesungen über Philosophie der Geschichte.* Stuttgart: Reclam.

Hofmann, H. 1974. *Repräsentation. Studien zur Wort- und Begriffsgeschichte von der Antike bis ins 19. Jahrhundert.* Berlin: Duncker und Humblot.

Illich, I. et al. 1979. *Entmündigung durch Experten.* Reinbek: Rowohlt.

Janssen, H. 1982. *Angeber Icks.* Hamburg: C. C. Verlag.

Keeley, K. W., and the Association of Space Explorers, eds. 1989. *Der Heimatplanet.* Frankfurt: Zweitausendeins.

Kolakowski, L. 1969. "Intellectuals and the Communist Movement." In *Toward a Marxist Humanism: Essays on the Left Today.* New York: Ever Grove.

Löwith, K. 1984. "Burckhardts Stellung zu Hegels Geschichtsphilosophie." In *Sämtliche Schriften.* Vol. 7. Stuttgart: Metzler.

Luther, M. 1983. "Daß eine christliche Versammlung oder Gemeinde Recht und Macht habe, alle Lehre zu beurteilen und Lehrer zu berufen, ein- und abzusetzen, Grund und Ursache aus der Schrift" (1523). *Ausgewählte Schriften.* Vol. 5. In Bornkamm, K., and G. Ebeling. Frankfurt: Insel.

Lyotard, I. F. 1979. *La Condition Postmoderne.* Paris: Ed. de Minuit (Collection Critique).

Marx, K. 1962. *Frühe Schriften.* Vol. 1. Darmstadt: Cotta.

Neidhardt, F. 1986. "Kollegialität und Kontrolle—am Beispiel der Gutachter der Deutschen Forschungsgemeinschaft (DFG)." *Kölner Zeitschrift für Soziologie und Sozialpsychologie* 38: 3–12.

Schwarzer, A. 1983. *Simone de Beauvoir heute. Gespräche auz zehn Jahren.* Reinbek: Rowohlt.

Thompson, E. P. 1972. *The Making of the English Working Class.* Harmondsworth: Penguin.

Weber, M. 1965. *Wirtschaft und Gesellschaft.* Studienausgabe, Köln/Berlin: Kiepenheuer und Witsch.

———. 1968. *Wissenschaft als Beruf.* In *Gesammelte Aufsätze zur Wissenschaftslehre.* 3d ed. Tübingen: Mohr.

Weiss, J. 1984. "Stellvertretung. Überlegungen zu einer vernachlässigten soziologischen Kategorie." *Kölner Zeitschrift für Soziologie und Sozialpsychologie* 36: 43–55.

————. 1987. "Der allgemeine Repräsentant. Zur Selbstdeutung der Intellektuellen in der kommunistischen Bewegung." In *Kulturtypen, Kulturcharaktere. Träger, Mittler und Stifter von Kultur,* edited by W. Lipp, 205. Berlin: D. Reimer.

6

Infrastructure and Superstructure
Revisions in Marxist Sociology of Culture
Robert Wuthnow

> *Between the general theory of superstructures and their relationship to the base and the concrete study of each specific ideological phenomenon there seems to be a certain gap, a shifting and hazy area that the scholar picks his way through at his own risk, or often simply skips over, shutting his eyes to all difficulties and ambiguities. The result is that either the specificity of the phenomenon suffers . . . or an "immanent" analysis which takes account of specificity but has nothing to do with sociology is artificially fitted to the economic base. And it is precisely a developed sociological doctrine of the distinctive features of the material, forms, and purposes of each area of ideological creation which is lacking.*
>
> Mikhail Bakhtin (1928:3)

It is a commonplace that Marx turned Hegel's view of cultural determination on its head. "Life is not determined by consciousness, but consciousness by life," he and Engels asserted in a much-quoted passage (1846:15). Or as one student of Marx explains:

[T]here are only two ways to understand history. Either we start from consciousness; in which case we fail to account for real life. Or we start from real life; then we come up against this ideological consciousness that has no reality, and must account for it. Historical materialism puts an end to the speculation which starts from consciousness, from representations, and hence from illusions (Lefebvre 1968:65).

In short, the material base of society determines the shape of its culture, not the other way around.

It is equally commonplace, however, to find assertions that hedge Marx's views, rendering them less vulgar, and pointing toward more complex, interactive relations between society's material base and its cultural superstructure. Raymond Williams (1977:79–80), for example, has argued that Marx's own usage of the terms *base* and *superstructure* was flexible and relational, and that it is mistaken to think of these concepts as enclosed categories or enclosed areas of activities. He also calls for a more active role for ideology in the shaping of the societal base, citing as evidence a letter to Bloch in September 1890 in which Engels states:

The economic situation is the basis, but the various elements of the superstructure—political forms of the class struggle and its results, to wit: constitutions established by the victorious class after a successful battle, etc., juridical forms, and even the reflexes of all these actual struggles in the brains of the participants, political, juristic, philosophical theories, religious views and their further development into systems of dogma—also exercise their influence upon the course of the historical struggles and in many cases preponderate in determining their form.

Another writer, Martin Seliger (1977:202), concludes from a lengthy survey of the ways in which culture has been discussed in the Marxist tradition that the evidence "calls in question the assumption that the contents and categories of thought can be unequivocally related to a specific class structure and the specific conditions of an epoch." In a similar vein, Göran Therborn (1980:viii) has expressed dissatisfaction with the manner in which Marxists themselves have dealt with the material determination of ideologies, either bypassing it "in embarrassed silence" or repeating it "in an endless series of Marxological exegeses" and has called for a wholly "new formulation of a theory of material determination and of class ideologies." And still another writer, approaching the subject as a Marxist literary critic, has noted that Marxist theory has often been interpreted in ways that have "failed to gain significant purchase on literature as a distinct, semi-autonomous social practice" (Sprinker 1987:238). The relation between culture and material conditions, it appears from these statements, is often more complex than the theoretical literature portrays. But if the complexity of this relation needs to be recognized, it has been only in relatively recent work that efforts have been made to sort out this complexity.

The problems that appear most in need of further reflection in order to understand cultural criticism within this perspective fall into four broad categories. First, a number of scholars, both those concerned with culture and those oriented toward other aspects of Marxist theory, have suggested that the nature of the material base, and especially the concept of class, should be clarified. Second, recent discussions have challenged subjectivist concepts of culture and ideology and have suggested the value of respecifying these concepts as elements of practice, as varieties of social production, or as social formations. Third, greater attention has been called for in specifying analytic and empirical variations within culture itself. And fourth, a stronger emphasis on the dynamic or interactive relations between infrastructure and superstructure has been suggested.

The first of these issues—the question of class—can largely be dispensed with here because it has received ample treatment in the writings of Seliger, Therborn, and others. The value of moving from subjectivist to more objective concepts of ideology will be accepted as a given: rather than defend it here, we will examine writers who have emphasized an objective concept of ideology in general and of cultural criticism in particular. It is for this reason that we concentrate on writers whose contributions to the general discussion have come from literary criticism: in focusing on literature, they have inevitably stressed the concrete and explicitly produced character of cultural criticism. The main focus of the present discussion is on the remaining two issues: the problems of specifying the internal structure of cultural criticism more carefully and of relating these patterns to social structure more interactively.

These considerations provide a valuable perspective for better understanding cultural criticism. The contributions of Terry Eagleton, Fredric Jameson, and Mikhail Bakhtin provide useful starting points for considering these issues. After reviewing the main lines of development evident in these contributions, some concepts of a more synthetic nature will be presented.

Terry Eagleton

The most relevant aspects of Terry Eagleton's work for rethinking the Marxist sociology of culture are contained in his essays

"Categories for a Materialist Criticism" and "Towards a Science of the Text" (in Eagleton 1976). Eagleton's starting point is the work of Raymond Williams, which he argues is flawed by an overly abstract, subjectivist conception of culture that conflates it with its material base. As a remedy, Eagleton advances a more concrete conception of culture, one that relies on the more categorical way of thinking that Williams criticizes, but seeks to avoid oversimplifying the relation between base and superstructure by specifying several subdivisions of each. Culture—that which is to be explained—is conceived of not as some ephemeral orientation in society but as a specific material practice or object, namely, a text.

At the same time, Eagleton denies the possibility of relating a specific text directly to the social context in which it is produced. Intervening factors that must be considered include some of the more implicit beliefs and assumptions on which subjectivist approaches to culture have focused. Eagleton identifies six "major constituents" that must be related to one another: the general mode of production (GMP), the literary mode of production (LMP), general ideology (GI), authorial ideology (AuI), aesthetic ideology (AI), and text.

The first five of the constituents are the structures, Eagleton says, that produce the text. Their relations with one another and with the text do not, however, form a causal system (a recursive model of the kind sometimes imagined by statistical sociologists). Eagleton (1976:45) suggests instead that the task of criticism is to analyze "the complex historical articulations of these structures." The term *articulation* is, of course, reminiscent of Louis Althusser and Etienne Balibar (1970), although Eagleton makes no specific mention of them at this point.

For Althusser, the notion of articulation arises specifically in the context of discussing the relations among modes of production that are not entirely integrated with one another but that can be understood by the theorist as part of a single system. Their relations emerge not only in the historical evolution of capitalism itself but also in the theorist's efforts to reconstruct the internal mechanisms of capitalism. Rather than specific binary relations being most at issue, it is the larger system of interrelationships that Althusser claims determines the course of history. It is, of course, this notion of a broader system that distinguishes Althusser's approach from the more limited materialist interpretations of Marxism, and Eagleton follows Althusser in adopting this general perspective in dealing with culture.

More generally, the idea of articulation as a way of thinking about relations among concepts also appears to underlie Eagleton's discussion. In this sense, articulation connotes dual, opposing tendencies, a fitting together of elements to form an interrelated system and yet a retention of distinct identities that prevent a system from becoming entirely integrated. As Maurice Bloch (1983:153) states, articulation refers to "a type of connection where what is joined does not consequently form a whole. The articulated elements remain fundamentally unchanged as if ready to detach themselves. The notion of articulation therefore stresses the idea of several elements whose different natures will lead to contradiction and therefore revolutionary change." Eagleton (1976:45) echoes this idea, although he places less emphasis on revolutionary change in suggesting that the primary relations of articulation that may occur among literary modes of production are "homology, conflict and contradiction." The idea of elements that remain unchanged, detachable, and contradictory is, as we shall see, evident in Bakhtin's discussion of the features of texts themselves, a theme that will prove helpful for understanding the specific nature of cultural criticism.

Eagleton passes quickly over the general mode of production, pausing only to assert that he considers it dominant, historically specific, and general only in the sense of referring to economic production broadly as opposed to literary production more narrowly. He thus assumes the Marxist position—that mode of production is the most salient feature of the social environment—as a starting point, rather than leaving this assumption open to historical investigation. In doing so, he of course leaves his discussion open to criticism on precisely these grounds. His analysis of the social environment in which cultural production takes place consists of asserting little more than that this environment is capitalist or bourgeois. Therefore, the value of his approach lies more in specifying the relations between cultural production and cultural products than in suggesting innovative conceptions of the relevant features of bourgeois society.

In his discussion of the concept of literary modes of production, Eagleton becomes more specific and of course more relevant to the immediate issue of cultural criticism. It emphasizes the fact, perhaps obvious yet often neglected in sociological theories of culture, that culture does not simply bear a kind of general affinity with its societal environment but is produced in specific contexts. It is to these contexts that closest attention must be paid to understand how social factors shape the form and content of culture. A literary mode of production, moreover, is not, in Eagleton's view, reducible to some mechanical or technological determinant, such as the printing press and movable type. It is rather constituted by a set of social interactions among the occupants of concrete social roles: the relations among cultural critics, patrons, suppliers of materials, publishers, disseminators, opponents, and consumers. This is one of Eagleton's most useful observations, although it is by no means original to him. Whether one takes a Marxist approach to culture or some other approach, the point is the same: culture originates in specific social settings and is likely to bear the imprint of these settings.

In addition, Eagleton cites and distinguishes among some historical examples of the ways in which literary modes of production may differ.

The tribal bard professionally authorised to produce for his king or chieftain; the "amateur" medieval poet presenting to his patron a personally requested product for private remuneration; the peripatetic minstrel housed and fed by his peasant audience; the ecclesiastically or royally patronised producer, or the author who sells his product to an aristocratic patron for a dedication fee; the "independent" author who sells his commodity to a bookseller-publisher or to a capitalist publishing firm; the state-patronised producer (1976:47).

Clearly these correspond generally to the level of economic development (general mode of production), and they in turn limit the kinds of texts that are likely to be produced. Texts produced under ecclesiastical patronage are likely to be devoutly didactic, to take the most obvious cases, while novels produced for sale to a commercial audience of bourgeois consumers are more likely to cater to the private tastes of these consumers. Authors' conceptions of their audiences and the means of reaching these audiences will, Eagleton suggests, shape both the choice of genre and the actual content of the works produced.

Beyond the effects of the experienced social relations in which culture producers are engaged, texts are also shaped by the three varieties of ideology, which Eagleton identifies as general, authorial, and aesthetic. All three pertain to the specific social relations in which culture producers are embedded and differ primarily in terms of which social relations are at issue. General ideology is defined as "a relatively coherent set of 'discourses' of values, representations and beliefs which, realised in certain material apparatuses and related to the structures of material production, so reflect the experiential relations of individual subjects to their social conditions as to guarantee those misperceptions of the 'real' which contribute to the reproduction of the dominant social relations" (1976:54). Authorial ideology, Eagleton states, is "the effect of the author's specific mode of biographical insertion into GI, a mode of insertion overdetermined by a series of distinct factors: social class, sex, nationality, religion, geographical region and so on." Aesthetic ideology, by comparison, is not defined formally but is described by typical examples of its content: "theories of literature, critical practices, literary traditions, *genres,* conventions, devices and discourses" (1976:60).

Each of these definitions, of course, raises a host of conceptual and theoretical questions that could become the focus of extensive discussion. Eagleton himself appears more interested in subsuming virtually everything that might shape the production of cultural texts under these rubrics than in delimiting the range of relevant considerations. Nevertheless, several important points can be extracted that may be useful in redirecting sociological thinking about cultural criticism and its relations to the social environment in which it is produced.

To begin with, Eagleton's conception of ideology differs radically from what might be considered in more standard sociological treatments of literary production to be the worldview, or even the internalized norms and values, of the literary producer. This point is worth underscoring because Eagleton does employ terms, such as *beliefs, values,* and *misperceptions,* and emphasizes what might be understood as the author's self-perception. All of this may seem reminiscent of a subjectivist conception of ideology. Nevertheless, Eagleton's emphasis is on a more objectivated form of ideology. In particular, he uses the phrase "discourses about values" rather than simply saying "values"; he asserts that these discourses are "realized in certain material apparatuses"; he discusses authorial ideology not as self-image but as literary expression, that is, as the way in which the author is represented within the text itself; and he again refers to concrete elements of discourse—conventions, genres, practices, and so on—in discussing aesthetic ideology.

Although ideology has an objective existence in the social world, it is analytically distinguishable from the social world, in Eagleton's view. Ideology is a discursive structure, a form of practice characterized by speech and the material artifacts of speech. It is discourse about the experienced world but not that world itself. The experienced world, perhaps ironically, is less observable for Eagleton than is the realm of discourse. Experience has a reality of its own, but it is observable only through the coordinates of the mode of production, on the one hand, and discourse, on the other hand. The mode of production, moreover, is a theoretical inference, an abstraction from the material conditions of the observed world. Thus the relation between base and superstructure becomes for Eagleton, in effect, a relation between a theoretical construct concerning modes of production and the actual discursive structures observed in the texts produced within that context.

To state it this way, however, creates too sharp a distinction between infrastructure and superstructure. The social world is real, in Eagleton's outline, apart from discourse. But it is also incorporated into the realm of discourse. Or put differently, ideology does not simply reflect the social world; ideology draws the world of experience into itself, turning these experiences into categories that shape the production of specific texts. There is, in short, a social horizon built into the discursive structure of ideology. For Eagleton (1976:54), ideology is "strewn with the relics of imperialist, nationalist, regionalist and class combat." That is, political categories from the experienced world become discursive categories in ideology, both directly in the words that are used and indirectly in language and colloquial expressions. There are also "cultural" elements or, more precisely, antecedents drawn from the social environment about the ways in which knowledge is to be packaged and communicated, styles of discourse, genres, and literary standards. These are, to a certain degree, evident in the concrete texts of culture producers themselves.

The relation between ideology and infrastructure is, most importantly, mediated by the immediate social relations that Eagleton calls the *literary mode of production*. This is an apparatus that includes, he says,

the specific institutions of literary production and distribution (publishing houses, bookshops, libraries and salons), but it also encompasses a range of "secondary," supportive institutions whose function is more directly ideological, concerned with the definition and dissemination of literary "standards" and assumptions. Among these are literary academies, societies and book-clubs, associations of literary producers, distributors and consumers, censoring bodies, and literary journals and reviews (1976:56).

He also argues that the communications industry and educational apparatus play an important role.

Eagleton's point, however, is not to propose studies, such as those that have become common among both sociologists of culture and cultural historians, that focus primarily on the institutional aspects of printing, publishing, reading clubs, book fairs, literary academies, and the like. The point is rather to emphasize the form and content of the texts produced, to discover the categories that are emphasized and deemphasized, and to determine the ways in which these categories illuminate or obscure features of the world of social experience. For the last of these especially, comparisons must be made between base and super-structure. Ideology, Eagleton assumes, will partially incorporate the experienced world into itself and will partially transform that world into something else. Ideology is not, therefore, simply a matter of false consciousness. As Eagleton (1976:69) explains, "Ideology is not just the bad dream of the infrastructure: in *deformatively* 'producing' the real, it nevertheless carries elements of reality within itself."

The elements of the real that are brought into the ideological realm are selectively processed through the institutional relations that comprise the literary mode of production. But again Eagleton stresses the interactive character of this process. He rejects a straightforward positivist view in which the real is seen as something external to ideology, a characteristic of the infrastructure that is merely reflected in ideology. The real is instead constituted by the discursive structure of ideology itself.

The real is by necessity empirically imperceptible, concealing itself in the phenomenal categories (commodity, wage-relation, exchange-value and so on) it offers spontaneously for inspection. Ideology, rather, so produces and constructs the real as to cast the shadow of its absence over the perception of its presence. It is not merely that certain aspects of the real are illuminated and others obscured; it is rather that the presence of the real is a presence constituted by its absences, and *vice versa* (1976:69).

Ultimately, then, the focus of analysis must be on the interplay of categories within the text itself. For it is here that the social world is reconstructed; here that reality is created—a reality that in some ways may correspond directly with the theorized character of the materialist infrastructure of history, but that also, by virtue of its textuality, escapes this direct form of determination, providing instead a defamiliarization of experience, "a sportive flight from history, a reversal and resistence of history, a momentarily liberated zone in which the exigencies of the real seem to evaporate, an enclave of freedom enclosed within the realm of necessity" (1976:72).

Fredric Jameson

Like Terry Eagleton, Fredric Jameson has emphasized the double determination of ideological texts—their determination through the internal logic of the text's content and their determination through the broader contexts in which they are produced. For Jameson, the general mode of economic production and the class relations arising within this mode constitute the theoretical environment in which to situate the analysis of ideology. But he too is especially concerned with the ways in which the social environment becomes articulated within the structure of ideology itself.

Because Jameson's oeuvre is broad and has itself become the subject of a number of secondary works, only a sketch of those aspects that bear most directly on the sociology of culture need be considered here. Jameson's work, like Eagleton's, falls squarely within the Marxist tradition of criticism, and he is especially interested in the complex relations between infrastructure and ideology. As a literary critic, his work is perhaps limited to those features of ideology that gain expression in formalized texts. He is, however, sensitive to the importance of treating ideology as a kind of practice—"symbolic art" is a phrase he uses repeatedly—rather than as a vague set of beliefs or a taken for granted worldview. As symbolic acts, texts constitute a special kind of practice. They have an intentional or instrumental aspect; that is, they do things to the world, manipulate it, change it. At the same time, they leave the social world untouched. Their action remains within the realm of discourse. They change the world not directly but by drawing the world into its own texture. To an even greater extent than Eagleton, Jameson is thus interested in how the social comes to be incorporated into ideological practice (an interest he shares, as we shall see, with Bakhtin). Indeed, Jameson takes the work of Northrop Frye as a starting point because he recognizes the value of Frye's emphasis on community. Rather than work within Frye's framework, however, he attempts to subsume Frye into a broader Marxist perspective (Jameson 1981; Dowling 1984).

Jameson's view of ideology resembles Marx's earlier treatment of ideology as a response to the alienated life elements of capitalism more closely than it resembles Marxist theories, such as those of Althusser and Jacques Lacan, that have borrowed insights from Freud to examine the manner in which ideology functions as a form of false consciousness. For Jameson, ideology is not so much a distortion of a perceivable reality as it is an attempt to come to terms with and to transcend the unbearable relationships of social life. In short, ideology is vision, not simply a reflection of reality or a description of it, and as such it acts symbolically upon the world. Ideology is a form of storytelling (Jameson 1981:105). It is at least potentially liberating and redemptive. The manner in which ideology articulates with history and the experience of social life is therefore crucial: ideology identifies certain features of experience and yet extricates itself from experience in such a way that experience can be transformed.

Though opting for a Marxist perspective, Jameson immediately declares his dissatisfaction with standard interpretations of the relations between infrastructure and superstructure. The latter does not merely reflect social structures that are somehow more basic, Jameson argues. The two are not levels of empirical reality than can be related causally or historically. Jameson, like Eagleton, is an Althusserian in that he takes Marxism as a theoretical framework that creates a certain view of reality rather than as a scientific description of something external to itself. He is also an Althusserian in stressing that the categories of Marxist thought should be related, not as elements of a causal system, but as components of a totality. Base does not, as it were, determine superstructure. The two, rather, articulate with one another, and the manner of their articulation is consequential for understanding the totality of society and for predicting the direction of its development. Most generally, Marxism is a source of "insight." It provides a conceptual scaffold for reconstructing relevant relationships. The concept of mode of production, for example, does not refer to actual historical development but serves as a model for understanding historical development. And Jameson adds to it a conceptual framework of his own that is aimed at revealing more of the internal structure of texts themselves.

A text can be rendered intelligible—or, we might say, meaningful—by apprehending it within three concentric frameworks, or "horizons." These consist of (1) political history, (2) the relevant social context, and (3) "history now conceived in its vastest sense of the sequence of modes of production and the succession and destiny of the various social formations, from prehistoric life to whatever far future history has in store for us" (1981:75). Each horizon may be understood in two ways: as a framework that the analyst imposes on the text and as a framework built into the text itself or definable as a set of relations among the text's elements. It is the second of these that most concerns us here. Jameson provides not only a general description of each of the three horizons but also a discussion of their relations with one another and with the external social environment.

The first horizon may be likened to the historical setting of the text that would be of interest in ordinary literary criticism. It is constituted by actors and events with which the text is concerned. These of course may be the same as those composing the author's contemporary experience, or they may be quite different, as in narratives about the past or about some imagined future. In either case, some parallels are likely to exist between the social environment of the author and the social horizon depicted in the narrative. Neither will exactly reflect the other, but certain resemblances, analogies, and dual meanings are likely to be present. Jameson argues especially for careful examination of narrative content as a starting point, but his discussion implicitly acknowledges the importance of knowledge about the context of the narrative's production as clues to this analysis. The conflicts and contradictions that can be observed within the narrative are particularly important according to Jameson.

At the second level, Jameson turns at once to a more general notion of social order within the text and a more specific notion of the salient features of this social order. Social order is essentially a matter of struggle between classes and among various class fractions. At a crude level, the conflicts evident in the text are read through the lens of class antagonism—an exercise that clearly runs into dangers of misinterpretation in dealing with many kinds of texts. The more useful point Jameson makes is that the relations among actors in the text, whether conflictual or harmonious, can be understood as a kind of dialogue. That is, social order at this level can be conceived of as discourse. And this discourse is likely to reveal both the substantive antagonisms or polarities around which discussion takes place and the shared codes that make discussion possible in the first place. The emphasis here on discourse is clearly the key. We can look at the institutional settings in which narrative action takes place and even compare these narrational settings with their historic counterparts. But over and above that, it is necessary to focus on the categories of speech that actors in these settings use and the ways in which these discourses are presented in the text. In addition, discourse always implies counterdiscourse. What is said must be read against what is not said, especially if we are interested in comprehending the hegemonic character of a dominant culture. Just as in Eagleton's discussion, then, Jameson emphasizes the negations and polarities that construct discourse.

Jameson's third framework or horizon is least clearly formulated and perhaps of less immediate programmatic relevance to the sociology of culture. It invokes the broad evolution of history conceived of in Marxist theory itself and asks the interpreter to seek traces of historical evolution within the various systems of discourse evident in the text. In one sense the specification of this horizon does nothing more than challenge the analyst to see the class antagonisms that have already been posited at the second level as part of a larger evolutionary process. In a different sense the analyst may be encouraged to recognize that historical evolution is no orderly or linear process but is a movement of fits and spurts, of continuous transition involving negotiation among class fractions and competing modes of discourse. From this perspective it appears that Jameson's third horizon, while partially evident in textual content, is primarily a horizon that the analyst must develop for himself or herself from an independent study of history.

Jameson's second horizon, then, offers the greatest degree of innovativeness to the study of ideology. Working within the larger historical-evolutionary framework suggested by the third horizon, and taking into account the standard social elements incorporated into the text itself (the first horizon), the analyst then engages in an act of discourse analysis that identifies basic categories of discourse, conflicts and polarities, and an internal dialogue among these polarities. This task is, of course, not merely an inductive operation, but an interpretation, a search for "an abstraction nowhere completely present in any body of texts or utterances and something that must always be reconstructed from partial evidence" (Dowling 1984:132). It is, nevertheless, an abstraction that organizes—and is organized by—the actions, events, and utterances that comprise the text itself.

The purpose of this reconstructive task is partially, for Jameson, to illuminate the ways in which basic class conflicts gain expression as intratextual dialogue. There is, however, a deeper purpose as well: to understand how it is possible for certain things to be said and others not to be said. In other words, the utterances of which ideology is comprised are shaped, not by the social infrastructure, but by the possibilities and limitations built into the framework of discourse itself. Characters in the text, therefore, do not emerge simply as actors appropriated directly from the experienced world; they are transformed into characters by being placed within a particular framework of discourse, and their speech and actions are oriented primarily to this framework.

This is the point, incidentally, at which Jameson's discussion intersects most directly with Eagleton's. The possibilities for intratextual dialogue between different discourses are, to a degree, contingent on the genre of the text, and the genre employed will invariably reflect the relations between culture producers and consumers that constitute the prevailing mode of literary production. Jameson points out, for example, that the modern novel is particularly suitable for mixing generic conventions and setting up dialogue that represents alternative points of view. It incorporates older genres as raw materials, combines them with realistic accounts of everyday life, and yet imposes its own ideological form as an organizing device. The general point is that genre becomes relevant to the analysis of ideology, both as a substructure on which surface conflicts are overlaid and as a mode of articulating the relations between texts and historical events (see also Eagleton 1981a).

Mikhail Bakhtin

In Mikhail Bakhtin we confront a theorist not only from a different era but also from a school of criticism to which some Marxists themselves have taken exception (see Carroll 1983; De Man 1983; and Young 1985, for overviews). The difference between these approaches is, however, considerably less severe in the case of Althusserian Marxists such as Eagleton and Jameson than it has been in the past. Indeed, it is Bakhtin to whom Jameson (1981:84) refers in suggesting the importance of examining the internal dialogue between opposing discourses in texts, and Eagleton (1981b, 1982) has also favorably appraised Bakhtin's work. For our present purposes, Bakhtin helps us understand the structure of cultural criticism by providing additional insights about the ways in which social horizons become incorporated into literary texts.

Although his early work stands half a century closer to Marx's than to Eagleton's or Jameson's, Bakhtin stresses the objective, material aspects of ideology and draws on Marx's scattered remarks about the production of culture in much the same way as Eagleton and Jameson, rather than subjectivizing ideology in relation to its infrastructural roots. In fact, Bakhtin argues explicitly for a perspective that emphasizes the materiality of cultural objects. He states, for instance, that "all the products of ideological creation—works of art, scientific works, religious symbols and rites, etc.—are material things, part of the practical reality that surrounds man" (Bakhtin and Medvedev 1928:7). They may have, as he says, "significance, meaning, inner value." But these meanings are "embodied in material things and actions." He also indicates specifically that his remarks should not be construed to pertain only to the more explicitly produced, tangible artifacts of culture:

> Nor do philosophical views, beliefs, or even shifting ideological moods exist within man, in his head or in his "soul." They become ideological reality only by being realized in words, actions, clothing, manners, and organizations of people and things—in a word: in some definite semiotic material. Through this material they become a practical part of the reality surrounding man (7).

It is fallacious, he asserts, to accept the prevalent social psychological approaches that regard ideology as the creation and comprehension of individuals. Terms such as *meaning* and *consciousness* should be rejected as elements of bourgeois ideology itself and replaced with a sociological approach that emphasizes the relations between social interaction and ideology as practice. Ideology, he concludes, "is not within us, but between us" (8).

If superstructure cannot be distinguished from infrastructure by its subjectivity, it is nevertheless, for Bakhtin, distinguishable. Ideology should not be approached like any other variety of social production. The danger is to treat it so much as a material object that it stands entirely apart from social interaction. This is the tendency, Bakhtin claims, in utilitarian positivist theories—even in utilitarian positivist interpretations of Marx. Cultural products should not be regarded as objects that have only uses—"external purposes"—that can be understood entirely from the outside and primarily in terms of technical organization. Cultural products are distinguished by their expressive dimension, by the fact that they become important in the relations among people. It is for this reason that terms such as *ideological intercourse, dialogue,* and especially *discourse* dominate Bakhtin's work.

What Bakhtin seeks is a richer, more variegated understanding of the "ideological environment," as he calls it. The ideological environment is a layer of reality that should be understood as the critical mediating context between economic modes of production on the one hand and human thought and action on the other.

> Social man is surrounded by ideological phenomena, by objects-signs of various types and categories: by words in the multifarious forms of their realization (sounds, writing, and the others), by scientific statements, religious symbols and beliefs, works of art, and so on. All of these things in their totality comprise the ideological environment, which forms a solid ring around man (14).

Our experience, in his view, is shaped, not directly by our existence, but through the medium of this ideological environment.

Bakhtin's perspective is thus similar in one sense to theories of reality construction and symbolic interactionism that emphasize the symbolically mediated realities in which we live. The ideological environment can be understood as the same world of symbols that has been stressed in these approaches. In another sense, however, Bakhtin's emphasis is quite different. His concern is not principally with explaining individual consciousness or even with showing how individual worldviews are constructed from symbolic material. It is with the contours of the ideological environment itself. This environment has a unity of its own, a structure, and it is in constant flux, constant interaction, always influenced by and influencing the economic and political relations with which it is associated.

Bakhtin is particularly helpful in demonstrating how the characters and events that compose literary texts are related to the broader ideological environment and to the economic base. He points out that these characters and events cannot be understood by projecting them directly into life, that is, by imagining they reflect actual characters and events in the real world. Nor can they be understood strictly in terms of some broad philosophical outlook of a certain period. A literary figure is instead an "ideological refraction of a given social type" (Bakhtin and Medvedev 1928:21). We must know something of the actual historical circumstances in which a literary figure is situated, and Marxist theory provides a starting point for ascertaining which of these circumstances to emphasize (for example, feudal relations or bourgeois class fractions). There is also a kind of semantic horizon, identifiable at several levels (the levels Jameson discusses), that can be seen in literary texts associated with these historical circumstances. This *ideologeme,* as Bakhtin calls it, sets the ideological context in which a literary figure can be expressed. It consists of genre, of certain conceptions of action and agency, of artistic standards, and more substantively, of dominant problems, constraints, and resources that shape the literary figure's actions. Character becomes characteristic within this framework and action becomes representative. Bakhtin insists that characters and events be understood as structural elements of the artistic work itself. The analyst's task, therefore, must always be twofold: to examine the relations between the broad economic modes of production that make up the societal infrastructure and the structure of the ideological system that Bakhtin variously refers to as the *ideological horizon, ideologeme, semantic horizon,* or *artistic totality* (all of which have been specified and drawn systematically into the models proposed by Eagleton and Jameson) and to examine the relations between these broader structures and the specific characters and actions that become defined within these structures. Both are appropriate foci of sociological investigation.

How then does Bakhtin suggest going about these dual analytic tasks? Only the more general guidelines can be mentioned here, but his own substantive discussions are replete with specific insights. As a starting point, we must recognize that the social situations in which ideological products are produced do not remain entirely external to these products themselves. The situation, Bakhtin asserts, "enters into the utterance as a necessary constitutive element of its semantic structure" (in Todorov 1984:41). This does not mean, of course, that the social situation will be reflected accurately in textual utterances; indeed, the text inevitably transforms the materials it draws from the external social world. Nevertheless, the sociologist must be attuned to the existence of a social world within the text as well as to the social world outside the text. Bakhtin suggests several important features of this intratextual world: the spatial and temporal horizons that constitute the situation in which action and dialogue occur, the social relations signaled by words such as *I* and *we,* the objects that are known and appropriate for discussion, and the relations between actors and what is happening, especially those that suggest an evaluative stance.

Further, the social relations incorporated into ideological products can be understood as a complex, multilayered series of discourses. At a minimum, primary discourse in the text may take the form of verbal dialogue, written correspondence, or a series of gestures exchanged between two or more of its characters. There may also be secondary levels of discourse: discourse about discourse, such as the direct quotation of other actors' (external or literary) discourse, commentaries on previous discourses, or even discussions about styles and modes of discourse. Then a number of implied discourses may have to be inferred from parallel forms of construction and other literary devices: a discourse between the author and an intended reader, discourse between the author and his or her own representation or voice within the text, discourse between either of these and other textual voices, and discourse between textual voices and the reader. All are forms of social interaction to which sociologists should be especially attentive. They also constitute much of the structure of texts, that is, the essential categories, frames, voices, contrasts, and parallels that impose order on the text (Bakhtin 1981:284). Furthermore, Bakhtin stresses the importance of considering the degree to which these structures envelop themselves to form a tight, monolithic sense of form and content or the degree to which heterology is evident in the variety of social forms, voices, and opinions expressed.

The analysis of discursive patterns is for Bakhtin, therefore, the most fruitful arena in which to explore how social conditions are incorporated into literary products and how these products define representative actions and agents. The dialogue contained in texts is likely to be framed concretely within various authoritative languages: "the language of the lawyer, the doctor, the businessman, the politician, the public education teacher and so forth" (1981:289). These may be elements of the class relations of the broader society that are expressed textually. They may also set up certain oppositions within the text that are artistically resolved, heightened, or objectified in the actions of representative characters. Again, it is essential to recognize that these intratextual relations are objects worthy of investigation in themselves. They do not precede the text but are created by it. Markers must distinguish alternative voices or positions, symbols of authority must be attached concretely to particular characters or opinions, and even categories of thought must be objectively signaled to the reader by parallel constructions, binary oppositions, polemical negations and counternegations, and so on.

Bakhtin, then, does not go so far as to champion a kind of superstructuralism that neglects the importance of infrastructural relations. He remains broadly within the Marxist framework. But he stresses the existence of a social infrastructure within the superstructure itself in addition to the external one. And he points to the importance of a closer reading of texts themselves. Ideology cannot be understood in terms of either its general thematic content or the patterns of beliefs and values that form an individual's consciousness. Ideology has its own internal structure, a structure that is at least as complex as the structures composing the economic base of society and that is as fully relevant and amenable to sociological investigation.

Causal Determination and the Problem of Meaning

Before turning to the task of extracting some common substantive themes from Eagleton, Jameson, and Bakhtin, some note must be made of the essential theoretical logic that emerges in their work. In Eagleton and Jameson particularly, standard assumptions about causality and the social determination of culture come explicitly into question. Rather than being superstructural elements shaped in some temporal or mechanistically causal way by elements of the infrastructure, the elements at both levels stand in an articulated relation to one another as parts of a larger totality. This manner of speaking may appear to undermine traditional Marxist theory, converting it to a kind of bland Hegelianism, at the same time that it tries to preserve the language of conventional Marxism. The basic challenge, however, should be a critique of empirical positivism rather than an attack on Marxist theory. Even Jameson, who has been accused most strongly of turning Marx upside down, holds firmly to the assumption that the historical movement among capitalist modes of production, as posited in Marxist theory, constitutes the most fundamental starting point for any analysis of cultural production. The materialist infrastructure, however, is no longer conceived of as something merely evident in the empirical world and discoverable through the positive application of scientific methods. It is rather an analytic feature of reality that becomes a reality only in interaction with the application of Marxist theory itself. Only with the benefit of this theoretical framework does the totality of the base and superstructure components become evident. This perspective more nearly represents a post-positivist or hermeneutic understanding of the relations between evidence and interpretation. It in no way rules out the study of empirical relations to determine how they relate to the posited totality and, within this totality, to one another.

The point of examining relations between base and superstructure, therefore, ceases to be one of explanation, in the sense of finding the true causes of ideological expressions, or of reduction, in the sense of showing that these expressions are mere epiphenomena in the larger scheme of objective social structural relations. It is essentially a task of interpretation, a task accomplished by determining whether the various elements of base and superstructure relate to one another to form a single, dominant totality or whether there are internal contradictions and conflicts, or even openings, that provide room for creative, redemptive—dare we say, revolutionary—alternatives. For this purpose, the notion of *articulation* appears to provide a convenient summary term. It connotes mutual accommodation or adaptation, a fitting together, as it were, of the various puzzle pieces to form a coherent whole. Base and superstructure interact dynamically in this process on many levels. Ideology may not ultimately transform the prevailing mode of production, but its internal structure shapes the degree of articulation that can develop with elements of the infrastructure, and it acts to control the resources and actions that its adherents can take. At the same time, pressures against articulation must be recognized. Base and superstructure are prevented from forming a wholly integrated system by the various contradictions, the alternative logics, that impinge upon them at any moment in historical development. Indeed, the very notion of totality must, since Althusser, be taken less as an integrated whole than as a conception that emerges from the complex, sedimentary or layered, interactions of what is present and what is absent.

If the fundamental point of studying ideology ceases to be one of causal explanation, then it can no longer be taken simply as a matter of interpreting the meaning of cultural symbols. Jameson, for instance, near the beginning of his discussion of literary texts, argues that a whole new approach to ideology must be found that goes beyond the quest for meaning. He cites a passage from Gilles Deleuze and Félix Guattari (1977), who assert a "general collapse of the question 'What does it mean?'" and argue that studies of linguistic structure have advanced only "to the extent that linguists and logicians have first eliminated meaning." Only in the broadest sense, that in which the interpreter provides an interpretation of base and superstructure by relating them to the theoretical framework provided by a Marxist (or some other) conception of history, can it be said that meaning has been ascribed to the cultural elements under scrutiny. Eagleton, Jameson, and Bakhtin emphasize the internal relations among the elements of texts and broader ideologies and the relations between these internal ones and those that constitute the social contexts in which the cultural products arise. The quest is for patterns of intelligibility rather than meaning.

These theorists do not go so far as to become what E. D. Hirsch (1976) has termed, referring to the deconstructionists, *cognitive atheists,* that is, interpreters who deny entirely the possibility of knowing what texts mean. Their view of meaning, however, focuses on relations rather than on some substratum of substantive truth. Jameson (1972:215), for example, specifically denies the simple semiotic method of discovering meaning by looking for the deeper "signified" that underlies the "signifier." Instead, he posits an "infinite regress from signifier to signified, from linguistic object to metalanguage." The shift is from meanings to sentences, from the content of substance to the content of relations. Rather than attempt to identify the meaning of a text, he writes about "meaning-effect" and "meaning-process." He rejects the notion of predixcursive meaning and focuses instead on meaning as the possibility of transcoding from one level of structure to another (Mohanty 1982:35). Meaning from this perspective is thus deprived of any ontological status; it is approached through "a basic reformulation of substance into process and form, into structured movement and production" (Mohanty 1982:36).

Common Directions and Problematic Foci

For a sociology of culture, particularly one claiming ties to the Marxist tradition, the relation between infrastructure and superstructure must remain central. There are, however, several emphases in the approaches, of which Eagleton, Jameson, and Bakhtin have been taken as representatives, in recent Marxist literary analysis that merit greater consideration from a sociological perspective. A useful starting point is to conceive of culture as practice, process, or product rather than as something more general, vague, or even subjective that bears only the broadest analytic correspondence to the social environment. This orientation is evident in Eagleton, Jameson, and Bakhtin and has been prominent in recent thinking about culture among sociologists as well. It is particularly appropriate to conceive of culture in this manner when the focus of inquiry is a particular ideology or ideological movement, the advent of a new idea or mode of discourse, or the social role of genre, discourse, or communities of artistic, literary, or religious expression. Less clear, of course, is whether this perspective can be applied successfully to studies of broad cultural orientations, such as individualism and rationality, or to patterns of generalized value orientations, such as universalism and particularism. At the very least, two considerations may be important when these broader conceptions of culture are at issue. First, the most generalized cultural patterns still become most real when they are manifested in concrete social situations. They are produced and disseminated, gain expression in concrete social processes, and influence behavior insofar as they govern discourse and other social resources in institutional settings. Second, traces of more generalized cultural patterns are likely to be observed both in the intellectual antecedents that shape specific cultural processes and in the theoretical perspectives that shape the interpretation of these processes.

An emphasis on specific cultural practices merely directs attention to the ways in which these patterns actually are manifested as traces.

An explicit feature of this approach is the importance it attaches to specifying the institutional contexts in which culture is produced and has its effects. Eagleton's distinction between general modes of production and literary modes of production is most helpful in this regard. However much the process of cultural production may be shaped by its general location within a social environment that may be termed *bourgeois, modern, industrial,* or whatever, its character will also be affected by the social relations that arise among producers, patrons, audiences, and wielders of power. These relations connect the social infrastructure, as it were, with the production of superstructural elements. The two are distinguishable, not in the sense of one being somehow real and the other being somehow distorted or epiphenomenal, but as manifestations of the Marxist framework itself. Infrastructure consists of historic behavioral patterns that the observer reconstructs from evidence at least partly, if not primarily, separate from the cultural products that arise from these patterns. At the same time, superstructure consists of the behavioral patterns in discourse, texts, and other symbolic-expressive media, which are also reconstructed by the observer according to certain preconceived theoretical categories of analysis. The analyst, then, also reconstructs a certain kind of articulation between infrastructure and superstructure by identifying homologies and noting patterns of covariation. This reconstruction, however, constitutes only the crudest level of analysis in determining the modes of articulation between base and superstructure. Neither category is hermetically sealed from the other. Superstructure becomes a feature of infrastructural relations, as it is said, when life imitates art, or when genres of discourse become, as it were, genres of social interaction. Similarly, and of greater interest in the present literature, features of the infrastructure become incorporated into the superstructure, comprising elements of its content and form and gaining textual transformation in the process.

As a guide to sociological investigations of these dynamic relations between base and superstructure, we might simplify the more nuanced discussions of Eagleton, Jameson, and Bakhtin by suggesting the term *social horizon* to encompass those features of the social environment that become incorporated into the cultural products under scrutiny. The social horizon of a text, therefore, encompasses the textual representation, in Eagleton's terms, of the mode of production, class relations, the author, and the author's relations to significant actors and events constituting the literary mode of production. In Jameson's terms, it encompasses the specific elements of political history and the more general symbolizations of class relations and discourse about class relations. In Bakhtin, the social horizon is expressed mainly in reflective levels of intratextual discourse and discourse about discourse. Different theoretical interpretations clearly will shape the particular ways in which the social horizon is reconstructed. At a minimal level of interpretation, primary emphasis should be given to the ways in which social events, actors, and relations are modeled in the text as settings, plots, characters, poignant examples, and so on.

In contrast with social horizons, the term *discursive fields* might be used to designate an underlying polarity, framework, or set of categories around which discourse is organized. Discursive fields are objectified in the internal dialogue that Bakhtin identifies and in the opposition of voices to which Jameson refers. If a Lévi-Straussian argument is followed, it may be argued that discursive fields are evident in all texts insofar as thought and speech are inherently dependent on binary oppositions. Discursive fields, however, constitute a more elaborate feature of texts than mere binary oppositions. They cannot be reduced to mutually exclusive conceptual categories or to dialectical moments that are ultimately synthesized and resolved. Discursive fields are instead defined by alterity, by poles that remain apart, and, indeed, by an opposition of words, genres, contexts, and voices that are, as Bakhtin suggests, set against each other dialogically. Especially in ideological discourse of the kind that Marxist theory has generally found interesting, discursive fields appear to represent one of the more fundamental structures that articulates (and disarticulates) the relation between base and superstructure.

A final conceptual component that is worth special attention in this context consists of what might be referred to as *figural action*. Within the symbolic polarity defined by a discursive field, ideological discourse typically identifies representative, prescriptive behaviors that reflect and resolve the dilemmas inherent in the symbolism of the discursive field itself. These behaviors, however, typically receive objectification over and above mere abstract idealization through an association with characters and characteristic actions that serve as exemplars or models. These figurative constructions, it appears, play an important dual role: on the one hand, they draw ideology into a specific relation of relevance with the social setting in which it is produced; on the other hand, they elevate ideology—emancipate it—by suggesting more complex, textually referential modes of action.

In conclusion, the perspectives on ideology evident in the writings of Eagleton, Jameson, Bakhtin, and other Marxist literary critics differ significantly from the dominant sociological conceptions of the relations between infrastructure and superstructure. At its worst, sociological theory has posited a broad homology or isomorphism between the stages of capitalism and the varieties of ideology alleged to be associated with these stages. At its best, sociology has gone beyond such general assertions mainly by specifying more detailed conceptions of social structure and suggesting relations between these contextual factors and various attitudinal themes or ideological dispositions. The sociological poetics of Bakhtin and the post-Althusserian formulations of Eagleton and Jameson allow for the development of more nuanced theories of the relations between infrastructure and superstructure. The general epistemological perspective of this literature focuses on theoretically constructed categories and the reconstruction of relations—relations of articulation and disarticulation—among these categories, rather than on raw empiricism, induction, or positivist methods. Ideology is conceived of as a form of social practice rather than as a subjective feature of consciousness, and questions of meaning are referred to the reconstructive or interpretive process itself. A more nuanced view of social structure is encouraged, particularly one that privileges the institutional contexts in which tangible ideological practices and objects are produced. The relation between base and ideology becomes more interactive as well, but not simply in terms of mechanical or historical causal influences between the two. Closer attention is paid to the fact that social contexts become incorporated into ideological texts rather than remaining external to these texts. The internal structure of texts, therefore, imposes its own mode of organization on this material and is in turn organized by it. A sociological theory of culture must, for this reason, demonstrate greater awareness of textual construction itself: of genre, methods of objectification, voice, dialogue, interpolation and interpellation, textual authority, redundancy, embedding, parallels, and contrasts. Discursive fields, it has been suggested, may be a particularly important textual pattern to observe. It has also been suggested that many of the specific behavioral prescriptions—models of ethical behavior, representative social actors, characters to emulate—emerge in ideological constructions, less as the direct prototypes of the social world and more as the products of the particular discursive fields that frame their options and provide the problems with which they struggle. In this sense, the focus of ideological analysis shifts from a metaphor of reflection—

superstructure as a reflection of infrastructure—to a metaphor of space. The thematic orientations that constitute the moral discourse of ideology, this perspective would suggest, bear an indirect or mediated relation to their social environment. The critical mediating link is a discursive field that creates the space, as it were, in which figural action can be identified.

References

Althusser, L., and E. Balibar. 1970. *Reading Capital*. London: Verso.

Bakhtin, M. M. 1981. *The Dialogic Imagination: Four Essays*. Austin: University of Texas Press.

Bakhtin, M. M., and P. M. Medvedev. 1928 [1985]. *The Formal Method in Literary Scholarship: A Critical Introduction to Sociological Poetics*. Cambridge: Harvard University Press.

Bloch, M. 1983. *Marxism and Anthropology*. Oxford: Oxford University Press.

Carroll, D. 1983. "The Alterity of Discourse: Form, History, and the Question of the Political in M. M. Bakhtin." *Diacritics* 13: 65–83.

Deleuze, G., and F. Guattari. 1977. *The Anti-Oedipus*. New York: Viking.

De Man, P. 1983. "Dialogue and Dialogism." *Poetics Today* 4: 99–107.

Dowling, W. C. 1984. *Jameson, Althusser, Marx: An Introduction to the Political Unconscious*. Ithaca: Cornell University Press.

Eagleton, T. 1976. *Criticism and Ideology*. London: Verso.

————. 1981a. "The Idealism of American Criticism." *New Left Review* 127: 60–65.

————. 1981b. *Walter Benjamin, or Towards a Revolutionary Criticism*. London: New Left Books.

————. 1982. "Wittgenstein's Friends." *New Left Review* 135: 64–90.

Hirsch, E. D. 1976. *The Aims of Interpretation*. Chicago: University of Chicago Press.

Jameson, F. 1972. *The Prison-House of Language*. Princeton: Princeton University Press.

————. 1981. *The Political Unconscious: Narrative as a Socially Symbolic Act*. Ithaca: Cornell University Press.

Lefebvre, H. 1968. *The Sociology of Marx*. New York: Vintage.

Marx, K., and F. Engels. 1846 [1947]. *The German Ideology*. New York: International Publishers.

Mohanty, S. P. 1982. "History at the Edge of Discourse: Marxism, Culture, Interpretation." *Diacritics* 12: 35–44.

Seliger, M. 1977. *The Marxist Conception of Ideology: A Critical Essay*. Cambridge: Cambridge University Press.

Sprinker, M. 1987. *Imaginary Relations: Aesthetics and Ideology in the Theory of Historical Materialism.* London: Verso.

Therborn, G. 1980. *The Ideology of Power and the Power of Ideology.* London: Verso.

Todorov, T. 1984. *Mikhail Bakhtin: The Dialogic Principle.* Minneapolis: University of Minnesota Press.

Williams, R. 1977. *Marxism and Literature.* Oxford: Oxford University Press.

Young, R. 1985. "Back to Bakhtin." *Cultural Critique* 2: 71–92.

PART TWO

Culture, Collective Purpose, and Polity

7

Collective Purpose and Culture
Findings and Implications from Some Studies of Societies

Guy E. Swanson

Seen historically, sociology's project is the strengthening in modern societies of compelling and normative meaning. Its contribution is to show that meaning and normativity emerge from the directed vitality of collective life—with the collective relations, commitments, and efforts that Durkheim introduced as "dynamic density," "collective spirit," "collective soul," and, most broadly, *conscience collective*.

The *Grand Larousse* (1972:913) says that *conscience collective* refers to the manners of thinking, feeling, and acting specific to social groups and different from those of individuals. It points simultaneously to consciousness, conscience, and conscientiousness, to the spread of perceptions and beliefs among individuals, and to the generating of new perceptions and beliefs through interaction. It points especially to the collective ends or values that emerge in interaction, ends or values that can become the core of collective motivations and that can shape the later course of social relations. These collective motivations are what, for simplicity, I call *collective purposes*.

Collective purposes have a central role in the analysis of culture, whichever of three common meanings of *culture* we prefer. These purposes seem identical with what is meant when culture is called "the 'informing spirit' of a whole way of life, which is manifest over the whole range of social activities" (Williams 1981:11). Collective purposes are also essential elements of those analyses in which culture is identified with collectively developed interpretations of the relevance that things have for collective purpose or in which culture refers to the collective processes through which such interpretations emerge.[1] Indeed, the properties customarily associated with culture as purpose, product, or process are related to one another through their association with collective purposes. This is evident, for example, in the four major properties of social relations and interpretations termed *cultural* in Jaeger and Selznick's (1964) well-known treatment:[2]

—*Meaningfulness.* Social arrangements are meaningful. This means that they embody the relevance, formal and empirical, that participants have for personal and collective goals.

—*Normativity.* As Durkheim so often stressed, social arrangements are to some degree normative. Normativity is a special form of relevance; it is the *degree of worth* that something has for the attainment of collective purposes.[3]

—*Agency.* Participants in social relations must serve those relations as their agents if their association is to survive. The very notion of agency involves acting in the interest of another, in this case in the interest of collective purposes.[4] (It is, of course, a critical property of collective motivations that they can, through learning, become aspects of the cognitive and motivational organization of individuals. That makes it possible for individuals to serve collective interests more effectively, taking whatever steps seem profitable in the face of changing problems and opportunities.)

—*Collective competencies and potentialities.* People often act as though collectivities had competencies and potentialities, a hidden character that is only partially expressed in existing structures, norms, or understandings. One example is the idea, common in simple or early societies, that there exist unknown laws that are there to be "found." Another appears in ecclesiastical efforts to recognize the "true mind" of the church. All notions of ideal ways of organizing a group belong here. In each case, something is considered to be at work in existing social relations, something which, if discovered, can be realized all the better. That something is always the collective enterprise and purpose, pressing now for incarnation.

I want to look at the nature of collective purposes and at some of the ways in which variations in these purposes, or in the structures that embody them, can affect collective interpretations and the process of making those interpretations. I begin by identifying what is meant by purpose, by collective purpose, and by structures devoted especially to them. Then I describe two sets of empirical studies. In the first set, cultural interpretations help us to identify variations in the presence and role of collective purposes. In the second set, variations in collective purposes and related structures are a basis for explaining variations in the process and products of collective interpretation. Taken together, these studies provide analyses of culture in three of its more common meanings.

In all of these studies I focus especially on whole societies: on the sense in which societies can be thought to have purposes and on relations between societies' purposes and other aspects of their cultures and organizations. We often assume that societies have purposes, but these have proven elusive; they are hard to operationalize and hard to explain.

The research on which I draw is primarily my own. Four of the studies are old but are now reanalyzed or extended and given a broader meaning (the studies numbered 1, 3, 4, and 8 in later sections of this chapter). Four others are new. All of them were designed to catch the presence and operation of collective purposes and to do so when using systematic cross-societal samples. Along the way, I examine some questions about research on this subject and about the way in which I have gone about it.*

What Is Collective Purpose?

I use the word *purpose* to refer to motivation, highlighting its directedness and, in people as selves, its reflexivity. Whether in collective or individual behavior, motivation refers to a range of phenomena. At one extreme is the pursuit of articulated and self-conscious goals; at the other, the mere tendency to move toward preferences that are barely sensed. Motivation also refers to a range of intensity, including everything from passionate involvement to near indifference. Any definition suited to so wide a range will give a very special meaning to the word *purpose*.

Motivation necessarily involves value and motive. Value is the rele-

*A supplement to this chapter, Swanson (1990), includes statistical tables, lists of societies arranged by particular codings, relations between findings reported here and related specialized literature, and appendices containing extended documentation. This document is available from the ASIS National Auxiliary Publications Service, P.O. Box 3513, Grand Central Station, New York, NY 10163–3513.

vance of things for blocking or facilitating behavior. Motives are expectations of a change in value contingent upon one's own activity. Motivation is the actual commitment to the activity entailed in motives and the guidance by motives of the performance of that activity (Swanson 1989).

Value, motives, and motivation can be collective in origin and reference. The root idea is that of collective relations (Swanson 1980b:4): "Social relations are relations among people as persons [or selves]: relations in which people take account of what is on their own minds and the minds of others and seek to articulate the two. . . . Social relations are collective to the extent that the persons [or selves] are engaged, whether knowingly or not, in a common undertaking: are taking account of concerns, capacities, and potentialities, both common and personal, and are trying to articulate these and to promote or change the common life."

This definition pictures the collective as a variable element within the social and is general enough to encompass the collective element in instances of social relations ranging from large, formal collectivities and whole societies to the casual encounters and communities memorialized by Goffman (1963). What, however, are the "common" undertakings on which the definition turns?

They are, at minimum, states of interdependence among persons. In social interaction we have persons influencing themselves and one another. In social interdependence, interacting persons are drawn to one another by their wanting to maintain their relationship. They share the desire to benefit from that relationship and the appreciation, however indistinct, that this will involve them in doing things together—in fitting their behavior to one another so that they sustain their mutual attractiveness and, at least for the moment, forgo alternative courses of action. A collectivity, whether a society or any other, is a population whose members are socially interdependent.

In this minimal definition, collective relations are those in which people are involved in a common pursuit, a joint enterprise, and, in that sense, are acting from a collective purpose. Collective value is then the relevance of things for blocking or facilitating collective action. Collective motives are expectations of a change in value for collective relations as contingent upon collective action. Collective motivation is the commitment to the collective action entailed in such motives and the guidance of that action by these motives. To me, collective purpose refers to collective motivation.

By this definition, collective purpose exists substantially and is not a reified abstraction. It is a defining property of collective relations and action, namely the commitment of a collectivity to a course of action and the guidance by motives of action that creates, supports, and employs a joint enterprise.[5]

The view of collective purpose that I propose resembles other conceptions but is importantly different. It does not involve assumptions that often accompany ideas of "group goals" or "common values." It assumes nothing about the extent to which personal and collective interests coincide except that participants must see some measure of joint action as being in their interests. As in Niklas Luhmann's (1982, 1985) vision of human association (he calls it *society*), it leaves open whether such action is specific and immediate or only a course that people want to have available as a possibility. The conception also leaves open whether people in a collectivity will have one or several collective purposes and, if several, whether those purposes will be fully compatible with one another (Stromberg 1986:4–20, 78). It leaves open whether participants are correct or incorrect in any interpretation they make as to the presence, nature, or importance of collective purposes.[6] The purposes that participants do interpret as collective may in fact be imposed by individuals or coalitions (Perrow 1968, 1972) or may be cases of false consciousness or cultural hegemony, but that need not preclude people's acting as though these purposes were authentically collective. The participants may see environmental contingencies, rather than purposes of any sort, as shaping their activities (Jones and Davis 1965); however, if they use collective criteria to assess their performance, then my definition classifies their behavior as collectively purposeful.

The definition also leaves open whether the purposes entail well-specified and highly self-conscious objectives. Scientists who think of collective purposes as having these specific properties—as, for example, in "management by objectives" (Cyert and March 1963; Swanson 1980a)—are likely to downplay their practical importance. Thus March and Olsen (1976) are disenchanted with the conception of collective goals because they find collective life more often tentative or irrational rather than conscious or planful. Hannan and Freeman (1977) and Pfeffer (1982) note that well-defined goals of organizations are often rendered of little consequence by the obscurity or fluidity of linkages among the resources, facilities, and intergroup relations on which organizations depend. Durkheim and Weber understood that the goals that groups specifically adopt are often inauthentic and are never more than a small fraction of those that seem to guide their actions. It is important to keep these considerations in mind, but I do not see them as grounds for giving collective purposes a less than central place in analyses of collective relations and behavior. In any case, the conception of collective purpose that I propose is not limited in the ways these analysts find objectionable because it allows us to treat the presence and role of collective purposes as a variable and one that is linked to wide variations in the coherence, contents, and potency of those purposes.

Collective Purpose and Social Structure

Motivation exists as a system of processes. Motivational processes are activities, whether overt or covert: the activities entailed in becoming committed, in evaluating, maintaining, or modifying existing commitments, and in guiding performance by its relevance for commitments. These activities are possible only if there are structures that set them in motion and carry them on. Such structures are occasioned and partially shaped by existing values and motives and by experiences, and they then act back upon the values and motives themselves. They also help determine the role and force of values and motives in behavior.

In the psychological systems of individuals, these structures include hierarchical and other relations among values and motives: for example, their comprehensiveness, their urgency, and their temporal sequencing. They include cognitive structures through which the relations of values and motives to environmental conditions are specified and through which implications are drawn. (Among these are the structures through which the impetus to action is judged as internal or external, as controllable or uncontrollable, as stable or unstable, and as intentional or unintentional (Hamilton 1983:125–207; Weiner 1986:43–78). And there are the cognitive-motivational structures that protect the individual's ability to make and monitor commitments, including the self-protective activities found in ego defenses (Swanson 1988) and in what Brehm (1966; Brehm and Brehm 1981) has called *psychological reactance*.

In collectivities the most immediately relevant structures include arrangements for setting joint goals and for selecting the basic terms on which they will be implemented. These are "policy-level" arrangements: the arrangements for policy-making or policy-control that are a part of the activities of all collectivities, however transient or enduring, formal or informal, and that become specified and differentiated in complex organizations. As motivation in individuals is distinguished from "knowing" (for example, information processing, memory) and from overt motor activity (performance), so collective arrangements for policy-making and control are distinguished from arrangements for acquiring and storing information, from arrangements for making information available when needed, and from arrangements for coordinating and conducting implementations of policy (from "lower management," "production," "marketing," or "service delivery"). I build on these points in studies of the cultures of societies.

The Place of Purpose in the Action of Societies

One might agree that collective purposes exist and are important and nonetheless wonder whether *societies* have such purposes and, if they do, how can they be identified and studied. Much depends on what one means by a "society."

To me, a society is a collectivity that a population treats as ultimately sovereign. Collectivities are sovereign if they exercise original and independent jurisdiction over some sphere of social life. The members, or their representatives, meet on regular occasions, and they have established procedures, formal or informal, for making choices on significant matters. A society is the most embracive of the sovereign collectivities that are recognized in a given population.

This conceptualization is not specifically "political" (Perczynski 1984). A group is different from an aggregation of people in being a collectivity—some people trying to do something together—and in these peoples' having some arrangements for taking coordinated action in matters of common interest. My definition says only that a society is a kind of group.

My conception of societies allows for many variations. Distinct societies may be similar or quite different in culture. Some societies are very large. Others are small: villages or extended families, for example. The boundaries of societies may be clear or relatively ambiguous, and people's attachments to societies may be rather tentative. (That was true in Europe in the early Middle Ages.) There may, as in medieval Christendom, be unclear boundaries between such competing and ultimate sovereignties as those associated with church and state. Likewise the "purposes" of society may be extensive or limited; they may be implicit or, as in the constitutions of modern nations, spelled out in at least a general way. In most cases the purposes include the resolving of some forms of disputes, the facing of some types of problems (for example, defense or setting a date for planting crops or trekking to new pastures), and the performance of certain rituals.

Although collective purposes differ from society to society and although the purposes of any given society can change over time, it is possible to ask and answer questions about the degree to which societies act purposefully and about the role of collective purposes in their activities. That is what I want to do in the next sections of this chapter. To do this, I rely particularly on information from samples of nonliterate, "primitive" societies. These societies are valuable in providing a range of observations on degree of purposefulness that is not readily available for more complex societies and a kind of "testimony" from their people about the presence of collective purposes and about the formal properties, modes of operation, and impact of those purposes. This testimony is found in the beliefs about gods and other spirits—a set of collective interpretations—that are held in these societies.[7] These interpretations can be used as indicators of the workings of societal purposes if we follow Durkheim's (1912) suggestion that beliefs about supernatural beings are strongly influenced by peoples' experiences with such purposes. (We need not concur with his conclusion that societal purposes are the sole referent or implication of these beliefs.)

As Durkheim noted, gods and other spirits are purposive beings. Like collective (or individual) purposes, they are invisible but potent. Like the purposes of societies and of many other collectivities, they are perceived as having an unbounded future—as being, in that sense, immortal. Like all purposes, they can simultaneously affect many specific activities and, by affecting many people or, perhaps, subsidiary groups, can be in many places at a given moment. Given these assumptions, differences in the degree of purposefulness of supernatural beings direct us to look for comparable differences in the societies or other groups with which they are associated.[8] So do differences in the way in which these various spirits operate.

Most of the studies I review employ either representative samples of societies or samples that include most cases of the type of society in question. That provides some confidence in the generality of the findings. The representative samples are also "diffusion-minimal." Thanks to efforts by Murdock (1967; Murdock and White 1980) and Naroll (1965), procedures are available for selecting samples of primitive societies that make it less likely that the independence of the cases will be compromised by intersocietal influences.

I now turn to the first set of my studies of societies. I show how differences among societies in structures vital for central policy-making and policy control affect the nature and differentiation of the purposes of those societies and the potency of their purposes in shaping societal action. More exactly, I show that differences in these structures are related to differences among societies in their collective interpretations of the nature and role of the collective purposes with which they operate. The second set of these studies will illustrate how differences in these structures can affect the process of interpreting when it is a collective enterprise.

Studies on Policy-Level Structures and Societies' Interpretations of the Nature and Role of Their Collective Purposes

Collective behavior is more fully purposeful when it involves more of the components of motivation. Such differences in purposefulness can be found in samples of societies and other collectivities. Thus some of the simpler societies have few arrangements for defining collective interests or making collective choices. Others are organized to arrive at choices but have no regular means for implementing them. Still others have difficulty in making or pursuing collective choices because these activities are weakened by individuals or subgroups pursuing other interests.

Conceptions of gods and other spirits direct our attention to differences in the presence, power, and operation of collective purpose under these varying conditions. These supernatural persons are more likely to be seen as present and as acting "intelligently" when associated with collectivities that are organized to make and implement choices. Associations of this kind appear in the first five studies I review. Each study offers *partial evidence* for the generalization about the nature and role of societal and other collective purposes under which it appears.

STUDY I

Collectivities are experienced as more purposeful than social categories. The very conception of collective purpose suggests that this statement should be true, but conceptualizations do not always fit "reality." Observations on ancestral spirits and kinship groups provide some evidence. Further evidence appears in several of the studies that follow.

In many of the simpler societies, every person is classified within some categories of kinship that extend beyond the nuclear family; for example, within a particular lineage (that is, descendants of a common ancestor whose core members normally live in a single community or a part thereof [Murdock 1981:95]) or a particular clan (lineages whose members reside in more than one community). In some of these societies, the people in these categories are organized as groups: their members meet, make choices, and implement those choices. In short, they engage collectively in purposeful activity. In other societies, these categories of kinship serve only as criteria for classifying people. The criteria may be important. (They may be like age roles or sex roles in modern societies in that they set constraints on whom one chooses as a partner in marriage. Or they may determine who can inherit from whom.) But the people in any one of these categories are not organized to do things together: they do not meet as a lineage or clan and do not collectively choose or implement choices. In sum, they do not engage collectively in purposeful action any more than, for example, all men or all persons aged twenty-one to forty in a modern society.

In some societies, ancestral spirits are active in human affairs. Belief in these spirits can be read as a report on the existence of collective purposes based upon kinship in these societies. That is because these spirits are active, not as the unique individuals each once was, but in their roles as ancestors, that is, as participants in relations based on descent or marriage. They aid or punish the living according to their status as relatives and not on the basis of other ties they may have had with them. Similarly, it is as relatives, and not as friends, neighbors, or coworkers, that the spirits make claims on the living: claims for food, honor, or a release from earthly bondage.

My suggestion, then, is that beliefs in ancestral spirits record experiences with the purposiveness of organized groups based on kinship. Such purposiveness is associated with organized kinship groups and not with mere categories based on kinship. The groups must be larger than the nuclear family because such families, or groups approaching them in size and transience, are found in almost all societies whereas beliefs in ancestral spirits are not.

To pursue this suggestion, I looked at fifty primitive societies in a worldwide, diffusion-minimal sample (Swanson 1960:97–108). I found a correlation of .80 ($p < .001$) between the presence in a society of these organized kinship groups and a belief in active ancestral spirits. By contrast, there is *no* significant relationship between that belief and the number of *social categories* based on kinship.

Other Difficulties in Purposeful Action

The next three studies look at policy-level properties of societies that make it difficult for them to act in fully purposeful ways: the absence of a stable organization through which choices can be made and monitored, the presence of exceptionally powerful divisive forces that limit the development of collective interests and enterprises, and, in somewhat more complex societies, the absence of organizational links between the organization that makes collective choices and the structures that will have to implement them. These three difficulties come to light when we reflect on the meaning of certain myths of societal origins, on the conspicuous role that trickster spirits have in some societies' pantheons, and on the existence of "high" gods who have no power over the universe they created. Myths of origin help us to lay out the problem addressed in study 2.

STUDY 2

Collectivities with populations that recurrently disperse and reassemble and that lack a continuing organizational center are less likely to engage in fully purposeful collective action. In some myths of origin, reality emerges from creation. That means that one or more spirits *produce* or *shape* the components of the natural world in a way that serves the end these spirits desire (Hepburn 1967). In other myths, spirits assemble *preexisting* components (sometimes after stealing them)—stars, water, fire, bits of land, and so on—to form a new whole. Both actions are purposeful, but those in creation are more fully guided by purpose. Creation is found in the origin myths of some relatively simple and some highly complex societies.[9] Origin through assembling is more likely in the myths of quite simple societies.[10]

Origin through assembling suggests the coming together of independently existing components to form meaningful (purposefully relevant) order. That is what happens in some very simple societies. Each year their populations disperse, and small bands or families or individuals break off to seek game or pasture. Then, periodically, the people reassemble to await the passing of winter, to find marriage partners, or to perform rituals, and their society becomes visible once more.

Origin through assembling is also a pattern in which meaningful order emerges without strong central direction. That would seem more likely in very simple societies that are also unstratified.

Mac Ricketts (1964, 1966) has assembled the origin myths of Native Americans north of the Rio Grande. This part of the world held a disproportionate number of the very simplest primitive societies. Murdock (1981: columns 30 and 67) provides codes that enable us to identify the presence of nomadic or seminomadic patterns of settlement and of stratification in forty-one of these societies. Analyses (Swanson [1990], table A-1) show that nomadic societies and those that are unstratified are more likely to picture meaningful order as emerging from assembling rather than from creation (the values of the respective βs are .40 ($p < .01$) and .33 ($p < .05$): $R = .56$ ($p < .001$).[11]

STUDY 3

Collectivities embodying unintegrated, divisive forces are experienced as less purposeful. Research on mythic tricksters directs us to a *weakness* of purposefulness *that results from internal divisiveness.*

Trickster figures appear in many mythic systems. In some they have a central position: creator, culture hero, or even powerful high god. It is surprising to find tricksters in such important roles because they tend to be childish, shortsighted, self-centered, and impulsive. They are purposeful but in only fitful, selfish, irresponsible, and generally ineffective ways.[12] On the other hand, they do endure. As I noted in an earlier report (1987:260–261),

A trickster is . . . a kind of fool . . . egocentric, cocky, and enjoying limitless appetites; childish and childlike; lacking in judgment and pathetically desirous of respect; an innocent, but one so impulsive and demanding as to be a nuisance or even dangerous. If the trickster is sometimes shrewd in exploiting an opponent's character or in evading social rules—and not every trickster is—he is also self-limiting. His ends are usually immediate, he underestimates the risks in what he does and his gains, if any, are short-lived. If he has a good plan, it is likely to play no part in what happens. He mislays, forgets, or bungles it. If he succeeds, it is more from happenstance than competence. If he is not defeated by failure, it is because he remains naively hopeful about his prospects and because his appetites are undiminished.

But a powerful trickster is also amazing; sometimes awesome.

Being indomitable, he cannot be ignored. He is a force and his force is original with his being . . . not dependent on allies or on training and reflection. What is more, he often gets what he wants. And his enjoyments are huge and uncomplicated and his trials are forgotten in any present success. . . . He may be limited to the short view, but he is fully alive.

Ricketts (1964) notes that these tricksters are far more likely to have a *central* role in relatively simple primitive societies of the type that were common in North America, and he provides us with an almost exhaustive catalog of North American trickster myths.

Wherever mythic tricksters have a leading role, they pursue independent objectives but depend on others for resources, help, and praise. They live collectively with others only to gratify personal needs. Their ego-centeredness then weakens their social ties. As we shall find, tricksters tend to have a *leading* position in the myths of those quite simple primitive societies whose members are able to pursue important personal and special interests outside the collective relations that constitute their society—interests that both draw them to other people and divide them from their fellows.

In the simpler primitive societies, interests of this sort are often associated with three conditions: an economy based primarily upon hunting and fishing, certain incompatibilities in the integration of special and common interests with collective action, and a stratification based upon differences in achieved wealth. (In more complex primitive societies, strong divisive interests can sometimes be integrated through overarching controls and organizations. [See, for example, the discussion in study 7.] In simpler primitive societies they remain but little integrated with the broadest collective interests.)

As many ethnographers (for example, Barry, Child and Bacon 1959) observe, economies based on hunting and fishing are often associated with strong, rather egocentric, self-reliance and independence in individuals and families. In these societies resources are often slim. Survival depends on individual and familial effort, skill, and risk taking, and people may be off by themselves for long periods. These people nonetheless need wider social connections (for example, for mutual aid or for marriage partners), and they contribute to wider collectivities. They therefore are tied to others in collective relations and are powerfully divided from them.

The power of collective ties and purposes can also be weakened if a society has inconsistent arrangements for integrating personal and special interests with collective interests. This inconsistency appears in some simple societies, such as those in which powerful tricksters are likely to be found. The people in these societies are organized principally through systems of governance and of descent. I proposed in earlier studies (1968, 1969, 1971a, 1974a, 1986, 1987) that some systems of descent are especially compatible with some systems of governance: both patrilineal systems and some forms of governance tend to legitimate the pursuit of special as well as common interests, matrilineal systems are similar to some patterns of governance in legitimating the pursuit of common, but not special, interests, and bilateral systems of descent and certain forms of governance are alike in permitting the pursuit of special interests but subordinating it to a concern for the common interest. (A review of the rationale and supporting evidence for this proposal would divert us from our immediate concerns.) The proposal's present importance is in the suggestion that certain patterns of descent and governance are similar in the roles they provide for the pursuit of special, as against common, interests and that other patterns are not. (As we shall see, inconsistent combinations of descent and governance are not uncommon among the *simpler* primitive societies. (Data in Swanson 1968, 1969, and 1974a, and Paige 1974 show that they are *far less* common in the *more complex* primitive societies and in literate societies.) When these social arrangements are *inconsistent,* they both draw people together for collective action and lead them in divergent directions.

In the simpler societies, appreciable differences among individuals and families in achieved wealth tend also to reflect both social ties and an independent pursuit of special interests—and the ability, or good fortune, to succeed in those personal efforts. In these societies, wealth draws people to one another as leaders and followers, patrons and clients, as sources of honor or respect, and as sources of supplies. It simultaneously separates people from one another as dangerously powerful or as dangerously jealous or dependent.

Codes on these three integrating, but divisive, conditions were available for fifty-nine of the North American societies in Rickett's catalog of trickster myths. Murdock's (1981) codes for a worldwide sample contained information about the dependence for sustenance upon hunting and fishing in societies (his column 7), about rules of descent (his columns 20, 22, 24), and about stratification by achieved wealth (his column 67). I had developed codes on patterns of governance in these societies.

Analyses (Swanson 1990, table A-2) show that, for the sample as a whole, powerful tricksters are more likely in the myths of those societies that gain at least 50 percent of their sustenance from hunting and fishing ($\beta = .33$, $p < .01$) and of those in which the patterns of descent and governance are incompatible ($\beta = .32$, $p < .01$): $R = .49$ ($p < .001$). Among the societies that depend heavily upon hunting or fishing *or* that have incompatible systems of governance and descent, the existence of stratification by achieved wealth is related to the importance of mythic tricksters: $r = .36$, $p < .05$. (As I report elsewhere [1987], powerful mythic tricksters tend to appear outside North America in societies with the same characteristics.)

STUDY 4

Collectivities organized to implement purposes are experienced as more purposeful. Groups organized around kinship usually have the means to take collective action, such as conducting rituals, planting crops, or raiding their neighbors, and the ancestral spirits associated with them are usually pictured as acting intentionally. In studies of high gods we see the possibility that collective purposes can be present in the absence of the ability to act on these purposes.

High gods are those that create all reality or serve as its supreme governors. They differ in which of these activities they perform. Indeed, some are inactive. Having created or ordered the universe, they do nothing more. Others are active rulers. What conditions make the appearance of high gods more likely and under what circumstances are they likely to be seen as active rather than inactive?

My suggestion in an earlier study (1960) was that high gods in some sense integrate diverse purposes or enterprises. They are "high" in that people or other purposeful beings go about their several undertakings and that these undertakings come to be integrated under a more comprehensive set of purposes, namely those of the high god.

As I have defined societies, all of them have arrangements for purposive action and every society embraces diverse purposes that could be integrated. But all societies do not have a high god. What makes the difference?

I proposed that high gods are most likely to appear when *strongly defined* differences in purposive activity are integrated under a superordinate purpose. Differences in purposive activity would have such a clear definition if they were associated with groups rather than individuals and with groups that had some measure of sovereignty—some sphere of original and independent jurisdiction in which the group's exercise of power may not legitimately be abrogated by other groups. In the United States, many groups have sovereignty in some sphere: the national state, of course, but also the several states, local communities, voluntary associations, families, and so on. In simpler societies, sovereignty is often associated with villages, families, larger kinship groups, chieftainships, and many other groups. By definition, each form of group having sovereignty is a center of distinctive collective purposes. I suggested that high gods would appear in societies having at least two types of groups having sovereignty, these being integrated by a more inclusive sovereign group. Coders working on a worldwide sample of fifty primitive and ancient societies counted the number of such groups in each society, working outward from the individual to consider the nuclear or extended family, other kin groupings, communities, regional organizations, and so to the total society itself.

As always in such efforts, cases are lost because some societies are not adequately described on some variables. In the end, thirty-nine of the fifty societies could be coded on indigenous beliefs concerning the presence of a high god. More recently, I drew a second worldwide, random sample of forty-six societies from Murdock and White's (1980) "minimal-diffusion" sample. (A graduate student in anthropology[13] coded the monographic literature for the number of types of sovereign groups and for other organizational features of these societies. She did not know the variables with which these were to be associated. I read the "religious" sections of this literature to code for the presence of high gods and certain other religious beliefs described below. I arrived at these ratings before my assistant's codes were available.) Murdock (1967) had coded the presence and characteristics of high gods for these societies and I have used his coding unless I found clear and overwhelming evidence to the contrary. Five cases of this sort were found.[14] Adequate data for my purposes were present for thirty of the forty-six societies.[15]

Tabulations (Swanson [1990], table A-3) show that there is a highly significant relationship between a society's having three or more types of sovereign groups and its having a belief in a high god. The correlations from the two samples are, respectively, .75 (p <.001) and .80 (p <.001).[16] In both samples, there are insignificant correlations between the presence of this kind of deity and measures of societal complexity such as size of population, the number of specialized occupations, or the percentage of sustenance obtained from agriculture.[17]

Some of these deities are inactive. Others are active rulers. In earlier research, I proposed that high gods might be active in societies that had standing organizations that served as agents of whatever sovereign groups are present: for example, police, courts, administrative cadres, or religious organizations. These bodies, which I called *communal groups,* are not themselves sovereign but serve as the hands and feet of groups that are.[18] Analyses (Swanson 1990, table A-4) show that in both samples, and among societies having at least three types of sovereign groups, societies having two or more such standing agencies are more likely to conceive of a high god as active. The respective correlations are .67 (p <.01) and .66 (p <.01). (In neither sample is there a significant correlation between the number of types of sovereign groups and the activity of the high god!)

These studies of high gods remind us that societies themselves and groups within them deal with many collective purposes. A consideration of pantheons of important deities leads us to some of the conditions under which specialized purposes become differentiated, organizationally and culturally. That is the focus of the last study in this first set, study 5.

STUDY 5

Collectivities are more likely to distinguish important subordinate aims within their overarching purposes if they have administrative and other organizational links that connect those over-arching purposes with the activities through which they are implemented. Active high gods draw our attention to organizational arrangements for carrying out collective purposes. So do pantheons of other gods in which each deity has some broad aspects of nature and culture as his or her province and none is limited in powers to a particular locality, species, or set of kin. The greater gods of classical Greece—Poseidon, Apollo, Ceres, Hermes, and the others—are cases in point. Unlike Zeus, the high god, these deities did not create and/or ultimately govern all or most of reality. I call them *superior* gods.

Each superior god is concerned with a cluster of specialized activities that people find important. (In ancient Greece, Ceres was concerned with agriculture, Artemis with hunting, Ares with war, Apollo with prophecy and purification, Themis with justice, and so on.) Each pursues specialized aims that fall within a society's general objectives of maintaining itself and mastering its environment.

All societies have such specialized aims. What determines whether these aims will be discriminated from one another as clearly as when they are represented by superior gods? Whatever the answer, it cannot rest solely upon just any form of societal complexity. In the first of the samples I used when studying high gods (the only one for which I have a count of superior gods), the correlation between number of superior gods and number of sovereign groups is an insignificant .17 ($N = 49$).

Why is this correlation so low? Sovereign groups are distinguished by having sole and original jurisdiction over some sphere of social relations. Therefore, less inclusive sovereign groups (say, families) are not creatures of more inclusive sovereign groups (say, villages or chieftainships), serving mainly to implement the programs of those inclusive groups. Perhaps the numbers of superior gods and of sovereign groups in societies are unrelated because the less inclusive sovereign groups are *not* seen as constituted to serve some specialized purposes of the society itself.

We found, however, that some societies have communal groups and that these society-wide collectivities specialize in serving one or another society-wide purpose. We found that, among societies having three or more sovereign groups, those that also had two or more communal groups were likely to have a high god who was active rather than inactive. If communal groups embody specialized society-wide activities, are they also associated with the presence of superior gods? In the sample of primitive societies for which I have relevant data, the overall correlation between the two is a statistically insignificant .26. However, the number of superior gods and of communal groups are related significantly ($r = .59$, $p < .05$) for the thirteen societies having four or more sovereign groups.

Perhaps, then, communal groups make visible some of the subordinate, specialized aims within overarching societal purposes, enabling people to deal better with the distinctive requirements of these specialized objectives. But communal groups have this role only in the more complex societies. Are there organizational arrangements that have the same effect and that can be operative in quite simple societies?

Parsons's (1966) discussion of what he called "the cybernetic hierarchy" provides one possibility. Parsons notes that all action, individual or collective, involves relations between actors' purposes and the adaptive activities through which those purposes are implemented. As he says, purposes and adaptive activities are connected through processes of specification and generalization. In specification, actors choose or develop adaptive activities according to their appropriateness for the implementation of one or another purpose (for example, adopting a ritual or a method of hunting because it seems suited for its purpose). In generalization, actors treat adaptive activities as belonging together because they serve the same or related purposes (for example, they distinguish economic activities from those that are political, judicial, religious, or whatever).

Specification and generalization thus group adaptive activities around specific aims or purposes and they sharpen awareness of the differences among purposes. Communal groups can be thought of as organizational embodiments or *outcomes* of specification and generalization, each communal group serving a cluster of special purposes and thereby making that cluster a distinctive object of action.

Specification and generalization also have an organizational embodiment in multipurpose arrangements for administration. Such arrangements can be found in societies that differ widely in complexity. Administration involves the guidance or coordination of others for the joint implementation of some established purpose. If there are specialized arrangements that regularly serve administrative purposes, these arrangements may be quite formal as in the administrative districts into which a chiefdom is divided for the local implementation of statewide policies. They may, however, be quite casual, as in the informal clustering of people in some sovereign groups (villages, for example) into smaller groupings (neighborhoods, wards) that are not themselves sovereign but that serve locally to implement wider sentiments, customs, and policies (for example, preparing for a ritual, readying young people for their initiation, and assembling tools for planting).

These administrative arrangements serve *many* purposes, not just one or a few. As a result, they constantly specify and generalize, linking overarching purposes with adaptive activities and, in the process, identifying specialized, subordinate purposes and the activities specific to each (for example, activities specific to clearing paths, tilling land, settling disputes, appeasing the spirits). My suggestion, then, is that standing administrative arrangements serve organizationally to discriminate among the major purposes of collectivities and to identify adaptive activities suited to each. As such, they may provide a basis for the specification of the specialized purposive domains that we find reported in pantheons of superior gods.

I looked for a relationship between such administrative arrangements and number of superior gods. The index for the presence of differentiated multipurpose administrative arrangements was derived from Murdock's (1981, column 32) code for the number of jurisdictional levels in primitive societies. This code includes *both* the number of sovereign groups *and* any additional levels of administration through which superordinate jurisdictions order affairs within or below them. I subtracted my count of the number of sovereign groups from Murdock's count of the number of levels of jurisdiction. Societies having *more* levels of jurisdiction than of sovereign groups were taken to have differentiated administrative arrangements. The data show that such societies are more likely to have two or more superior gods: $r = .49, p < .001$.

To this point we have found that two forms of organization that bring specialized, subordinate purposes to light are associated with beliefs in superior gods. They are communal groups and differentiated administrative arrangements. (The association between superior gods and communal groups holds only for societies with four or more sovereign groups.)

Table 7.1 shows a final development in this analysis. Whereas levels of jurisdiction devoted specifically to administration can make the presence of a cybernetic hierarchy more explicit and effective, the presence within a society (or other collectivity) of purposes that are hostile and alien may weaken the operation of that hierarchy. In many primitive societies, alien purposes are pervasive. For example, people may be required to marry someone from another society (usually another village or clan whose members see it as ultimately sovereign). This practice forges a link between members of societies that tend also to be near one another and competitors. In that situation, spouses come from groups that do not fall under the same normative controls and that have conflicting interests. A similar result is produced by a rule that people from another society must participate in rituals for worshiping the spirits or initiating the young. Will the alien participants play their part to the local inhabitants' benefit or exploit the situation for their own ends? As I reported in an earlier study of the societies represented in table 7.1 (Swanson 1960:137–152), the presence in a society of such alien purposes correlates strongly with the prevalence of witchcraft ($r = .66$, $p < .001$). Table 7.1 shows that societies that have *not* incorporated such

Table 7.1 *Number of Superior Gods by Presence of Alien Purposes, Number of Sovereign Groups, and Administrative Levels*

Presence of Hostile, Alien Purposes	Number of Sovereign Groups	More Administrative Levels Than Sovereign Groups	Number of Superior Gods	
			0–1	*2 or more*
Present	4 or more*	yes	3	2
		no	1	0
	3*	yes	1	1
		no	2	0
	2*	yes	5	4
		no	6	0
Absent	4 or more[+]	yes	1	3
		no	2	1
	3[+]	yes	1	5
		no	4	0
	2[+]	yes	1	6
		no	0	1

*,[+]Combined for correlational analysis.

alien purposes are more likely to have two or more superior gods. A multiple regression analysis finds that the value of β between absence of alien purposes and number of superior gods is .34 ($p < .01$); the β for the presence of one or more differentiated levels of administration is .48 ($p < .001$), and R is .60 ($p < .001$).

SUMMARY OF STUDIES I THROUGH 5

These studies show that it is possible and useful to examine societies as collectivities, to describe the degree to which their activities are purposeful, and to look for conditions associated with differences in purposefulness. Action is defined as more fully purposeful according to the number of components of motivation that are present: for example, assessments of the relevance of collective action and of situations for collective values, commitments of standing organizational arrangements to the representation and monitoring of those assessments, the existence of organizational arrangements for implementing choices, and the presence of organizational arrangements that represent and pursue subordinate purposes within larger purposes. Studies based on the normative testimony—the collective interpretations—of participants show that fully purposive collective action is less likely under the following conditions:

—People are organized as social categories rather than as collectivities (for example, classifications of a population by categories of kinship versus organization of that population into large groups based on the same categories of kinship).

—Collectivities recurrently disperse and reassemble and also lack a continuing organizational center (for example, societies whose people regularly disperse for nomadic treks and also lack continuing elites or officials).

—Collectivities lack a continuing organizational center and are also organized on principles that simultaneously divide and unite their members (for example, societies that lack officials, depend heavily on hunting and fishing, are stratified by achieved wealth, or have systems of descent that are inconsistent with their "political" arrangements).

—Collectivities have an organizational center but lack continuing organizational arrangements for implementing that center's purposes (for example, societies with a hierarchy of at least three types of sovereign groups but one or no commmunal groups).

—Collectivities lack organizational structures devoted to implementing the cybernetic hierarchy entailed in purposive activity (for example, societies without standing administrative arrangements).

Some of the studies suggest ways in which people will act collectively in the absence of arrangements required for more fully purposive action: for example, people may solve problems by assembling the necessary components rather than by creating them, or participants may conduct collective relations more by getting things from one another than by explicit efforts to do things together. Most of the possibilities of identifying and studying these and other less than fully purposive activities remain to be exploited (Swanson 1970).

Collective Purposes and the Structuring of Collective Interpretation

Collectivities differ in their abilities to take purposeful action. Among the collectivities capable of such action, there are differences in the place and interrelations of collective purposes. These differences have consequences. In this section I look at some ways in which collective interpretation is affected by inconsistencies in a collectivity's purposes; specifically, some effects of the following:

—The collectivity itself having inconsistent purposes (an effect: fewer social norms).

—The collectivity having within it collectivity-wide subgroups whose purposes conflict (an effect: the development, under certain conditions, of more communal groups to tie people together).

—The embracing by the collectivity of organized and competitive special interests that have a formal role in formulating its overarching purposes or in implementing them (an effect: a sharper differentiation within the collectivity and in its interpretations between overarching purposes and the organizational arrangements that bear them).

STUDY 6

Collectivities with consistent collective purposes have more social norms. Normativity is the degree to which something affects the realization of a value. Social norms are socially sanctioned judgments about the degree to which things affect the realization of collective purposes.

Other things being equal, it should be easier to make these judgments if collective purposes are consistent: judgments should take less time and agreement on them should be easier to reach. It also seems likely—other things being equal—that more judgments will be made if it is easy to make them. Therefore, the more consistent a collectivity's purposes, the more norms it will produce.

Robert Barnes developed codes that catch certain consistencies and inconsistencies among collective purposes and that provide a count of certain social norms.[19] He then applied these codes to a worldwide sample of forty primitive societies.

Barnes's argument can be seen as building on a point found in Durkheim and Weber. Both note that social solidarity based upon consistent immersion in an established way of life is different in character from solidarity based importantly upon formal authority. Both forms of solidarity embody collective purposes, but, as Barnes says, societies having the first form of solidarity (he calls it "ritualistic") view effective behavior as depending upon a person's being immersed in overt participation with others in common and customary activities, whereas societies having the second kind of solidarity (he calls it "traditional") stress the importance of a person's guidance by existing authorities or by authoritative institutions and their pronouncements.

Barnes based a code for these two kinds of solidarity on societies' theories about the causes of crime and other forms of deviance and on their methods for "reforming" and controlling deviants. Tabulations (Swanson 1990, table A-5) show that there is a strong relationship ($r = .68, p < .001$) between Barnes's coding of a society as traditional rather than as ritualistic and Murdock's (1980, column 32) coding of that society as having a structure of governance that transcends local communities.[20]

Like Durkheim and Weber, Barnes sees traditionalism and ritualism as incompatible and not merely as different. Authorities and authoritative institutions typically try to strengthen their own resources and operations by modifying some features of customary ways of doing things and are resisted when they do so. If the two forms of solidarity are inconsistent, it should follow that collectivities with strong elements of *both* kinds of solidarity should have *fewer* social norms than those with just one form of solidarity.

Barnes's coders counted the number of norms concerning eating, dress, and adornment found in each society in his sample. (He focused on these areas of normativity because they are not as dependent as, say, technological inventions, on the presence of environmental conditions required for their production.) In his sample, societies with strong elements of *both* ritualistic and traditional solidarity have *fewer* norms concerning eating and apparel than do societies based primarily on one form of solidarity: $r = -.56, p < .01$. This finding is especially interesting because the societies based importantly on both forms of solidarity are not, on the average, as simple in number of jurisdictional levels or technology or as small in population as those coded as ritualistic. The data are consistent, therefore, with the argument that incompatible collective purposes lead to the production of fewer social norms—fewer collective interpretations.

STUDY 7

Groups that implement the purposes of a superordinate sovereign group are more likely to develop if the members of that superordinate group are cross-pressured by the requirements of less embracive sovereign groups that compete with one another for support. Ethnographers are often impressed by the elaborate normative and organizational systems found among some peoples whose cultures are very simple in other respects. As we have seen, an efflorescence of norms is more likely in simple or complex societies that have consistent collective purposes. Societies, some of them simple, also differ in the number of communal groups in their populations. (We were introduced to these groups in study 4.) For example, the Timbira, a Brazilian society of about three hundred people, are reported (Nimuendaju 1946) as having twenty-seven communal groups, including age classes, groups of clowns, curing societies, and other groups having specialized rituals.

What determines the appearance of such groups? They are, of course, more prevalent in societies that are complex in other respects. In the samples I used in studying high gods, the correlation between number of sovereign groups and number of communal groups is .72 ($p < .001$). Eighty-eight percent of the societies having five or more types of sovereign groups have at least two communal groups; 94 percent of those having two or fewer sovereign groups have no communal groups or only one. In the remaining societies, however, the number of communal groups varies considerably.

Some years ago, S. N. Eisenstadt (1956) offered an explanation for the presence of one type of communal group: age sets or classes. It can be generalized to encompass others. Eisenstadt noted that age classes bring together members of different kinship groups and of different economic or other groupings, obliging them to live and act together in the service of society-wide purposes. That tends to be the role of *all* communal groups (Jorgensen 1980, 1987).

Eisenstadt noted that the demands made on individuals by kinship groups often compete with those made by economic groupings and that age groups serve to unite people across these conflicting purposes. Using a very large, worldwide sample, he showed that age groups are likely in societies in which large, organized kinship groups and also groups based upon other, especially economic, ties are important.

It seems plausible that communal groups of many kinds will help to overcome the sorts of cross-pressures that Eisenstadt identified and that cross-pressures other than those involving kinship and economic relations can have similar outcomes. Certainly conflicts that people experience between (a) their attachments to one another as members of a society and (b) their interests as occupants of competing positions in any developed system of stratification would seem to provide such cross-pressures.

Data relevant for this line of argument are available for the peoples included in the study of high gods. I will focus on the thirty-six of those peoples who are intermediate in number of sovereign groups (those having three or four such groups) and for whom there are codes on the number of communal groups. Approximate indices for Eisenstadt's "independent" variables are available in Murdock's (1981) codes on the presence of organized kinship groups larger than the nuclear family (his columns 20, 22, and 24) and on the presence in a society of social classes (his column 67), the latter indicating bases for relations other than those grounded in kinship. Among my own codes is one indicating whether the ultimately sovereign group (the "society") in these thirty-six populations is itself organized on the basis of kinship (for example, as a lineage or phratry).

If we generalize Eisenstadt's explanation, it predicts that communal groups will be more prevalent where people are cross-pressured as members of groupings that are society-wide and that make conflicting demands on individuals. The results in table 7.2 are broadly consistent with that prediction.

The cross-pressures Eisenstadt has in mind are presumably *less likely* in (a) societies organized preponderantly by kinship (those organized on kinship principles and also having corporate kinship groups) and (b) societies that are not so organized and that also lack cross-pressures associated with social classes. Table 7.2 shows that only one of the nine societies in these categories has two or more communal groups.[21]

By Eisenstadt's reasoning, the relevant cross-pressures are *most likely* in societies having social classes and also strong but *not preponderant* sets of kinship ties. Twelve of the eighteen societies having those characteristics have two or more communal groups. (Overall, the thirty-six societies in table 7.2 tend to have more communal groups if they *have* social classes and *are not* based preponderantly on kinship; $r = .45$: $p < .01$.)

The data do not allow us to decide whether this association is due to *cross-pressures* associated with classes that are not subordinated to kinship. That question will require further study. We can say that, for these thirty-six societies, the distinctions noted in table 2 are not related to indicators of "cultural complexity" identified by Murdock and Provost (1980): for example, size of settlements, density of population, development of agriculture, and number of occupational specializations. We must look elsewhere for an explanation of the pattern in table 7.2.

Table 7.2 *Number of Communal Groups**

Ultimately Sovereign Group Is Kin-based	Presence of Large Kinship Groups	Presence of Social Classes	Number of Communal Groups	
			0–1	*2 or more*
yes	yes	yes	5	1
		no	2	0
	no	yes	0	0
		no	0	0
no	yes	yes	5	10
		no	6	3
	no	yes	1	2
		no	1	0

*In societies having 3 or 4 types of sovereign groups.

STUDY 8

The purposes of a collectivity are more likely to be sharply distinguished in interpretations from its organization, acts, and agents if special interest groups have an important formal role in forming and implementing those purposes. This study, like studies 6 and 7, shows some consequences of inconsistencies or incompatibilities in collective purposes. In study 6, the purposes seemed those of the society itself, and their inconsistency was related to the production of fewer social norms. In study 7, society-wide organizations made conflicting demands on individuals and on subgroups. Communal organizations were seen as being formed to provide bonds that united people across those conflicts. In this study, the overarching purposes of societal collectivities are contrasted with the purposes of other groups in the population. My proposal here is that, if those more specialized groups have an important role in formulating or implementing the society's purposes, a sharper distinction will be made between societal purposes and the organization that bears and serves them.

I first saw this pattern when studying the spread of Protestantism through the states of Europe from 1520 through 1685 (Swanson 1967). A comparison of essential differences in Protestant and Catholic doctrine set the problem of relations between collective purposes and a collectivity's organization.

By the sixteenth century, the Western church (and the Eastern as well) had defined its sacramental acts as those of God. Thus, when the

Church acted through its ordained agents and in its sacral capacity, God himself was acting: forgiving, baptizing, marrying, confirming, ordaining. And it was the very essence of God in Christ that the communicant received in the eucharistic elements. What is more, the "mind" of the Church as embodied in its authoritative experience and teaching was one with the Bible as a source of ultimate truth—whether the Church recognized that truth immediately or only later. Many doctrines were validated by this experience and by reflection upon it rather than by the Bible; for example, beliefs in the nature and the salvific role of the Virgin and the saints, in Purgatory, in the efficacy of prayers for the souls of the dead, and in the power of the Church's acts of "indulgence" to remit punishments for sin.

Protestantism denied or qualified each of these claims. In its view, no historically existing person or organization could legitimately claim to be God in action or claim to be able, at its discretion, to dispense any portion of God's good will or personal essence. To Protestants, God had promised to be with his people, an active participant with them in the sacraments and in everyday life, but his presence was at his own discretion and took the form of a divine personality offering a personal relationship and never, even in the Eucharist, of a kind of "medicine." As concerns salvation, God in Christ had said and done what was necessary and anything beyond the scriptural account was unjustified.

Whatever else it meant, the spread of Protestantism indicated disbelief in many of Catholicism's claims or of indifference to them, in particular, the claim that God's divine essence or will was embodied in the organization or acts of the historically existing church and was available to be drawn upon, dispensed, or interpreted by ecclesiastical authorities. This difference between Catholic and Protestant views was what I tried to understand.

I cast the problem as one of the acceptance and spread of Protestantism rather than as one of origin. The origins of the Reformation, as of any social movement, involve many factors and many contingencies (Bouwsma 1974; Kouri and Scott 1987; Spitz 1985): the competition between the Church and emerging national states, the spread of learning, the Church's difficulties in preparing, sustaining, and disciplining its clergy, the role of the Church as a secular power in European affairs, and so on. In the end, explanations of a particular social movement are limited by the difficulties of dealing with a singular case. It may be possible, however, to identify conditions that lead to the acceptance or rejection of a movement's orientations. A range of cases can be examined, "variables" can be controlled, and explanations can be evaluated against comparative evidence. The results may even have implications for the question of origin.

In thinking about the spread of Protestantism, I drew on the type of research I have been reviewing here. Because God is a high god, I focused on differences in the ultimately sovereign decision-making structures of European societies, especially the structures that were most embracive. I interpreted the Protestant-Catholic differences as concerned with the role of societal purposes in the decision-making structures supposedly designed to serve them.

What leads people to doubt that the structure and the acts of an organization are authentic embodiments of collective purpose? Such doubts are common. They arise from signs that special interests, and not just the common interest, are being served and that they are being served illegitimately.

How is an organization able to retain credibility and loyalty despite such doubts? In many cases, it is not challenged because people think that the organization is what it should be despite its being misused. Misuses can be corrected without fundamental changes in the organization.

The situation is different, however, if people find that service to special interests, as well as to overarching collective purposes, is built into the very structure of the organization. In this circumstance, the organization's structure and acts will represent some mixture of common and special interests and people must be wary about confusing one with the other. The two must be distinguished and differentiated.

Given this reasoning, the pre-Reformation decision-making structures of societies that *adopted* Protestantism should embody an important, even legitimate, role for special interests in the definition and implementation of overarching collective purposes. Because Calvinism and Zwinglianism are more thoroughgoing than Lutheranism or Anglicanism in their versions of Protestant themes, their acceptance should be associated with an even stronger participation of special interests in the formulation and pursuit of societal purposes.

These expectations were confirmed in the history of religious and political developments in most of the societies I studied. I examined the historical record for forty-two states of Europe that had sufficient independence at some period between 1520 and 1685 to develop and implement an indigenous response to the Reformation. This sample included all of the major states, including the larger states in Germany, and many smaller ones, among them the several Swiss cantons and, in Italy, the city-states of Venice and Florence. By current estimates (De Vries 1984:36, 269–287; McEvedy and Jones 1978), these states encompassed about 77 percent of the European population (about sixty-two million people) of Western Christendom as of 1500 and more than 90 percent of the people in the politically independent states of the area.[22]

My sample did not include any of the Imperial Free Cities, and it has been suggested (Midelfort and Edwards 1972; Ozment, 1975; Wuthnow 1985, 1987:299–330) that the story there might have been different from the one I found for larger states. There were more than sixty such cities, most of them very small, and they varied in their degree of independence from Imperial control. In a supplement to this chapter (Swanson 1990), I show that the relations found in my original study appeared again for the eight imperial cities that were by far the largest. All of them were relatively independent in settling on a response to the Reformation.

Compared with most primitive societies, the European states in my samples had more differentiated structures for making authoritative decisions and all of them had come to distinguish between what Bracton (circa 1250–1256) and other medieval thinkers called *gubernaculum* and what they called *jurisdictio*. I found this distinction helpful when thinking about operational definitions of the penetration of societal purposes by special interests. For present purposes, an abbreviated description of this distinction must suffice.

Speaking broadly, *gubernaculum* corresponds to the principal executive and higher judicial powers. In principle, these maintain and implement collective purposes. In the states of early modern Europe they would have included the power to make war or conclude a peace, to create supreme magistrates, to establish a system of judicial appeals, to pardon adjudged offenders, to coin money, to receive allegiance or fealty or homage, to grant patents, including those of monopoly, and to convoke and control the militia of the state. *Jurisdictio,* by contrast, included rights to define the range of subjects over which *gubernaculum* might be exercised, to set the level of financial and other support that the population would provide for collective activities, and to consent to, or to reject, actions that might determine the future existence or basic organization of the society as a collective enterprise. In early modern times these actions included all or more of the following: approval of the making or changing of laws, consent to codifications of law, exercise of ultimate judicial functions in cases affecting the existence or basic structure of the state (for example, treason, rebellion, or lese majesty), approval of declarations of war or of treaties of peace, and approval of proposals to levy or renew taxes or to make or obtain loans.

By these definitions, *jurisdictio* refers to the continuous establishing of a collectivity's boundaries and of bonds between collective interests and personal and special interests. In *jurisdictio*, people and groups appear as the creators of a societal collectivity and as continuously reestablishing that collective relationship. *Gubernaculum*, however, refers to the formulation and guidance of collective acts based upon the *prior* existence of collective relations. By this reasoning, the existence and operation of collective purposes is most evident in the exercise of *gubernaculum*. If those purposes are less clearly expressed in the organization and the acts of societies in which special interests play an important role in the specification and implementation of collective purposes, then it is the legitimated role of special interests in the exercise of *gubernaculum* that should have special attention. That was my focus in studying the spread of the Reformation.

I found that Protestantism was officially (and, usually, popularly) accepted in those societies in which groups pursuing special interests had *previously* come to have an important, legitimate role in *gubernaculum* and that Catholicism was retained in those in which this was not the case. The involvement of special interests in the exercise of *gubernaculum* varied in nature from one society to another. In some, it meant that representatives of special interest groups (for example, guilds, circles of nobles, city wards, counties) comprised a council that had ultimate authority. That was the case, for example, in such Swiss cantons as Basel or Zurich and in the United Provinces of the Netherlands. In other societies, a deep penetration of *gubernaculum* was effected by having representatives of special interests serve as the king's council or by requiring that the consent of those representatives be obtained before the king's nominees to his council, or to major administrative posts, could take office. Patterns of this sort appeared in Bohemia, Hungary, Transylvania, and, with a small self-perpetuating council serving as chief magistrate, Geneva. In still other societies, representatives of special interest groups were designated as the proper implementers of the state's programs; thus they served as the hands and feet of legitimate action: assessing and collecting taxes, raising militia, enforcing the law, adjudicating in important legal questions, building roads, supporting the poor, regulating markets, and so on. That was the role of people representing their localities in England, Sweden, Brandenburg, Prussia, Hesse, Saxony, Wurttemberg, and Denmark. (In a separate report [1990], I consider a question raised about my coding of these matters in England and France.)

There were, of course, powerful special interest groups in all of the other European societies, and their struggles comprise a large part of the history of those societies. They did not, however, as special interests, have the formal prerogative to choose representatives who could, of right, promote special, as well as common, interests. In some societies *gubernaculum* was exercised through a council that was legitimated as representing the common interests, this legitimation being implemented by the requirement that decisions be made through unanimity or very large majorities, by providing very short terms for major officials, and by selecting councillors or other officials by lot. These types of practices appeared in such Swiss cantons as Schwyz, Unterwalden, and Fribourg, in Venice and Florence, and, for a considerable time, in Poland.[23] (As these cases show, my account does *not* turn simply on an association between "democracy" and Protestantism [Brady 1978:10–11, 20; Ozment 1975: 9–11].) In other societies, all powers in *gubernaculum* were formally vested in a prince and the agents whom he chose and whose powers could be withdrawn at his discretion. That was the arrangement in France, Spain, Austria, Bavaria, and several smaller states.

Table 7.3 shows the chief results. All societies having a *formal* role for special interests in the *central* exercise of *gubernaculum* became Zwinglian or Calvinist; all providing such a role in the *local implementation of central programs* became Lutheran or Anglican; eighteen of the twenty-one societies that provided neither role for special interests remained Catholic: $\eta = .86, p < .001$.

Certain additional findings (including those for the Imperial cities in Swanson 1990) sustain the likely importance of this correlation in understanding the spread of the Reformation. First, before the period from 1450 to 1480, none of these societies provided the role for special interests in *gubernaculum* that I associated with Protestantism. Second, the special interests concerned varied in character from one society to another (for example, upper nobility, all landowners, merchants, guildsmen), but it is the way in which they were involved in acting on collective purposes and not their other characteristics that is associated with the form of religion that was adopted. Third, before 1620 there were several important shifts in the role of special interests in the central operations of the state in Poland and in Austria. In both countries, each shift was soon followed by the adoption of a specific version of Protes-

Table 7.3 *Adoption of Protestantism and the Role of Special Interests in the Exercise of* Gubernaculum

Role of Special Interests in Exercise of *Gubernaculum*	Final Reformation Settlement		
	Roman Catholic	*Anglican or Lutheran*	*Calvinist or Zwinglian*
Role in its exercise by central authorities	0	0	12
Role in its exercise by local authorities	0	7	0
No formal role	18	1	2

tantism, or by a return to Catholicism, as predicted in the patterns in table 7.3. Fourth, since the completion of this study of the Reformation, I have found that several phenomena that distinguish Protestant and Catholic outlooks are correlated with the role of special interests in other samples of societies or in families. (For a review of these, see Swanson 1986; Swanson and Phillips 1989.)

SUMMARY OF STUDIES 6 THROUGH 8

Studies 1 through 5 showed that we can identify differences in the degree to which collectivities are capable of acting purposively and some consequences of those differences. Studies 6 through 8 show that relations among collective purposes, and relations between overarching purposes and special interests, can be identified and that hypotheses about their effects can be tested.

As always, these findings hold within certain constraints. Some constraints are unknown; others can be stated. Thus the societies that form communal groups to overcome cross-pressures from incompatible subordinate groups must have resources to make that possible. The development of communal groups may be less likely in the very simple primitive societies that contain the internal divisiveness described in connection with the appearance of tricksters (study 3). Again, sharp distinctions between ultimate sources of purpose and organizational arrangements inferred from Protestantism are unlikely in societies less differentiated than those that appeared in early modern Europe (Swanson 1971b). The discovery of such requisite contexts for any relationship is, of course, a continuous process.

On the Place and Study of Collective Purpose and Interpretation

The studies I have presented show that it is useful to think of collective action as purposeful. They offer some hypotheses about the sources and effects of those purposes, and they show that one can test these hypotheses even when the purposes are those of whole societies.

These demonstrations are, necessarily, limited. Some important topics would be difficult or impossible to address with the types of data I have used. For example, the ethnographic reports rarely allow us the historical depth or the detailed information on collective processes (discussed in Swanson 1970) that we would need to study the development of collective purposes: the processes through which participants come to feel that they must act together and decide upon one rather than another set of objectives as adequate or as the only possibility—on a "one-possibility world" (Geertz 1966:24–40). (The data on the Reformation are longitudinal and therefore better suited to studies of process or causation.) My ethnographic findings do show that collective purposes, like other collective phenomena, rarely have the simple, direct relations with phenomena at other levels of analysis that Hamnett (1984), Underhill (1974, 1976), Swanson, (1974b, 1976), or Simpson (1979, 1984) propose when they suggest that societal purposes are directly grounded in geography, demography, technology, or the ecological distribution of other organisms. Indeed, I have repeatedly noted the absence of such connections with conceptions of spirits.

The data I have used have another limitation. They would not take us far if we wanted to get at the microprocesses through which people arrive at their *interpretations* of the collective purposes they encounter. It is useful to show that particular interpretations, for example, those found in conceptions of gods and other spirits, are associated with specific ways in which purposeful collective activity is organized (Bergesen 1984; Robertson and Lechner 1984; Winter 1984).[24] If we want instead to show the steps by which people arrived at these interpretations and became committed to them, we shall again need information on collective processes. The existence of collectively purposeful action does not, of itself, produce an interpretation of that action any more than the mere use of a language by adults produces linguistic skills in a child. And the existence of collective purposes is not sufficient to produce one interpretation as against another: for example, in the studies I have presented, an interpretation framed in the action of deities rather than a secular interpretation.

Nor are my studies exceptions to the rule that research on motivation must, at some points, employ indirect evidence. This is the case for research on the motivations of individuals as well as of collectivities.

In studying motivation in individuals, evidence of many kinds has a role. It includes signs of motivational arousal (physiological signs, signs from projective and other inquiries, and so on), signs that the individual uses the same criteria in formulating behavior across widely differing situations, signs that the individual is trying to manage the strength of arousal (to heighten, dampen, or otherwise control it), signs of satiety or of dissatisfaction, and so on (Sorrentino and Higgins 1986). The more points on which there is supporting evidence, the greater the confidence about the presence of motives and about their nature and role (Swanson 1989).

In the end, all of this evidence is indirect. There is no direct access to psychological processes as such. But the indirect evidence has often proven sufficient to develop and test hypotheses, some of which seem to order wide ranges of observations that are otherwise problematic. (For a recent, powerful example on motivational matters, see Petty and Cacioppo's [1986] systematization of research on persuasion and attitude change.)

I make these points because questions about collective purpose are sometimes avoided on the ground that one cannot obtain "objective, direct" evidence, especially on the purposes of whole societies. If all motivational phenomena entail subjective processes, then the "evidence" for them will always involve inference as well as observation. The results of research on individuals' motivations and the studies of societal purposes that I have presented suggest that the consequences are not fatal: that we need not join Wuthnow (1985:804) in despairing of the possibility of scientific research on these subjects.[25] (Despite his reliance on indirect evidence, it can be "objectively" shown that Wuthnow's own account of the spread of the Reformation must be incorrect.[26]

Research on collective purposes, including my own studies, does make clear that collective purposes can serve as reasons, causes, or consequences, and it thereby sets aside long-standing debates as to whether collective values, motives, and motivation should be placed in "infrastructure" or "superstructure." The question at stake in these debates is that of the role or weightiness of collective purpose in causation or of the extent to which its ontological status is formal or empirical.

Like other aspects of collective relations, collective purpose emerges from social interdependence. Social interdependence is a necessary, but not sufficient, condition for the appearance of collective relations. On the other hand, the existence of collective purposes, and of organizational arrangements through which they are implemented, makes it more likely that collective relations will persist. Collective purposes are also preconditions for processes of organizational differentiation and reintegration and for the appearance of normativity based on collective values. If "infrastructure" stands for causal priority, collective purposes sometimes have that role and they sometimes do not.

Again, individuals and collectivities are actors, whereas collective purposes are aspects of action and are defining properties of collectivities. But there are no collectivities without individuals or collective purposes. And, as motivations, collective purposes structure action processes and are structured by them. The structuring is both formal and empirical. Thus, depending upon where we enter the connections among these entities, we highlight the role of collective purposes as reasons, causes, or consequences: as aspects of collective actors or as themselves developed through social relations among actors, individual or collective.

A failure to make these distinctions can lead to explanations that are clearly insufficient. Wallerstein's (1974) provocative account of the "origins of the European world economy in the sixteenth century" provides an example that deals with events I have treated in this chapter.

Wallerstein follows most historians in saying that western and northern Europe were afforded an opportunity for commercial expansion by, among other things, their demographic growth, the emergence of strong national states (France and Spain are his chief examples), and the weakening of Italian and other southern commercial powers by military threats from Turkey and North Africa. He fails to consider whether the most commercially successful of the northern states had organizational and cultural characteristics that enabled them to take advantage of these opportunities. (This omission stems, in part, from his effort to show that the new centers obtained their predominance by exploiting an "unearned" position rather than through any "virtues" of their own, virtues that might be emulated by countries seeking a comparable prosperity.)

For Wallerstein (1974:156, 207, 353), the Reformation was irrelevant to commercial expansion. It was simply an expression of nationalism that was imposed by states such as England where the king and other elites had until then been too weak to establish the control over ecclesiastical properties and preferments that had been won earlier by the strong monarchies in France and Spain. Whatever the correctness of Wallerstein's argument (I think it wrong), an interpretation that accounts for the organization of societal purposes suggests other, or additional, sources of the economic growth of northern and western Europe. It opens the possibility (Swanson 1967:247–252) that the guilds, regions, and other centers of purposes and "interests" were legitimized in entrepreneurial efforts by their greater importance in the central polities of these countries—that it was entrepreneurial efforts so legitimized that enabled these countries to exploit their opportunities. It raises the possibility that Protestant formulations of societal purposes as guides of societal activities, but as differentiated from the current organization for promoting those activities, may have been important in integrating societies in which "special interests" associated with commerce were to have an unusually free play. (And an account that takes collective purpose seriously seems also to provide grounds for understanding the significance of specifically religious doctrines such as those on predestination or on the nature of the Eucharist.)

My point, of course, is not that the considerations with which Wallerstein deals are unimportant but rather that they are insufficient for his purpose. An approach from collective purpose seems to help us understand what happened.

I began by saying that I would focus on collective purpose because it is often identified with culture or is itself the focus of collective interpretation and interpretations in which culture is often said to consist. This approach from collective purpose is stimulating because it opens new opportunities for dealing with basic questions. Many phenomena that have resisted systematic understanding seem importantly constituted by collective purpose and await studies that take it into account. Some of these phenomena are general and fundamental to all social relations: for example, the emergence of normativity and of its variant forms and the processes through which normativity becomes attached to collective acts or becomes attached to interpersonal relations and to principles for adjudicating between them. Equally basic and puzzling are such related topics as collective irrationality or the dynamics of mythic plots or the experience of being empowered for a life career. Every social scientist can add to the list.

Some questions are equally critical but less general. They center on the purposes of whole societies: for example, the nature and grounding of secularization, the underpinnings of the purposes of societies that are unable to exercise their sovereignty (for example, Poland or Ireland in the long periods when they were occupied by foreign powers), the existence in a society of norms and values that are universal in reference rather than particular to that society, and the denigration of magic and spiritualism in modern societies and the recent popular appeal of such beliefs in many of those societies. The agenda is immense.

Notes

1. There are, of course, other conceptions of culture (Kroeber and Kluckhohn 1952; Williams 1981). Many anthropologists equate it with social heritage or with systems of symbols. Some writers confine it to metaculture: the making of authoritative interpretations of authoritative interpretations (for example, specifying criteria of validity, proffering a systematic of representations, identifying the ordering entailed in cybernetic hierarchies). Still others include in culture one possible outcome of authoritative interpretations: the making accessible of authoritatively validated experiences of meaning and value. A few (Bellah 1970) include the objects so experienced (Bellah regards these as *symbolic realities*).

2. An explicit conception of collective purpose seems to provide the missing framework for the phenomena treated in Jaeger and Selznick's paper and one within which they can be ordered and studied.

3. Although he never uses words like *collective motivation* or *purpose*, Durkheim constantly relies on these conceptions. In *Suicide* (1897), he links self-destruction to a person's having ties with collective purpose that are too strong or too weak. In *The Elementary Forms of Religious Life* (1912), he sees the totemic plants and insects of aboriginal Australia as symbols of collective unity in directed action. He interprets the native rituals as a generating, regenerating, and intensification of collective purposes: as a making immediate and palpable the "spirit" that empowers collective life and gives meaning to all particular norms and practices. In *The Division of Labor* (1893), it is not the increase of rates of social interaction that leads to specialization in roles and institutions but of interaction as entailed in joint undertakings and therefore of interaction that has what Durkheim calls *moral* properties. People may move toward a specialization in their activities for the very reason that Durkheim suggests, that is, to enhance their competitive positions. But, for Durkheim, it is people's participation in collective life that first puts them in the position of being potential competitors and that then provides them with the possibility for specialized contributions that can transform the meaning of their specialization from competition into collaboration. Durkheim sees people's joint undertakings as making available the activities in which they will find it profitable to specialize and

as relating specialized roles and institutions to one another. These joint under-takings and their goals are the source of that form of normativity that he calls *organic solidarity* and on which he builds in the famous preface to the second edition of *The Division of Labor*. (Contrary to Schnore [1958], there is only a superficial resemblance between this analysis and the one typical among human ecologists where ideas of collective relations and purpose play no part.)

4. More specifically, collective purpose refers to the collectively developed motives that people serve when acting as agents of a collectivity. People find that to have a collective relationship they must do more than create and use it. They must meet its requirements and serve its interests. They become the agents of the relationship and not just its creators and users. It is in the actions of participants as agents that a collectivity is sometimes considered a collective actor: as having purposes or interests distinguishable from those of its partici-pants when considered individually and as engaging in a course of collective action.

5. All embracive theories of collective action—the "classical texts," old and new—give collective purpose a central place in analyses of collective organiza-tion and action. (None gives it an exclusive place. All recognize that behavior-istic and other considerations [Buxton 1985] must be taken into account along with the role of values, motives, and motivation.) Durkheim's treatments are only the most extended (see note 1). For Marx (Jay 1984:60–66), collective purposes embody the true nature and situation of mankind; one that is dis-torted by the dominant position of special interests and by the purposelessness of free markets; one that, like Luther's "true" church, is invisible, authoritative, and certain to prevail but perhaps only at the end of history. For Weber (1925), collective consciousness as focused in collective purposes is the basis for treating the "totality" (Jay 1984; Yack 1986) of a society or civilization through ideal types (Burger 1976:160–179; Hekman 1983). For Park (1938, 1939), it af-fords the distinction between the ecological order and the cultural, between community and society. For Parsons (1961, 1966), it is a necessary source of the phases of collective action and of the four great spheres of institutionaliza-tion, each sphere being an aspect of a larger set of collective efforts and ends. For students of collective behavior and social change, the development of collec-tive beliefs and motivations, and of an organization through which they can be implemented, is a central problem (Smelser 1963:71–73; Swanson 1970). For students of complex organizations, the efforts of organizations to find and employ suitable goals is a major concern (March and Olsen 1976; Mohr 1982; Zander 1985).

6. It is, of course, a truism that individuals have values, motives, and motivations of which they are in some sense unaware (cf. Freud 1900; Kahne-man and Tversky 1973; Nisbett and Wilson 1977).

7. Swanson (1990) presents evidence against Mary Douglas's (1970) claim that certain tribal societies were secularized.

8. The conditions under which these normative considerations extend to personal life and personalized relations, or to private contracts, may be quite specialized. What Lukes (1985) treats as Marx's failure to provide a morality omits Marx's stress on collective values and fulfillments (Marcuse 1941).

9. Myths that picture reality as an aspect of deity rather than as its product seem to appear only in rather complex societies (for example, Collins 1982).

10. A note on representations of collective purpose in the most complex societies appears in Swanson (1990).

11. Swanson (1990) contains a listing of sampled societies according to their origin myths.

12. Elsewhere (1987) I discuss the formal similarities between these tricksters and what Freud called *pregenital* characteristics.

13. Cheryl Shelmadine.

14. Swanson (1990) provides a review of evidence where Murdock's code seems incorrect.

15. There is a listing of sampled societies according to presence and activity of high gods in Swanson (1990).

16. Hamnett's (1984), Pickering's (1984), and Wuthnow's (1983) criticisms of the methodology of these studies seem not to jeopardize the essential findings. (1) The replication of earlier results in a new sample, and with blind coding, increases both the number of cases and the likelihood that the relations obtained hold for the relevant universe of cases. (2) Whatever the limitations of some ethnographic accounts, they seem adequate for meaningful research on this subject. How, otherwise, could these replicated findings be obtained? (3) The codes used to define sovereign groups were developed for my first study of high gods through my reading of the ethnography on a small sample of simple societies. I did not use those societies in the sample I originally employed to test the hypotheses. Some of those societies in my small "feasibility" sample were stateless, and I found it necessary to be quite circumstantial in detailing the conditions under which such societies did or did not have a wide and embracive level of decision making despite the absence in them of formal and continuously operative political structures. Wuthnow is correct in noting that such specific details are not derivable specifically from a conception of a society or its collective purposes. To permit that derivation, the operational details need to be stated more generally, but they seem to catch the sort of phenomena that are sought in testing these hypotheses. And they direct us to the relevant observations in each of two samples. (4) As I indicate elsewhere (1974b, 1976, 1986), alternative accounts by Simpson and Underhill are insufficient to explain the relationships I report.

17. Simpson's suggestion that high gods appear in societies that depend upon the raising or hunting of small animals for their food need not trouble us because the correlation he reports is not statistically significant.

18. Jorgensen (1980, 1987) refers to them as *sodalities*.

19. I appreciate Dr. Barnes's permission to use the data from which my analyses were developed.

20. There is a listing of sampled societies by code in Swanson (1990).

21. There is a listing of sampled societies by number of nonsovereign, communal groups in Swanson (1990).

22. Wuthnow (1983:354, 1985, 1987) regrets my not taking up the regimes and religious developments in several parts of Europe. One of these, Russia (but see my discussion, 1967:242–243) was omitted because it was not

within the sphere of the Western church; others were omitted (Flanders, Norway, Finland, and Wallachia) because they were controlled by outside regimes and not able to develop religious positions based upon indigenous conditions. He is wrong in saying that I omitted Moravia (it was considered a part of the kingdom of Bohemia) and the Holy Roman Empire (I treated all of the principal states of Germany, including all electoral states [apart from the archbishoprics]: the Palatinate, Bohemia, Brandenburg, and Saxony). It therefore seems unnecessary to share Wuthnow's concern (1985:805) that the sampling was too limited to be taken seriously as evidence.

23. Ozment's (1975:9–11) suggestion that what truth there is in my account is due to the acceptance of the Reformation by governments under "popular" control leaves mysterious the retention of Catholicism in places such as the inner Swiss cantons or Poland during the period of the *liberum veto*.

24. Wuthnow must surely misunderstand when he suggests (1985:804) that my not taking that step indicates that I work with a "correspondence" theory.

25. Wuthnow overstates when he suggests (1985:803–804) that for collective criteria to be involved people must be self-consciously aware of the criteria to which their interpretations must be faithful. It is unlikely that the people concerned were self-aware of the features of their society that I find are related to their religious interpretations in any of the studies in this paper. With collectivities as with individuals, people often relate in orderly ways to conditions they cannot articulate or, for whatever reason, they misinterpret.

26. Wuthnow's own interpretation of the Reformation also relies on indirect evidence. He suggests (1985:804, 812) that Protestantism tended to be accepted where it could be imposed by a strong central authority because "the nobility everywhere remained overwhelmingly resistant to the Reformation." He argues, in elaboration, that the nobility were thus resistant because they did not want to give up the ability to control the resources of the Church or to control appointments to its offices. Wuthnow does not provide direct evidence of any nobleman's making these calculations and, as a consequence, rejecting Protestant views. Fortunately, in his case as in many others, indirect evidence is useful. It shows that his account is incorrect. In or near the first half of the sixteenth century, the period he specifies as relevant, the Reformation had from strong to overwhelming support from the nobility in the following states (dates for the legalization of Protestantism are also given): Prussia, 1525; Wurttemberg, 1535; Denmark, 1536; Sweden, 1536; Brandenburg, 1539; Saxony, 1539; Hungary, 1540; England, 1547–1553; Inner Austria, 1549; Poland, 1555; Transylvania, 1557; Scotland, 1560.

References

Barry, H., I. L. Child, and M. K. Bacon. 1959. "Relation of Child Training to Subsistence Economy." *American Anthropologist* 61: 51–63.

Bellah, R. N. 1970. "Christianity and Symbolic Realism." *Journal for the Scientific Study of Religion* 9: 89–96.

Bergesen, A. 1984. "Swanson's Neo-Durkheimian Sociology of Religion." *Sociological Analysis* 45: 179–184.

Bouwsma, W. J. 1974. "Renaissance and Reformation, An Essay in Their Affinities and Connections." In *Luther and the Dawn of the Modern Era,* edited by H. A. Oberman, 127–149. Leiden: Brill.

Brady, T. A. 1978. *Ruling Class, Regime and Reformation at Strasbourg 1520–1555.* Leiden: Brill.

Brehm, J. W. 1966. *A Theory of Psychological Reactance.* New York: Academic Press.

Brehm, S. S., and J. W. Brehm. 1981. *Psychological Reactance: A Theory of Freedom and Control.* New York: Academic Press.

Burger, T. 1976. *Max Weber's Theory of Concept Formation: History, Laws, and Ideal Types.* Durham: Duke University Press.

Buxton, C. E. 1985. "American Functionalism." In *Points of View in the Modern History of Psychology,* edited by C. E. Buxton, 113–148. Orlando: Academic Press.

Collins, S. 1982. *Selfless Persons, Imagery and Thought in Theravada Buddhism.* Cambridge: Cambridge University Press.

Cyert, R. M., and J. G. March. 1963. *A Behavioral Theory of the Firm.* Englewood Cliffs: Prentice-Hall.

De Vries, J. 1984. *European Urbanization 1500–1800.* Cambridge: Harvard University Press.

Douglas, M. 1970. *Natural Symbols, Explorations in Cosmology.* New York: Pantheon.

Durkheim, E. 1893. *De la Division du Travail Social: Étude sur l'Organisation des Sociétés supérieures.* Paris: Alcan.

———. 1897. *Le Suicide: Étude de Sociologie.* Paris: Alcan.

———. 1912. *Les Formes Élémentaires de la Vie Religieuse: Le Système Totemique en Australie.* Paris: Alcan.

Eisenstadt, S. N. 1956. *From Generation to Generation.* Glencoe: Free Press.

Freud, S. 1990. *The Interpretation of Dreams.* Vol. 5 of *The Standard Edition of the Complete Psychological Works of Sigmund Freud.* Edited and translated by J. Strachey, 1938. London: Hogarth Press.

Geertz, C. 1966. "Religion as a Cultural System." In *Anthropological Approaches to the Study of Religion,* edited by M. Banton, 1–46. New York: Praeger.

Goffman, E. 1963. *Behavior in Public Places, Notes on the Social Organization of Gatherings.* New York: Free Press.

Grand Larousse. 1972. *Grand Larousse de la Langue Française.* Paris: Librarie Larousse.

Hamilton, V. 1983. *The Cognitive Structures and Processes of Human Motivation and Personality.* New York: Wiley.

Hamnett, I. 1984. "Durkheim and the Study of Religion." In *Durkheim and Modern Sociology,* edited by S. Fenton, 202–218. Cambridge: Cambridge University Press.

Hannan, M. T., and J. Freeman. 1977. "The Population Ecology of Organizations." *American Journal of Sociology* 82: 929–964.

Hekman, S. J. 1983. *Weber, the Ideal Type, and Contemporary Social Theory.* Notre Dame: University of Notre Dame Press.

Hepburn, R. W. 1967. "Creation: Religious Doctrine of." In *The Encyclopedia of Philosophy*, Vol. 2, 252–256. New York: Free Press.

Jaeger, G., and P. Selznick. 1964. "A Normative Theory of Culture." *American Sociological Review* 29: 653–669.

Jay, M. 1984. *Marxism and Totality, The Adventures of a Concept from Lukács to Habermas.* Berkeley and Los Angeles: University of California Press.

Jones, E. E., and K. E. Davis. 1965. "From Acts to Dispositions: The Attribution Process in Person Perception." In *Advances in Experimental Social Psychology*, Vol. 2, edited by L. Berkowitz, 220–266. New York: Academic Press.

Jorgensen, J. G. 1980. *Western Indians: Comparative Environments, Languages, and Cultures of Aboriginal Western North America.* San Francisco: Freeman.

———. 1987. "Political Society in Aboriginal Western North America." In *Themes in Ethnology and Culture History*, edited by L. Donald, 175–226. Berkeley: Folklore Institute.

Kahneman, D., and A. Tversky. 1973. "On the Psychology of Prediction." *Psychological Review* 80: 237–251.

Kouri, E. I., and T. Scott. 1987. *Politics and Society in Reformation Europe.* London: Macmillan.

Kroeber, A. L., and C. Kluckhohn. 1952. "Culture: A Critical Review of Concepts and Definitions." *Papers of the Peabody Museum*, Vol. 47. Cambridge: Harvard University.

Luhmann, N. 1982. *The Differentiation of Society.* Translated by S. Holmes and C. Larmore. New York: Columbia University Press.

———. 1985. "Society, Meaning, Religion—Based on Self-Reference." *Sociological Analysis* 46: 5–20.

Lukes, S. 1985. *Marxism and Morality.* Oxford: Clarendon.

March, J. G., and J. P. Olsen. 1976. *Ambiguity and Choice in Organizations.* Oslo: Universitetsforlaget.

Marcuse, H. 1941. *Reason and Revolution: Hegel and the Rise of Social Theory.* New York: Oxford University Press.

McEvedy, C., and R. Jones. 1978. *Atlas of World Population History.* Hardmondsworth: Penguin.

Midelfort, H. C. E., and M. U. Edwards. 1972. "Introduction." In *Imperial Cities and the Reformation*, by B. Moeller, vii–xi. Philadelphia: Fortress.

Mohr, L. B. 1982. *Explaining Organizational Behavior.* San Francisco: Jossey-Bass.

Murdock, G. P. 1967. "Ethnographic Atlas: A Summary." *Ethnology* 6: 109–236.

———. 1981. *Atlas of World Cultures.* Pittsburgh: University of Pittsburgh Press.

Murdock, G. P., and C. Provost. 1980. "Measurement of Cultural Complexity." In *Cross-Cultural Samples and Codes,* edited by H. Barry and A. Schlegel, 147–160. Pittsburgh: University of Pittsburgh Press.

Murdock, G. P., and D. P. White. 1980. "Standard Cross-Cultural Sample." In *Cross-Cultural Samples and Codes,* edited by H. Barry and A. Schlegel, 3–43. Pittsburgh: University of Pittsburgh Press.

Murdock, G. P., and S. F. Wilson. 1980. "Settlement Patterns and Community Organization: Cross-Cultural Codes 3." In *Cross-Cultural Samples and Codes,* edited by H. Barry and A. Schlegel, 75–116. Pittsburgh: University of Pittsburgh Press.

Naroll, R. 1965. "Galton's Problem: The Logic of Cross-Cultural Analysis." *Social Research* 32: 428–451.

Nimuendaju, C. 1946. "The Eastern Timbira." Translated by R. H. Lowie. *University of California Publications in American Archaeology and Ethnology,* Vol. 41.

Nisbett, R. E., and T. D. Wilson. 1977. "Telling More Than We Can Know: Verbal Reports on Mental Processes." *Psychological Review* 84: 231–259.

Ozment, S. E. 1975. *The Reformation in the Cities.* New Haven: Yale University Press.

Paige, J. M. 1974. "Kinship and Polity in Stateless Societies." *American Journal of Sociology* 80: 301–328.

Park, R. E. 1938. "Reflections on Communication and Culture." *American Journal of Sociology* 44: 187–205.

———. 1939. "Symbiosis and Socialization: A Frame of Reference for the Study of Society." *American Journal of Sociology* 45: 1–25.

Parsons, T. 1961 [1965]. "An Outline of the Social System: Culture and the Social System: Introduction." In *Theories of Society, Foundations of Modern Sociological Theory,* edited by T. Parsons et al., 30–79, 963–993. New York: Free Press.

———. 1966. *Societies: Evolutionary and Comparative Perspectives.* Englewood Cliffs: Prentice-Hall.

Perczynski, Z. A., ed. 1984. *The State and Civil Society: Studies in Hegel's Political Philosophy.* Cambridge: Cambridge University Press.

Perrow, C. 1968. "Organizational Goals." In *International Encyclopedia of the Social Sciences,* Vol. 11, 305–311. New York: Macmillan.

———. 1972. *Complex Organizations, A Critical Essay.* Glenview: Scott, Foresman.

Petty, R. E., and J. T. Cacioppo. 1986. *Communication and Persuasion: Central and Peripheral Routes to Attitude Change.* New York: Springer-Verlag.

Pfeffer, J. 1982. *Organizations and Organization Theory.* Marshfield: Pitman.

Pickering, W. S. F. 1984. *Durkheim's Sociology of Religion: Themes and Theories.* Boston: Routledge and Kegan Paul.

Ricketts, M. L. 1964. *The Structure and Religious Significance of the Trickster-Transformer-Culture Hero in the Mythology of the North American Indians.* Doctoral Dissertation, Divinity School, University of Chicago.

———. 1966. "The North American Indian Trickster." *History of Religions* 5: 327–350.

Robertson, R., and F. Lechner. 1984. "On Swanson: An Appreciation and Appraisal." *Sociological Analysis* 45: 205–211.

Schnore, L. F. 1958. "Social Morphology and Human Ecology." *American Journal of Sociology* 63: 620–634.

Simpson, J. H. 1979. "Sovereign Groups, Subsistence Activities, and the Presence of a High God in Primitive Societies." In *The Religious Dimension: New Directions in Quantitative Research,* edited by R. Wuthnow, 299–310. New York: Academic.

———. 1983. "Power Transfigured: Guy Swanson's Analysis of Religion." *Religious Studies Review* 9: 349–352.

———. 1984. "High Gods and the Means of Subsistence." *Sociological Analysis,* 45: 213–222.

Smelser, N. J. 1963. *Theory of Collective Behavior.* New York: Free Press.

Sorrentino, R. M., and E. T. Higgins, eds. 1986. *Handbook of Motivation and Cognition: Foundations of Social Behavior.* New York: Guilford.

Spitz, L. 1985. *The Protestant Reformation, 1517–1559.* New York: Harper.

Stromberg, P. G. 1986. *Symbols of Community, The Cultural System of a Swedish Church.* Tucson: University of Arizona Press.

Swanson, G. E. 1960. *The Birth of the Gods: Origins of Primitive Beliefs.* Ann Arbor: University of Michigan Press.

———. 1967. *Religion and Regime, A Sociological Account of the Reformation.* Ann Arbor: University of Michigan Press.

———. 1968. "To Live in Concord with a Society: Two Empirical Studies of Primary Relations." In *Cooley and Sociological Analysis,* edited by A. J. Reiss, 87–150. Ann Arbor: University of Michigan Press.

———. 1969. "Rules of Descent, Studies in the Sociology of Parentage." *Anthropological Papers,* Museum of Anthropology, University of Michigan, No. 39.

———. 1970. "Toward Corporate Action: A Reconstruction of Elementary Collective Processes." In *Human Nature and Collective Behavior,* edited by T. Shibutani, 124–144. Englewood Cliffs: Prentice-Hall.

———. 1971a. "An Organizational Analysis of Collectivities." *American Sociological Review* 36: 607–623.

———. 1971b. "Interpreting the Reformation." *Journal of Interdisciplinary History* 1: 419–446.

———. 1974a. "Descent and Polity: The Meaning of Paige's Findings." *American Journal of Sociology* 80: 321–328.

———. 1974b. "Monotheism, Materialism and Collective Purpose: An Analysis of Underhill's Correlations." *American Journal of Sociology* 80: 862–869.

———. 1976. "Comment on Underhill's Reply." *American Journal of Sociology* 82: 421–423.

———. 1980a. "A Basis of Authority and Identity in Post-Industrial Society." In *Authority and Identity,* edited by B. Holzner and R. Robertson, 190–217. Oxford: Blackwell.

———. 1980b. "For General Sociology." In *Sociological Theory and Research, A Critical Approach,* edited by H. M. Blalock, 3–16. New York: Free Press.

————. 1986. "Immanence and Transcendence: Connections with Personality and Personal Life." *Sociological Analysis* 47: 189–213.

————. 1987. "Tricksters in Myths and Families: Studies on the Meaning and Sources of 'Pregenital' Relations." In *Themes in Ethnology and Culture History*, edited by L. Donald, 259–308. Berkeley: Folklore Institute.

————. 1988. *Ego Defenses and the Legitimation of Behavior.* Cambridge: Cambridge University Press.

————. 1989. "The Motives and Motivation of Selves." In *The Sociology of Emotions*, edited by D. D. Franks and E. D. McCarthy, 3–32. Greenwich: JAI Press.

————. 1990. "Additional Tables and Documentation to Accompany 'Collective Purpose and Culture: Findings and Implications from Some Studies of Societies.' " New York: ASIS National Auxiliary Publications Service.

Swanson, G. E., and S. S. Phillips. 1989. "Will Surveillance, Replacement, and Withdrawal: Some Social Correlates." Forthcoming, *Psychiatry*.

Underhill, R. 1974. "Economic and Political Antecedents of Monotheism: A Cross-Cultural Study." *American Journal of Sociology* 80: 841–861.

————. 1976. "Economy, Polity, and Monotheism: Reply to Swanson." *American Journal of Sociology* 82: 418–421.

Wallerstein, I. 1974. *The Modern World-System: Capitalist Agriculture and the Origins of the European World-Economy in the Sixteenth Century.* New York: Academic Press.

Weber, M. 1925 [1968]. *Economy and Society,* Vol. 1. Translated by G. Roth and C. Wittich. New York: Bedminster.

Weiner, B. 1986. *An Attributional Theory of Motivation and Emotion.* New York: Springer-Verlag.

Williams, R. 1981. *The Sociology of Culture.* New York: Schocken.

Winter, J. A. 1984. "Toward a Fuller Version of Swanson's Sociology of Religion." *Sociological Analysis* 45: 205–211.

Wuthnow, R. 1983. "Durkheim via Swanson." *Religious Studies Review* 9: 352–356.

————. 1985. "State Structures and Ideology." *American Sociological Review* 50: 799–821.

————. 1987. *Meaning and Moral Order: Explorations in Cultural Analysis.* Berkeley and Los Angeles: University of California Press.

Yack, B. 1986. *The Longing for Total Revolution: Philosophic Sources of Social Discontent from Rousseau to Marx and Nietzsche.* Princeton: Princeton University Press.

Zander, A. 1985. *The Purposes of Groups and Organizations.* San Francisco: Jossey-Bass.

8

Social Norms in the Institutional Culture of the German Federal Parliament

Renate Mayntz

Concepts of Culture and the Object of This Study

Whenever a group of sociologists meets to discuss *culture,* it becomes quickly apparent that there is (still) no agreement on the meaning of this core term of sociological analysis. At one time or another, myths, values, eating and dressing habits, scientific theories, social norms, novels, and situational definitions have all been treated as elements of culture. Keesing's challenge "to narrow the concept of 'culture' so that it includes less and reveals more" (Keesing 1974) is still being met in different ways by different schools of thinking.

One important step in the direction of terminological specification has been the analytical distinction between social system and cultural system that has become a hallmark of the Parsonian tradition of thinking. When Kroeber and Parsons advocated this distinction, they did so in contrast to a view prevalent among cultural anthropologists that regards societies as sociocultural systems in which social and cultural elements are inextricably intertwined, forming one integrated whole (Kroeber & Parsons 1958). The analytical distinction between culture and social system (or social structure) excludes observable behavior patterns from the concept and characterizes culture as an idea system. Such systems, however, can still be conceptualized and circumscribed in different ways, for instance, with respect to the emphasis placed on the ideas in people's heads or on collective representations such as myths or doctrines or with respect to the (relative or even exclusive) emphasis on symbolic, cognitive/interpretive, or evaluative elements. As Michael Schmid points out in chapter 4, Parsons himself was inconsistent in this and has emphasized different elements on different occasions. Regardless of these unresolved conceptual issues, the Parsonian distinction between cultural and social systems has the advantage of directing attention to the relationship between them. Two sets of questions are thus raised, one referring to the causal linkage between both systems, the other to the delimitation of the social basis (or scope) of a culture.

Both issues are familiar. With respect to the first, Marxist orthodoxy assumes that the ideational superstructure is determined by the socioeconomic basis; Parsons in contrast ascribes a regulative function to the cultural system (Parsons 1951). If one wants to avoid both materialist and idealist determinism by assuming the relationship between culture and social structure to be one of mutual influence rather than of one-sided dependence, it becomes an empirical challenge to trace the shaping influence of situational (structural, institutional) constraints upon cultural elements.

The major issue in debates over the scope of cultural systems is whether and to what extent subsystems of society possess a culture of their own.[1] One answer has been that cultural differentiation is a correlate of social differentiation, and that it is hence meaningful to speak, for instance, of different regional, ethnic, class, and professional cultures within a given society. But where the integrative function of culture is stressed, social subsystems have instead been viewed as societies *en miniature* and attempts have been made to identify the manifestations of the encompassing cultural system of the society at large in the smaller unit. This has been true for local communities as well as for organizations (for example, Arensberg 1954; Lammers & Hickson 1979). Of course these views are not mutually exclusive. Subcultures may well have specific or even unique traits and manifest a wider societal culture at the same time.

In the sociology of organizations, both of these analytical routes have been pursued. Efforts have been made to identify how different national cultures affect the structure and functioning of organizations (Hofstede 1981) and, likewise, to prove the existence, and explain the genesis, of an endogenous "organizational culture" that is specific to individual organizations (Allaire & Firsirotu 1984; Ouchi & Wilkins 1985). In this literature it is assumed that organizational cultures develop in the course of an organization's history and are heavily influenced by its leaders and particularly by the experience of successful mastery of an important challenge.[2] It is also interesting to note that myths, legends, and shared cognitive maps are emphasized much more than evaluative and especially normative elements—occasionally to the virtual exclusion of social norms from the concept of organizational culture (for example, Smircich 1983). This tendency is probably related to the critical function served by the concept of organizational culture in the context of a research tradition that has long focused on aspects of structure and their normative underpinnings in the form of rules and regulations.

Empirical studies of organizational culture have mostly dealt with industrial firms or business corporations, but the same questions can obviously be asked about any other organized social group, including political institutions such as legislatures. In fact, scientific interest in "political culture" is fairly widespread. True, most studies of political culture are concerned with orientations of the population at large (for example, Almond & Verba 1965); here politicians enter the picture only as objects of popular orientations. But there is growing interest also in the specific values and beliefs of policymakers impinging upon policy formulation (Sturm 1985; Feick & Jann 1988). In much of this particular literature, elements of political culture are inferred from the observed characteristics of specific policy decisions. Where the orientations of policymakers—politicians and higher civil servants—have been investigated directly, it has mostly been done in the form of attitude and opinion surveys of *categories* of social actors (for example, Aberbach et al. 1981) rather than in studies of institutional subcultures. Exceptions are occasional analyses of informal social norms in legislative bodies (for example, Crowe 1983; Kornberg 1964; Loewenberg & Mans 1988; Matthews 1960).

The research on which the following discussion is based belongs to the small group of studies of parliamentary cultures. Though the German Federal Parliament has never before been studied, the research did not aim at comparison with other legislatures but pursued a set of more theoretically oriented questions about the existence and nature of a parliamentary subculture, which will be examined in the following section.

The Institutional Culture of the Bundestag: Research Questions and Methods

The most general question to be raised about parliamentary cultures concerns the possibility of their empirical existence. Legislatures are problem-solving and decision-producing organizations with a high degree of institutionalized, internal conflict and a high turnover rate of their members. According to Wilkins and Ouchi (1983), the growth of an organizational culture is encouraged by a long history and stable membership, frequent interaction among members, and the absence of exposure to contradictory sets of expectations. That none of these conditions are met in the case of the German Bundestag might impede the emergence of an institutional subculture. Also, the extreme competitiveness of the milieu might militate against the development of shared values and meanings. On the other hand it could be argued that the very instability and tension-ridden nature of the setting should increase the need for shared beliefs and social norms that regulate the behavior and mutual relations of deputies. Similarly, the role characteristics of deputies might engender the need for strong in-group ties to balance status insecurity and role stress (Mester-Grün 1979:10). In view of such countervailing tendencies (or at least contrasting hypotheses), the existence—and substantive content—of a parliamentary subculture, beyond the formal rules guiding the behavior of deputies and the cognitive and evaluative orientations they might share by virtue of their social origin and general political socialization, is an interesting empirical question, and one that has not yet found a conclusive answer. Thus Wahlke and others (1962) found a relatively low degree of consensus among state legislators in the United States with respect to the forty-two subjectively held norms they identified. On the other hand, "research on non-American legislatures has frequently discovered that the party loyalty of legislators is structured by clear norms of a sort rarely found in the United States" (Loewenberg & Mans 1988:157).

The empirical investigation that I conducted with a colleague (see Mayntz & Neidhardt 1989) aimed, therefore, first of all to identify informal social norms in the behavior of deputies of the German Bundestag. In doing so, we intended to use any empirical evidence of shared or divergent normative beliefs not only to measure group consensus or dissensus but also to inquire more deeply into the character of the normative system thus emerging: the substantive reference points of norms, their formal characteristics, and so on.

A second major question involved the forces shaping the parliamentary culture we might find. This question has many aspects, for example, the extent to which subcultural norms are an outgrowth of more general cultural standards or are unique to the institution investigated and the extent to which subcultural norms reflect individual needs rather than social (functional) imperatives. While remaining sensitive to these issues, we were mainly interested in yet another aspect of the same general question: the relationship of such informal norms as we might find to the specific institutional setting of the German Federal Parliament. Finally, we hoped that even though our data referred directly only to perceptions and beliefs, it might be possible to interpret them in light of the question about the relationship of subcultural norms to observable behavioral practice. Structural functionalism, or more generally theorists following the normative paradigm, tends to emphasize the guiding effect of shared beliefs and social norms on behavior, whereas the influence of situational constraints tends to be played down and even neglected. In contrast, actor-oriented approaches often insist that the opportunity structure of action situations is decisive for the choice of behavioral alternatives (for example, Crozier & Friedberg 1977) and the elements of culture serve mainly a legitimating, rather than a guiding, function.

While these questions may sound ambitious, the study itself was small and exploratory. The data base consisted of thirty intensive interviews with a stratified sample of deputies and written sources such as biographical material and newspaper articles.[3] Our analytical categories highlighted selected aspects of group structure and culture, while we were less interested in the process of legislative decision making. As for the parliamentary culture, we emphasized norms over shared cognitive maps of deputies and focused on intrainstitutional behavior and relations. In contrast, we did not attempt to delve into substantive policy orientations and political ideologies, questions about legitimating beliefs (for example, representation versus trusteeship), and norms relating to constituents, the party organization, the bureaucracy, and organized interests. Such a selective approach can uncover only a relatively small segment of an institutional subculture. This holds particularly for all taken-for-granted elements of shared interpretive frames, such as those that ethnographers and ethnomethodologists might find through observation. The strong, though not exclusive, emphasis on normative beliefs also precluded any attempt to approach the (often neglected) issue of the internal structure of cultural systems.

Features of the Institutional Context

With 520 members who, when it is in session, are expected to be present and even together in one room during plenary meetings, the German Federal Parliament is a very large face-to-face group. Internally, this group is segmented along political party lines, as the German Bundestag is formally organized into parliamentary party groups (*Fraktionen*). These party groups have not only an elected leadership (*Fraktionsvorstand*) who controls the parliamentary activities of deputies, assigns tasks, distributes resources, and tries to ensure party discipline, but also an elaborate system of permanent committees that meet regularly to prepare for the work in the corresponding parliamentary committees. The Bundestag is known to be more a "working" than a "debating" parliament. Of course there are debates (nearly 610 hours of debate during the 139 plenary meetings of the eighth legislative period), but relatively few parliamentary decisions depend on them.

A number of formal rules regulate the status of deputies: some paragraphs of the constitution, the election law, a section in the general procedural rules of parliament, and the *Abgeordnetengesetz* of 1977.[4] In substantive content, these rules refer to the nature of representation (deputies represent the electorate at large and are not bound by imperative mandates), indemnity and immunity, financial matters (salary, pension rights, other benefits), and permitted or prohibited economic activities, additional gainful employment, contractual relations, and so on. The purpose of most of these formal rules is to safeguard the independence of the deputies in their legislative engagement. The "allowances" (*Diäten*) of federal deputies are today a—relatively high—salary, their activities being legally considered a full-time profession (or job).

Though extensively, if quite selectively, regulated, the general status of a deputy is much less salient for the individual than is membership in one of the *Fraktionen*. Deputies hardly perceive a "deputy role" separate from their role as "deputy of party X," and the assembly as a whole is an arena rather than an integrated social group. Plenary meetings and even the equally frequent meetings of parliamentary committees are carefully prepared *encounters* of *groups;* only committees may over time achieve a certain amount of social integration across party lines, a process supported by their relatively small size and low membership turnover, and by official travel of the whole committee or of delegations. For most deputies, the parliamentary committee is in fact the most important arena of participation in the legislative process; it is the main locus of meaningful activity and of productive work.

Outside plenary and parliamentary committee meetings, the deputies of different party groups do not interact much. There exist interparliamentary associations (German-British, German-American, and so on) to which deputies of different parties belong, the Parliamentary Society, a kind of club where deputies can meet informally, some bars that, though mainly frequented by members of one specific party, also serve as informal meeting places across party lines, and receptions at embassies and similar occasions, but most of these have at best a tenuous group character and do not constitute an arena for serious debate and concerted action.

The parliamentary group is the deputy's most important reference group in Bonn. Its own social integration, however, is impeded by ideological diversity (the different intraparty currents) and, above all, by strong internal rivalry. Such rivalry results from competition for membership in important committees, for elective offices, for speaking time in plenary debates, and for a number of important resources and material rewards that the leadership of the parliamentary party group can distribute; above all, there is competition for publicity, for chances to increase one's visibility to all those on whose support the deputy's political career (or at least reelection) depends. As competition both contributes to and is reinforced by ideological differences (or differences of views on specific policy issues), in-group conflict tends to be self-reinforcing. At the same time, of course, party opposition generates a strong pressure for intraparty solidarity. It is the resulting coincidence of and permanent tension between strong forces making for group solidarity and equally strong competitive impulses that characterize the parliamentary party group. A spirit of conflict pervades the parliamentary arena and makes task-oriented cooperation in the fulfillment of legislative functions, that is, problem solving rather than confrontation, difficult.[5]

The imperative of securing reelection as a necessary prerequisite of any further "success" is probably the most important situational constraint for deputies, though its absolute weight differs among individuals. Deputies with a personally satisfying alternative—such as a profession or job, a family to raise—are obviously less subject to the pressures of this imperative, but these deputies tend to become increasingly a minority given the ascendance of the professional (career) politician who lives not only for, but first and foremost off, politics. The reelection imperative implies dependence relations, which differ according to the primarily local or primarily national orientation of deputies. For deputies who have a "safe" district and/or are genuine district candidates firmly rooted in the local party organization, a different kind of performance spells success than for deputies who owe their reelection to the national (or regional) party organization.[6] The parliamentary arena thus has a different significance for them, which will influence their social identification with the Bundestag and their sensitivity to the rewards and punishments distributed there. For most deputies, incidentally, the parliament in Bonn and their local constituency are *both* salient reference points, and the weekly travel between these two different worlds seriously strains the chances of social integration in Bonn.

Informal Social Norms in the Bundestag

We can now turn to the informal social norms operative in this institutional setting. Informal expectations may relate to different aspects of the deputy role. It seems useful to distinguish three major categories: norms relating to group membership, norms relating to interpersonal relations, and norms relating to task performance.

Beginning with the first kind of informal expectations, we may ask what is expected of the deputy as a member of the Bundestag, irrespective of party group membership, office, sex, and age. Are deputies expected to comply, to preserve the legitimacy of their elevated political status, with normative expectations of exemplary behavior in such areas as sexual relations, alcohol consumption, and financial comportment? It may be surprising to Americans that this is not the case. More precisely, there is no normative expectation among deputies that they should conform to middle-class norms of sexual behavior and alcohol consumption, and there is no readiness to criticize, much less to sanction, infringement of such norms by colleagues. The only norm that does exist, and that is felt strongly and violated rarely, is that the infringement of such middle-class norms should not be made public. This means both that deputies must take care not to be publicly observed in irregular behavior, as it may harm the public image of their party, and that such "private sins" are not to be used as instruments in the political struggle, a norm that covers members of the parliamentary opposition as well as those of one's own party. Remarkably, the norm to keep silent about the private sins of politicians is also shared by journalists, and for them to deviate from this norm means to renounce the claim to privileged professional status.

The situation is somewhat different with respect to irregular financial behavior. While debt is a private sin and is treated as such, using the political office for personal enrichment is not. One purpose of formal rules is to prevent such abuse. But because deputies legally enjoy a number of material privileges and have legal opportunities for economic gain, there exists a "gray zone" where formal rules are not sufficient to distinguish the permissible from the unacceptable. It is in this zone that informal social norms might be looked to for guidance. To get at the corresponding normative expectations, we discussed some well-known cases of financial misdemeanor with our respondents. The degree of consensus in judgment that we found was high—surprisingly high given that our respondents were unable to formulate in positive terms specific injunctions regarding the financial behavior of deputies.

One case concerned a high-ranking member of the Christian Democrats, a former minister and president of the federal parliament (a prestigious formal position without much political power), who had to step down from this office under pressure from his own party when a lucrative contract he had negotiated with a legal firm became publicly known. Since, in terms of existing legal norms, Rainer Barzel, himself a lawyer by training, had done nothing wrong, he must have violated an important informal norm to be sanctioned so severely—unless, of course, the incident was used as an excuse to get rid of an incumbent. In fact, considerations of this kind may have been a reinforcing condition, but the vast majority of our respondents agreed that Barzel's behavior in this particular matter had been decidedly objectionable. To draw financial or generally economic advantage from one's political position—one's prestige, public visibility, acquired expertise, and personal relations—is acceptable up to a certain point, but it constitutes a norm violation when a threshold is passed. The problem is to define this threshold. Apparently, it cannot be formulated generally but must be established case by case by a complex reckoning of several factors. It was felt that Barzel had obtained a high additional income *out of proportion to the service actually rendered,* that is, an *unjust* advantage *in exchange terms,* cashing in on his political prestige alone. Worse, he himself had been inclined to moralize, that is, a discrepancy was felt to exist between his own behavior and the normative standards he publicly espoused; apparently the cutoff point between acceptable and unacceptable behavior varies with the level of moral aspiration of the actor. Yet another circumstance further aggravated his case: he had violated expectations of the proper relationship of a deputy to the party group leaders by not having informed them of this contract when he had asked for their help in a situation of economic insecurity.

While in this particular case legally correct behavior constituted deviance from informal social norms, the reverse is also possible. A second case we discussed with our respondents concerned a widely diffused, but legally dubious, fund-raising practice for political parties that became a scandal when attention was publicly drawn to it while its post-hoc legalization was sought—unsuccessfully. Eventually even some high-ranking politicians had to appear in court. Although this practice was recognized as illegal, most deputies (except for a few reacting with strong moral convictions) agreed that no social norm had been violated. Almost everyone thought that practice acceptable, possibly because it was in the interest of the party organization and not in the economic interest of individual politicians.

Although little evidence exists of informal norms referring to "private" aspects of a deputy's behavior, recognized rules exist with respect to the more political aspects of a deputy's role. There are, of course, many formal rules of procedure instructing deputies how to behave in debates, at question time, when taking votes, and so on. These formal norms are hardly controversial and, apparently, there are no strong forces that make for deviance. However, these norms give only the answers to easy how-to questions. The entry of the Green party into the federal parliament and the general irritation caused by the unorthodox behavior of Green deputies provided a good opportunity to discover the more implicit normative expectations of the parliamentary culture. The perception that the Greens violate implicit norms is widely shared among deputies, including the Greens themselves. The Greens' widely publicized, unorthodox way of dressing (tennis shoes, jeans, and never a tie), bringing of flowers and knitting to parliament, and generally informal behavior were considered to be relatively unimportant deviations per se, but they were sometimes resented because they made the well-behaved majority look like Philistines. They also provoked fierce objections when it was feared that by making the parliament as a whole look ridiculous, the Greens would seriously damage its image—the "dignity of the house" (*Würde des Hauses*)—which in fact *needs* visible demonstration to a skeptical electorate. The most severely judged norm infringements of the Greens, however, refer to the rules on which the parliamentary system as such is based, for example, readiness to abide by majority decisions, acceptance of the state's legitimate monopoly on the use of force, and tolerance for minority views. In addition, we found resentment of the moralizing stance of the Greens, who keep voicing obvious, but unattainable, ideals as if they alone believe in them. This resentment reflects an implicit expectation of realism or pragmatism, a widespread view that politics is the art of the possible, and that dream dancers make poor deputies. A related matter is the criticism that the Greens claim credit for initiatives and popular positions that they were not the first to support, thus stealing the show from other party groups. Understandably, this criticism was felt most strongly by Social Democrats, who are in ideological proximity to certain Green positions.

Norms related to group membership concern the correct behavior of a member *as* member. The most prominent of these norms, while shared at the level of the parliament, refer not to parliament as a whole—that is, the deputy's role as such—but to the parliamentary party group. Normative expectations with respect to the deputy-party group relationship specify a general norm of group solidarity or, more precisely, the expectation that the deputy should support his or her party in the struggle with the parliamentary opposition. Formulated negatively, this means avoiding behavior harmful to one's party, a norm that is even explicitly stated in party constitutions and serves as a basis for the formal procedure of ousting a member. Of course this general maxim needs to be specified, and in fact there is relatively high consensus on the types of behavior that help or harm a party group. One important expectation is support for the party group's position on legislative issues, both when voting in a plenary meeting and when talking to the press or to constituents. It is also considered harmful—and therefore to be avoided—to make pronouncements about issues on which the party has not yet established its position, because doing so might restrict its room for action.

The motives to deviate from these norms are strong because they restrict the deputy's maneuvering space in the public assertion of his or her individuality—personal judgment, values, engagement for certain causes, and so on—and hence in the pursuit of a career. The strong informal expectation to vote with one's party group (*Fraktionsdisziplin*) even stands in contrast to the constitutional norm of independence of the deputy who is formally only bound by conscience (and existing laws). This strong tension between the (uncontested) need for group solidarity and personal career interests apparently can temper normative standards by including in the formulation of norms the conditions under which they definitely ought to be respected or the acceptable forms of deviating from them if such pressure becomes very strong. For instance, not to vote with one's party group is particularly objectionable when the margin of majority is small and/or the issue attracts much publicity and when the deputy has not informed the party group's leadership beforehand of his or her intention to defect. Similarly, taking a personal stand becomes increasingly acceptable as the centrality of the issue to basic party values decreases. On the other hand, defection is particularly objectionable if the party group's official position has been reached with difficulty, and represents a compromise with party ideals. To behave as an ideological purist in such a case means trying to win personal acclaim at the expense of one's party; it is this behavior that constitutes the offense.

Another interesting feature of the norms of party group solidarity is that they often refer specifically to *representational* aspects, that is, the public, or front stage, part of behavior. If intragroup dissension cannot be avoided, as it obviously cannot, it is important at least to demonstrate unity in the face of the opposition. Thus, deputies should not inform outsiders about dissension within the party group. There is also an informal rule that one should avoid receiving applause from the opposition benches in plenary meetings. Although this contributes to the highly polemical character of parliamentary debates, it demonstratively affirms group integration and group membership.

In the relationship between deputies of the same political party, fair-play norms restricting intragroup rivalry are prominent. One shared and fairly straightforward expectation is respect for the legitimate substantive (or policy) domain of party colleagues. Several deputies reported instances where they themselves had—often unwittingly—invaded another's domain, such as a public statement on some matter, and where this had brought forth not only criticism but also stronger sanctions. A second important expectation is that deputies should not monopolize opportunities for positive self-presentation or seek publicity at the expense of colleagues; however, they should help junior or lower ranking colleagues in their quests for positive public images, for example, in their constituencies, when it can be done at little personal cost. This expectation highlights again the focal importance of the *public* dimension of political action. In contrast, attempts to obtain a bigger share of the common pool of material rewards (office space, assistance, attractive invitations, and so on) were rarely mentioned as objectionable.

The norm restricting attempts to increase one's public visibility was repeatedly formulated in another version, not as a proscription to monopolize scarce opportunities but as an injunction not to overdo the search for publicity and a positive public image. This variant of the norm is interesting insofar as it is again a "threshold norm" where the cutoff point needs to be defined—and can obviously only be defined with respect to specific cases and situations. Such a norm seems to reflect the strong forces that make conformity difficult, as with the norms of group solidarity, because what is at issue is a basic condition of individual career success.

Though what one might call "solidarity norms" clearly predominate with respect to intragroup behavior, there is also evidence of some other normative expectations, notably with respect to deference. Obviously, the prerogatives of the elected party group leadership and the committee chairs should be respected, but this is a formal, rather than an informal, norm. However, deference from newcomers toward their elders is also expected. While they are still new to the job, deputies should avoid attempts to occupy center stage, to claim superior competence in some area, or to compete for highly valued assignments. "Lie low, learn, and build up a reputation of competence and trustworthiness" is how one might summarize the advice experienced deputies would give a newcomer wanting to "make it" in Bonn. But the fact that deference rules were mentioned in the context of an "advice to newcomers" question, rather than in the informal rules one should observe to avoid censure by colleagues, indicates that they are norms with a relatively low moral intensity. To violate deference rules is a strategic mistake rather than a misdemeanor met with moral indignation.

Although strong expectations restrain intraparty rivalry and conflict, we have found surprisingly little evidence of informal norms restricting conflict between majority and opposition parties and securing their cooperation in the legislative process. Thus no informal norm restricting polemics in plenary debates seems to exist. Parliamentary polemics arise from a combination of individual motives and situational features that make for an intensely antagonistic style of verbal exchange between deputies of the governing and the opposition parties, such as is rarely found in normal professional life. Insults can be sanctioned by formal reprimand, the reprimand even being entered into the official record. But even when the formal rule is applied, it does not carry informal censure with it, although many, perhaps a majority, of deputies find these polemics at times painful and know that the electorate following them on radio or television consider them offensive. Discussions in the parliamentary committees are mostly much less polemical, though here, too, the style of interaction seems to be more often confrontational than cooperative. The lower level of expressed antagonism between deputies of different parties in committee is hardly the result of a strongly felt norm of intergroup solidarity. For one thing, some of the situational factors inducing polemics in plenary debates, such as the presence of the mass media (especially television), are absent in committee meetings. More important, the parliamentary committees are task-oriented groups, which means that in committee meetings the logic of task-related cooperation suffuses the logic of political opposition. Not surprisingly, therefore, we were told repeatedly of instances of tacit cooperation and informal premeeting contacts across party lines. But such cooperation does not seem to follow specific normative expectations to this effect; rather, it is guided by strategic considerations and a very general *do ut des* norm, that is, the rationality of fair exchange.

The Nature of the Parliamentary Subculture: Conclusions

This inquiry into the institutional subculture of the German Federal Parliament has, first of all, confirmed the existence of subcultural norms. Behavioral expectations, which the deputies themselves designated as "informal rules of the game," are widely shared. While the formulations often differed, there was a high degree of substantive consensus about such rules, irrespective of the age, sex, rank, length of experience, and political affiliation of deputies. This finding has a high validity: since no checklist of normative statements was used, deputies produced what actually came to mind when we discussed specific instances or asked what might discredit deputies in the eyes of their colleagues.

Second, the informal behavioral norms identified by this study are evidently related to the group structure of the German parliament. The most highly emphasized norms have the parliamentary party group as a reference point or refer to relations among its members. This dominance of solidarity norms referring to the parliamentary party group reflects both the high subjective salience of party group membership for the individual deputy and the much higher interaction density within, rather than between, party groups—two factors that derive from the specific institutional context. In contrast, there is strikingly less emphasis on solidarity among deputies of different parties and in parliament as a whole. The result is a clear differentiation between "in-group" and "out-group" directed behavior: acts proscribed within the party group are permitted against (deputies of) currently opposing party groups.

Of course, that does not imply that parliament as a whole *lacks* cultural integration. A number of the expectations we found are in fact attached to the role of deputy in general, for example, the expectation to overlook private sins and the normative beliefs articulated in analyzing the irritation caused by the Greens. It is quite likely that, in addition, deputies of all political parties share basic political values, which were not explicitly addressed in the interviews. But ideological and social integration evidently do not go together—at least in the German Bundestag.

What is striking about the most prominent of the behavioral expectations we found is not only their social reference point but also their specific content. The normative expectations of which deputies are particularly conscious are the rules restricting intragroup competition and the uninhibited pursuit of individual career goals. They thus constitute a kind of "social contract" that inhibits the disintegrative forces of personal rivalry and allows the party group to confront opposition from other parties. In contrast, performance-related norms, if they exist at all, seem to possess such a low priority that they did not surface when we discussed with our respondents at length the kinds of behavior that discredit or enhance a deputy in the eyes of other deputies. Even though no attempt was made in this study to discover all subcultural norms referring to different activities, relations, and so on, the substantive selectiveness of the norms we did find is in all likelihood not a methodological artifact. In fact, this finding of a selective emphasis on group-related norms is corroborated by a conclusion that Loewenberg and Mans (1988:157–158) draw from existing research, which has "demonstrated the existence of norms governing the personal relationships of legislators to each other, but showed fewer traces of norms to promote the transaction of legislative business." Of course lack of prominence does not mean nonexistence. There is, for instance, occasional reference to the norm of reciprocity, which is applied not only to career-related favors but also to task-related interactions among deputies, even across party lines. In general, however, it seems that legislative performance, the task fulfillment of deputies, is structured more by shared *cognitive* orientations, including knowledge about strategies, than by social norms.

There is, for instance, virtual unanimity among deputies in their perception of the strategic prerequisites of success in promoting policy initiatives. Deputies share the view that success is here a matter of collective effort, so that coalition formation and consensus building are generally and explicitly recognized as the preeminent conditions of securing desired policy decisions. Another generally perceived prerequisite of the successful promotion of an issue is the possession of widely acknowledged expertise on the matter. Expertise thus has an instrumental value for the deputy. In fact, to acquire expertise in a field that is both substantively promising and not yet overcrowded is advice that deputies would consensually give to a newcomer wanting to know the secret of success.

An important *formal* characteristic of the subcultural norms we found is a lack of specificity. Most accepted and easily reproducible "rules of the game" were phrased in general terms rather than in casuistic detail, that is, as specific descriptions of proscribed or desired behavior, in spite of the fact that the formulation of our questions not only permitted but indeed stimulated the mention of *specific* injunctions. That norm specificity tends to decrease with increasing status is generally accepted in role theory. However, low specificity may also be a characteristic of normative expectations that refer to membership roles rather than to task roles (positions in a functionally differentiated system). Of course, general maxims such as "Do not damage the public image of your party group" or "Do not exaggerate in seeking public visibility" provide no clear instructions for behavior in actual situations—and yet they apparently permit the widely shared evaluation of specific instances. They do so because the general maxim is fleshed out with more specific conditions of its applicability, turning it into conditional prescriptions or proscriptions. The transformation rule that turns a general maxim into specific injunctions takes the form of a statement of relaxing or intensifying conditions (that is, "the norm is applicable unless . . ." or "definitely applicable if . . ."), which means there is a threshold beyond which a tolerated behavior becomes objectionable. Thus normative expectations assume the character of a more or less complex evaluative algorithm, which may even involve difficult causal judgments concerning the fulfillment of a limiting condition (for example, whether a specific action will harm the party). In this way, it also becomes possible to apply the norm to different arenas, different types of interaction partners, and so on because specific situational features can be accommodated among the set of applicability conditions. But because it is difficult to establish exact cutoff points and to balance mitigating and exacerbating conditions objectively, conditional norms of the kind described permit negotiations about the fulfillment of the applicability conditions or the location of the threshold. As a form of social discourse, these negotiations must obviously take place post hoc, that is, when a decision has to be made on whether a given instance violates a norm, but as a form of inner monologue negotiation may also precede action. In any case, when the applicability of an injunction is negotiable, it makes for both flexible behavior and flexible norms.

Most of the behavioral maxims of the parliamentary subculture seem to be avoidance rules (or proscriptions) rather than prescriptions. They serve mainly to *curb* spontaneous behaviors, rather than to incite action. Behavior in the parliamentary situation is motivated, not by internalized norms, but by individual drives, personal interests, and possibly values on the one hand and by the incentives implied in the institutional context—the opportunity structure—on the other hand. The majority of the deputies we interviewed appeared to be motivated primarily by individual political success, which can mean both the achievement of a position and/or the shaping of policy, where "leaving a trace" is important per se and the specific area in which that occurs may be of secondary importance. This generalized power motivation, which corresponds well with the notion of a specific kind of political rationality that aims at power as an end in itself, is a likely outcome of self-selective tendencies to become a politician, of the lessons learned while climbing the career ladder, and of the institutional setting characteristic of parliamentary democracies with multiparty systems.[7]

If the behavioral norms of which deputies are most conscious serve to control and restrain behavior rather than to motivate it positively, then they present a view that contrasts sharply with the "oversocialized conception of man" implied in much of role theory (Wrong 1961), in which internalized norms are regarded as the driving force of social action. The basically restrictive character of informal behavioral norms in the Bundestag is underscored by the observation that even very strongly felt injunctions are continuously violated in the everyday interactions among deputies, which does not seem to detract from their validity as indicated by the fact that such violations continue to be sanctioned.[8] The permanent tension between strong personal motives and strong restrictive norms, together with the uncertainty about the exact dividing line between the permissible and the impermissible, turn everyday parliamentary behavior into a "tightrope walk," as one respondent expressed the feeling shared by many.

However, a word of caution should again be added. This study has been able to uncover only those elements of a common culture of deputies of which our respondents were fairly conscious. It is plausible that norms that *conflict* with personal interests and spontaneous inclinations and that are noticeably sanctioned are registered more consciously than, for instance, basic interpretive schemes, worldviews, and values, which become part of one's own motivational structure. The only legitimate conclusion is that the *easily reproducible norms* that are part of the parliamentary subculture tend to be restrictive in nature; the same cannot be said of this subculture as a whole.

The focus of this study has been the nature, rather than the genesis and functions, of subcultural norms. Nevertheless, we briefly address the two latter issues. At the beginning the general question of the link between a subculture and the encompassing culture of the society at large was raised. The empirical case reviewed here has shown evidence both of a close linkage and of specific subcultural traits. In many cases, subcultural norms appear to be situationally specific variations on a common cultural theme; examples were the expectation of reciprocity (mutual help) and the norms of group solidarity. We also found evidence of more specifically national cultural traits. Thus the rather strict separation between "private sins" that are irrelevant and not to be sanctioned in the parliamentary arena and deviations from standards considered binding *for parliamentarians* may well reflect a cultural tradition of separation between the private and the public spheres, which has no counterpart in the United States.[9] In contrast, the extremely high sensitivity to the public visibility of behavior is an arena-specific aspect of the parliamentary subculture. In the case of private sins, public visibility itself constitutes the norm violation; in cases of deviance from subcultural norms, it is an aggravating circumstance; and in the case of the expectation of a demonstrative in-group/out-group difference in behavior (in public one must applaud deputies of one's party and criticize or denigrate deputies of the opposition party), visibility even becomes the basis of a behavioral norm. In all these cases, the arena-specific elements of subcultural norms are clearly shaped by the institutional context, for example, the reelection imperative and the related need to present a favorable image to the electorate.

This last observation immediately raises the issue of functionality. In the Parsonian tradition of thinking, the cultural system fulfills essential integrative and adaptive functions by controlling and coordinating social action (Parsons 1951:26–45). As is also evident in other contributions to this volume, the assumption of a general cultural functionality has often been challenged—without therefore denying the directive effects of culture on human behavior. In studies of organizational culture, there is likewise no general assumption of functionality: organizational cultures can also obstruct change and the necessary adaptation to new situations (for example, Bate 1984). In light of the empirical evidence presented here, it does appear that the subcultural norms reflect the needs of political survival and political success in the given institutional context. But these are power-related needs of individuals and social groups, which may conflict with the prerequisites of an optimal fulfillment of legislative functions. In this respect, we have seen that norms that would contribute to such task performance are absent or possess a low priority; this holds both for performance-related norms and for norms ensuring cooperation in legislative work across party lines. Some of the strong norms we found, on the other hand, can be dysfunctional in this regard. This is true, for instance, of the norm of demonstrative antagonism to the out-group which can result in obstruction of legislative procedures for the sake of obstruction alone rather than for substantive reasons. Though the available evidence does not definitely show whether the high level of individual competition and the normatively supported antagonism between party groups negatively affects the inherent quality of legislative performance, such as the timeliness, innovativeness, and problem-solving capacity of policy decisions, this study does raise some doubt on the functionality of the parliamentary subculture for effective legislation. This implies that subcultural norms might generally respond more to the imperatives of system maintenance than to those of system performance.

Notes

---

1. This homogeneity-differentiation issue should be clearly distinguished from the coherence-incoherence issue; see Neil Smelser, chapter 1 of this volume.
2. This comes out very clearly in Dierkes's (1988) survey of the literature; see, particularly, Schein (1983).
3. The sample was stratified by sex, party affiliation, and length of service in the Bundestag. We interviewed five women and twenty-five men; seven were deputies of the Christian Democrats, three of its Bavarian sister party the CSU, eleven of the Social Democrats, four of the Free Democrats, and five of the Green party. Of the thirty interviews, all but eight were conducted by Friedhelm Neidhardt and myself, the remaining ones by Peter Stadler, a part-time collaborator on the project whose main job was parliamentary assistant. The interview period extended over twenty-two months, with most interviews conducted between the summer of 1986 and the fall of 1987. All interviews were guided by a schedule containing twenty questions, though they were not always in a standard sequence and sometimes varied in their phrasing. To undercut the defenses of interview partners as highly skilled impression managers (as parlia-

mentarians are), we used no preformulated statements and only open questions and avoided asking for the verbalization of prescriptions. Instead we asked for proscriptions and sanctions (from general disapproval over open criticism and withdrawal of support to ostracism) and discussed the reactions to well-known "scandalous" incidents and the irritations caused by the behavior of Green deputies in order to get at the normative expectations underlying them.

4. Gesetz über die Rechtsverhältnisse der Mitglieder des Deutschen Bundestages, passed on 18 February 1977.

5. For this distinction of decision styles and their implications for decision outcomes see Scharpf (1988).

6. The existence of these two categories of deputies, those elected by majority vote in their district and those getting into parliament via a party's list of candidates, follows from the German election law, which mixes elements of proportional and majoritarian representation.

7. It would require a separate discussion to establish whether power per se can also be called a subcultural *value*. We have found hints that striving for power for oneself and for one's group are accepted among deputies, while the person who confuses politics with a morality play is regarded with suspicion and ridicule. But toward the electorate and the public, it is still necessary to display a primary *policy* orientation and to convey the impression of working for the common welfare. One also should not discount completely the effects of the disappointment that deputies strongly motivated to shape some aspect of reality experience invariably when they realize that individually attributable success in policy matters is virtually impossible. This disappointment may lead to a displacement of the criteria defining success from policy to power.

8. The cutting edge of available social sanctions, incidentally, aims precisely at that type of deputy who is under the strongest pressure to infringe the norms curbing disintegrative tendencies, that is, the career politician who wants to "make it" *in Bonn*. Within a parliamentary party group, task-oriented cooperation and special resources cannot be withdrawn without harming the effectiveness of the group, as both are to a large extent functionally determined. Other sanctions, such as publicly reprimanding or ousting a member, would be to the direct advantage of the opposition. What remains is, above all, the withdrawal of support in seeking offices and in reelection—the very core of the careerist's striving.

9. This cultural difference is time and again experienced by Europeans in contact with Americans, whose immediate and direct inquiry into matters considered private, and therefore to be raised at the utmost only by close friends, they consider indiscreet and difficult to deal with.

References

Aberbach, Joel D., Robert D. Putnam, and Bert A. Rockman. 1981. *Bureaucrats and politicians in western democracies*. Cambridge, Mass.: Harvard University Press.

Allaire, Y., and M. E. Firsirotu. 1984. Theories of organizational culture. *Organization Studies* 5: 193–226.

Almond, G. A., and S. Verba. 1965. *The civic culture: Political attitudes and democracy in five nations.* Boston: Little, Brown.

Arensberg, C. C. 1954. The community study method. *American Journal of Sociology.* 60: 109–124.

Bate, P. 1984. The impact of organizational culture on approaches to organizational problem-solving. *Organization Studies* 5: 43–66.

Crowe, E. W. 1983. Consensus and structure in legislative norms: Party discipline in the House of Commons. *Journal of Politics* 45: 907–931.

Crozier, M., and E. Friedberg. 1977. *L'acteur et le système.* Paris: Éditions du Seuil.

Dierkes, M. 1988. Unternehmenskultur und Unternehmensführung. *Zeitschrift für Betriebswirtschaft* 58: 554–575.

Feick, J., and W. Jann. 1989. Comparative policy research—Eclecticism or systematic integration? Max-Planck Institut für Gesellschaftsforschung discussion paper.

Hofstede, G. 1981. Culture and organizations. *International Studies of Management and Organizations* 10 (4): 15–41.

Keesing, R. 1974. Theories of culture. *Annual Review of Anthropology* 3: 73–97.

Kornberg, A. 1964. The rules of the game in the Canadian House of Commons. *Journal of Politics* 26: 358–380.

Kroeber, A., and T. Parsons. 1958. The concept of culture and of social system. *American Sociological Review* 23: 582–583.

Lammers, C. J., and D. J. Hickson. 1979. *Organizations alike and unlike: International and institutional studies in the sociology of organizations.* London: Routledge and Kegan Paul.

Loewenberg, G., and T. C. Mans. 1988. Individual and structural influences on the perception of legislative norms in three European parliaments. *American Journal of Politics* 155–177.

Matthews, D. 1960. *U.S. senators and their world.* Chapel Hill: University of North Carolina Press.

Mayntz, R., and F. Neidhardt. 1989. Parlamentskultur: Handlungs-orientierungen von Bundestagsabgeordneten. *Zeitschrift für Parlamentsfragen* 20 (3): 370–387.

Mester-Grün, M. 1979. *Beruf: Abgeordneter. Das einfache Mandat aus sozialwissenschaftlicher Sicht.* Bonn.

Ouchi, W. G., and A. L. Wilkins. 1985. Organizational culture. *American Review of Sociology* 11: 457–483.

Parsons, T. 1951. *The social system.* Glencoe, Ill.: Free Press.

Scharpf, F. W. 1988. The joint decision trap: Lessons from German federalism and European integration. *Journal of Public Administration* 66 (3): 239–289.

Schein, E. A. 1983. The role of the founder in creating corporate culture. *Organizational Dynamics* 12: 13–28.

Sturm, R. 1985. "Die Politikanalyse. Zur Konkretisierung des Konzeptes der politischen Kultur in der policy-analyse." In *Policy-Forschung in der Bundes-*

republik Deutschland, edited by H. G. Hartwich, 111–116. Opladen: Westdeutscher Verlag.

Wahlke, J. et al. 1962. *The legislative process.* New York: John Wiley.

Wilkins, A. L., and W. B. Ouchi. 1983. Efficient cultures: Exploring the relationship between culture and organizational performance. *Administrative Science Quarterly* 28: 468–481.

Wrong, D. H. 1961. The oversocialized conception of man in modern sociology. *American Sociological Review* 26: 183–193.

Smircich, L. 1983. Concepts of culture and organizational analysis. *Administrative Science Quarterly* 28: 339–358.

PART THREE

Culture, Inequality,
and Life-style

9

The Production and Reproduction of Inequality
A Theoretical Cultural Analysis
Richard Münch

Structures of social inequality are a traditional object of sociological research and theory building and have always received a good deal of attention. In the relatively recent past, empirical studies have been able to provide increasingly subtle insights into the changes occurring in these structures. This makes social inequality a well-researched sociological subject. Yet theoretical explanation has now been left behind by developments in empirical research. In many cases, the same tools that were most used during the 1950s and 1960s are still being bandied about: functionalistic approaches vie with conflict-theoretical ones or some combination of the two is used. However, the development of sociological theory has changed since the 1950s and 1960s. What is lacking is a link between the two developments. To change this latter situation is the purpose of a project upon which this paper reports. The objectives in carrying out the project are as follows:

—To formulate a sociological theory of the production and reproduction of structures of social inequality (by this I also mean the transformation of such structures).
—To formulate ideal-typical models of the various processes in which structures of social inequality are produced and reproduced.

I am grateful to Neil Johnson for his help in translating the German original of this article. Many thanks also to Claudia Flümann and Willy Viehöver for the bibliographical work.

243

—To clarify the ideal-typical models by taking selected societies as examples.

I begin with the premise that social structures of inequality, in terms of income, power, education, and prestige, are produced, reproduced, and transformed in interaction with the cultural code of a society, which entails the language, values, and norms used in discourses on questions of equality and inequality. This interaction is where culture meets social structure, exerts its influence on it, and is itself influenced by it. The cultural code sets the frame within which structures of inequality are produced, reproduced, and transformed into legitimate ones. The social structure of inequality, which exists at a certain place and time, sets the conditions from which any reproduction and transformation of inequalities starts.

The effects of the cultural code and of the existing social structure of inequality on each other are set in motion and mediated by processes of social interaction, which I differentiate analytically into four basic types according to my interpretation of the Parsonian AGIL-schema as an action space composed of four fields: market exchange (A), political struggle (G), processes of communal association (I), and cultural legitimation (L).[1]

An action space can be construed in terms of the interrelation of two basic elements: symbols (meaning constructions, norms, expressions, cognitions) and actions guided by these symbols. The sphere of symbols can be more or less ordered according to the number and interrelations of symbols: their complexity. The sphere of actions can be more or less ordered according to the number of actions that could possibly occur: their contingency. The complexity of symbols and the contingency of actions vary independently of each other. This makes possible four extreme combinations:

A. Adaptation. Opening of the scope for action. High symbolic complexity and high contingency of actions. In market exchange no limit to the wishes and actions could be imagined.

G. Goal attainment. Specification of the scope for action. High symbolic complexity and low contingency of actions. In political struggle the application of power restricts actions to what is commanded, though an unlimited set of alternatives could be imagined.

I. Integration. Closing of the scope for action. Low symbolic complexity and low contingency of actions. In communal association the horizon of imagination and the alternatives of action are limited to a self-evident life-world. Within the field of communal association solidarity relationships exert the greatest closing effects on action. Beliefs and life-styles provide for generalization, rites for opening, and cults for specification within the boundaries of the closed life-world of communal association. Generalization is extended by defining the legitimacy of beliefs and life-styles, opening by the change of associations, and specification by the settling of group conflict.

L. Latent pattern maintenance. Generalization of the scope for action. High symbolic complexity and high contingency of actions. In discursive cultural legitimation a broad set of different actions is subsumed under one single value or a small set of general values.

There are the basic fields of social interaction in which corresponding processes of interaction link the cultural code with existing structures of inequality. The latter are located in the solidarity relationships, the association and dissociation of people in society. The structure of inequality is a structure of solidarity relationships that initially limits access to associations and then to income, power, education, and prestige.

As indicated, this structure of inequality is reproduced and transformed in interaction with the cultural code of society. The latter provides the language for legitimating and delegitimating equality and inequality. Its relation to the structure of inequality is primarily one of symbolization, which is guided by the law of symbolic abstraction. This means that talking about structures of inequality in terms of the language of the cultural code tends toward abstraction in the sense of defining concrete inequalities in more general terms, for example, in terms of general rights to equality instead of particular wishes for equality. The more the reproduction and transformation of structures of inequalities is guided by symbolic abstraction, that is, by a system of general ideas, the more the particular interests will be channeled into the frame of general rights.

In addition to being guided by symbolic abstraction, the reproduction and the transformation of existing structures of inequality are also guided by cultural legitimation according to the law of discursive generalization, by market exchange according to the law of economic achievement, by political struggle according to the law of political accumulation, and by communal association according to the law of inertia and

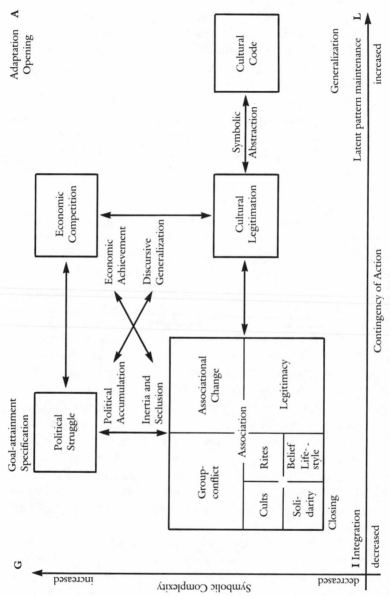

Figure 9.1. The production and reproduction of structures of inequality.

seclusion. The processes of communal association, political struggle, and market exchange are related to the cultural code via processes of cultural legitimation and symbolic abstraction, which are closest to the cultural code. The processes of symbolic abstraction, cultural legitimation, market exchange, and political struggle are related to social structures of inequality via processes of communal association, which are also closest to the cultural code (see figure 9.1).

Communal association is governed by the law of inertia and by communal exclusiveness:

The more people are linked together in a community, the more they will confine the circle in which they live to that community, and the greater will be the barriers that are reciprocally erected between different self-contained life-circles.

This communal exclusiveness then leads to a corresponding cultural exclusiveness reflected in common cultural symbols, ideas, and lifestyles, in the regular renewal of these via common rituals, and in their orientation to common goals via common cults. In turn, these common symbols, rituals, and cults also contribute to the reproduction of social exclusiveness. If the law of inertia and social exclusiveness were to be the only factor having an effect on society, its structure of classes, strata, social groupings, and social milieu would continually reproduce itself in the same way. This would be a traditionalistically determined society in which nothing ever changed.

The process of *market exchange* is governed by the law of market success (achievement):

The more people seek economic success and enter into market exchange and competition with one another, the more they will change the circles in which they live to suit changing degrees of success and the lower will be the barriers between different circles.

Because market success is the factor that decides to which life-circle one will belong and because it is a factor relatively prone to change, the membership of different life-circles changes rapidly, but this does not mean a change in the way society is differentiated according to variations in market success. Society is constantly characterized by inequality between those who are more successful and those who are less, yet a person's particular position of success is subject to continual change as long as market success is the only law in operation.

A precondition for the operation of the law of market success, however, is the existence of ideal market conditions, that is, of equal competitive opportunities for all. Yet because in practice market successes can be converted into advantageous starting positions for the continuing competition, there is a tendency for the successful to form an exclusive circle. This is the law of economic accumulation:

The more success someone has, the more successful he/she will be in future, and the converse for anyone who is less successful, provided that the available resources are deployed optimally.

Despite these conditions, the market is where the greatest mobility is permitted compared with any other social field, because the race to success is run afresh day after day, even if the starting conditions are not actually equal. In comparison with the market sphere, the communal, political, and cultural spheres are characterized by greater inertia, a greater tendency toward persistence, or a slower rate of change.

The process of *political struggle* is governed by the law of political accumulation:

The more people are determined to reach one particular goal and the more any one individual's actions have consequences for others, the more frequently one person's goal attainment will be at others' expense, or, in other words, the more frequently the various individuals come into conflict and the more frequently they have to mobilize power in order to achieve their aims.

In the event that the goal involved is to attain or retain a relatively high position within society, under these conditions the result will be a political struggle for the higher societal positions. Persons and groups higher up the scale use the power available to them to keep others away from their positions, while persons and groups occupying lower positions mobilize power (by forming coalitions of the relatively weak to confront the strong, for example) in a bid to gain access to the higher positions. Under these conditions, the law of political accumulation comes into effect:

The more power people already possess, the more they are able to augment their power in the political struggle.

Consequently, one can expect structures of social inequality to become proportionately more stable as the powerful become still more powerful and the weak still weaker. This naturally only applies to the extent that social inequality truly is reproduced by political struggle and other laws do not come into play. If the weaker parties make more intelligent use of the power available to them and/or if they form coalitions, they may succeed in overcoming the stronger ones after all. This is the point where changes can be made in social inequality, and these then take the form of revolutionary upheavals and shifts in power.

The process of *cultural legitimation* is governed by the law of discursive generalization:

The more the allocation of a position is subject to discursive reasoning, the more likely the allocation of a position is considered legitimate only if it is justified by generally valid principles.

Any person's or group's possession of more income, power, cultural competence (in the sense of "authoritativeness"), or prestige than others is no longer taken without question but has to be justified on generally accepted grounds. This means that inequality of income is only counted as legitimate if it flows from a corresponding inequality in achievement. Likewise, inequality of power is only taken to be legitimate if it is necessary for the attainment of common goals, inequality of competence or authoritativeness only if it is based on unequal levels of knowledge, and inequality of prestige only if it derives from the unequal realization of common values. These ideas—the apportionment of income according to achievement, power according to the need for leadership in order to attain common goals, cultural competence according to knowledge, and prestige according to the realization of common values—are the universal ideas through which inequalities need to be justified in modern society.

To the above must be added justification by the idea of equality. In a radical interpretation, this would give all inequalities the taint of illegitimacy. In a less radical view which acknowledges the previous requirements of the unequal allocation of positions, the idea of equality is narrowed down to the idea of equality of opportunity. If income is to be differentiated according to achievement, everyone must then be given an equal chance to achieve. If power is to be differentiated according to the need to attain common goals, everyone should be offered the same chance to be a candidate for the corresponding positions of power. If cultural competence (authoritativeness) is to be attributed with knowledge as the decisive standard, everyone should have the same opportunity to acquire that knowledge. If prestige is to be apportioned in line with the realization of common values, everyone should have the same opportunity to participate in realizing those values. In this sense, the effect of the compulsion to legitimate social inequality in modern society is the dismantling of inequalities of opportunity. This must not be confused with dismantling social inequality itself. It does not change the differentials in income, power, cultural competence, or prestige in the slightest. Moreover, the pressure of legitimation working toward reducing inequality of opportunity need not necessarily or immediately signify any actual reduction in such inequality. The wrong measures are often taken, and many attempts fall short of the goal or lose their effectiveness over time because the other sets of laws—the laws of inertia and social exclusiveness, of market success, and of political accumulation—act as countervailing forces to the equality of opportunity. However, this in its turn does not mean that the law of discursive generalization remains completely ineffective. Had it not exerted its effects, we would still be in a pre-Enlightenment society in which traditionally established inequalities of opportunity would be taken as self-evident. Modern society can at least be distinguished from such a situation insofar as inequality of opportunity now bears a stigma of illegitimacy.

The four laws discussed above that govern the production and reproduction of social inequality are ranked with different priorities in different societies and are combined in different ways. This gives rise to a complex structure composed of both basic laws and derived laws resulting from combinations of these laws. For example, in the struggle between classes and strata, the law of political accumulation combines with the law of inertia and social exclusiveness, whereas in the struggle for legitimation the former law combines with that of discursive generalization, and in the competitive struggle it combines with that of market success.

The four basic laws dominate to different degrees in different societies, taking the lead from and working in conjunction with the remaining basic laws in each case. That is, no society is determined exclusively by the working of one law; rather, a society is determined by a set of laws interrelated in a specific ranking. The ranking of laws may change during the historical development of a society. However, if we contrast societies to each other, then we may discern the primary effects of a specific leading law and the secondary effects of the other laws in a specific rank order in particular societies over the period of historical development since the onset of industrialization. In the following section, I illustrate the workings and interrelationships of the above laws with an example of the development of structures of inequality in German society since the nineteenth century, when the basic formation of its cultural code and social structure and their unique interrelationship took shape.

In doing so, I briefly describe the cultural code that underlies the structure of inequality and that, via the value conceptions and the language it embraces, represents the basis for processes that legitimate social inequality. Then follows a description of the structure of inequality and the symbols and life-styles, rituals and cults belonging to it, this being complemented by an identification of the unique characteristics of the legitimacy, change, and conflict associated with that structure of inequality. Finally, the structure and its unique characteristics are explained with reference to one particular law and the interplay between it and the other laws.[2]

A Historical Illustration: German Society

The cultural code of German society took shape during the nineteenth century under the leadership of the cultured, educated middle class (*Bildungsbürgertum*), comprising professors, teachers, and clergy, and its alliance with the state.[3] In this process, three ideas took on an especially significant role: the classical idea of education, the idea of a person's office, and the idea of synthesis, the latter two as an attempt to close the split between established bourgeois society and industrial society and as a specific form in which the postulate of equality established during the Enlightenment could be realized. Social rank is determined by the type and level of education people have received and the level of responsibility attached to the offices people hold within society. The differentiation of society into classes, strata, and groups is supposed to be overcome by a synthesis that leads to a new unity. Hegel saw this synthesis embodied in the state, Marx saw it in Communist society, the revisionists saw it in the social welfare state (*Sozialstaat*), and the National Socialists saw it in the popular state (*Volksstaat*). Following World War II, the role of synthesis has been played by the concepts of the social market economy, the leveled middle-class society and affluence for all.

By tradition, the structure of inequality in German society is characterized primarily by the differentiation of classes and status groups according to the type and level of education they have received.[4] In accordance with this tradition, which dates back to the nineteenth century, it has never been possible for those rising socially through economic or political success to claim the same legitimacy as those rising by way of education. The second traditional criterion for the allocation of status is the vesting of a person with an "office." The closer this office is located to the center of the state, the higher its rank. In the nineteenth century, the alliance between the cultured, educated middle class and the state allowed the well-read professor, the grammar school (*Gymnasium*) teacher, the pastor, lawyer or doctor, the civil servant, and the officer to emerge as and to remain for a long period the best respected status groups. In contrast, the classes and strata belonging to the business, industry, technology, and agriculture spheres were valued unfavorably because they possessed neither a classical education nor any kind of office. Officialdom itself is again differentiated according to the level of education attained, the categories being top-level, senior, middle-level, and junior officials. From the 1870s on, however, the alliance between heavy industry and the state, together with the overall economic and political ascendancy of the commercial, industrial, and technical strata, began to question the claims to higher status of the *Bildungsbürgertum* and officialdom, creating a situation of status insecurity.

In the postwar period, the flourishing of material consumption has encouraged the social advancement of higher-earning commercial, industrial, and technical strata.[5] Status today is no longer acquired solely via education or tenure of office, but it is also a function of the food, dress, living accommodations, furniture, automobiles, and vacations that people can afford. In this sense, society in West Germany has moved closest—among the European societies—to the principle of market success and the demonstrative consumption this implies, and hence it has also achieved the closest resemblance to U.S. society. In this situation, we see the traditional apportionment of status via education and office tenure existing side by side with the apportionment of status according to economic success and demonstrative consumption.

That is not to say, then, that the criterion of education has become totally insignificant. Rather, it also has penetrated the commercial and industrial strata as they have grown in importance and it determines internal differentiation within these strata. Training and academic certificates also determine social status here: occupational schools, technical schools, and technical degree colleges, together with advanced training and informational courses of all kinds, ensure that members of these strata are better trained and qualified than ever.

The manual working population, too, is typically divided into groups of unskilled, semiskilled, and skilled workers. Both trends—the greater significance of qualification in training overall and the constant increase in the level of consumption—have led to the traditional differentiation of society being replaced by a society in which the large majority of households can participate both in a relatively high level of consumption and in a constantly rising level of education and training. In comparison with other Western European countries, Germany exhibits the least hierarchical differentiation of society. Status is granted according to four criteria, with the first two increasingly pushed into the background by the latter two: (1) classical education before technical training, (2) civil service or "official" positions placed before self-employed, employees, and workers, (3) level of qualification within one's occupation, including technical training, and (4) level of consumption.

As more and more households attain relatively high levels of training and consumption, the society increasingly corresponds to what Schelsky termed the *leveled middle-class society* (*nivellierte Mittelstandsgesellschaft*).[6] This would appear to be the synthesis that has always been sought in Germany. It is now a society with a highly diffuse social structure in which, as a result of the change in criteria for the apportionment of status, one no longer really knows who belongs where. The place of collective groupings on different levels of rank is taken instead by individual destinies: factors such as occupational or economic failure, illness, divorce or separation, and unemployment influence the course of life far more than social stratum class does. A broadly cast center is taking shape that includes all those able to participate in consumption and education or training. It is surrounded by a periphery of marginal groups either unwilling or unable to participate in consumption and/or education and training. The term *the two-thirds society* has been coined to depict this situation.[7]

The same diffusivity found in the overall social edifice also characterizes general attitudes to life and life-styles. Whereas one might traditionally have relied on a clear differentiation between attitudes to life and life-styles, the lines have become increasingly blurred over time. The pride taken by the government official in serving the state, by the *Bildungsbürgertum* in its level of education, by the self-employed in their independence, by white-collar employees in the services they provide, by the industrial and technical strata in the usefulness of their work, by manual workers in the value of their physical effort, and by farmers in their tilling of the soil has since given way to an overall relativizing of these values and to efforts, regardless of the stratum to which one belongs, to reach a satisfying level of education or training, to work with a likeable team of people, and to enjoy a good life with time for consumption, vacations, and leisure activities. The same is true of the interpretational patterns with which people view society. The workers' dichotomous view of society is blurred by the diffuse notion that they, too, can join in the general process of consumption. Anyone who can afford the things that all others can afford will not have the feeling of being near the bottom of any social scale.[8]

Life-styles have converged to a tremendous extent, primarily because of the general improvement in education and income levels. This emerging cult of upgraded consumption may seem surprising for those who know Germany from its traditional class hierarchy. However, tremendous changes have occurred that began in the fifties and attained a very high level in the eighties. The recent literature on consumption styles and the "individualization" of life chances now pays overwhelming attention to this development.[9]

It is now so thoroughly widespread for people to participate in consumption of more "luxurious" goods and services—the home itself, household appliances, furniture, television, stereos, videos, personal computers, automobiles, good food, clothing, entertainment, sporting activities, vacations, and so on—that hardly any difference is visible between the household of a skilled worker couple, who between them may have monthly earnings of about DM 6,000, and the households of teachers, clergy, professors, business people, technicians, and engineers, for their disposable income will frequently not be so much higher. All of these groups share the same pleasure in consuming semiluxury and luxury goods.[10] Those who are unable to participate in this celebration of consumption are students, young trainees and apprentices, senior citizens with low pensions, those dependent on social assistance, low-income families with a single earner, the unemployed, and those who have consciously chosen an alternative, less materialistic life-style. These are the marginal groups who are unable or, in some cases, unwilling to be included in the overall celebration of consumption.[11] On the other hand, the ideals of high culture have also become part of widespread demonstrative consumption. Wherever they do still fulfill a demarcating function, they represent the life-style of marginal academics who are no longer able to claim any higher status for their love of literature, theater, or art. Therefore, there is no longer a hierarchical differentiation of value attitudes, worldviews, and life-styles, but there is the dominance of one broad and central complex of relatively luxurious consumption and a narrow periphery of marginal groups comprising poor and/or nonconforming people. This peculiar quality of value attitudes, worldviews, and life-styles has feedback effects on the apportionment of status. An ever-broader center develops when the internal differentiation of status becomes less pronounced because everyone has a similar opportunity to participate in education and consumption. Marginal groups remain excluded and, because they abstain from consumption either intentionally or unintentionally, are denied the status of belonging by the two-thirds majority.

An examination of the rituals that serve to renew the social structure shows developments similar to those that can be observed among value attitudes, worldviews, and life-styles. The tradition dating back to the nineteenth century gave rise to numerous rituals for the inward unification and outward demarcation of social classes, strata, and groups. A visit to the theater, the opera, or a classical concert, eating in restaurants, shopping in large stores, playing golf or tennis, riding, playing football, going on vacation, dinner parties—these are all activities in which particular classes, strata, or groups would stay among their own kind. In this sense, they did represent rituals of inward unification and outward demarcation. Though it is still possible to observe these rites today, they are on the decline. Engaging in these activities more frequently involves stepping beyond the confines of one's own class, stratum, or group. They are less often reserved for members of any particular class, stratum, or group, which in turn means that they rarely can function as demarcation rituals. Instead, they tend to serve as rituals of unification across a broader front. Other rituals in which class, stratum, or group boundaries are unknown can be added, such as strolling down the shopping streets and visiting a supermarket or shopping complex.[12] This decline in demarcation rituals, coupled with a simultaneous increase in rituals of unification beyond class, stratum, or group boundaries, is a development stemming from the changes in social structure, but it also has a positive feedback effect on those changes toward increasing diffusivity in the social structure. Traditionally, rituals of synthesis have made a decisive contribution to unification independent of class, stratum, or group, including large-scale events such as the German Festival of Gymnastics, the biannual national congress in the Lutheran church, choral festivals, and carnival processions in the main Rhineland centers. All of these events are open to anyone to take part.

Cults lend a specific identity to classes, strata, and groups, and to society as a whole. The cult that has traditionally fulfilled this function is that of education. *Abitur* ceremonies (the highest examination in secondary education), master's ceremonies in the craft trades, and graduation ceremonies of whatever kind publicly document the identity of the corresponding educational stratum. The modern cult is that of semi-luxurious and luxurious consumption. To belong, it is essential to join in this cult. By this means, the vast majority of the population confirms its membership not in any particular stratum, but in the mainstream, the center of society.

The traditional basis for the legitimacy of the structure of inequality described was the unequal distribution of educational certificates. Given this tradition, any status differential has to be justifiable in terms of different educational levels. Anyone with a poor education attaining a higher position or earning a higher income, or conversely anyone well educated taking up a low position or earning very little, will awaken doubts as to his or her legitimacy. This criterion for legitimacy has been accompanied increasingly by the criterion of participation in semiluxurious or luxurious consumption. The latter is normally a precondition for attaining prestige in the neighborhood.

In light of the idea of equality, the legitimacy of unequal access to educational institutions has increasingly been questioned. This situation, combined with a widespread desire for advancement, has led to a tremendous increase in the number of people with advanced educational qualifications. Hence, we are a little closer to the synthesis we had always dreamed of now that the number of higher educational qualifications has grown, but there has also been a counteracting consequence: the traditional link between a high degree of educational qualification and a higher status is being loosened. There is a growing number of people who, although they have achieved advanced educational qualifications, have not attained any higher status. This phenomenon is felt to represent, and is criticized as, status inconsistency and gives rise to doubts as to the legitimacy of existing status differentiation in light of traditional ideas. Yet as these developments continue, the old idea of status being accorded in terms of educational qualification will be undermined. Together with the general increase in the level of consumption, the vast number of people with advanced educational qualifications is leading to the differentiation of status being broken down in its entirety. The market, and hence the short-term allocation of status and income, is gradually replacing the long-term allocation of the two on the basis of having attained a given level of education.[13]

Traditionally, people's association in neighborhoods, political communities, and group leisure activities was differentiated along class and status-group lines. Accordingly, the cities are divided into workers' neighborhoods and those for the middle and upper strata. However, this picture has been substantially changed by the enormous growth in residential areas on the edges of the cities and outside the cities altogether. The groups mix together to a far higher degree in these new residential areas. Business people, various grades of white-collar employees or civil servants, and skilled workers all live next door to each other. The same can be increasingly said of sporting and other leisure activities. Thus, there is an increase in the number of associations that form as a result of the coincidental convergence of private interests and private decisions, and these associations accordingly introduce a greater dynamism into the structure of classes, strata, and groups and act as a countervailing force to the traditional differentiation of associations along status lines.[14]

Beginning with social legislation enacted during Bismarck's time, attempts have been made to solve the conflict between classes, strata, and groups by achieving a synthesis. However, Bismarck's policy of persecuting the socialists prevented the inclusion of the working class into society. Following the approaches to inclusion made during the Weimar Republic, which granted the Social Democrats access to government, and by the National Socialists, with the synthesis inherent in their idea of the popular state (*Volksstaat*), the inclusion of working people has progressed further in the Federal Republic of Germany, with the development of the social welfare state and the idea of social partnership, than in most comparable industrial nations. The class struggle has been displaced by class synthesis on a scale that surpasses even the dreams of the revisionists within the early socialist movement.[15] Together with the synthesis achieved by the welfare state and social partnership, the continual increase in the number of advanced educational qualifications has led to a growing educational synthesis. The decline in individual attachment to class or stratum and the traditionally high value placed on education indicate that more and more people have set out to gain a higher level of educational qualifications. As a consequence, competition to gain better occupational positions is greatly intensified. Even to belong to the center that comprises those able to participate in more luxurious consumption, it is absolutely essential to strive for higher educational qualifications. The traditional class struggle has long since been displaced by a universal struggle for educational and training certificates and for the qualified jobs that have now become so scarce. Traditionally, the three-class secondary education system—comprised of the *Hauptschule*, which is the most elementary form of secondary schooling, the *Realschule*, which provides a more thorough preparation for technical and practical careers, and the *Gymnasium*, with its classical academic education to prepare future university students—had the effect of securing the perpetuation of the old hierarchical status differentiation because family background exerts a major influence on students' success at school at the age of eleven years, when pupils are allocated to the various types of secondary schools. With the broadening of access to the *Realschule,* the *Gymnasium,* and later to universities and other institutions of further education, this tradition has been counteracted, but one consequence has undoubtedly been intensified competition in the labor market and a corresponding devaluation of advanced educational qualifications as a prerequisite to higher-placed careers. The struggle to gain educational qualifications and then qualified jobs is something that embraces the whole of society.

The law that primarily explains the production and reproduction of the structure of social inequality described above and its specific hallmarks is the law of discursive generalization. This law states that discourse on the legitimacy of social structures leads to a process in which the ideas underlying those structures are increasingly generalized, and this gives rise to increasing pressure on social structures to approach the more comprehensively interpreted ideas. Since the establishment of the alliance between the *Bildungsbürgertum* and the state in the nineteenth century, the ideas that have been used as a standard against which to measure structures of inequality in Germany are those of education and the holding of an "office." These ideas were used in societal discourse to justify social status. In light of these ideas it is only when there is a congruence between education and the responsibilities of office on the one hand and cultural competence (authoritativeness), power, income, and prestige on the other that this can be considered legitimate.

The *Bildungsbürgertum's* alliance with the state gave these ideas and the discourse associated with them such a priority that they decisively influenced the approach of the entire social structure during the nineteenth century as to what was conceived to be an ideal hierarchy of education and office. However, the economic and political ascendancy of the commercial, industrial, and technical strata, as well as the working class, also gave the value attitudes of these strata and classes a place in societal discourse. This meant that increasing significance was attached to the usefulness of education and material consumption when it came to the legitimation of status differentials. Advanced education in the classical sense then had to compete with the most varied, utility-oriented educational qualifications and could no longer claim higher status as a right. In this way, the understanding of education became discursively generalized: whereas education was traditionally understood in terms of classical education, it currently embraces everything from training received by skilled workers via the master's certificate and various technical schools and college diplomas to university degrees. Insofar as any hierarchy is still visible in this spectrum, it would appear to be a relic of classical education's traditional claim to élite status. However, this tradition has been so revised that society no longer has the appearance of being clearly divided according to an educational hierarchy, but it now contains a diffuse complex of improved educational qualifications that represent a broad center from which marginal groups without such qualifications are set apart.

Another effect of discursive generalization derives from the idea of equality as interpreted during the French Revolution, which was understood as a form of synthesis in nineteenth-century Germany and, hence, as a solution to the division of society into classes, strata, and groups. The idea of synthesis was in accordance with the worldview of an educated stratum allied with the state. Thus Hegel saw a synthesis of society's dissipation into particularized interests as being achievable by pledging the state to the general good. Through various stages of development, this idea of synthesis has retained its significance. It is possible to see the synthesis of present-day society in the constant broadening of education and in the integration of many educational qualifications into a more general understanding of the term *education*. A wider interpretation of the postulate of equality requires that the entire population be involved via a comprehensive concept of education.

The law of discursive generalization exerts strong pressure to change upon the structure of classes, strata, and groups, and it restricts the effectiveness of the law of inertia and social exclusiveness. The social structure began by developing a hierarchy of education and office tenure in the nineteenth century, which was later displaced more and more in the current century, especially since 1945, by a societal pattern in which a broad center where all kinds of educational qualifications exist is surrounded by a narrow periphery where the level of education is low. The consolidation of the hierarchy of education and of office tenure in the nineteenth century was made possible by the secondary role played by the law of inertia and social exclusiveness. The different educational levels formed delineated social milieus, each with its own type of school. Later on, however, the law of inertia and social exclusiveness was increasingly pushed into the background. While the hierarchy of education and office tenure is still supported by delineated value attitudes, worldviews, life-styles, rites, and cults, these are now being increasingly replaced by ones that at least embrace society's broad center.

The combination of the law of discursive generalization with that of market success has made a major contribution to the change from a society of education to one of both education and consumption. Through the commercial and industrial strata, material consumption has been admitted to the cultural horizon of values. This trend has evolved into the principle of "affluence for everyone" by the process of discursive generalization. Accordingly, a unique, generally high level of consumption has developed in Germany. Moreover, the higher value now placed upon market success has been accompanied by the trend for associations to form on the basis of individual interests rather than on the basis of any collectivity to which those individuals might belong. Because it is more and more usual to choose one's companions according to one's current interests, changes in the overall edifice of the social structure are being infused with a growing dynamism.

In conjunction with political processes, the law of discursive generalization has assigned to the state the task of bringing peace to the class struggle by removing class distinctions. Typical of the ideas with which this synthesis has been expressed are those of the *Kulturstaat* (*Kultur* in the sense not only of "culture" but also of education), the *Rechtsstaat* (state of law and justice), and the *Sozialstaat* (state of social welfare). To the extent that these ideas have been successfully realized, the law of political accumulation has been relegated to its proper place. The apportionment and deployment of power are only determined by the law of political accumulation within the limits marked by the above types of order. Now that the social welfare state and the concept of social partnership in industry have been developed, the class struggle has been led into peaceful channels governed by annual negotiations over pay and conditions. The broadened access to advanced education and the overall increase in the level of educational qualification have replaced the class struggle by a universal struggle to obtain educational certificates.

This chapter was written during a time when German reunification was inconceivable. Reunified Germany is now struggling with a new type of inequality between the affluent western Germans and the poorer eastern Germans. The country is attempting to correct this inequality as soon as possible. Such rapid transformation produces new strains and conflicts, which display an overall tendency toward the model of market success. This transformation, however, is an entirely different subject matter and is not elaborated on here.

Notes

1. These theoretical foundations are further elaborated in Münch (1987, 1988).

2. This essay works on the comparative study elaborated in Münch (1986).

3. On the shaping of the cultural code of German society in the nineteenth century see Plessner (1959), Dahrendorf (1965), Ringer (1969), Krieger (1957), Münch (1986, 683–846).

4. On the shaping of German social structure in the nineteenth century see Ringer (1969, 14–80).

5. On the substantial rise of living standards and the increasing role of consumption in the Federal Republic of Germany, see Kreikebaum and Rinsche (1961), Mooser (1983), Thränhardt (1986), and Glaser (1986).

6. On the long-term trend toward income and status leveling, see Hardach (1985), Wilensky (1986), Thränhardt (1986), and Glaser (1986, 75–80).

7. Additional material on the social structure of the Federal Republic of Germany is provided by Lepsius (1974, 1978), Bolte and Hradil (1984), and Franz, Kruse, and Rolff (1986). On the "two-thirds society," see Kleining (1975, 273) and Schäfers (1985, 87).

8. According to Klingemann's (1984) analysis of workers' subjective stratum identification, German workers tend to regard themselves as middle class to a substantially higher degree than British and American workers.

9. On individualization see Beck (1983, 1986) and Hradil (1983).

10. At least in parts of society, an "outward life-style" was able to develop (Thränhardt 1986, 168), though that does not mean consumption has lost its distinctive function, as is shown by Pappi (1978) for example. Furthermore, according to Mooser (1983, 287–88) and Handl, Mayer, and Müller (1977, 60–62), the workers' participation in consumption is by no means universal.

11. The "marginal groups" have been investigated by Roth (1979), Hauser, Cremer-Schäfer, and Nouvertne (1981), and Kührt (1982).

12. On the development of mass culture via television, see Knilli (1972) and Eurich and Würzberg (1983). The development of tourism in Federal Germany exemplifies almost all of the phenomena that determine overall societal developments: the increased standard of living, broadened participation, demonstrative consumption, rituals of association and also of distinction, and the exclusion of the "periphery." See Datzer (1981), Weymar (1983), Maase (1983, 214), and Glaser (1986, 145–152).

13. For an introduction to the discussion on the "educational emergency" of the 1960s, see Dahrendorf (1963) and Picht (1964). According to Bolder (1978) and Klemm and Rolff (1986), worker participation in the competitive struggle for educational certificates is not yet universal—a presumption that applies for women as well: see Blossfeld (1983), Frevert (1986), and Müller, Willms, and Handl (1983).

14. On the mixture of social groups and strata in residential areas, see Niethammer (1979) and Mooser (1983, 297), who identify a fundamental change in this respect during the 1960s.

15. On the sphere of conflict in the Federal Republic of Germany, see Erd (1978), Kudera, Ruff, and Schmidt (1982), Uffelmann (1982), Müller-Jentsch (1986), and Abelshauser (1987).

References

Abelshauser, W. 1987. *Die langen Fünfziger Jahre. Wirtschaft und Gesellschaft der Bundesrepublik Deutschland 1949–1966.* Düsseldorf: Schwann.

Beck, U. 1983. "Jenseits von Stand und Klasse? Soziale Ungleichheit, gesellschaftliche Individualisierungsprozesse und die Entstehung neuer sozialer Formationen und Identitäten." In *Soziale Ungleichheiten. Soziale Welt,* special issue 2, edited by R. Kreckel, 35–74. Göttingen: Schwartz.

———, 1986. *Risikogesellschaft. Auf dem Weg in eine andere Moderne.* Frankfurt am Main: Suhrkamp.

Blossfeld, H. P. 1983. "Höherqualifizierung und Verdrängung— Konsequenzen der Bildungsexpansion in den siebziger Jahren." In *Beschäftigungssystem im gesellschaftlichen Wandel,* edited by M. Haller and W. Müller, 184–240. Frankfurt: Campus.

Bolder, A. 1978. *Bildungsentscheidungen im Arbeitermilieu.* Frankfurt and New York: Campus.

Bolte, K. M., and S. Hradil. 1984. *Soziale Ungleichheit in der Bundesrepublik Deutschland.* Opladen: Westdeutscher Verlag.

Dahrendorf, R. 1963. *Bildung ist Bürgerrecht.* Hamburg: Nannen.

———. 1965. *Gesellschaft und Demokratie in Deutschland.* Munich: Piper.

Datzer, R. 1981. *Urlaubsreisen 1980.* Starnberg: Studienkreis für Tourismus.

Erd, R. 1978. *Verrechtlichung industrieller Konflikte. Normative Rahmenbedingungen des dualen Systems der Interessenvertretung.* Frankfurt and New York: Campus.

Eurich, C., and G. Würzberg. 1983. *30 Jahre Fernsehalltag. Wie das Fernsehen unser Leben verändert hat.* Reinbek and Hamburg: Rowohlt.

Franz, H. W., W. Kruse, and H. G. Rolff, eds. 1986. *Neue alte soziale Ungleichheiten. Berichte zur sozialen Lage in der Bundesrepublik.* Opladen: Westdeutscher Verlag.

Frevert, U. 1986. *Frauen-Geschichte. Zwischen bürgerlicher Verbesserung und neuer Weiblichkeit.* Frankfurt: Suhrkamp.

Glaser, H. 1986. *Kulturgeschichte der Bundesrepublik Deutschland. Zwischen Grundgesetz und grosser Koalition 1949–1967.* Munich and Vienna: Hanser.

Handl, J., K. U. Mayer, and W. W. Müller. 1977. *Klassenlagen und Sozialstruktur.* Frankfurt and New York: Campus.

Hardach, G. 1985. "Die Wirtschaftsentwicklung der fünfziger Jahre. Restauration und Wirtschaftswunder." In *Die Fünfziger Jahre. Beiträge zu Politik und Kultur,* edited by D. Baensch, 57ff. Tübingen: Narr.

Hauser, R., H. Cremer-Schäfer, and U. Nouvertne. 1981. *Armut, Niedrig-*

einkommen und Unterversorgung in der Bundesrepublik Deutschland. Frankfurt: Campus.

Hradil, S. 1983. "Die Ungleichheit der 'Sozialen Lage.' " In *Soziale Ungleichheiten. Soziale Welt,* special issue 2, edited by R. Kreckel, 101–118. Göttingen: Schwartz.

Kleining, G. 1975. "Soziale Mobilität in der Bundesrepublik Deutschland. Part 2. Status und Prestigemobilität." *Kölner Zeitschrift für Soziologie und Sozialpsychologie* 27:273–292.

Klemm, K., and H. G. Rolff. 1986. "Ungleichheit der Bildungschancen in Schule und Hochschule." In *Neue alte Ungleichheiten,* edited by H. W. Franz, W. Kruse, and H. G. Rolff, 249–261. Opladen: Westdeutscher Verlag.

Klingemann, H. D. 1984. "Soziale Lagerung, Schichtbewußtsein und politisches Verhalten. Die Arbeiterschaft in der Bundesrepublik im historischen und internationalen Vergleich." In *Das Ende der Arbeiterbewegung in Deutschland,* edited by R. Ebbinghausen and F. Tiemann, 593–621. Opladen: Westdeutscher Verlag.

Knilli, F., ed. 1972. *Die Uterhaltung der deutschen Fernsehfamilie. Ideologiekritische Kurzanalysen von Serien.* Munich: Hanser.

Kreikebaum, H., and G. Rinsche. 1961. *Das Prestigemotiv in Konsum und Investition.* Berlin: Duncker & Humblot.

Krieger, L. 1957. *The German Idea of Freedom: History of a Political Tradition.* Boston: Beacon Press.

Kudera, W., K. Ruff, and R. Schmidt. 1982. "Soziale Lage und Bewußtsein von Arbeitern." In *Einführung in die Arbeits und Industriesoziologie,* edited by W. Littek, W. Rammert, and G. Wachtler, 269–283. New York: Campus.

Kührt, P. 1982. *Das Armutssyndrom. Die Entstehung und Verfestigung von Sozialhilfebedürftigkeit in der Bundesrepublik Deutschland.* Weinheim and Basel: Beltz.

Lepsius, M. R. 1974. "Sozialstruktur und soziale Schichtung in der Bundesrepublik." In *Die zweite Republik,* edited by R. Löwenthal and H. P. Schwartz, 263–288. Stuttgart: Seewald.

———. 1978. "Soziale Ungleichheit und Klassenstrukturen in der Bundesrepublik Deutschland." In *Klassen in der europäischen Sozialgeschichte,* edited by H. U. Wehler, 166–209. Göttingen: Vandenhoek & Ruprecht.

Maase, K. 1983. "Freizeit." In *Die Bundesrepublik Deutschland. Geschichte in drei Bänden.* Vol. 2, *Gesellschaft,* edited by W. Benz, 209–233. Frankfurt: Fischer.

Mooser, J. 1983. "Die Auflösung proletarischer Milieus. Klassenbindung und Individualisierung vom Kaiserreich bis in die Bundesrepublik Deutschland." *Soziale Welt* 34:270–306.

Müller, W., A. Willms, and J. Handl, 1983. *Strukturwandel der Frauenarbeit 1890–1980.* Frankfurt: Campus.

Müller-Jentsch, W. 1986. *Soziologie der industriellen Beziehungen.* Frankfurt and New York: Campus.

Münch, R. 1986. *Die Kultur der Moderne.* Vol. 1, *Ihre Grundlagen und ihre*

Entwicklung in England und in Amerika. Vol. 2, *Ihre Entwicklung in Frankreich und Deutschland.* Frankfurt: Suhrkamp.

—————. 1987. *Theory of Action. Toward a New Synthesis Going beyond Parsons.* London and New York: Routledge.

—————. 1988. *Understanding Modernity. Toward a New Perspective Going beyond Durkheim and Weber.* London and New York: Routledge.

Niethammer, L., ed. 1979. *Wohnen im Wandel. Beiträge zur Geschichte des Alltags in der bürgerlichen Gesellschaft.* Wuppertal: Hammer.

Pappi, F. U. 1978. "Sozialer Status und Konsumstil. Eine Fallstudie zur Wohnzimmereinrichtung." *Kölner Zeitschrift für Soziologie und Sozialpsychologie* 30:87–115.

Picht, G. 1964. *Die deutsche Bildungskatastrophe.* Freiburg: Walter.

Plessner, H. 1959. *Die verspätete Nation.* Stuttgart: Kohlhammer.

Ringer, F. 1969. *The Decline of the German Mandarins. The German Academic Community, 1890–1933.* Cambridge, Mass.: Harvard University Press.

Roth, J. 1979. *Armut in der Bundesrepublik.* Reinbek and Hamburg: Rowohlt.

Schäfers, B. 1985. *Sozialstruktur und Wandel der Bundesrepublik Deutschland.* Stuttgart: Enke.

Thränhardt, D. 1986. *Geschichte der Bundesrepublik Deutschland.* Frankfurt: Suhrkamp.

Uffelmann, U. 1982. "Wirtschaft und Gesellschaft in der Gründungsphase der Bundesrepublik Deutschland." *Aus Politik und Zeitgeschichte* 1–2:3–27.

Weymar, T. 1983. "Ein Volk auf Achse." *Wechselwirkungen* 19:25.

Wilensky, H.L. 1986. "Wird ökonomische Ungleichheit durch staatliches Handeln reduziert? Eine international vergleichende Analyse." In *Soziale Ungleichheit und Sozialpolitik. Legitimation, Wirkung, Programmatik*, edited by J. Krüger and H. Strasser, 143–169. Regensburg: Transfer.

10

Cultural Production, Consumption, and the Development of the Cultural Sphere

Mike Featherstone

Max Weber's theory of cultural rationalization and differentiation is well known. For Weber the development of modernity not only involved a long process of differentiation of the capitalist economy and the modern state but also entailed a cultural rationalization with the emergence of separate scientific, aesthetic, and moral value spheres. Weber's (1948) discussion of the differentiation of the cultural sphere from a more rudimentary, holistic, religious cultural core is conducted at a high level of abstraction. Although Weber provides brief glimpses of the way in which each aspect of the cultural sphere is relentlessly driven by its own logic, the way in which values relate to life-style and conduct, and the tensions experienced by intellectuals, the "cultivated man" and the cultural specialist, his prime purpose was to sketch out a typology (Weber 1948:323–24). While we do find fuller discussions of the cultural sphere in the writings of Bell (1976) and Habermas (1981), we need to build on these sources if we seek to understand the particular conjunction of culture in contemporary Western societies. In effect we need to investigate the conditions for the development of the cultural sphere by focusing on particular historical sequences and locations. First, we need to understand the emergence of relatively autonomous culture (knowledge and other symbolic media) in relation to the growth in the autonomy and power potential of specialists in symbolic production. We therefore need

I would like to thank Peter Bailey, Jose Bleicher, David Chaney, Mike Hepworth, Stephen Kalberg, Stephen Mennell, and Bryan S. Turner for commenting on an earlier version of this chapter.

to focus on the *carriers* of culture and the contradictory pressures that are generated by changing interdependencies and power struggles of the growing fraction within the middle class toward dual processes of (a) the monopolization and separation of a cultural enclave and (b) the demonopolization and diffusion of culture to wider publics. Second, we need to focus on the development of separate institutions and life-styles for cultural specialists and examine the relation between value complexes and conduct in the various life orders, not only in terms of a cultural sphere conceived as the arts and the academy ("high culture") but also in terms of the generation of oppositional countercultures (bohemias, artistic avant-gardes). Third, we need to comprehend the relational dynamic of a parallel development to that of the cultural sphere: the general expansion of cultural production via "culture industries" and the generation of a wider market for cultural and other symbolic goods to produce what has been termed a *mass culture* or a *consumer culture*. Both tendencies have contributed to the increasing prominence of culture within modern societies—tendencies that threaten to erode and domesticate everyday culture, the taken-for-granted stock of memories, traditions, and myths.

This suggests that cultural specialists are often caught in an ambivalent relationship toward the market that may lead to strategies of separation and distancing to sustain and promote the autonomy of the cultural sphere. At the same time, in terms of their interdependencies and power struggles with other groups (notably economic specialists), this may dispose them to use the marketplace to reach wider audiences to bolster their general societal power and increase the prestige and public value of their specialist cultural goods. Conditions that favor the autonomization of the cultural sphere will better allow cultural specialists to monopolize, regulate, and control cultural production, to seek to place cultural production above economic production, and to place art and intellectual pursuits above everyday life, popular uneducated tastes, and mass culture. Alternatively, conditions that threaten the autonomy of the cultural sphere, the demonopolization processes that discredit the "sacred" intellectual and artistic symbolic hierarchies, will tend to allow outsider groups of cultural specialists to endorse alternative tastes and to seek to legitimate an expanded repertoire that may include the formerly excluded popular traditions and mass cultural goods. Without an attempt to comprehend the rising and declining fortunes of particular groups of cultural specialists, it may be difficult to make sense of those who mourn or applaud present-day assertions, such as "the end of art," "the end of the avant-garde," "the end of the intellectuals," and "the end of culture" (Featherstone 1988, 1989a, 1989b, 1991).

In this paper we will look at various approaches that have addressed these issues. This will be done via an examination of three major conceptions of the development of an enlarged field of cultural production, which entails analyzing the interrelationship between the development of the cultural sphere and a mass consumer culture. First, we examine the production of culture perspective in which a mass culture that is presented as threatening to engulf and debase the culture sphere is seen as the logical outcome of the process of capitalist commodity production. Second, we examine a mode of consumption approach that draws on anthropological perspectives to argue that there are similarities in the consumption of culture in all societies and that we should refrain from negatively evaluating mass-produced culture. Rather, the classification of cultural goods and tastes (be they everyday consumer durables, life-style practices, or high cultural pursuits), must be understood as operating relationally within the same social space. This sociogenetic perspective focuses on how the symbolic aspects of goods and activities are used practically to draw the boundaries of social relationships. Third, we explore a psychogenetic perspective on cultural consumption that examines the genesis of the propensity and desire to consume new goods and experiences. Such a perspective, which focuses upon the middle class and draws upon Weber's notion of ideal interests, also raises the issue of the long-term process of the generation of habitus, dispositions, and means of orientation in different interdependent and competing groups of people. Finally, we return to a discussion of the cultural sphere and suggest some of the conditions that favor its formation and deformation and the generation of particular evaluations of mass culture by a set of cultural specialists. This attempt to identify how such issues should be addressed can help us to better understand the process of cultural development and to move beyond statically conceived notions of the cultural sphere, market culture, mass culture, consumer culture, everyday culture, and deeply ingrained cultural traditions and codes.

The Production of Consumption

The study of consumption has long been regarded as the province of economics, and, although Adam Smith argued that "consumption is the sole end and purpose of all production" (Minchinton 1982:219), the analysis of consumption has been largely neglected in favor of production and distribution. This neglect may have resulted from the assumption that consumption was unproblematic because it was based upon the concept of rational individuals buying goods to maximize their satisfaction. That rational choice might be modified by social pressures such as the customs and habits of the people was given only minor acknowledgment. In the late nineteenth century we find some interest in external effects on utility, such as conspicuous consumption, the snob effect, and the bandwagon effect (Minchinton 1982: 221). In general, sociological interest in the move to mass consumption in the second half of the nineteenth century has been restricted to indicating the limitations of strictly economic or market explanations of human behavior. This sociological critique of economics has sometimes been coupled with a concern that mass consumption brought about social deregulation and a threat to the social bond. The move to intensified mass production, mass consumption, and the extension of the market into more areas of life is thus generally seen as harmful to culture. The new culture produced for mass consumption, then, was often viewed negatively, especially by neo-Marxist critics, who regarded advertising, the mass media, and the entertainment industries as logical extensions of commodity production in which markets were monopolized to produce mass deception and a debased consumer culture. The tendency has been to deduce the effects on consumption of culture from the production of culture and, within the neo-Marxist framework, to follow variants of the base-superstructure model. From this perspective it is possible to regard the logic of capitalist mass production as leading to a more extensive mass society.

One of the clearest statements on the power of the productive forces in society to harness consumption to fit with its designs is the Frankfurt school's theory of the culture industry. Nonwork activities in general become subsumed under the same instrumental rationality and commodity logic of the workplace, and artistic and cultural goods become subjected to the same standardization and pseudoindividualization used in the production of other goods. Hence Horkheimer and Adorno (1972:137) state that "Amusement under late capitalism is the prolongation of work." Art, which formerly supplied the *promesse de bonheur,* the yearning for the otherness that transcends the existing reality, now openly becomes a commodity. As Horkheimer and Adorno remark, "What is new is not that it is a commodity, but that today it deliberately admits it is one; that art renounces its own autonomy and proudly takes its place among consumption goods constitutes the charm of novelty" (157). The culture industry offered the prospect of a manufactured culture in which discrimination and knowledge of culture (the high culture of the literati) was swamped and replaced by a mass culture (the prestige seeker replacing the connoisseur) in which reception was dictated by exchange value. For Adorno the increasing dominance of exchange value obliterated the original use value (in the case of art, the *promesse de bonheur,* the enjoyment, pleasure, or purposiveness without purpose with which the object was to be approached) and replaced it with exchange value (its instrumental market value or "currency"). This freed the commodity to take on a wide range of secondary or artificial associations, and advertising, in particular, took advantage of this capacity.

From this perspective advertising not only used, transformed, or replaced traditional high culture to promote the consumption of commodities and further mass deception but also drew attention to the symbolic aspect of commodities. The triumph of economic exchange need not just entail the eclipse of traditional culture and high.culture, but a new "artificial" culture was generated from "below," via the logic of commodity production, to replace them. Hence, a number of commentators have focused upon the centrality of advertising in the genesis of a consumer culture (Ewen 1976; Ewen and Ewen 1982; Leiss et al. 1986).

Another example of the interpretation of the culture of consumption in terms of the commodification of everyday life is found in the work of Fredric Jameson. Following the capital logic approach, which points to the profusion of a new artificial culture with the extension of commodity production, Jameson (1982:139) emphasizes that "culture is the very element of consumer society itself; no society has ever been saturated with signs and messages like this one . . . the omnipresence of the image in consumer capitalism today [means that] the priorities of the real become reversed, and everything is mediated by culture." This perspective is central in his influential paper "Postmodernism or the Cultural Logic of Late Capitalism," in which he outlines the contours of postmodern culture (Jameson 1984:87).

A similar emphasis upon cultural profusion and disorder, which threatens to obliterate the last vestiges of traditional popular culture or high culture, is found in the work of Jean Baudrillard, on which Jameson draws. Baudrillard (1970) builds on the commodification theory of

Lukács and Lefebvre, arguing that consumption involves the active manipulation of signs and that what is consumed is not objects but the system of objects, the sign system that makes up the code. Baudrillard draws on semiology to develop the cultural implications of commodity analysis and argues that in late capitalist society sign and commodity have fused to produce the commodity-sign. The logic of political economy for Baudrillard has therefore involved a semiological revolution entailing not just the replacement of use-value by exchange-value, but eventually the replacement of both by sign-value. This leads to the autonomization of the signifier, which can be manipulated (for example, through advertising) to float free from a stable relationship to objects and establish its own associative chains of meaning.

In Baudrillard's later writings (1983a, 1983b), references to economics, class, and mode of production disappear. Indeed at one point in *Simulations*, Baudrillard (1983a) tilts at Bourdieu when he argues that social analysis in terms of normativity or class is doomed to failure because it belongs to a stage of the system that we have now superseded. The new stage of the system is the postmodern simulational world in which television, the machine of simulation par excellence, endlessly reduplicates the world. This switch to the production and reproduction of copies for which there is no original, the simulacrum, effaces the distinction between the real and the imaginary. According to Baudrillard (1983a:148), we now live "in an 'aesthetic' hallucination of reality." The ultimate terminus of the expansion of the commodity production system is the triumph of signifying culture and the death of the social: a postsociety configuration that escapes sociological classification and explanation, an endless cycle of the reduplication and overproduction of signs, images, and simulations that leads to an implosion of meaning. We are now in the increasingly familiar territory of the transformation of reality into images in the postmodern, schizoid, depthless culture. All that remains on the human level is the masses, the silent majority, which acts as a "black hole" (Baudrillard 1983b:9), absorbing the overproduction of energy and information from the media and cynically watching the fascinating endless play of signs. Baudrillard's conception of mass has taken us a long way from mass culture theory, in which the manipulation of the masses through the popular media plays a central role. For him the logic of commodity development has seen the triumph of culture, a new postmodern phase of cultural disorder in which the distinctions between levels of culture—high, folk, popular, or class—give way to a glutinous mass that simulates and plays with the overproduction of signs.

Today the high culture/mass culture debate arouses little passion in academic life. Since the mid-1970s the attacks on the distinction between high culture and mass culture have proceeded apace. Particularly influential in the British context has been the work of the Birmingham Centre for Contemporary Cultural Studies (see Hall et al. 1980) and the Open University (see Bennett et al. 1977; Bennett et al. 1981). One finds a wide range of criticisms. There is the alleged elitism of the Frankfurt school's pro-high-culture distinction between individuality and pseudo-individuality, which condemns the masses to manipulation (Bennett et al. 1977; Swingewood 1977). Other criticisms include the puritanism and prudery of those arguments that favor notions of creative production against the right of the masses to enjoy its consumption and pleasures (Leiss 1983; New Formations 1983); the invalidity of the distinction between true and false needs found in the critiques of consumer society and its culture in the work of Marcuse (1964), Debord (1970), and Ewen (1976) (see Sahlins 1976; Leiss 1983; Springborg 1981); and the neglect of the egalitarian and democratic currents in mass culture, the process of leveling up and not down, that finds one of its strongest statements in Shils (1960) (see also Swingewood 1977; Kellner 1983). There have also been criticisms that the foundation of the critique of mass culture is to be found in an essentially nostalgic *Kulturpessimismus* perspective on the part of intellectuals who were entrapped in a myth of premodern stability, coherence, and community (Stauth and Turner 1988) or a nostalgia for a premodern, precommodity form of symbolic exchange or a presimulational reality such as we find in Baudrillard's work. The critics of mass culture theories also have neglected complex social differentiations (Wilensky 1964), the ways in which mass-produced commodities can be customized or signs can be reversed with their meanings renegotiated critically or oppositionally. See the work on youth subcultures by the Birmingham Centre for Contemporary Cultural Studies, especially Hebdige (1979 on punk; also de Certeau 1981). In addition there is Raymond Williams's (1961) pronouncement that "there are no masses, only other people." Such critiques point to the importance of transcending the view that uniformity of consumption is dictated by production and emphasize the need to investigate the actual use and reception of goods in various practices. Such critiques also entail a revaluation of popular practices, which are no longer to be seen as debased and vulgar. Rather, the integrity of the culture of the common people is defended and suspicion is cast upon the whole enterprise of the construction of an autonomous cultural sphere with its rigid symbolic hierarchies, exclusive canons, and classifications.

Modes of Consumption

Focusing on the consumption of culture rather than on production points us toward the differential reception and use of mass-produced cultural goods and experiences and the ways in which popular culture has failed to be eclipsed by mass culture. Indeed, if we take a long-term process approach to cultural formation it is clear that cultural objects are continually redesignated and move from popular to high to mass and vice versa. In this sense, popular and folk culture cannot provide a pristine baseline for culture because they have a long history of being packaged and commodified. Hence, the emphasis should switch from more abstract views of cultural production to the actual practices of cultural production on the part of particular groups of cultural specialists and the ways in which they relate to the actual practices of consumption on the part of different groups.

Considerable insight into this process is gained by analyzing anthropological research on consumption that focuses on the symbolic aspect of goods and their role as communicators. From this perspective, goods are used to mark boundaries between groups, to create and demarcate differences or communality between figurations of people (see Douglas and Isherwood 1980; Sahlins 1976; Leiss 1983; Appadurai 1986). Leiss (1978:19), for example, argues that, while utilities in all cultures are symbolic, goods are in effect *doubly* symbolic in contemporary Western societies: symbolism is consciously employed in the design and imagery attached to goods in the production and marketing process, and symbolic associations are used by consumers in using goods to construct differentiated life-style models.

The work of Douglas and Isherwood (1980) is particularly important in this respect because of their emphasis on how goods are used to draw the lines of social relationships. Our enjoyment of goods, they argue, is only partly related to physical consumption. It is also crucially linked to their use as *markers;* we enjoy, for example, sharing the names of goods with others (the sports fan or the wine connoisseur). In addition, the mastery of the cultural person entails a seemingly "natural" mastery, not only of information (the autodidact "memory man") but also of how to use and consume appropriately and with natural ease in every situation. In this sense the consumption of high cultural goods (art, novels, opera, philosophy), must be related to the ways in which other, more mundane, cultural goods (clothing, food, drink, leisure pursuits) are handled and consumed, and high culture must be inscribed into the same social space as everyday cultural consumption. In Douglas and Isherwood's (1980: 176ff.) discussion, consumption classes are defined in relation to the consumption of three sets of goods: a staple set (for example, food), a technology set (travel and capital equipment), and an information set (information goods, education, arts, and cultural and leisure pursuits). At the lower end of the social structure the poor are restricted to the staple set and have more time on their hands, but those in the top consumption class require not only a higher level of earnings but also a competence in judging information goods and services. This entails a considerable investment in time, both as a lifelong investment in cultural and symbolic capital and as an investment in maintaining consumption activities (it is in this sense that we refer to the title of Linder's [1970] book, *The Harried Leisure Class*). Hence the competition to acquire goods in the information class generates high admission barriers and effective techniques of exclusion.

The phasing, duration, and intensity of time invested in acquiring competences for handling information, goods, and services as well as the day-to-day practice, conservation, and maintenance of these competences are, as Halbwachs reminds us, useful criteria of social class. Our use of time in consumption practices conforms to our class habitus and, therefore, conveys an accurate idea of our class status (see the discussion of Halbwachs in Preteceille and Terrail 1985:23). This points us toward the importance of research on the different long-term investments in informational acquisition and cultural capital of particular groups. Such research has been carried out in detail by Bourdieu and his associates (Bourdieu et al. 1965; Bourdieu and Darbel 1966; Bourdieu and Passeron 1971; Bourdieu 1984). For Bourdieu (1984) particular constellations of taste, consumption preferences, and life-style practices are associated with specific occupation and class fractions, making it possible to map the universe of taste and life-styles with all its structured oppositions and finely graded distinctions that operate within a particular society at a particular point in history. Yet within capitalist societies the volume of production of new goods results in an endless struggle to obtain what Hirsch (1976) calls "positional goods," goods that define social status. The constant supply of new, fashionably desirable goods, or the usurpation of existing marker goods by lower groups, produces a paper-chase effect in which those above have to invest in new (informational) goods to reestablish the original social distance.

It is therefore possible to refer both to societies in which the tendency is for the progressive breakdown of the barriers that restrict the production of new goods and the capacity of commodities to travel and to societies with the countertendency to restrict, control, and channel exchange in order to establish enclaved commodities. In some societies, status systems are guarded and reproduced by restricting equivalences and exchange in a *stable* universe of commodities. In other societies with a fashion system, *taste* in an ever-changing universe of commodities is restricted and controlled, and at the same time there is the illusion of individual choice and unrestricted access. Sumptuary laws are an intermediate consumption-regulating device for societies with stable status displays which face the deregulation of the flow of commodities, for example, premodern Europe (Appadurai 1986:25). The tendencies noted by Jameson, Baudrillard, and others toward the overproduction of symbolic goods in contemporary societies suggest that the bewildering flow of signs, images, information, fashions, and styles would be impossible to subject to a final or coherent reading (see Featherstone 1988, 1989a, 1991).

Examples of this alleged cultural disorder are often taken from the media (as does, for example, Baudrillard), yet, apart from grand statements such as "television is the world," we are given little understanding of how this disorder affects the everyday practices of different figurations of people. It can be argued that as long as face-to-face encounters continue between embodied persons, attempts will be made to read a person's demeanor for clues as to his or her social standing. The different styles and labels of fashionable clothing and goods, however much subject to change, imitation, and copying, are one such set of clues. Yet as Bourdieu (1984) reminds us with his concept of symbolic capital, the signs of the dispositions and classificatory schemes that betray a person's origins and trajectory through life are manifest in body shape, size, weight, stance, walk, demeanor, tone of voice, style of speaking, sense of bodily ease or discomfort, and so on. Hence culture is incorporated, and it is not just a question of what clothes are worn but of how they are worn. Advice books on manners, taste, and etiquette—from Erasmus to Nancy Mitford's "U" and "Non-U"—impress on their subjects the need to naturalize dispositions and manners, to be completely at home with them. At the same time the newly arrived may display signs of the burden of attainment and the incompleteness of their cultural competence. Hence the new rich, who often adopt conspicuous consumption strategies, are recognizable and assigned their place in the social space. Their cultural practices are always in danger of being dismissed as vulgar and tasteless by the established upper class, the aristocracy, and those "rich in cultural goods"—the intellectuals and artists.

From one perspective, artistic and intellectual goods are enclaved commodities whose capacity to move around in the social space is limited by their ascribed sacred qualities. In this sense the specialists in symbolic production will seek to increase the autonomy of the cultural sphere and to restrict the supply and access to such goods, in effect creating and preserving an enclosure of high culture. This can take the form of rejecting the market and any economic use of the goods and adopting a life-style that is the opposite of the successful economic specialist (disorder versus order, the cultivation of transgressions strategies, the veneration of natural talent and genius against systematic achievement and work, and so on). Yet as Bourdieu (1984, 1979) indicates, there is an interest in disinterestedness, and it is possible to chart the hidden and misrecognized economy in cultural goods with its own forms of currency, rates of conversion to economic capital, and so on. The problem of the intellectuals in market situations is that they must achieve and retain this degree of closure and control that enables artistic and intellectual goods to remain enclaved commodities. Indeed, as many commentators have pointed out, this is the paradox of intellectuals and artists: their necessary dependence on, yet distaste for and desire for independence from, the market. Within situations of an overproduction of symbolic goods, there may be intensified competition from new cultural intermediaries (the expanding design, advertising, marketing, commercial art, graphics, journalistic, media, and fashion occupations) and other "outsider" intellectuals that have emerged from the postwar expansion of higher education in Western societies. This competition may lead to the inability of established intellectuals to maintain the stability of symbolic hierarchies, and the resultant phase of cultural declassification opens a space for the generation of interest in popular culture on what is proclaimed to be a more egalitarian and democratic basis.

We have therefore moved from considering the production of culture from a mode of production perspective to one that, following Preteceille and Terrail's (1985:36) depiction of Bourdieu's work, we can call a *mode of consumption* approach. From this point of view, demand and cultural consumption are not merely dictated by supply, but they must be understood within a social framework, that is, as sociogenetically induced. A perspective that emphasizes that "consumption is eminently social, relational, and active rather than private, atomic, or passive" (Appadurai 1986:31).

Romanticism, Desire, and Middle-class Consumption

The mode of consumption perspective emphasizes the continuities in the socially structured handling and use of goods between contemporary capitalist and other types of societies. The "psychogenetic" perspective, like the production of consumption approach, focuses on explaining the proliferation of new goods. In contrast to the latter's emphasis on *supply*, the psychogenetic approach concentrates on the problem of the *demand* for new goods. This entails a move from economic centered analysis to questions of desire—to the puzzle of the genesis of the propensity to consume anew, the motivational complex that develops a thirst for pleasure, poverty, self-expression, and self-realization through goods. In a manner reminiscent of Weber's *Protestant Ethic*, Campbell (1987) argues that the rise of consumption, like that of capitalist production, requires an ethic, and in this case it is romanticism, with its focus on imagination, fantasy, mysticism, creativity, and emotional exploration, and not Protestantism, that supplies the impetus.[1] He writes: "The essential activity of consumption is thus not actual selection, purchase or use of products, but the imaginative pleasure-seeking to which the product image lends itself, 'real' consumption being largely a result of this 'mentalistic' hedonism" (Campbell 1987:89). From this perspective, the pleasure derived from novels, paintings, plays, records, films, radio, television, and fashion is not the result of manipulation by the advertisers or an "obsession with social status," but it is the illusory enjoyment stimulated by daydreaming. The disposition to live out desires, fantasies, and daydreams, or the capacity to spend a good deal of time in pursuit of them, may vary among different social groups. Campbell locates its origins in relation to consumerism within the eighteenth-century English middle class. Groups that have achieved a high degree of literacy are likely to be more disposed to take ideas and character ideals seriously and, as Weber pointed out, to seek to achieve consistency in conduct. Yet how far can we understand mass consumption by focusing solely upon the development of a romantic ethic in the middle class? To understand the consumption habits of the middle class in the eighteenth century we need to locate the habits of this group in relation to those of the lower and the upper classes.

We have already referred to the contrast between societies that restrict the exchange of commodities in order to reproduce a stable status system and societies that have an ever-changing universe of commodities and a fashion system with the appearance of complete interchangeability, which actually can be considered in terms of socially structured taste. Consumption in the upper class or aristocracy tends more toward the reproduction of a stable status system, which also includes phases of liminal excess and transgression (carnivals, fairs, and so on.) Mennell (1987) reminds us that the aristocracy in court society became "specialists in the arts of consumption entrapped in a system of fine distinctions, status battles, and competitive expenditure from which they could not escape because their whole social identity depended upon it." Here the fashion code was restricted rather than elaborated and the courtier had to conform to strict rules of dress, manners, and deportment (Elias 1983:232). In court societies such as Versailles during the reign of Louis XIV, consumption was highly structured in terms of the regulation of etiquette, ceremony, taste, dress, manners, and conversation. Every detail was perceived as an instrument in the struggle for prestige. The ability to read appearance and gestures for slight giveaway clues and the time spent in decoding the demeanor and conversation of others indicate how a courtier's very existence depended on calculation.

These tight restrictions on behavior in court society produced a number of countermovements that sought to compensate for the suppression of feeling and court rationality by the emancipation of feeling. We are generally inclined to perceive these contrasting positions as involving class differences between the aristocracy (the dissimulating, artful, false courtier) and the middle class (the virtuous, sincere, honest citizen) and to formulate them in terms of other-directed and inner-directed qualities. Elias (1978:19), in the early part of *The Civilizing Process,* shows how the German middle class venerated *Kultur* with romantic ideals of love of nature, solitude, and surrender to the excitement of one's own heart. Here the middle-class outsiders, spatially dispersed and isolated, can be contrasted to the established court with its ideals drawn from French *civilisation*. From this a further series of contrasts can be made between the middle-class intelligentsia and the aristocratic courtier: inwardness and depth of feeling versus superficiality and ceremony; immersion in books and education and the development of personal identity versus formal conversation and courtly manners; and virtue versus honor (see Vowinckel 1987).

Yet there are also links between the middle-class romantic emphasis upon sincerity and the development of romantic tendencies within the aristocracy. Elias (1983:214ff.), in "The Sociogenesis of Aristocratic Romanticism," argues that one of the influential forerunners of bourgeois romanticism, Rousseau, owed some of his success to the ways in which his ideas were perceived as a reaction to court rationality and the suppression of "feeling" in court life. The idealization of nature and the melancholic longing for country life is found in the early eighteenth-century nobility at the court of Louis XIV. The sharp contrast between court and country, the complexity of court life, and the incessant self-control and necessary calculation contributed to a nostalgia for the idealized rural existence described in the romantic utopias filled with shepherds and shepherdesses in novels such as *L'Astrée* by Honoré d'Urfé. Elias (1983) can detect both clear discontinuities and similar processes in the sociogenesis of bourgeois and aristocratic romanticism. He refers (262) to the middle classes as "dual-front classes" that are exposed to social pressures from groups above who possess greater power, authority, and prestige and from groups below who are inferior in these qualities. The pressures for self-control in relation to the codes of professional life, coupled with pressures of being in a dual-front class, may help to generate an ambivalence toward the system of rules and self-constraints that nourish a dream-image of a more direct, spontaneous expression of emotion.

The implications of the role of the romantic ethic in the genesis of consumerism should now be clearer. Romanticism cannot be assumed just to work as a set of ideas that induced more direct emotional expression through fantasies and daydreaming and that translated into the desire for new commodities to nourish this longing. Rather, we need to understand the sociogenesis of romantic tendencies that were generated in the rivalries and interdependencies between the aristocracy and the middle classes. These pressures may have nourished a romantic longing for the unconstrained, expressive, and spontaneous life that was projected onto commodities and manifest in fashion, novel reading, and other popular entertainments catered for in the burgeoning public sphere. Yet the practicalities of everyday life, the social demands of sustaining one's acceptability, were also important forces. Social constraints demanded from middle-class professionals careful attention to etiquette, dress, demeanor, and an ordered, measured consumption. Unlike the courtier class, the middle classes enjoyed a private life in which they could be "off stage." Yet it is easy to overestimate the freedom and independence of the private sphere. The pressures to maintain a style of social life concomitant with one's status led to increasing pressures to codify and regulate domestic consumption, artistic taste, food, and festivities (see Elias 1983:116).

When we look more specifically at the middle class, we need to consider the different situations in particular nations in the eighteenth century. The situation of the English middle class was very different from that of the French and the German. England provided a middling case in which closer links existed between court life and country life and between a more differentiated aristocracy, the gentry, and the middle classes (Elias and Dunning 1987:35; Mennell 1985:119). In the eighteenth and early nineteenth centuries, landed London society was a reference group for those in the rising middle-class strata who emulated its tastes, manners, and fashions (Mennell 1985: 212). Davidoff (1973: 13) has noted in early nineteenth-century housekeeping manuals, etiquette books, and magazines how increased expenditures on ceremonial displays to maintain an expected life-style became requisite (see Mennell 1985:209).

Evidence suggests that the middle class in eighteenth-century England encountered increasing pressure for consumption from below. What has been referred to as the "consumer revolution" in the eighteenth century involved increased consumption of luxury goods, fashion, household goods, popular novels, magazines, newspapers, and entertainment and the means of marketing them through advertising to an enlarged buying public (see McKendrick et al. 1982). The lower classes were drawn into this expansion of consumption by adopting fashions that emulated the upper classes, and fashion diffused down the social scale much more widely in England than in other European countries (McKendrick et al. 1982:34ff.).

One important reason why emulation was possible and new fashion was transmitted so rapidly was that they took place within an urban milieu. London was the largest city in Europe in the eighteenth century and it exercised a considerable dominance over other European countries. Changing fashions, the display of new goods in shops, and conspicuous consumption were clearly visible and were topics of everyday conversation. The narrowing of social distances and the swing toward informal relations between the classes also became manifest in a new use of public space within London, which has come to be called the *public sphere*. The public sphere was comprised of social institutions: periodicals, journals, clubs, and coffeehouses in which individuals could gather for unconstrained discussion (see Habermas 1974; Eagleton 1984; Stallybrass and White 1986:80ff.). The emergence of the public sphere is closely tied to the development of the cultural sphere. The profession of literary criticism and the independent specialists in cultural production who wrote for newspapers and magazines and produced novels for their newly enlarged audiences developed dramatically by mid-eighteenth century (Williams 1961; Hohendahl 1982). The city coffeehouses became centers where people gathered to read or to hear newspapers and magazines read aloud and to discuss them (Lowenthal 1961:56). Not only were the coffeehouses democratic domains for free cultural discussion (cf. Mannheim 1956), but also they were spaces of civility, a cleansed discursive environment freed from the low-others, the "grotesque bodies," of the alehouses (Stallybrass and White 1986:95). The coffeehouses replaced "idle" and festive consumption with productive leisure. They were *decent*, ordered places that demanded a withdrawal from popular culture, which was increasingly viewed from a negative perspective.

While there was therefore a movement toward a democratization of cultural interchange *and* a differentiation of culture between the respectable, decent, and civil and the ill-controlled lower orders in the eighteenth century, this was a part of a long-term process. Burke (1978:24) argues that in the sixteenth century there were two traditions in culture: the classical tradition of philosophy and theology learned in schools and universities and the popular tradition contained in folksongs, folktales, devotional images, mystery plays, chapbooks, fairs, and festivals. Yet the upper levels directly participated in popular culture, and even in the early eighteenth century not all were disengaged from the culture of the common people. Burke (286) suggests that in 1500 the educated strata despised the common people although they shared their culture. Yet by 1800 their descendents had ceased to join spontaneously in popular culture and were rediscovering it as something exotic and interesting. The culture of the lower orders remained a source of fascination, and the symbolism of this tradition remained important as a strand within the high culture of the middle classes (Stallybrass and White 1986:

107). The *carnivalesque,* with its hybridization, mixing of codes, grotesque bodies, and transgressions, remained a fascinating spectacle for eighteenth-century writers, including Pope, Rousseau, and Wordsworth. While one part of this tradition emerged in the artistic bohemias of the mid-nineteenth century, with their deliberate transgressions of bourgeois culture and invocation of liminoid grotesque body symbolism associated with the *carnivalesque,* another developed into romanticism. When Frederick the Great published his *De la littérature allemande* in 1780, he protested against the social mixing and transgression and manifest lack of taste in "the abominable works of Shakespeare" over which "the whole audience goes into raptures when it listens to these ridiculous farces worthy of the savages in Canada" (quoted in Elias 1978:14). For the bourgeois intellectuals and their public against whom Frederick directed his remarks, the actual savages of North America (Voltaire's *L'Ingénu*) and of Tahiti (Bougainville's *Voyage*) held a growing fascination as "exotic otherness."

At the same time, then, that traditional popular culture was beginning to disappear, European intellectuals were discovering, recording, and formulating the culture of the people (see Burke 1978). In part this was a reaction against the enlightened gentility of the "civilized" classical culture of the court and the aristocracy (Lunn 1986) and the uniform rationalism and universalism of the Enlightenment. Herder, for example, was sensitive to cultural diversity, the particularity of each cultural community, and wanted the different cultures to be considered on an equal basis. This strand developed into a critique of the French sociocentric identification of their own culture, designated as "civilization" and "high culture," as *the* universal metaculture for mankind (Dumont 1986).

Concluding Remarks:
The Development of the Cultural Sphere

The development of the cultural sphere must be seen as part of a long-term process that involved the growth in the power potential of the specialists in symbolic production and that produced two contradictory consequences. There was a greater autonomy in the nature of the knowledge produced and the monopolization of production and consumption in specialist enclaves with the development of strong ritual classifications to exclude outsiders. There was also a greater expansion of knowledge and cultural goods produced for new audiences and markets in which existing hierarchical classifications were dismantled and specialist cultural goods were sold in similar ways to other "symbolic" commodities. It is these processes that point to the autonomy and heteronomy of the cultural sphere.

It would be useful to take Norbert Elias's observations (1971: 15) and examine the process of formation of the "autonomization" of particular spheres, which should be understood in terms of the changing power balances and the functional interdependencies between different social groups. To understand, therefore, the development of the economic sphere, we need to link the term *economic* to the rise of particular social strata and the theorization of the growing autonomous nexus of the relations generated by this group and other groups. Elias (1984) focuses on Quesney and the Physiocrats (who were soon followed by Adam Smith and others) as the first groups to synthesize empirical data in the belief that they could detect the effects of the laws of nature in society that would serve the welfare and prosperity of humankind. The ideas of the Physiocrats, according to Elias (1984:22), were positioned halfway between a social religion and a scientific hypothesis. They were able to fuse two, until then largely independent, streams of tradition: the large-scale philosophical concepts of book writers and the practical knowledge accumulated by administrators and merchants.

As the power of middle-class groups of economic specialists in commerce, trade, and industry increased, the object of inquiry changed in structure and formed the basis for a more autonomous scientific approach. Therefore the growing autonomy of social phenomena such as markets found expression in the gradual and growing autonomy of theory about these phenomena and in the formation of the science of economics that carved out a separate sphere with immanent, autonomous laws of its own. The claim of middle-class entrepreneurs that the economy ought to be autonomous and free from state intervention became actualized. (For an interesting account of the attempts to create a "market culture" and to persuade people that the theory was in line with actuality, see Reddy 1984). The idea developed that the economy was a separate sphere and was, in fact, autonomous within society. Elias (1984:29) suggests this claim for autonomy had at least three strands:

It was a claim asserting the autonomy of the nexus of functions which formed the subject-matter of the science of economics—of the autonomy in relation to

other functions, the subject-matter of other disciplines. It was a claim to autonomy of the science whose subject-matter this nexus was—of its theories and
methods in relation to those of other disciplines. And it was also a claim to
autonomy of the class of people who were specialists in the performance of
these functions in relation to other social groups and particularly in relation to
governments.

We can therefore attempt to understand the processes whereby the
economy became posited as an independent social sphere and the relative autonomous science of economics was developed. We have already
noted some ways in which the cultural sphere may also have moved in
the direction of autonomy, and this trend of course merits a much fuller
treatment. There are, however, important differences between the
spheres, not only in the level of autonomy achieved but also in the
deficit in the power potential of the specialists in symbolic production
(artists, intellectuals, academics) compared with economic specialists
and other groups and in the nature of the form, content, and social
effectivity of the symbols and cultural goods produced. As Bendix
(1970) points out, following Weber's reasoning, the religious specialists
who monopolized magical-mythical knowledge supplied beliefs that
had a mundane meaning and a practical usefulness as a means of orientation for ordinary people. The knowledge of artists and intellectuals did
not offer similar practical benefits, despite the convictions of their advocates. Although artists, by virtue of their skills, possessed mysteries that
made them formidable, these skills did not provide power in the religious sense, and arcane knowledge without apparent purpose may even
have made the cultural elites suspect to the populace (Bendix 1970:
145). Nevertheless, the demand for such goods may increase with the
shift toward a consumer and credential based society, with its wider
market for cultural goods and associated expansion of higher education.

The endeavor to establish an autonomous sphere of high culture may
conceal a series of tensions and interdependencies within the production of culture in general. Pierre Bourdieu (1984, 1985), for example,
has suggested that the major organizing principle in cultural production
is whether symbolic considerations (which generate what he calls the
"field of restricted cultural production") or economic considerations
(the "field of large-scale cultural production") come first. As mentioned, artists and intellectuals tend to emphasize their autonomy from
the market and economic life. For Bourdieu, however, a relational dynamic operates here, because the denial of the market and the relevance
of economic capital is based on "interests in disinterestedness," an inter-

est in the enhancement of the prestige and relevance of their cultural goods—of cultural capital over economic capital. The picture is further complicated by the fact that the subfield of artistic and intellectual production itself can be seen as part of a continuum. This continuum consists of four parts: (1) the tiny mutual admiration societies of avant-gardes and bohemians who follow myths of charismatic creation and distinction and who are highly autonomous from the market; (2) cultural institutions such as academics and museums that are relatively autonomous from the market and that establish and maintain their own symbolic hierarchies and canons; (3) the cultural producers who achieve "high-society" and upper-class endorsement and success and whose cultural success is closely tied to economic profit and market success; and (4) the cultural producers who achieve mass audience or "popular" success and whose production is closely tied to the dictates of the market (see Bourdieu 1983:329).

A number of points can be made about the interrelationships of the subfields and the notion of cultural production as a whole. First, such a model, which emphasizes the relative heteronomy and autonomy of the various subfields from the market, points to the relational determinism of the various parts of the cultural sphere as a whole. It suggests that the valuation of high culture, and the devaluation of popular culture, will vary with the extent to which cultural avant-gardes and cultural institutions develop and maintain autonomy and legitimacy. We therefore need to examine the interdependencies and shifting power balances between symbolic specialists and economic specialists in a manner that accounts for the differentiation of the various subfields of the cultural sphere.

Second, we should not focus exclusively on these groups. The processes that gave rise to the cultural sphere and mass market culture took place within different state formation processes and national traditions. Maravall (1986), for example, disputes that the development of a mass culture in seventeenth-century Spain should be understood solely in terms of economic factors. Rather, he conceives of the development of baroque culture as a conservative cultural reaction to the crisis faced by the Spanish state (in particular the monarchical and seignorial sectors), which manipulated culture production to generate a new culture of spectacles for the growing urban masses. Another example is directly relevant to the potential autonomy of culture. The peculiarities of the French state formation process, which attained a high degree of centralization and integration, also promoted the view that French culture represented universal civilization and the metaculture of humankind. This view not only facilitated a serious attitude toward culture through the development of cultural institutions but also favored the development of culture as a prestigious specialism and life-style. This was particularly true for those fractions within the middle class that were attracted to the cultural ideals of the Enlightenment and the life-style of the independent writer in the eighteenth century (Darnton 1983). It also provided the basis for the development of autonomous artistic and literary bohemians and avant-gardes in Paris from the 1830s onward (Seigel 1986). Hence, to understand different societal evaluations of "high culture" or the transcultural applicability of Bourdieu's notion of "cultural capital," we need to be aware that the acceptance and the social efficacy of recognizable forms of cultural capital vary in relation to the society's degree of social and cultural integration. Outside specific metropolitan centers in the United States, cultural capital, that is, knowledge of high culture and acquired dispositions and tastes that manifest such knowledge, is accorded less legitimacy and investment potential than in France (Lamont and Lareau 1988).

Third, although certain subfields of the cultural sphere attain relative autonomy, their cultural practices may still affect everyday culture and the formation of habitus and dispositions within broader groups outside the cultural sphere, as our French example indicates. It would be useful to investigate the place of cultural ideals such as "the artist as hero" and the veneration of the artist's and intellectual's life-style within different groups, education processes, and mass cultural media. For some commentators the cultural sphere is credited with a considerable influence on everyday culture. Bell (1976) asserts that artistic modernism, with its transgressive strategies, has strongly influenced consumer culture and threatens the basis of the social bond. Martin (1981) has also considered the effects of cultural modernism and the counterculture on mainstream British culture. We also need more systematic studies on the role of the cultural sphere in the formation of dispositions, habitus, and means of orientation for different groups. Such studies would help to explore the connections between sociogenetic and psychogenetic perspectives in that the formation of the cultured or cultivated person entails tendencies that parallel the way civilizing processes ensure the control of affects and the internalization of external controls. In addition we need to focus on the long-term processes that form larger audiences and publics for the particular types of cultural goods produced within the various subfields of the cultural sphere.

Our discussion of the cultural sphere therefore suggests the need for a more differentiated notion of the cultural sphere in which the relative autonomy of the various subfields is investigated. This would better enable us to understand the relationship between those sectors that seek to achieve greater autonomy (high culture) and those sectors that are more directly tied to production for the popular markets in cultural goods (mass consumer culture). As we have emphasized, the relationship between these sectors is not fixed or static but is best conceived of as a process. It is therefore important to consider various phases that entail spurts toward autonomy (which, as mentioned, was particularly marked in nineteenth-century France) and toward heteronomy (phases of cultural declassification in which cultural enclaves are pulled into wider economic markets for cultural goods such as postmodernism). We therefore need to focus upon certain phases in the history of particular societies to understand the processes that lead to the formation and deformation of the cultural sphere. This entails examining the particular intergroup and class fractional power struggles and interdependencies that increase or diminish the power potential of cultural specialists and the societal valuation of their cultural goods and theories.

Here it would be useful to investigate the relationship between particular theoretical conceptions of the nature, scope, and purpose of culture produced by cultural specialists and the differential pulls toward autonomy and heteronomy. The intention in this chapter has therefore been to argue for a long-term process perspective on culture in which the focus is on neither cultural production nor cultural consumption per se. Rather, we need to examine both their necessary interrelationship and the swings toward theorizations that emphasize the exclusivity of the explanatory value of either approach given the rise and fall of particular figurations of people involved in interdependencies and power struggles. In effect we need to focus on the long-term process of cultural production within Western societies that has enabled the development of a massive capacity for producing, circulating, and consuming symbolic goods.

Note

1. The relationship between values and action is complex, as the secondary literature on Weber's *Protestant Ethic* thesis attests (see Marshall 1982:64ff.). Bendix's (1970:146ff.) discussion of the *Protestant Ethic* is a useful clarification

of the different ways in which cultural values are transmitted to the populace under contrasting conditions of intense religiosity and secularization. Campbell's study unfortunately does not direct sufficient attention to the interpersonal nexus of conduct and the key role that cultural specialists play in attempting to promote, transmit, and sustain beliefs under conditions of increased secularization in which one can presume a greater hiatus between high culture and everyday experience. Although we do know that the middle classes have a greater capacity to take beliefs seriously, we need more evidence of the effects of beliefs on actual conduct.

References

Appadurai, A. 1986. "Introduction: Commodities and the politics of value." In *The social life of things*, edited by A. Appadurai. Cambridge: Cambridge University Press.

Baudrillard, J. 1970. *La société de consommation*. Paris: Gallimard.

———. 1983a. *Simulations*. New York: Semiotext(e).

———. 1983b. *In the shadow of the silent majorities*. New York: Semiotext(e).

Bell, D. 1976. *The cultural contradictions of capitalism*. London: Heinemann.

Bendix, R. 1970. "Culture, social structure and change." In *Embattled reason: essays on social knowledge*. New York: Oxford University Press.

Bennett, T. et al. 1977. *The study of culture*. Milton Keynes: Open University Press.

Bennett, T., G. Martin, C. Mercer, and T. Woollacott, eds. 1981. *Culture, ideology and social process*. London: Batsford.

Bourdieu, P. 1979. The production of belief: Contribution to an economy of symbolic goods. *Media, Culture and Society* 2:261–93.

———. 1983. The field of cultural production. *Poetics* 12:311–56.

———. 1984. *Distinction*. London: Routledge.

———. 1985. The market of symbolic goods. *Poetics* 14:13–44.

Bourdieu, P., L. Boltanski, R. Castel, and J. C. Chamboredon, 1965. *Un art moyen*. Paris: Minuit.

Bourdieu, P., and A. Darbel. 1966. *L'amour de l'art*. Paris: Minuit.

Bourdieu, P., and J. C. Passeron. 1971. *La reproduction*. Paris: Minuit.

Burke, P. 1978. *Popular culture in early modern Europe*. London: Temple Smith.

Campbell, C. 1987. *The romantic ethic and the spirit of modern consumerism*. Oxford: Blackwell.

Darnton, R. 1983. *The literary underground of the old regime*. Cambridge: Harvard University Press.

Davidoff, L. 1973. *The best circles: Society, etiquette and season*. London: Croom Helm.

Debord, G. 1970. *Society of the spectacle*. Detroit: Red & Black.

de Certeau, M. 1981. The discovery of everyday life, a sample. *Tabloid* 3:24–30.

Douglas, M., and B. Isherwood. 1980. *The world of goods.* Harmondsworth: Penguin.

Dumont, L. 1986. Collective identities and universalist ideology: The actual interplay. *Theory, Culture and Society* 3(3):25–34.

Eagleton, T. 1984. *The function of criticism.* London: Verso.

Elias, N. 1971. Sociology of knowledge: New perspectives, part 1. *Sociology* 5.

———. 1978. *The civilizing process.* Vol. 1, *The history of manners.* Oxford: Blackwell.

———. 1983. *The court society.* Oxford: Blackwell.

———. 1984. On the sociogenesis of sociology. *Sociologisch Tijdschrift* 11(1).

Elias, N., and E. Dunning. 1987. *Quest for excitement, sport and leisure in the civilizing process.* Oxford: Blackwell.

Ewen, S. 1976. *Captains of consciousness.* New York: McGraw-Hill.

Ewen, S., and E. Ewen. 1982. *Channels of desire.* New York: McGraw-Hill.

Featherstone, M. 1988. In pursuit of the postmodern. *Theory, Culture and Society* 5(2–3):195–215.

———. 1989a. Towards a sociology of postmodern culture. In *Culture and social structure,* edited by H. Haferkamp. Berlin: de Gruyter.

———. 1989b. Postmodernism, cultural change and social practice. In *Jameson/postmodernism/critique,* edited by D. Kellner. Washington, D.C.: Maisoneuve Press.

———. 1991. *Consumer culture and postmodernism.* London: Sage.

Habermas, J. 1974. The public sphere. *New German Critique* 3.

———. 1981. *The theory of communicative action,* Vol. 1. London: Heinemann.

Hall, S., D. Hobson, D. Lowe, and P. Willis, eds. 1980. *Culture, media and language.* London: Hutchinson.

Hebdige, D. 1979. *Subculture: The meaning of style.* London: Methuen.

Hirsch, F. 1976. *The social limits to growth.* London: Routledge.

Hohendahl, P. U. 1982. *The institution of criticism.* Ithaca: Cornell University Press.

Horkheimer, M., and T. Adorno. 1972. *Dialectic of enlightenment.* New York: Herder & Herder.

Jameson, F. 1982. Reification and utopia in mass culture. *Social Text* 1(1):130–148.

———. 1984. Postmodernism or the cultural logic of late capitalism. *New Left Review* 146:52–92.

Kellner, D. 1983. Critical theory, commodities and the consumer society. *Theory, Culture and Society* 3(3):66–83.

Lamont, M., and A. Lareau. 1988. Cultural capital: Allisons, gaps and glissandos in recent theoretical developments. *Sociological Theory* 6(2):153–168.

Leiss, W. 1978. *The limits to satisfaction.* London: Marion Boyars.

———. 1983. The icons of the marketplace. *Theory, Culture and Society* 1(3):10–21.

Leiss, W., S. Kline, and S. Jhally. 1986. *Social communication in advertising.* London: Methuen.

Linder, S. 1970. *The harried leisure class.* New York: Columbia University Press.

Lowenthal, L. 1961. *Literature, popular culture, and society.* Palo Alto, Calif.: Pacific Books.

Lunn, E. 1986. Cultural populism and egalitarian democracy. *Theory and Society* 15:479–517.

McKendrick, N., J. Brewer, and J. H. Plumb. 1982. *The birth of a consumer society.* London: Hutchinson.

Mannheim, K. 1956. The problem of the intelligentsia. In *Essays on the sociology of culture,* edited by E. Mannheim and P. Kecskemeti. London: Routledge.

Maravall, J. A. 1986. *The culture of the baroque.* Manchester: Manchester University Press.

Marcuse, H. 1964. *One-dimensional man.* London: Routledge.

Marshall, G. 1982. *In search of the spirit of capitalism.* London: Hutchinson.

Martin, B. 1981. *A sociology of contemporary cultural change.* Oxford: Blackwell.

Mennell, S. 1985. *All manners of food.* Oxford: Blackwell.

———. 1987. On the civilizing of appetite. *Theory, Culture and Society* 4(2–3):373–403.

Minchinton, W. 1982. Convention, fashion and consumption: Aspects of British experience since 1750. In *Consumer behaviour and economic growth,* edited by H. Baudel and H. van der Meulen. London: Croom Helm.

New Formations. 1983. *Formations of pleasure.* London: Routledge.

Preteceille, E., and J. P. Terrail. 1985. *Capitalism, consumption and needs.* Oxford: Blackwell.

Reddy, W. M. 1984. *The rise of market culture.* Cambridge: Cambridge University Press.

Sahlins, M. 1976. *Culture and practical reason.* Chicago: Chicago University Press.

Seigel, J. 1986. *Bohemian Paris.* New York: Viking.

Shils, E. 1960. Mass society and its culture. *Daedalus* 89(2):288–314.

Springborg, P. 1981. *The problem of human needs and the critique of civilisation.* London: Allen and Unwin.

Stallybrass, P., and A. White. 1986. *The political and poetics of transgression.* London: Methuen.

Stauth, G., and B. S. Turner. 1988. Nostalgia, postmodernism and the critique of mass culture. *Theory, Culture and Society* 5(203):509–526.

Swingewood, A. 1977. *The myth of mass culture.* London: Macmillan.

Vowinckel, G. 1987. Command or refine? Culture patterns of cognitively organizing emotions. *Theory, Culture and Society* 4(2–3):489–514.

Weber, M. 1948. The religious rejections of the world and their directions. In *From Max Weber,* edited by H. H. Gerth and C. Wright Mills. London: Routledge.

Wilensky, H. L. 1964. Mass society and mass culture: Interdependencies or dependencies. *American Sociological Review* 29(2):173–97.

Williams, R. 1961. *Culture and society 1780–1950.* Harmondsworth: Penguin.

PART FOUR

Culture, Technology, and Work

11

The Promise
of a Cultural Sociology
Technological Discourse and the Sacred
and Profane Information Machine
Jeffrey C. Alexander

The gradual permeation of the computer into the pores of modern life deepens what Max Weber called the "rationalization of the world." The computer converts every message—regardless of its substantive meaning, metaphysical remoteness, or emotional allure—into a series of numerical bits and bytes. These series are connected to others through electrical impulses. Eventually these impulses are converted back into the media of human life.

Can there be any better example of the subjection of worldly activity to impersonal rational control? Can there be any more forceful illustration of the disenchantment of the world that Weber warned would be the result? Much depends on the answer to this portentous question, for discourse about the meaning of advanced technology demarcates one of the central ideological penumbra of the age. If the answer is yes, we are not only trapped inside of Weber's cage of iron but also bound by the laws of exchange that Marx asserted would eventually force everything human into a commodity form.

This query about the rationalization of the world poses theoretical questions, not just existential ones. Can there really exist a world of purely technical rationality? Although this question may be ideologically compelling for critics of the modern world, I will argue that the theory underlying such a proposition is not correct. Because both action and its environments (Alexander 1982–1983, 1988a) are indelibly interpenetrated by the nonrational, a pure technically rational world cannot exist. Certainly the growing centrality of the digital computer is

293

an empirical fact. This fact, however, remains to be interpreted and explained.

It is theory that provides the framework for interpretation and explanation. In the following section I outline a theoretical model that provides a more accurate understanding and that points to a more culturally sensitive sociology. On the basis of this model, I will argue against the validity of Weber's conception of rationalization. First, I critically examine sociological accounts of technology in general, arguing that by eliminating technology's symbolic status, these accounts reduce it to a cog in the social system. From there I turn to an empirical examination of the social understandings of the computer that have emerged over the last half century. Far from leading to (or from) the rationalization of society, this prototype of modern technology has been caught within a deep and traditional cultural web. I conclude that the rationalization thesis is a reflection of this web of symbolism rather than an explanation of it. It crystallizes the sentiments and symbolic meanings that underlie what is perceived to be peculiarly modern about our world.

Taking Meaning Seriously

Contemporary sociology is almost entirely the study of social elements from the perspective of their place in the social system. The promise of a cultural sociology is that a more multidimensional perspective can be attained. From this multidimensional perspective, social elements would no longer be seen naturalistically, as things that can exist, in and of themselves, without the mediation of cultural codes. Although this naturalistic view seems pragmatically justified in terms of how we experience the world (Rochberg-Halton 1986), in fact, it reifies persons and institutions.[1]

Such reification is most obvious in the theoretical traditions that have emerged from the dichotomies of the post-Parsonian world (Alexander 1987: chaps. 8–20). Microtheorists tend to see actors as omnipowerful meaning-creators, as hard-headed rationalizers, as participants in networks that have immediate situational relevance. Macrotheorists are inclined to see the world in terms of *Realpolitik*.[2] In more subtle ways, this pragmatic reification has vitiated the contributions of theorists who have given the cultural realm more serious attention. From Simmel to Parsons, theorists have justified an exclusively social system reference for sociology—its self-limitation to institutions, interactions, and institutionalized values—by apportioning disciplinary specialties. Anthropology or literary studies explain symbolic patterns; sociologists focus on real interactions.[3]

While Simmel and Parsons described this specialization as an analytic one, the argument is closely connected to the approach that makes culture into a concrete variable. In the worst case this variable is high culture. From this perspective, "cultural sociologists" are limited to research on art museums and musical taste, and mass society theorists speak about the decline of culture in the modern world.[4] More common, but just as misleading, culture is equated with ideological attitudes and contrasted to—measured against the effect of—economic interests; it is equated with values and contrasted with norms; it is equated with religion and weighted against the effects of political position. Common to all these approaches is the "everything else" argument. Other than this particular variable, their adherents suggest, everything else is noncultural. Everything else exists in its social system form.

The alternative to such "type analysis" is an analytic approach, but one that will not relegate symbolic status to disciplines outside sociology. This approach, rather than understanding symbolic and material forces in a pluralistic and "generous" way, assumes that both are always present as analytical dimensions of the same empirical unit. From the analytic perspective, every social object can be analyzed as a cultural object, every social structure as a "culture structure" (for this concept, see Rambo and Chan 1990; for a general defense of the analytic approach to culture, see Kane 1991). Events, actors, roles, groups, and institutions, as elements in a concrete society, are part of a social system; they are simultaneously, however, part of a cultural system that overlaps, but is not contiguous with, the society. I define culture as an organized set of meaningfully understood symbolic patterns. It is because of their location in such an organized set that every social interaction can also be understood as a text (Ricoeur 1971).

Only if these analytical transformations are made, can the thickness of human life (Geertz 1973), its dimensionality and nuance, enter into the language of social science. Dilthey (1976) prepared us to respect this density by insisting that all social action rests upon the reservoir of our inner experience of life. Because we experience the world rather than simply behave in it, the world is meaningful. As social scientists, we must describe the world's inner life or we will fail to describe "it" at all. We cannot, moreover, handle the problem of meaning cavalierly, taking its character for granted as something obvious and shifting our attention to this meaning's cause or effects, as does the culture-as-variable approach.[5] Rather, we must willingly inhabit the world of meaning itself.

To try to inhabit this world does not mean orienting ourselves to the idiosyncratic attitudes of individuals. This is the "getting into the actor's head" approach advocated by microtheorists such as symbolic interactionists.[6] Because culture is an environment of every action, to inhabit the world of meaning is, rather, to enter into the organized sets of symbolic patterns that these actors meaningfully understand. This is not to say that social science aims to describe cultural patterns in and of themselves. In the first place, mere description is impossible; cultural analysis consists of interpretation and reconstruction. In the second place, to attempt a complex understanding of meaningful sets is not to eschew a fuller explanatory goal. Indeed, my contention here is quite the opposite. Only with a more muscular understanding of culture can we gain a real, multidimensional understanding of the relation between symbolic systems and more traditional sociological referents.[7]

We cannot enter this world of meaning armed only with methodologies, our sensibilities and hermeneutical circles well in hand. We can do so only with strong theories about how the cultural system actually works. For this, hermeneutics, whether Dilthey's or Gadamer's, is hopelessly unprepared. Sociological theories of modern culture are not much better. Beyond the death of meaning, Weber (1958) suggests its fragmentation into autonomous spheres of cognitive, moral, and aesthetic knowledge. This perspective leads us to understand the antagonism, or paradoxes, between different beliefs and competing social actions (Schluchter 1979). It does not lead us to pattern-interpretation, the effort to understand these patterns in and of themselves.[8] For his part, Durkheim (1951) often endorses a complementary view of the dissolution of meaning. In the best-known examples to the contrary, he (1933, 1973) theorizes the generalization and growing abstraction of the collective conscience. This approach lends itself to the blurring and vulgarization of the symbolic patterns in organized sets, leading the analyst to look at culture from the outside, in terms of its social effects.

Parsons draws on both Weber's and Durkheim's theories, transmuting them (for example, Parsons 1966) into accounts of cultural differentiation and value generalization. The precision of his theorizing makes the implications of this approach much clearer than in classical work. Parsons (for example, Parsons and Shils 1951) declares that he is not concerned with the internal geography of the culture structure, which he calls *symbol systems*. Rather, he says, sociology should study only the institutionalized segment of culture, in Parsons's terms not the *cultural system*, but the *latency*, or *pattern maintenance*, *subsystem* of the social system. These specialized elements are called *values* in Parsons's theory.[9] Parsons examined socialization and specification to study the manner in which differentiated and generalized values affect the organization of the social system: the support for politics, the motivation for work, the nature of professions, and the operation of universities. He studied, in other words, not the internal structure of symbolic systems, but the processes by which a given culture structure becomes institutionalized in society.[10]

Contemporary critical theory is similar in surprising respects, though it hardly gives institutionalization its due. For Habermas, neither meaning nor culture structure is the real object of analysis. On the basis of Weber's and Parsons's evolutionary theory, the existence of a small number of abstract, differentiated, and specific normative patterns is assumed (Habermas 1984). The concern is not with interpreting normative patterns but with tracing how actors refer to patterns and, particularly, with the effect this reference has on the relations between actors and institutions. Recreating the inner world of modern objects, however, involves much more rigorous and internally complex theoretical resources. To acquire these resources, we must turn to extrasociological traditions and to sociological theories of premodern life.

If we begin with the notion that culture is a form of language, we can make use of the conceptual architecture provided by Saussure's semiotics, his "science of signs." Though they perhaps are not as tightly organized as real languages (but see Barthes 1983), cultural sets have definite codelike properties. They are composed of strongly structured symbolic relationships that are largely independent of any particular actor's volition or speech. Cultural codes, like linguistic languages, are built upon signs, which contain both signifier and signified. Technology, for example, is not only a thing, a signified object to which others refer, it is also a signifier, a signal, an internal expectation. The relation between signifier and signified, Saussure insists, is "arbitrary." When he writes (1964) that the former "has no natural connection with the signified," he is suggesting that the meaning or nature of the sign—its name or internal dimension—cannot be understood as being dictated by the nature of the signified, that is, by the sign's external, material dimension.

If the meaning of the sign cannot be observed or induced from examining the signified, or objective, referents, then how is it established? By its relation to other signifiers, Saussure insists. Systems of signs are composed of endless such relationships. At their most primitive, these relationships are binary. In any actual system of cultural sets, they become long strings, or webs, of interwoven analogies and antitheses, what Eco (1979) calls the "similitude of signifiers" that compose the "global semantic field."[11] Structural anthropology has illustrated the usefulness of this architecture, most famously in the work of Lévi-Strauss (1967) and most usefully in the work of Sahlins (1976, 1981).

Yet, even at its most socially embedded, semiotics can never be enough. By definition it abstracts from the social world, taking organized symbolic sets as psychologically unmotivated and as socially uncaused. By contrast, for the purposes of cultural sociology, semiotic codes must be tied into both social and psychological environments and into action itself. I will term the result of this specification *discourses,* in appreciation of, though not identification with, the phenomena conceptualized by Foucault. Discourses are symbolic sets that embody clear references to social system relationships, whether defined in terms of power, solidarity, or other organizational forms (cf. Sewell 1980; Hunt 1984).[12] As social languages, they relate binary symbolic associations with social forms. In doing so, they provide a vocabulary for members to speak graphically about a society's highest values, its relevant groups, its boundaries vis-à-vis conflict, creativity, and internal dissent. Discourse socializes semiotic codes and emerges as a series of narratives (Ricoeur 1984)—myths that specify and stereotype a society's founding and founders (Eliade 1959; Bellah 1970a), its critical events (Alexander 1988b), and utopian aspirations (Smith 1950).

In their theories of premodern cultures, classical sociologists constructed powerful models of how this social construction of semiotic codes can proceed. They did so in terms of their theories of religion. Thus, drawing from primitive totemism, Durkheim (1964) argued that every religion organizes social things into both binary relations and deeply felt antitheses between sacred and profane. Because sacred objects have to be protected, the "society" maintains a distance between them and other objects, either routine or profane. Actors not only try to protect themselves from coming into contact with polluted (Douglas 1966) or profane (Caillois 1959) objects, but also seek a real, if mediated, contact with the sacred. This is one primary function of ritual behavior (Turner 1969; cf. Alexander 1988c).

While Weber's better-known theory of religion overlaps with Durkheim's, it is historically and comparatively specific. Given the emergence of a more formal and rationalized religion, the goal of believers becomes salvation from worldly suffering (Weber 1946a). Salvation creates the problem of theodicy, "from what" and "for what" one will be saved. Theodicy involves the image of God. If the gods or God is immanent, worshipers seek salvation through an internal experience of mystical contact. If God is transcendent, salvation is achieved more ascetically, by correctly divining God's will and following his commands. Each of these mandates can be pursued, moreover, in either a this-worldly or an otherworldly direction.

While Durkheim and Weber generally limited the application of these cultural theories to premodern religious life, it is possible to extend them to secular phenomena. This possibility is clarified when we define religions as types of semiotic systems, as discourses that reveal how the psychological and social structuring of culture proceeds.[13]

In this section I have briefly sketched a model for examining the cultural dimension of social life. I hope merely that this discussion provides an introduction to what follows. Before examining the construction of the computer as a cultural object in the postwar world, however, I look at a range of earlier sociological treatments of technology to sense the difficulties that a more culturally sensitive approach must overcome.

Sociological Accounts of Technology: The Dead Hand of the Social System

Considered in its social system reference, technology is a thing that can be touched, observed, interacted with, and calculated in an objectively rational way. Analytically, however, technology is also part of the cultural system. It is a sign, both a signifier and a signified, in relation to which actors cannot entirely separate their subjective states of mind. Social scientists have not usually considered technology in this more subjective way. Indeed, they have not typically considered it as a cultural object at all. It has appeared as the material variable par excellence, not as a point of sacrality, but as the most routine of the routine, not a sign, but an antisign, the essence of a modernity that has undermined the very possibility for cultural understanding itself.

In the postmodern era, Marx has become infamous for his effusive praise in *The Communist Manifesto* of technology as the embodiment of scientific rationality. Marx believed that modern industrial technique, as the harbinger of progress, was breaking down the barriers of primitive and magical thought. Stripped of its capitalist integument, Marx predicted, advanced technology would be the mainspring of industrial communism, which he defined as the administration of *things* rather than *people*.[14] Despite the central role he gives to technology, for Marx it is not a form of knowledge, even of the most rational sort. It is a material variable, a "force of production" (Marx 1962). As an element of the base, technology is something actors relate to mechanistically. It is produced because the laws of the capitalist economy force factory owners to lower their costs. The effects of this incorporation are equally objective. As technology replaces human labor, the organic composition of capital changes and the rate of profit falls; barring mitigating factors, this falling rate causes the collapse of the capitalist system.

While neo-Marxism has revised the determining relationship Marx posits between economy and technology, it continues to accept Marx's view of technology as a purely material fact. In Rueschemeyer's recent work on the relation between power and the division of labor, for example, neither general symbolic patterns nor the internal trajectory of rational knowledge are conceived of as affecting technological growth. "It is the inexorability of interest and power constellations," Rueschemeyer (1986: 117–118) argues, "which shape even fundamental research and which determine translations of knowledge into new products and new ways of production." We would expect modern functionalism to view technology very differently, but this is true in an only limited sense. Of course, Parsons (1967) criticized Marx for putting technology into the base; functionalists have always been aware that technology belongs in a more intermediate position in the social system. They have, however, never looked at it as anything other than the product of rational knowledge, and they have often conceived of its efficient causes and specific effects in material terms.

In *Science, Technology, and Society in Seventeenth-Century England,* Merton emphasizes the role that puritanism played in inspiring scientific inventions. Within the context of this inventive climate, however, the immediate cause of technology was economic benefit. The "relation between a problem raised by economic development and technologic endeavor is clear-cut and definite," Merton argues (1970: 144), suggesting that "importance in the realm of technology is often concretely allied with economic estimations." It was the "vigorous economic development" of the time that led to effective inventions, because it "posed the most imperative problems for solution" (146). In Smelser's (1959) later account of the industrial revolution, the perspective is exactly the same. Methodist values form a background input to technological innovation, but they are not involved in the creation or the effects of technology itself. Innovation is problem driven, not culture driven, and the immediate cause is economic demand. The effect of technology is also concrete and material. By resolving strain at the social system level, innovation allows collective behavior to leave the level of generalized behavior—wish fulfillment, fantasy, utopian aspirations—and return to the more mundane and rational attitudes of the everyday (Smelser 1959: 21–50).

Parsons himself is more sensitive to the subjective environment of technology. While acknowledging that it is "a product of productive processes," he insists (1960: 135) that it depends ultimately on cultural resources. In a characteristic move, he turns his discussion of technology from economic issues to a focus on the origins of "usable knowledge." He describes the latter as "produced by two processes which, though economic factors play a part, are clearly predominantly noneconomic, namely research and education" (135). In other words, while Parsons recognizes that technology is, in the most important sense, a product of subjective knowledge rather than material force, this recognition leads him, not to the analysis of symbolic processes, but to the study of institutional processes, namely research and education. When Parsons and Platt explore these processes in *The American University* (1973), they take the input from culture—the "rationality value"—as a given, focusing instead on how this value becomes institutionalized in the social system.

Critical theory, drawing from Weber's rationalization theme, differs from orthodox Marxism in its attention to the relation between technology and consciousness. But whereas Weber (for example, 1946b) viewed the machine as the objectification of discipline, calculation, and rational organization, critical theorists reverse the causal relation, asserting that it is technology that creates rationalized culture by virtue of its brute physical and economic power. "If we follow the path taken by labour in its development from handicraft [to] manufacture to machine industry," Lukács writes (1971: 88), "we can see a continuous trend toward greater rationalization [as] the process of labour is progressively broken down into abstract, rational, specialized operations." This technologically driven rationalization eventually spreads to all social spheres, leading to the objectification of society and the "reified mind" (93). Lukács insists that he is concerned "with the *principle* at work here" (88, original italics), but the principle is the result of technology conceived as a material force.

This shift toward the pivotal ideological role of technology, without giving up its materialist conceptualization or its economic cause, culminates in Marcuse's later work. To explain the reasons for "one-dimensional society," Marcuse actually focuses more on technological production per se than on its capitalist form. Again, that technology is a purely instrumental, rational phenomenon Marcuse takes completely for granted. Its "sweeping rationality," Marcuse writes (1963: xiii), "propels efficiency and growth." The problem, once again, is that this "technical progress [is] extended to a whole system of domination and coordination" (xii). When it is, it institutionalizes throughout the society a purely formal and abstract norm of rationality. This technological "culture" suppresses any ability to imagine social alternatives. As Marcuse states (xvi), "technological rationality has become political rationality."

New class and postindustrial theories make this critical theory more nuanced and sophisticated, but they do not overcome its fatal anticultural flaw. Gouldner accepts the notion that scientists, engineers, and government planners have a rational worldview because of the technical nature of their work. Technocratic competence depends on higher education, and the expansion of higher education depends in the last analysis on production driven by technology. Indeed, Gouldner finds no fault with technocratic competence in and of itself; he takes it as a paradigm of universalism, criticism, and rationality. When he attacks the technocrats' false consciousness, he does so because they extend this rationality beyond their sphere of technical competence: "The new ideology holds [that] the *society's* problems are solvable on a technological basis, with the use of educationally acquired technical competence" (1979: 24, italics added). By pretending to understand society at large, the new class can provide a patina of rationality for the entire society. Gouldner also emphasizes, of course, that this very expansion of technical rationality can create a new kind of class conflict and a "rational" source of social change. This notion, of course, is simply the old contradiction between (technological) forces and relations of production, dressed in postindustrial garb. When Szelenyi and Martin (1987) criticize Gouldner's theory as economistic, they have touched its theoretical core.

Using similar theoretical distinctions, conservative theorists have reached different ideological conclusions. In his postindustrial theory, Bell (1976) also emphasizes the growing cultural rationality of modern societies, a cultural pattern he, too, ties directly to technological and productive demands. In order to produce and maintain the advanced technologies that are at the basis of postindustrial economic and political institutions, scientific values and scientific education have become central to modern life. In the political and economic spheres of modern societies, therefore, sober, rational, and instrumental culture is the rule. It is only in reaction against this technological sphere that there develop, according to Bell (1976), irrational, postmodern values, which create the cultural contradictions of capitalist society. Here the contradiction between (technological) forces and relations is dressed in other garb. Because Ellul, the other, more conservative, theorist of "technological society," wrote before the 1960s, he views the social effects of technology as more thoroughly instrumental and rational than does Bell. Propelled by "the search for greater efficiency" (Ellul 1964: 19), technique "clarifies, arranges, and rationalizes" (5). It exists in "the domain of the abstract" (5) and has no relation to cultural values or to the real needs of human life.

It is fitting to close this section with Habermas, for the distinction between the world of technique (variously defined as work, organization, or system) and the world of humanity (communication, norms, or lifeworld) has marked a fateful contrast throughout his work. Habermas (1968a: 57) defines technology in what is by now a familiar way. He believes it to be the "scientifically rationalized control of objectified processes" and contrasts it with phenomena that are related to "the practical question of how men can and want to live." With the increasing centrality of technology, the meaningful organization of the world is displaced by purposive-rational organization. "To the extent that technology and science permeate social institutions and thus transform them," Habermas (1968b: 81) insists, "old legitimations are destroyed."

These old legitimations were based on tradition, "the older mythic, religious, and metaphysical worldviews" that addressed "the central questions of men's collective existence [for example] justice and freedom, violence and oppression, happiness and gratification . . . love and hate, salvation and damnation (96)." After technology has done its work, however, these questions can no longer be asked: "The culturally defined self-understanding of a social life-world is replaced by the self-reification of men under categories of purposive-rational action and adaptive behavior" (105–6). There has ensued a "horizontal extension of subsystems of purposive-rational action," such that "traditional structures are increasingly subordinated to conditions of instrumental or strategic rationality" (98). In this particular sense, Habermas (111) argues, the ideology of technology has displaced all previous ideologies. Because it is so stubbornly rationalistic, this new ideology does not exhibit "the opaque force of a delusion" or a "wish-fulfilling fantasy," nor is it "based in the same way [as earlier ideologies] on the causality of dissociated symbols and unconscious motives." This ideology, Habermas believes, has abandoned any attempt to "express a projection of the 'good life.' "

In the discussion that follows, I will demonstrate that these suppositions about technological consciousness are false. Only because Habermas has accepted the possibility of a radical historicization of consciousness can he believe them to be true. My own discussion begins from quite the opposite understanding. It is impossible for a society to be dominated by technical rationality because the mental structures of humankind cannot be radically historicized; in crucial respects, they are unchanging. Human beings continue to experience the need to invest the world with metaphysical meaning and to experience solidarity with objects outside the self. Certainly, the ability to calculate objectively and impersonally is perhaps the clearest demarcation of modernity. But this remains one institutionalized complex (Parsons 1951) of motives, actions, and meanings among many others. Individuals can exercise scientifically rational orientations in certain situations, but even in these instances their actions are not scientifically rational as such. Objectivity is a cultural norm, a system of social sanctions and rewards, a motivational impulse of the personality. It remains nested, however, within deeply irrational systems of psychological defense and cultural systems of an enduringly primordial kind.

This is not to deny that technological production has become more central with the advent of postindustrial society. There has been a quickening in the substitution of information for physical energy, which Marx described as a shift in the organic composition of capital, with dramatic consequences. The shift from manual to mental labor has transformed the class structure and the typical strains of capitalist and socialist societies. The increased capacity for storing information has strengthened the control of bureaucracy over the information that it constantly needs. But the sociological approaches to technology, which we have examined in this section, extend much further than such empirical observations. The stronger version of Marxist and critical theory describes a technologically obsessed society whose consciousness is so narrowed that the meaningful concerns of traditional life are no longer possible. The weaker versions of functionalist and postindustrial theory describe technology as a variable that has a merely material status and orientations to technology as cognitively rational and routine. From my point of view, however, neither of these positions is correct. The ideas that inform even modern society are not cognitive repositories of verified facts; they are symbols that continue to be shaped by deep emotional impulses and molded by meaningful constraints.

Technological Discourse and Salvation

We must learn to see technology as a discourse, as a sign system that is subject to semiotic constraints and responsive to social and psychological demands. The first step to this alternative conception of modern technology is to reconceptualize its introduction so that it is open to metaphysical terms. Ironically, perhaps, Weber himself provided the best indication of how this can be done.

Weber argued that those who created modern industrial society did so in order to pursue salvation. The Puritan capitalists practiced what Weber (1958) called *this-worldly asceticism*. Through hard work and self-denial they produced wealth as proof that God had predestined them to be saved. Weber (1963) demonstrated, indeed, that salvation has been a central concern of humankind for millennia. Whether it be heaven or nirvana, the great religions have promised human beings an escape from toil and suffering and a release from earthly constraints—only if humans conceived of the world in certain terms and strove to act in certain ways. In order to historicize this conception of salvation and to allow comparative explanation of it, Weber developed the typology of this-worldly versus otherworldly paths to salvation, which he interwove with the distinction between ascetic and mystical. The disciplined, self-denying, and impersonal action upon which modernization depended, Weber argued, could be achieved only by acting in a this-worldly, ascetic way. Compared to Buddhist or Hindu holy men, the Puritan saints focused their attention much more completely on this world. Rather than allowing themselves the direct experience of God and striving to become vessels of his spirit, they believed that they would be saved by becoming practical instruments for carrying out his will. This-worldly salvation was the cultural precursor for the impersonal rationality and objectivism that, in Weber's view (1958: 181–183), eventually dominated the world.

While Weber's religious theory is of fundamental importance, it has two substantial weaknesses. First, Weber conceived the modern style of salvation in a caricatured way. It has never been as one-sidedly ascetic as he suggests. This-worldly activity is permeated by desires to escape from the world, just as the ascetic self-denial of grace is punctuated by episodes of mystical intimacy. In an anomalous strain in his writing about modernity (Alexander 1986), Weber acknowledged that industrial society is shot through with "flights from the world," in which category he included things such as the surrender by moderns to religious belief or ideological fanaticism and the escape provided by eroticism or aestheticism. Although Weber condemned these flights as irresponsible, however, he was never able to incorporate them into his sociology of modern life. They represented a force with which his historicist and overly ideal-typical theory could not contend.

In truth, modern attempts to pursue salvation in purely ascetic ways have always short-circuited, not only in overtly escapist forms but also in the everyday world itself. We would never know from Weber's account, for example, that the Puritans conceived of their relationship to God in terms of the intimacies of holy matrimony (Morgan 1958); nor would we be aware that outbursts of mystical "antinomianism" were a constant, recurring danger in Puritan life. The post-Puritan tradition of evangelical Protestantism, which developed in Germany, England, and the United States in the late eighteenth and early nineteenth centuries, was distinguished by its significant opening to mystical experience. One of its cultural offshoots, the modern ideology of romantic love (Lewis 1983), reflected the continuing demand for immediate, transformative salvation in the very heart of the industrial age.

This last example points to the second major problem in Weber's religious theory, its historicism. Weber believed that a concern with salvation could permeate and organize worldly experience only so long as scientific understanding had not undermined the possibility of accepting an extramundane, divine telos for progress on earth. As I suggested previously, this mistaken effort to rationalize contemporary discourse can be corrected by incorporating the more structural understandings of Durkheim's religious sociology. Durkheim believed that human beings continue to divide the world into sacred and profane and that even modern men and women need to experience mystical centers directly through ritual encounters with the sacred. In the modern context, then, Weber's salvation theory can be elaborated and sustained only by turning to Durkheim. The fit can be made even tighter if we make the alteration in Durkheim's theory suggested by Caillois (1959), who argued that alongside sacred and profane there was a third term, *routine*. Whereas routine life does not partake of ritual experience, sacred and profane experiences are both highly charged. Whereas the sacred provides an image of the good with which social actors seek community and strive to protect, the profane defines an image of evil from which human beings must be saved. This conception allows us to be more true to Weber's understanding of theodicy, even when we shift it onto the modern state. Secular salvation "religions" provide escape not only from earthly suffering in general but also more specifically from evil. Every salvation religion has conceived not only God and death, in other words, but also the devil.

It is in terms of these reconstructed arenas for symbolic discourse that our examination of the introduction of technology will proceed.

The Sacred and Profane Information Machine

Expectations for salvation were inseparable from the technological innovations of industrial capitalism. Major inventions like the steam engine, railroad, telegraph, and telephone (Pool 1983) were hailed by elites and masses as vehicles for secular transcendence. Their speed and power, it was widely proclaimed, would undermine the earthly constraints of time, space, and scarcity. In their early halcyon days, they became vessels for experiencing ecstatic release, instruments for bringing the glories of heaven down to earth. The technicians and engineers who understood this new technology were elevated to the status of worldly priests. In this technological discourse, however, the machine has been not only God but also the devil. In the early nineteenth century, Luddites lashed out at spinning machines as if they were the idols that the Hebrew fathers had condemned. William Blake decried "dark Satanic mills." Mary Shelley wrote *Frankenstein, or, the Modern Prometheus,* about the terrifying results of Victor Frankenstein's effort to build the world's most "gigantic" machine. The Gothic genre presented a revolt against the Age of Reason and insisted that dark forces were still brewing, forces that were often embodied by the engine of technology itself. It was, ironically, from such forces that the modern age had to be saved. There is a direct line from that gothic revival to Steven Spielberg's wildly popular movie, *Star Wars* (Pynchon 1984). Today's science fiction mixes technology with medieval Gothic themes, pits evil against good, and promises salvation from space, from time, and even from mortality itself.

The computer is the newest and certainly one of the most potent technological innovations of the modern age, but its symbolization has been much the same. The culture structure of technological discourse has been firmly set. In theoretical terms, the introduction of the computer into Western society resembles the much more tumultuous entrance of Captain Cook into the Sandwich Islands: it was an event "given significance and effect by the system in place" (Sahlins 1981: 21).[15]

While there were certainly "routine" assessments of the computer from 1944 to 1975—assessments that talked about it in rational, scientific, and "realistic" tones—they paled in comparison to the transcendental and mythical discourse that was filled with wish-fulfilling rhetoric of salvation and damnation. In a *Time* magazine report on the first encounter between computer and public in 1944, the machine was treated as a sacred and mysterious object. What was "unveiled" was a "bewildering 50-foot panel of knobs, wires, counters, gears and switches." The connection to higher, even cosmic, forces immediately suggested itself. *Time* described it as having been unveiled "in the presence of high officers in the Navy" and promised its readers that the new machine would solve problems "on earth as well as those posed by the celestial universe" (T8/44). This sacred status was elaborated in the years that followed. To be sacred, an object must be sharply separated from contact with the routine world. Popular literature continually recounted the distance that separated the computer from the lay public and the mystery attendant on this. In another report on the 1944 unveiling, for example, *Popular Science,* a leading lay technology magazine, described the first computer as an electrical brain whirring "behind its polished panels" secluded in "an air-conditioned basement" (PS10/44). Twenty years later the image had not changed. In 1965, a new and far more powerful computer was conceptualized in the same way, as an "isolated marvel" working in "the air-conditioned seclusion of the company's data-programming room." In unmistakable terms, *Time* elaborated this discourse of the sacred technology.

Arranged row upon row in air-conditioned rooms, waited upon by crisp young white-shirted men who move softly among them like priests serving in a shrine, the computers go about their work quietly and, for the most part, unseen from the public (T4/65).

Objects are isolated because they are thought to possess mysterious power. The connection between computer and established centers of charismatic power is repeated constantly in the popular literature. Occasionally, an analogy is made between the computer and sacred things on earth. Reporting on the unveiling of a new and more sophisticated computer in 1949, *Newsweek* called it "the real hero" of the occasion and described it, like royalty, as "holding court in the computer lab upstairs" (11/49). Often, however, more direct references to the computer's cosmic powers and even to its extrahuman status were made. In an article about the first computer, *Popular Science* reported that "everybody's notion of the universe and everything in it will be upset by the columns of figures this monster will type out" (PS10/44). Fifteen years later, a famous technical expert asserted in a widely circulated feature magazine that "forces will be set in motion whose ultimate effects for good and evil are incalculable" (RD3/60).

As the machine became more sophisticated, and more awesome, references to godly powers were openly made. The new computers "render unto Caesar by sending out the monthly bills and . . . unto God by counting the ballots of the world's Catholic bishops" (T4/65). A joke circulated to the effect that a scientist tried to stump his computer with the question: Is there a God? "The computer was silent for a moment. Then it answered: 'Now there is' " (N1/66). After describing the computer in superhuman terms—"infallible in memory, incredibly swift in math [and] utterly impartial in judgment"—a mass weekly made the obvious deduction: "This transistorized prophet can help the church adapt to modern spiritual needs" (T3/68). A leader of one national church described the Bible as a "distillation of human experience" and asserted that computers are capable of correlating an even greater range "of experience about how people ought to behave." The conclusion that was drawn underscored the deeply established connection between the computer and cosmic power: "When we want to consult the deity, we go to the computer because it's the closest thing to God to come along" (T3/68).

If an object is sacred and sealed off from the profane world, gaining access to its powers becomes a problem in itself. Priests emerge as intermediaries between divinity and laity. As one leading expert suggested, while there were many who appreciated the computer, "only specialists yet realize how these elements will all be combined and [the] far-reaching social, economic, and political implications" (RD5/60). Typically, erroneous predictions about the computer were usually attributed to "nonspecialists" (BW3/65). To possess knowledge of computing, it was emphasized time and again, requires incredible training and seclusion. Difficult new procedures must be developed. To learn how to operate a new computer introduced in 1949, specialists "spent months literally studying day and night" (N8/49). The number of people capable of undergoing such rigorous training was highly restricted. The forging of "links between human society and the robot brain" (N9/49) called for "a new race of scientists." The "new breed of specialists [which] has grown up to tend the machines," *Time* wrote sixteen years later, "have formed themselves into a solemn priesthood of the computer, purposely separated from ordinary laymen [and] speak[ing] an esoteric language that some suspect is just their way of mystifying outsiders" (T4/65). The article predicted: "There will be a small, almost separate society of people in rapport with the advanced computer. They will have established a relationship with their machines that cannot be shared with the average man. Those with talent for the work will have to develop it from childhood and will be trained as intensively as the classical ballerina." Is it surprising that, reporting on computer news ten years later, *Time* (1/74) decided its readers would be interested in learning that among this esoteric group of programmers there had emerged a new and wildly popular computer game called "the game of life"? The identification of the computer with God and of computer operators with sacred intermediaries signifies culture structures that had not changed in forty years.

The contact with the cosmic computer that these technological priests provided would, then, certainly transform earthly life. Like the revolutionary technologies that preceded it, however, the computer embodied within itself both superhuman evil and superhuman good. As Lévi-Strauss (1963) emphasized, it is through naming that the cultural codes defining an object are first constructed. In the years immediately following the introduction of the computer, efforts to name this new thinking machine were intense, and they followed the binary pattern that Durkheim and Lévi-Strauss described. The result was a "similitude of signifiers," an amplified series of sacred and profane associations that created for technological discourse a thick semantic field. One series revealed dreadful proportions and dire implications. The computer was called a "colossal gadget" (T8/44, N8/49), a "figure factory" (PS10/44), a "mountain of machinery" (PS10/44), a "monster" (PS10/44, SEP2/50), a "mathematical dreadnought" (PS10/44), a "portentous contrivance" (PS10/44), a "giant" (N8/49), a "math robot" (N8/49), a "wonder-working robot" (SEP2/50), the "Maniac" (SEP2/50), and the "Franken-stein-monster" (SEP2/50). In announcing a new and bigger computer in 1949, *Time* (9/49) hailed the "great machines that eat their way through oceans of figures like whale grazing on plankton" and described them as roaring like "a hive of mechanical insects."

In direct opposition to this profane realm, journalists and technicians also named the computer and its parts through analogies to the presumptively innocent and assuredly sacred human being. It was called a "super-brain" (PS10/44) and a "giant brain" (N8/49). Attached to an audio instrument, it was described as "a brain child with a temporary voice" and as "the only mechanical brain with a soft heart" (N10/49). Its "physiology" (SEP2/50) became a topic of debate. Computers were given an "inner memory" (T9/49), "eyes," a "nervous system" (SEP2/50), a "spinning heart" (T2/51), and a "female temperament" (SEP2/50) in addition to the brain with which they were already endowed. It was announced that they were to have "descendants" (N4/50), and in later years "families" and "generations" (T4/65) emerged. Finally, there were the developmental phrases. "Just out of its teens," *Time* announced (T4/65), the computer was about to enter a "formidable adulthood." It might do so, however, in a neurotic way, for its designers had "made a pampered and all but adored child" out of him (or her).[16]

The period of compulsive naming quickly abated, but the awesome forces for good and evil that the names symbolized have been locked in deadly combat to this day. Salvation rhetoric overcomes this dualism in one direction, apocalyptic rhetoric in another. Both moves can be seen in structural terms as overcoming binary opposition by providing a third term. But more profound emotional and metaphysical issues are also at stake. Computer discourse was eschatological because the computer was seen as involving matters of life and death.

At first, salvation was defined in narrowly mathematical terms. The new computer would "solve in a flash" (T9/49) problems that had "baffled men for years" (PS10/44). By 1950, salvation had already become much more broadly defined. "Come the Revolution!" read the headline to a story about these new predictions (T11/50). A broad and visionary ideal of progress was laid out: "Thinking machines will bring a healthier, happier civilization than any known heretofore" (SEP2/ 50). People would now be able to "solve their problems the painless electronic way" (N7/54). Airplanes, for example, would be able to reach their destinations "without one bit of help from the pilot" (PS1/55).

By 1960, public discourse about the computer had become truly millennial. "A new age in human relations has opened," a reigning expert announced (RD3/60). Like all eschatological rhetoric, the timing of this promised salvation is imprecise. It has not yet occurred, but it has already begun. It is coming in five years or ten, its effects will be felt soon, the transformation is imminent. Whatever the timing, the end result is certain. "There will be a social effect of unbelievable proportions" (RD3/60). "By surmounting the last great barrier of distance," the computer's effect on the natural world will be just as great (RD3/ 60). Most human labor will be eliminated, and people will finally be set "free to undertake completely new tasks, most of them directed toward perfecting ourselves, creating beauty, and understanding one another" (Mc5/65).[17]

The convictions were confirmed in still more sweeping tones in the late 1960s and early 1970s. The new computers had such "awesome power" (RD5/71) that, as God was recorded in the book of Genesis, they would bring "order out of chaos" (BW7/71). That "the computer age is dawning" is certain. One sign of this millennium will be that "the common way of thinking in terms of cause and effect [will be] replaced by a new awareness" (RD5/71). That this was the stuff of which "dreams are made" (USN6/67) cannot be denied. Computers would transform all natural forces. They would cure diseases and guarantee long life. They would allow everyone to know everything at all times. They would allow all students to learn easily and the best to learn perfectly. They would produce a world community and end war. They would overturn stratification and allow equality to reign. They would make government responsible and efficient, business productive and profitable, work creative, and leisure endlessly satisfying.

As for apocalypse, there was also much to say. The machine has always embodied not only the transcendental hopes but also the fear and loathing generated by industrial society. *Time* once articulated this deep ambiguity in a truly Gothic way. Viewed from the front, computers exhibit a "clean, serene dignity." This is deceptive, however, for "behind there hides a nightmare of pulsing, twitching, flashing complexity" (9/49).

Whereas contact with the sacred side of the computer is the vehicle for salvation, the profane side threatens destruction. It is something from which human beings must be saved. First, the computer creates the fear of degradation. "People are scared" (N8/68) because the computer has the power to "blot or diminish man" (RD3/60). People feel "rage and helpless frustration" (N9/69). The computer degrades because it objectifies; this is the second great fear. It will "lead to mechanical men who replace humans" (T11/50). Students will be "treated as impersonal machines" (RD1/71). Computers are inseparable from "the image of slavery" (USN11/67). It is because they are seen as objectifying human beings that computers present a concrete danger. In 1975, one popular author described his personal computer as a "humming thing poised to rip me apart" (RD11/75). More typically the danger is not mutilation but manipulation. With computers "markets can be scientifically rigged . . . with an efficiency that would make dictators blush" (SEP2/50). Their intelligence can turn them into "instruments for massive subversion" (RD3/60). They could "lead us to that ultimate horror—chains of plastic tape" (N8/66).

Finally there is the cataclysm, the final judgment on earthly technological folly that has been predicted from 1944 until the present day. Computers are "Frankenstein (monsters) which can . . . wreck the very foundations of our society" (T11/50). They can lead to "disorders [that may] pass beyond control" (RD4/60). There is a "storm brewing" (BW1/68). There are "nightmarish stories" about the "light that failed" (BW7/71). "Incapable of making allowances for error," the "Christian notion of redemption is incomprehensible to the computer" (N8/66). The computer has become the Antichrist.

I have taken the computer story to 1975. This was the eve of the "personal computer," the very name of which demonstrates how the battle between human and antihuman continued to fuel the discourse that surrounded the computer's birth. In the decade of discussion that followed, utopian and antiutopian themes remained prominent (for example, Turkle 1984: 165–196). Disappointment and "realism," however, also became more frequently expressed. In the present day, computer news has passed from the cover of *Time* to advertisements in the sports pages of daily newspapers. This is routinization. We may, indeed, be watching this latest episode in the history of technological discourse pass into history.

Conclusion

Social scientists have looked at the computer through the framework of their rationalizing discourse on modernity. For Ellul (1964: 89), it represented a phase of "technical progress" that "seems limitless" because it "consists primarily in the efficient systematization of society and the conquest of the human being." In the analysis of Lyotard, who proposes a postmodern theory, the same kind of extravagant modernizing claims are made. "It is common knowledge," according to Lyotard (1984: 4), "that the miniaturization and commercialization of machines is already changing the way in which learning is acquired, classified, made available, and exploited." With the advent of computerization, learning that cannot be "translated into quantities of information" will be abandoned. In contrast to the opacity of traditional culture, computerization produces "the ideology of communicational 'transparency' " (5), which signals the decline of the "grand narrative" and will lead to a crisis of legitimation (66–67).

I have tried to refute such rationalistic theorizing, first by developing a framework for cultural sociology and second by applying it to the technological domain. In theoretical terms, I have shown that technology is never in the social system alone. It is also a sign and possesses an internal subjective referent. Technology, in other words, is an element in the culture and the personality systems as well; it is both meaningful and motivated. In my examination of the popular literature about the computer, I have shown that this ideology is rarely factual, rational, or abstract. It is concrete, imagistic, utopian, and satanic—a discourse that is filled, indeed, with the grand narratives of life.

Let us return, in conclusion, to the sociological understandings of technology I have recounted above. Far from being empirical accounts based on objective observations and interpretations, they represent simply another version of technocratic discourse itself. The apocalyptic strain of that discourse fears degradation, objectification, slavery, and manipulation. Has not critical theory merely translated this evaluation into the empirical language of social science? The same goes for those sociological analyses that take a more benign form: they provide social scientific translations of the discourse about salvation.[18]

At stake is more than the accuracy or the distortion of social scientific statements. That the rationalization hypothesis is wrong does not make technology a benign force. The great danger that technology poses to modern life is neither the flattening out of human consciousness nor its enslavement to economic or political reality. To the contrary, it is because technology is lodged in the unreal fantasies of salvation and apocalypse that the dangers are real.

For Freud, psychoanalysis was a rational theory of the irrational, even while it did not promise an ultimate escape from unconscious life. Psychoanalysis aimed to provide a distance from irrationality, if not the high ground of conscious rationality itself. Cultural sociology can provide a similar distance and some of the same cure. Only by understanding the omnipresent shaping of technological consciousness by discourse can we hope to gain control over technology in its material form. To do so, we must gain some distance from the visions of salvation and apocalypse in which technology is so deeply embedded.[19]

Notes

1. In this respect, I could not disagree more with Rochberg-Halton's assertion that it is the semiotic and Parsonian position that leads to reification and that the pragmatic one is their antidote. It is Rochberg-Halton's commitment to Peircean semiotics that underlines his naturalism. Saussurian semiotics, by contrast, make it possible to see naturalism's fatal weaknesses. Where Saussure and Parsons emphasize the constructed meaning of objects, Peirce (1985) is obsessed with the relative "realness" of signs, in the sense of both their scientific truthfulness and their tactile representatives. On the one hand, this emphasis on the motivated, rather than the arbitrary, relation of signifier and signified (see the discussion of Saussure below) is an advantage, as demonstrated by Peirce's extremely interesting theorizing about icons and indexes. At the same time, Peirce's emphasis on the growing truthfulness of signs—*symbols* in his vocabulary—and their relationship to experience can cause serious problems, allowing Peircean analysts to emphasize the pragmatics of culture in place of the semiotics.

2. Mann's (1985) work attempts to blend micro and macro sides of the post-Parsonian response, even while it begins to move beyond them. While I believe the historical aspects of his account of the Western world are not only highly original but also largely correct, the work suffers from an anticultural theoretical bias despite the significant empirical openings it makes to religion. Mann insists that one can and should study the infrastructures of ideas, the concrete networks and communications systems through which ideas are expressed rather than the ideas themselves. His premise is that ideas are not in themselves legitimate social causes. Yet one of the major sociological explanations for these infrastructures must always be the influence of the ideas themselves.

3. I have criticized Parsons's repeated effort to apportion different variables to different disciplines in Alexander 1983: 272–276. In that discussion, how-

ever, I related this tendency to Parsons's idealism, for he apportioned to sociology the specialization in normative rather than material forces (in his later work, it was the study of the integrative subsystem of general action, which specializes in affect). Here I criticize this disciplinary apportionment because it allowed Parsons to escape from a true confrontation with symbolic codes. Although Parsons provided the baseline for any contemporary effort to create a multidimensional cultural sociology, he blocked its development by insisting that sociology focus only on the institutionalized segment of culture, in his terms not the *cultural system,* but the *latency,* or *pattern maintenance, subsystem* of the social system. Only these specialized elements are called *values* in Parsons's theory, as Bellah (1970b) makes particularly clear in some of his work. Yet, as I have argued elsewhere (1988a, 1990), values are only one of several areas of focus for a true cultural sociology.

4. This concrete approach to culture as high culture has been subject to criticism by Greenfield (1987) in a recent round of discussion about approaches to cultural sociology in the newsletter of the Culture Section of the American Sociological Association.

5. Such a treatment is manifest, for example, in much of Wuthnow's (1987) recent work. Although Wuthnow sets out to reinsert culture into sociology, and provides some important illustrations of how to do so, he throws a roadblock in his own path by insisting that cultural analysis should take an "objective" approach that avoids the problem of meaning. This avoidance is epistemologically impossible, for any effort to understand a social element, even from the outside, is based upon assumptions about its subjective orientation or inner patterns, that is, its meaning (see Alexander 1987: 281–301). An analyst can no more avoid the meaning problem than an actor can. Indeed, in the methodologically ideal case, the same organized set provides a reference point for both.

The principle of avoiding meaning allows Wuthnow a rationale for not entering into the "thicket of symbolism." With some important exceptions (1987: 66–96), this has the effect of undermining the authenticity of his references to cultural patterns, which he often reduces to such vague and general themes as *individualism, socialism,* and *rationality* (for example, 1987: 187–214), that is, he glosses over meaningful sets rather than attempts to understand them. Not surprisingly, as his book progresses, Wuthnow's theorizing of culture as variable gives increasing, and eventually almost exclusive, attention to the institutional and ecological forces in culture's environment. For an insightful discussion of the limitations of what they call Wuthnow's "positive structuralism," see Rambo and Chan 1990.

6. By orthodox interactionists, I am referring to those, such as Blumer, who manifest the individualist current (see Alexander 1987: 215–237). An attractive counterexample within the interactionist tradition is found in Fine's (1987) interpretation of the culture of little league baseball players in the United States. Motivated by interactionist theory, Fine develops the concept of *idioculture* to describe the specific and unique belief set developed within each team; yet this individualizing variant is placed deftly within a more general cultural framework that Fine interprets and finds to be widely shared.

7. Swidler takes quite the opposite position, criticizing recent movements toward thicker cultural analysis as mere efforts "to *describe* the features of cultural products and experiences" (italics added) in contrast to efforts at "*cultural explanation*," which she prefers (Swidler 1986: 273, original italics). By searching for "effects" and "causes" and by offering "an image of culture as a 'tool kit' of symbols," Swidler moves from culture to the levels of social system and action. Her essay actually reinforces the very tendencies that have prevented social science from taking culture seriously. Kane's (1991) theoretical essay is the most systematic and successful effort to argue that the analytic autonomy of culture is essential for any realistic assessment of its relation to more structural variables to be attained.

8. Indeed, rather than investigate the texture of new meaning configurations, most contemporary Weberians take over the ideal-typical patterns of modernity that Weber identified at the beginning of this century, for example, value rationality, ethic of responsibility, and so on.

9. Bellah emphasized this distinction between symbols and values in his early work on Japan (Bellah 1970b). As he moved toward symbolic realism and his civil religion concept, this distinction became blurred for he became less interested in institutionalized systems and more interested in symbolic references in and of themselves. In Bellah's most recent work, the internal analysis of meaning systems has received less attention.

10. Eisenstadt is one of the few contemporary sociologists of culture who continues this early Parsonian focus on institutionalization. By incorporating elements of Shils's more cultural program and by expanding the Weberian elements that are incorporated into institutionalization theory, however, Eisenstadt has significantly extended the Parsonian cultural program (see Alexander and Colomy 1985). For a critique by Eisenstadt of contemporary macrosociological analyses on the grounds they take an *ontological* approach to culture rather than an analytical one—a critique parallel to my discussion of the problems with the culture-as-variable approach—see Eisenstadt 1987.

11. For an extremely interesting study of contemporary society that makes use of Eco's conception of an interwoven web of symbols, see Edles's (1990) study of Spanish political culture in the transition to democracy after Franco's death.

12. Rather than a relation between symbolic and social systems, Foucault would call this the manner in which discourse is shaped by discursive relations.

Discursive relations are, in a sense, at the limit of discourse: they offer it objects of which it can speak, or rather . . . they determine the group of relations that discourse must establish in order to speak of this or that object, in order to deal with them, name them, analyze them, classify them, explain them, etc. These relations characterize . . . rules that are immanent in a practice, and define it in its specificity (1972: 47).

This last sentence shows the difficulty in Foucault's approach. After defining discursive relations as something that offers objects to discourse, he collapses the distinction between these relations and discursive patterns by calling relations *rules*, on the one hand, and arguing that they (these rules, or symbolic codes) are at the same time immanent in practices, on the other. Reductionistic idealism and materialism are both at work in Foucault's analysis, for reasons of both theoretical confusion and ideological interest. Rather than following Foucault's lead to establish the "power-culture link," as Lamont (1988) advises, we must learn how to separate the two spheres analytically in order to understand just what it is that power links to.

13. Among contemporary social theorists, Shils (for example, 1975) is virtually alone in his effort to elaborate the secular extension of Durkheim's and Weber's religious theories. Shils argues that modern societies still retain "centers" of sacred and transcendent significance and that social status is determined by the distribution of charisma from these sacred centers. The power of this vocabulary to clarify cultural sociology is partly neutralized by the awkward concreteness of Shils's vocabulary, its concentration on charisma, its inexplicable rejection of Durkheimian theory, and its failure to consider more general issues of semiotic thought.

14. As Habermas (1968a: 58) wonderingly puts it, "Marx equates the practical insight of a political public with successful technical control."

15. The data in the following are samples from the thousands of articles written about the computer from its introduction in 1944 up until 1984. I selected for analysis ninety-seven articles drawn from ten popular American mass magazines: *Time* (T), *Newsweek* (N), *Business Week* (BW), *Fortune* (F), *The Saturday Evening Post* (SEP), *Popular Science* (PS), *Reader's Digest* (RD), *U.S. News and World Report* (USN), *McCall's* (Mc), and *Esquire* (E). In quoting or referring to these sources, I cite first the magazine, then the month and year; for example, T8/63 indicates an article in *Time* magazine that appeared in August 1963. These sampled articles were not randomly selected but chosen by their value relevance to the interpretive themes of this work. I would like to thank David Wooline for his assistance.

16. Many of these anthropomorphic references, which originated in the "charismatic" phase of the computer, have since become routine in the technical literature, for example, in terms such as *memory* and *generations*.

17. Technological discourse has always portrayed a transformation that would eliminate human labor and allow human perfection, love, and mutual understanding, as the rhetoric of Marx's descriptions of communism amply demonstrates.

18. While we examined several neutral accounts of technology, we did not spend much time on truly benign accounts. Marx was the only writer we examined who qualifies for this category, and his account is double-edged. An outstanding recent example of the social scientific translation of salvation discourse is Turkle's (1984) widely read pop-sociology discussion. Her account, presented as objective data gleaned from her informants, is breathless in its sense of imminent possibility.

Technology catalyzes changes not only in what we do but in how we think. It changes people's awareness of themselves, of one another, of their relationship with the world. The new machine that stands beyond the flashing digital signal, unlike the clock, the telescope, or the train, is a machine that "thinks." It challenges our notions not only of time and distance, but of mind (1984: 13).

Among a wide range of adults, getting involved with computers opens up long-closed questions. It can stimulate them to reconsider ideas about themselves and can provide a bias for thinking about large and puzzling philosophical issues (165).

The effect is subversive. It calls into question our ways of thinking about ourselves (308).

19. World War II was brought to an end on 10 August 1945 by the surrender of Japan, which followed quickly after the atomic bomb attacks on Hiroshima and Nagasaki. The very next day there appeared in *The Times* of London an article by Niels Bohr, which presented a prescient perspective on how efforts to control the bomb should proceed. Even while he notes the apocalyptic strain in the public's comprehension of this terrible technological achievement, Bohr warns that, above all, a distance from this fantasy is necessary if rational control efforts are to be made.

The grim realities which are being revealed to the world in these days will no doubt, in the minds of many, revive terrifying prospects forecast in fiction. With all admiration for such imagination, it is, however, most essential to appreciate the contrast between these fantasies and the actual situation confronting us (1985 [1945]: 264).

Bohr was just as concerned to counter the utopian discourse so prevalent among Los Alamos scientists during the war, which portrayed the much hoped for bomb as the only means for ensuring future peace (Rhoades 1987: 528–538).

References

Alexander, Jeffrey C. 1982–1983. *Theoretical Logic in Sociology.* 4 Vols. Berkeley and Los Angeles: University of California Press.

———. 1983. *The Modern Reconstruction of Classical Thought: Talcott Parsons.* Berkeley and Los Angeles: University of California Press.

———. 1986. "The Dialectic of Individuation and Domination: Max Weber's Rationalization Theory and Beyond." In *Max Weber and Rationality*, edited by Sam Whipster and Scott Lash. London: Allen and Unwin.

———. 1987. *Twenty Lectures: Sociological Theory Since World War II.* New York: Columbia University Press.

———. 1988a. "Action and Its Environments." In *Action and Its Environments: Toward a New Synthesis*, edited by J. Alexander, 301–333. New York: Columbia University Press.

———. 1988b. "Culture and Political Crisis: 'Watergate' and Durkheimian Sociology." In *Durkheimian Sociology: Cultural Studies*, edited by J. Alexander, 187–224. New York: Cambridge University Press.

———, ed. 1988c. *Durkheimian Sociology: Cultural Studies.* New York: Cambridge University Press.

————. 1990. "Analytic Debates: Understanding the Autonomy of Culture."
In *Culture and Society: Contemporary Debates,* edited by J. Alexander and
Steven Seidman. New York: Cambridge University Press.

Alexander, Jeffrey C., and Paul Colomy. 1985. "Towards Neofunctionalism:
Eisenstadt's Change Theory and Symbolic Interaction." *Sociological Theory*
3 (2): 11–23.

Barthes, Roland. 1983. *The Fashion System.* New York: Hill and Wang.

Bell, Daniel. 1973. *The Coming of Post-Industrial Society.* New York: Basic
Books.

————. 1976. *The Cultural Contradictions of Capitalism.* New York: Basic
Books.

Bellah, Robert. 1970a. "Civil Religion in America." In Bellah, *Beyond Belief,*
168–189. New York: Harper and Row.

————. 1970b. "Values and Social Change in Modern Japan." In Bellah,
Beyond Belief, 114–145. New York: Harper and Row.

Bohr, Niels. 1985 [1945]. "Energy from the Atom: An Opportunity and a
Challenge." In *Niels Bohr: A Centenary Volume,* edited by A. P. French and
P. J. Kennedy, 261–265. Cambridge: Harvard University Press.

Caillois, Roger. 1959 [1939]. Man and the Sacred. New York: Free Press.

Dilthey, Wilhelm. 1976. "The Construction of the Historical World in the
Human Studies." In *Selected Writings,* 168–245. New York and Cambridge: Cambridge University Press.

Douglas, Mary. 1966. *Purity and Danger.* London: Penguin.

Durkheim, Emile. 1933. *The Division of Labor in Society.* New York: Free
Press.

————. 1951. *Suicide.* New York: Free Press.

————. 1963. *The Elementary Forms of Religious Life.* New York: Free Press.

————. 1973. "Individualism and the Intellectuals." In *Emile Durkheim on
Morality and Society,* edited by Robert N. Bellah, 48–56. Chicago: University of Chicago Press.

Eco, Umberto. 1979. "The Semantics of Metaphor." In *The Role of the
Reader,* edited by U. Eco. Bloomington: Indiana University Press.

Edles, Laura. 1990. "Political Culture and the Transition to Democracy in
Spain." Unpublished Ph.D. Dissertation, Department of Sociology,
UCLA.

Eisenstadt, S. N. 1987. "Macrosociology and Sociological Theory: Some
New Directions." *Contemporary Sociology* 16: 602–610.

————. 1987. *International Sociology.*

Eliade, Mircea. 1959. *The Sacred and the Profane.* New York: Harcourt,
Brace, and World.

Ellul, Jacques. 1964. *The Technological Society.* New York: Vintage.

Fine, Gary Alan. 1987. *With the Boys: Little League and Preadolescent Culture.*
Chicago: University of Chicago Press.

Foucault, Michel. 1972. *The Archaeology of Knowledge.* New York: Pantheon
Books.

Geertz, Clifford. 1973. "Thick Description: Toward an Interpretive Theory of Culture." In Geertz, *The Interpretation of Cultures*, 3–32. New York: Basic Books.

Gouldner, Alvin. 1979. *The Future of Intellectuals and the Rise of the New Class*. New York: Seabury.

Greenfeld, Liah. 1987. "Sociology of Culture: Perspective Not Speciality." *Newsletter of the Culture Section of the American Sociological Association* 2 (1): 2.

Habermas, Jürgen. 1968a. "Technical Progress and the Social Life-World." In Habermas, *Toward a Rational Society*, 50–61. Boston: Beacon.

———. 1968b. "Technology and Science as 'Ideology.'" In Habermas, *Toward a Rational Society*, 31–122. Boston: Beacon.

———. 1981. *The Theory of Communicative Action*. Vol. 1, *Reason and the Rationalization of Society*. Boston: Beacon.

Hunt, Lynn. 1984. *Politics, Culture, and Class in the French Revolution*. Berkeley and Los Angeles: University of California Press.

Kane, Anne. 1991. "Cultural Analysis in Historical Sociology: The Analytic and Concrete Forms of the Autonomy of Culture." *Sociological Theory* 9:1 (spring): 53–69.

Lamont, Michele. 1988. "The Power-Culture Link in a Comparative Perspective." Paper prepared for the Third German-American Theory Conference in Bremen, West Germany.

Lévi-Strauss, Claude. 1963. *Structural Anthropology*. New York: Basic Books.

———. 1967. *The Savage Mind*. Chicago: University of Chicago Press.

Lewis, Jan. 1983. *The Pursuit of Happiness: Family and Values in Jefferson's Virginia*. New York: Cambridge University Press.

Lukács, Georg. 1971. "Reification and the Consciousness of the Proletariat." In Lukács, *History and Class Consciousness*, Cambridge, Mass.: MIT Press.

Lyotard, Jean-François. 1984. *The Postmodern Condition: A Report on Knowledge*. Minneapolis: University of Minnesota Press.

Mann, Michael. 1985. *The Origins of Social Power*. Vol. 1. New York: Cambridge University Press.

Marcuse, Herbert. 1963. *One-Dimensional Man*. Boston: Beacon.

Marx, Karl. 1962. "Preface to a Contribution to the Critique of Political Economy." In *Selected Works*, Vol. 1, K. Marx and F. Engels, 361–365. Moscow: International Publishing House.

Merton, Robert K. 1970. *Science, Technology and Society in Seventeenth-Century England*. New York: Harper and Row.

Morgan, Edmund. 1958. *The Puritan Dilemma*. Boston: Little, Brown.

Parsons, Talcott. 1937. *The Structure of Social Action*. New York: Free Press.

———. 1951. *The Social System*. New York: Free Press.

———. 1960. "Some Principal Characteristics of Industrial Societies." In *Structure and Process in Modern Societies*, edited by T. Parsons, 132–168. New York: Free Press.

———. 1966. *Societies: Evolutionary and Comparative Perspectives*. Englewood Cliffs, N.J.: Prentice-Hall.

———. 1967. "Some Comments on the Sociology of Karl Marx." In *Socio-

logical Theory and Modern Society, edited by T. Parsons. New York: Free Press.

Parsons, Talcott, and Gerald Platt. 1973. *The American University.* Cambridge: Harvard University Press.

Parsons, Talcott, and Edward Shils. 1951. "Values, Motives, and Systems of Action." In *Towards a General Theory of Action,* edited by T. Parsons and E. Shils. New York: Harper and Row.

Peirce, Charles. 1985. "Logic as Semiotic: The Theory of Signs." In *Semiotics,* edited by Robert E. Innis, 1–23. Bloomington: Indiana University Press.

Pool, Ithiel de Sola. 1983. *Forecasting the Telephone.* Norwood, N.J.: Ablex.

Pynchon, Thomas. 1984. "Is It O.K. to Be a Luddite?" *New York Times Book Review,* 23 October, 1.

Rambo, Eric, and Elaine Chan. 1990. "Text, Structure, and Action in Cultural Sociology: A Commentary on 'Positive Objectivity' in Wuthnow and Archer." *Theory and Society* 19 (1990): 635–648.

Rhoades, Richard. 1987. *The Making of the Atomic Bomb.* New York: Simon and Schuster.

Ricoeur, Paul. 1984. *Time and Narrative,* Vol. 1. Chicago: University of Chicago Press.

———. 1971. "The Model of a Text: Meaningful Action Considered as a Text." *Social Research* 38: 529–562.

Rochberg-Halton, E. 1986. *Meaning and Modernity.* Chicago: University of Chicago Press.

Rueschemeyer, Dietrich. 1986. *Power and the Division of Labor.* Stanford: Stanford University Press.

Sahlins, Marshall. 1976. *Culture and Practical Reason.* Chicago: University of Chicago Press.

———. 1981. *Historical Metaphors and Mythical Realities: Structure in the Early History of the Sandwich Islands Kingdom.* Ann Arbor: University of Michigan Press.

Saussure, Ferdinand de. 1964. *A Course in General Linguistics.* London: Owen.

Schluchter, Wolfgang. 1979. "The Paradoxes of Rationalization." In *Max Weber's Vision of History,* edited by Guenther Roth and W. Schluchter, 11–64. Berkeley and Los Angeles: University of California Press.

Sewell, William, Jr. 1980. *Work and Revolution in France.* New York: Cambridge University Press.

Shils, Edward. 1975. *Center and Periphery: Essays in Macrosociology.* Chicago: University of Chicago Press.

Smelser, Neil. 1959. *Social Change in the Industrial Revolution.* Chicago: University of Chicago Press.

Smith, Henry Nash. 1950. *Virgin Land.* Cambridge: Harvard University Press.

Swidler, Ann. 1986. "Culture in Action: Symbols and Strategies." *American Sociological Review* 51: 273–286.

Szelenyi, Ivan, and Bill Martin. 1987. "Theories of Cultural Capital and Beyond." In *Intellectuals, Universities, and the State in Western Modern Societies,* edited by Ron Eyerman, L. G. Svensson, and T. Soderquist, 16–49. Berkeley and Los Angeles: University of California Press.

Turkle, Sherry. 1984. *The Second Self: Computers and the Human Spirit.* New York: Simon and Schuster.

Turner, Victor. 1969. *The Ritual Process.* Chicago: Aldine.

Weber, Max. 1946a. "Religious Rejections of the World and Their Directions." In *From Max Weber,* edited by Hans Berth and C. Wright Mills, 323–359. New York: Oxford University Press.

———. 1946b. "The Meaning of Discipline." In *From Max Weber,* edited by H. Gerth and C. W. Mills, 253–264. New York: Oxford University Press.

———. 1958. *The Protestant Ethic and the Spirit of Capitalism.* New York: Scribners.

———. 1963. *The Sociology of Religion.* Boston: Beacon Press.

Wuthnow, Robert. 1987. *Meaning and Moral Order.* Berkeley and Los Angeles: University of California Press.

12

Culture and the Locus of Work in Contemporary Western Germany
A Weberian Configurational Analysis
Stephen Kalberg

An intense discussion in the Federal Republic of Germany (FRG) in the past fifteen years has crystallized around the theme of "the crisis of working society" (*Krise der Arbeitsgesellschaft*). Although the debate has offered various unorthodox proposals to combat unemployment (for example, Benseler, Heinze, and Klönne 1982; Bonß and Heinze 1984; Matthes 1983; Offe 1984), a far more fundamental issue has been central: the *proper place* of work in the postindustrial society. The pivotal concept of *de-coupling* stands at its center.

In this discussion, work in the postindustrial epoch is understood as constituting only one in a series of activities significant in the formation of a stable sense of self-worth. A de-coupling of work from social status is argued for, indeed to such an extent that occupational life is denied the capacity to monopolize the formation of meaning and self-esteem. Amidst this decline in the hegemonic position of work and the drifting apart, or de-coupling, of meaning and work, other aspects of modern life—leisure, the family, personal relationships, and hobbies—are viewed as significant arenas in reference to which the formation of a sense of self-worth and adequate life-styles can, and should, take place. Thus, the traditionally close relationship among work, income, meaning, and social status is radically called

I would like to thank Hans-Jürgen Giegel, Elliott Krause, Renate Mayntz, Hans-Peter Müller, Richard Münch, Joachim Savelsberg, Neil Smelser, Willfried Spohn, Johannes Weiss, Ansgar Weymann, and Claudia Wies-Kalberg for helpful comments.

into question as work becomes simply one important realm of activity among others (Bahrdt 1983; Dahrendorf 1980, 1983; Guggenberger 1982; Benseler, Heinze, and Klönne 1982). Despite high levels of unemployment throughout Europe, only the German debate has addressed in a sustained manner the fundamental issue of the *place* of work *in principle* in postindustrial society. Why, despite high levels of unemployment throughout Europe, has this question arisen in only one postindustrial nation?

This singular debate may unveil aspects of German society of great sociological interest. It may point to the manner in which work is *situated* in Western Germany[1]; that is, it may constitute evidence for the existence of a unique *locus* for occupational life. Is occupational life in the FRG in fact somehow less elevated than, for example, in the United States and less central for the formation of satisfactory personal identities? Might the radical de-coupling notion that work must be viewed as one sphere among many, all of which should *equally* contribute to meaning, self-worth, and social status, point indeed to a particular configuration of sociological factors prominent only in contemporary Western Germany?

Does the prestige and centrality of work vary in different postindustrial societies within a dynamic web of past and present cultural and structural forces? The de-coupling debate poses in particular the question of the precise locus for work in present-day German society.[2] Moreover, it as well raises the question of whether motivation to work in occupational life may vary decisively.

The *locus* for work in Western German society can be established only in reference to a theoretical framework that inventories not only diverse structural and cultural macrosociological variables but also an analytic typology that surveys the varying *possible* motivations that stand behind work. Construction of such a theoretical framework constitutes our first task. In reference to this heuristic construct, the precise *locus* for work in contemporary Western Germany can be established. Procedures in this investigation are highly indebted to those used by Max Weber in his comparative historical writings.[3] The power of the Weberian framework to capture the significance of *cultural* variables constitutes one of the major reasons for its use here. Indeed, Weber's configurational strategy of research, as employed here, examines the roles of both structural and cultural forces and the impact of their synchronic and diachronic interaction. In addition, it links macro forces systematically to the intensity of motives to work.

A Weberian Theoretical Framework

___

MOTIVES FOR WORK

An analytic framework used by Weber, which stands at the foundation of his analysis of the origins of the "spirit" of capitalism (1930), illustrates the ways in which individuals work for different reasons. He distinguishes four analytically distinct motivations behind work.[4]

The *traditional economic ethic* sanctifies customary means to satisfy needs. Age-old practices are viewed as fully legitimate simply as a result of their familiarity, proven effectiveness since time immemorial, and enduring usefulness. Workers imbued with this traditional spirit tend to view labor as a necessary evil. For this reason, once the minimum requirements for subsistence are fulfilled, no further incentive exists to work. Because less work is valued more than increased earnings, an increase in wages or piecework rates cannot alter this situation. Indeed, even a doubling of wages will not accelerate production; on the contrary, workers realize that the subsistence wage can be earned in half the time, leaving more time for leisure (Weber 1930, 51, 65–68).

Weber contrasts the traditional economic ethic to the *charismatic ethic* of "economic supermen" and "adventure capitalists." Whether a Rockefeller, a Fugger, or a Cecil Rhodes, the extraordinary capitalist can be found in an entire array of epochs and civilizations. These "heroic entrepreneurs" work harder than anyone else, systematically run their own businesses, and reinvest profit, which they seek for its own sake and, very often, by whatever means necessary (Weber 1968, 613, 1118, 1930, 51). Means-end rational *(zweckrational)* action characterizes this ethic.

Weber also discovered a *practical rational ethic.* Although devoid of the heroic element, an orientation to sheer means-end rational calculations of advantage prevails here as well. This type of action appears, even in the natural economy, wherever exchange takes place. Wherever the bonds of the traditional economic ethic are loosened or, on the other hand, the "spirit" of capitalism loses its grip upon modern workers and entrepreneurs, this utilitarian ethos of self-interest often arises (Weber 1930, 48–54).

The *rational economic ethic,* or "spirit" of capitalism, diverges radically in its unequivocal orientation to values *(wertrationales Handeln)* and its understanding of methodical labor as a duty—an internally felt obligation positively valued as an end in itself. As carried by members of Calvinist sects and churches, this economic ethic understands labor as a calling, with punctuality, reliability, industry, self-control, discipline, and frugality as virtues. Neither leisure nor a comfortable life prevails over diligence and systematic labor by entrepreneurs and workers alike, all of whom pursue the goal of continuously increasing wealth. Similarly, honesty is expected in all transactions, and the unscrupulous as well as the ruthless means of acquisition universally present in trade relationships are rejected absolutely. Action in reference to all these values is viewed as part of the individual's moral obligation to his or her calling. Indeed, the specifically ethical character of this rational ethos is evident in its prohibition against using the riches acquired as a result of systematic work, particularly in an ostentatious manner, as well as against the acquisition of luxuries (Weber 1930, 47–58, 62–73; Kalberg 1983).

Due to its great resilience, the traditional work ethic, Weber argues, could be shattered only by orientations to work much stronger than those founded in the calculation of advantage and the sheer pursuit of worldly self-interests. Weber discovered the requisite methodical element only in the rational economic ethic anchored in value-rational action. This anchoring infuses the motivation to work with a greater *intensity and stability* (Weber 1968, 31, 1930, 75–77, 1951, 226–49). Weber argues that, under certain circumstances, distinctions at the level of motives may well be significant with respect to social change and even to long-range developments, such as the unfolding of modern capitalism.

Thus, his analysis stresses the macrosociological significance of motives. Weber's most salient distinction for a discussion of work in the postindustrial epoch is that between means-end rational—or utilitarian/instrumental—action (the practical rational economic ethic) and value-rational action (the rational economic ethic). A wide *variety* of instrumental considerations may lie at the base of work motivations, such as the understanding of hard labor as constituting a viable *means* toward higher status, wealth and increased consumption power, and "the better life" in general. In these cases, purely utilitarian considerations dominate, as occurs whenever individuals view work and the workplace simply as an efficient and even indispensable means toward full social integration. Of course, social integration may be perceived by some persons as a value in itself, as may high social status, the better life, and even the acquisition of wealth. If this occurs empirically and work is perceived as the valid means toward these values, then work itself becomes endowed with a value premium. Other persons may award a high value premium to a notion of self-realization; if work is perceived as the valid means toward such self-fulfillment, then work again becomes imbued with a value premium. Finally, this occurs as well when individuals believe in the values of disciplined, reliable, and honest work not simply as utilitarian virtues but also as ideals and valid *ends* and orient their actions accordingly (see Weber 1968, 31, 36).

In these ways, an orientation to values may serve as a significant motivating force. In all these examples work is viewed primarily neither in terms of accustomed modes of life nor in reference to means-end rational calculations of advantage. Frequently, cultural factors (for example, religion and status ethics) bear the responsibility for such a *sublimation* of work-oriented action from traditional and means-end rational to value-rational motives. Conversely, if the Weberian framework is used, a "decline of the work ethic" can be conceptualized as involving a *routinization* from predominantly value-rational to utilitarian orientations to work.

This analytic discussion of the diverse possible motivations that underlie work provides a conceptual foundation for this study. Yet this typology of work motives is acontextual. If the locus for work in Western German society is to be identified, it must be supplemented by a macrosociological theoretical framework. Moreover, this framework must be capable of furnishing a *configurational* component that identifies the manner in which, and despite certain structural tendencies toward homogeneity, the locus of occupational life in postindustrial societies *may vary*. Just in this respect, as will be noted, cultural forces come to the fore. Only after such an orientational framework has been constructed can an analysis of the sociological location of work in a particular society—the Western German—proceed. Because it is underpinned by the typology of motives just discussed, this analysis will allow as well an assessment of *likelihoods* regarding the prevalence and intensity of different motives.

WEBER'S PRACTICED METHODOLOGY: A CONFIGURATIONAL MACROSOCIOLOGY

An assessment of the manner in which the locus of occupational life varies in the different postindustrial societies turns us away from the traditional structural-functional theories of modernization (Almond and Coleman 1960; Almond and Powell 1966) as well as from the structuralism of Moore (1966) and Skocpol (1979). These schools fail to offer a theoretical framework that assists precise conceptualization of the ways in which significant sociological developments—for example, of citizenship (Kalberg 1992a), public trust, public ethics (Kalberg 1987a), and motivations toward work—*diverge* in the separate industrial and postindustrial nations. This results in part from an omission of methodologies that conceptualize and identify precisely the *interaction* of cultural and institutional factors and, particularly in the case of structural functionalism, from an underlying proclivity to see a convergence and fundamental homogeneity across industrial societies. A less linear and more *configurational* analytic framework is required. Modes of procedures and the methodology Weber employs in his comparative historical sociology provide such a framework. His basic view of society must first be scrutinized. His emphasis upon the *interaction* of historical forces with the present will next be examined and, then, his allocation of a central role, in all macrosociological analysis, to *social carriers*.

Social Domains: Weber's View of Society. Weber sees fragmentation, tension, rulership, power, and conflict and rejects at the outset the notion of societies as constituting unified entities; he focuses instead upon a broad array of delimited "domains of action" (*Bereiche*). For him, because patterned action orientations of individuals—his fundamental unit of analysis in his comparative historical sociology—occur in reference to analytically identifiable spheres of life (the rulership, religious, legal, and economic), universal organizations (the family, the sibling group, and the traditional neighborhood), and status groups rather than in "society," these domains and the subtypes within them constitute the important level of analysis.[5] Continuous fluctuation, rather than lawfulness of any sort or the priority of a particular domain, characterizes the analytic relationships of these domains to one another, and the *patterned*—that is, sociologically significant—action orientations of individuals within them captures his attention. He kept the question continuously in mind of whether *domain-specific opportunities and constraints*—typical social conditions, routine everyday experiences, pragmatic life chances, all of which can be charted as ideal types—could conceivably, and with an identifiable likelihood, call forth analytically specifiable regularities of action.

Economy and Society (Weber 1968) comprises the bountiful yield of his effort to do so. On a truly universal scale, this analytic treatise examines in great detail all sociologically significant domains within which patterned action occurs. To Weber, persons are "placed into various life-spheres, each of which is governed by different laws" (Weber 1946, 123). Moreover, he (1968) investigates thoroughly the *analytic interaction* of action regularities that occur between the various arenas. Weber maps these hypothetical interactions—such as those between legal and rulership organizations, diverse paths to salvation and types of law, the family and the types of rulership, law and universal organizations, and the status ethics of various status groups and the realms of religion, law, and rulership—in terms of *elective affinity* and *antagonism* relationships.

This focus upon a pluralistic array of delimited social domains, the constraints and opportunities that call forth various patterned action orientations within them, and the interactions across realms provides a differentiated theoretical framework that is capable of defining, when employed as a matrix, the distinct and unique contours of the postindustrial society under investigation. Although some combinations of the regular action indigenous to each domain are empirically unlikely, all are analytically possible. Weber attaches a modest purpose to this analytic framework: it offers only a differentiated means of orientation for sociological investigation rather than either a closed conceptual scheme or a knowledge of a *particular* postindustrial society.

When employed as a theoretical framework, this heuristic matrix is empowered to isolate, inventory, and clearly define sociologically significant empirical variation across postindustrial societies. When used as a means of orientation, it identifies the unique *weightings* of the various domains, the diverse delimited factors in the particular society under investigation, and the prevalent *interactions* between the various domains on the one hand and between the various domains and demarcated historical forces on the other. In doing so, this broad-ranging grid locates delineated features, such as citizenship, public trust, or work motivation, in a given postindustrial society. In addition, through comparisons to other postindustrial societies, this analytic framework enables assessments of the extent to which the location of citizenship, public trust, and motivations toward work *diverge* across societies. As will become apparent, the locus of work can be conceptualized as standing at the intersection of a variety of domains, such as religion, state, prominent status ethics, and family, and society-specific historical factors. This locus varies in each postindustrial society depending upon the dominant patterns of action typical in these domains, the relationship of the domains to one another, and demarcated past and present factors.

Before undertaking an analysis in reference to contemporary Western German society, a further overriding aspect of Weber's practiced methodology must be explained if the locus of work is to be more precisely ascertained. He attends systematically not only to the *synchronic* interaction of domains with one another and with delineated historical factors but also to the manner in which the past influences the present.

Past and Present Interaction: The Fundamental Importance of Legacies. Weber's understanding of societies as only loosely held together and as constituted from numerous and diverse competing and reciprocally interacting social domains and demarcated events naturally convinces him of the pivotal significance of the past for any examination of the present. Established domain-specific patterns of action permeate regularly and in multiple, often clandestine, ways into the present. For this reason, he dismisses all dichotomies, such as *Gemeinschaft/Gesell-schaft*, particularism/universalism, and tradition/modernity, as far too global, and he opposes as well the view that the impact of the past upon the present remains circumscribed and of little sociological consequence.

Although their sources can be located in a particular epoch, certain regular action orientations always endure and cast legacies across subsequent epochs. Even drastic metamorphoses and the abrupt advent of the "new" never fully rupture ties to the past (Weber 1968, 29). Should a cluster of forces undergo just a slight shift as a result of a discrete event or even a charismatic individual, a reverberating effect may be set into motion and developments that were presumed to have disappeared entirely "may come to light in an entirely new context" (Weber 1976, 366). History, for Weber, is far from banished; it frames the present and interacts repeatedly and significantly with it, indeed to such a degree that any attempt to explain the uniqueness of the present without acknowledgment of historical legacies remains a hopeless task. Even the monumental structural transformations called forth by industrialization failed to sweep away the past. Viable legacies remain.[6]

Weber's examination of the influence of legacies emphasizes not only the impact of the past upon the present but also the *dynamic* interaction of past and present. For him—and not surprisingly in light of his view of societies as loosely connected and often conflicting social domains— the *interaction itself* may introduce an independent, significant, and even autonomous causal thrust, one capable of reorienting patterned action in unexpected ways.

Social Carriers: The Anchoring of Patterned Action. The practiced methodology of Weber's comparative historical sociology also stresses the importance of social carriers. Patterned action orientations of every imaginable variety have arisen in every epoch and civilization. Yet, if the regular action indigenous to any domain is to become influential and sociologically significant, cohesive and powerful carriers (*Träger*) for it must crystallize. In every society, only certain traditional, affectual, value-rational, and means-end rational patterns of action acquire strong exponents and become institutionalized in the social fabric.

Status groups, classes, and organizations with articulated boundaries serve, in Weber's substantive sociology, as the most prominent bearers of action. Each "carries" a configuration of delineated action orientations. Weber notes, for example, the ideal-typical status ethic of the civil servant stratum (duty, punctuality, the orderly performance of tasks, disciplined work habits) (Weber 1968, 956–1003), the ethos of the neighborhood organization (mutual assistance and a "sombre economic 'brotherhood' practised in case of need" [363]), and the class ethos of the bourgeoisie (opposition to privileges based upon birth and status and a favoring of formal legal equality [477–80; see Kalberg 1985]). Attention to such carriers is characteristic of Weber's substantive sociology. It leads him to investigate, for example, whether a powerful bourgeois class arose in China to promote an ethic of formal equality (Weber 1951, 137, 142) and whether such a class *could* crystallize to "serve as a political force and promote a 'civic' development in the occidental sense" (Weber 1958, 273) in a pre-Meiji Japan dominated by an antagonistic status group: the samurai. If the institutionalization of regular action orientations is to be ascertained, a focus upon carriers is indispensable.

These central postulates and procedures of Weber's comparative historical sociology—an understanding of societies as constituted primarily from delimited social domains, a charting of the manner in which action orientations of varying intensity occur in reference to these domains, an emphasis upon the *interaction* of action orientations (including those with their sources in the past), and an assessment of the extent to which patterned action becomes institutionalized in strong social carriers—establish a macrosociological framework for examining the diverse possible motives that underlie work. Moreover, these fundamental features of Weber's methodology provide a differentiated means of orientation that assists identification of the locus of work in the western states of contemporary Germany.

This theoretical framework directs our analysis toward a pluralistic array of social domains and the question of which domains played particularly prominent roles in German society. It points as well to the necessity for an acknowledgment of the configurational *dynamic* that results from interdomain interaction and the interaction of domain-specific action orientations with delimited events. In addition, it advises that systematic attention to the diverse ways in which prominent historical legacies interact with and influence the present is necessary. Finally, in arguing for an assessment of whether strong social carriers appeared, it evaluates the extent to which regular action orientations become anchored in firm status groups, classes, and organizations. Far from attending simply to structural factors or the present, Weber's configurational analysis perpetually interweaves culture and structure as well as past and present. Only such a mode of analysis is empowered to establish the distinct locus of work in contemporary Western Germany.

Establishing the Locus of Work in Contemporary Western Germany: A Weberian Configurational Analysis

An identification of the major social domains that influenced work motivations in German history constitutes the first task. Religion and its carriers—churches and sects—are central in this respect. The manner in which action orientations indigenous to this cultural realm interacted with the dominant status groups—the civil servants, or *Beamtentum,* and the university based literati, or *Bildungsbürgertum*—in German society on the one hand and the state on the other next captures our attention. The way in which present configurational interactions containing clear historical legacies established a particular locus for work in German society is then addressed in reference to two periods: the end of the nineteenth century and the post-World War II era. By taking special note of the diverse ways in which the rise of a large middle class, postwar affluence, and the various legacies of National Socialism created a unique and dynamic juxtaposition of past and present, in comparison to the early twentieth-century period, the latter discussion establishes the locus of occupational life in the FRG.

The major features of the religious realm in Germany, prominent social carriers, the state, and the singular "weighting" and configurational interactions of domains with one another and historical forces, cannot be defined precisely without a comparative case. The *particularity* of a given social context cannot be established in isolation; rather, its boundaries and distinctive features become isolated and visible only through comparisons. If uniqueness is to be established, a comparative case is indispensable. Comparisons to the United States at every step of this analysis enable a more exact definition of the locus of work in contemporary Western Germany.[7] Just such comparisons will illuminate the great importance of *cultural* factors for the establishment of the locus of work in all postindustrial societies.

PROMINENT SOCIAL DOMAINS AND SOCIAL CARRIERS: RELIGION, SOCIAL STRATA, AND THE STATE

The Sublimation of Work Motives through the Cultural Sphere of Religion: Lutheranism Versus Ascetic Protestantism. Motivations behind work in both Germany and the American colonies were sublimated from traditional and means-end rational motives and infused with values. Religious beliefs were instrumental in this process. Both in respect to the *intensity* of the regular action orientations they called forth among believers and the *content* of the values they articulated, the religious traditions in these countries diverged distinctly. The premiums they placed upon work constitute our exclusive concern here.

What values typically motivated the Lutheran to work? This salvation religion adopted feudalism's respect for craftsmanship and endowed it with systematic qualities. Every believer required a vocation (*Beruf*), and the disciplined and reliable performance of tasks in accord with the given standards of one's vocation became a religious duty. Only faith was necessary, in addition, for salvation (Weber 1930, 63–73; Troeltsch 1931; Dillenberger 1961).

Although Luther's notion of *Beruf* made for clear differences between the Lutheran and the Catholic economic ethics, both churches strongly opposed the impersonality of modern economic relationships and both were designated by Weber as traditional. Weber also notes that the position of Lutheranism with respect to the two classes that grew out of modern capitalism, the bourgeoisie and the proletariat, does not in principle vary from the Catholic attitude (Weber 1968,

1197–1198). From the beginning, Luther's concept of worldly vocation stressed that work in the world was itself the factor of utmost importance for salvation. No consequence could be attributed to the particular vocation taken up by a believer, if only because the "pilgrimage of life" was a short one (Weber 1930, 84, 212n.). Thus, no "psychological premiums" adhered to occupational mobility. On the contrary, as Luther's theological thinking developed, he increasingly viewed the particular calling pursued by individuals as the result of a divinely ordered special decree. After the Peasant War, he understood even the entire historical order of things within which each person is placed as a direct manifestation of God's will. As this providential element penetrated more deeply into even the particular events of daily life, the traditional conception of the vocation as well as of social status came to prevail (see Weber 1930, 85).

Because the calling was given by divine ordinance, believers could contemplate the best manner in which to be obedient to God and adapt themselves to their vocations, but they could never entertain the idea of changing their calling or ponder how they could either increase productivity or, through achievement, ensure upward mobility. Unlike Calvinism, Lutheran doctrine placed no strong premium on "success" in the calling; instead, it emphasized the reliable, punctual, and efficient performance of the tasks and duties given by the vocation itself. Nor did religious rewards adhere either to work outside the vocation or to an intensification of labor beyond the standards set by each calling. Moreover, God firmly set the needs for each station in life (*Stand*), and Luther saw the acquisition of goods beyond this level as morally suspect and sinful (Weber 1930, 216n., 82n., 213n.). For all these reasons, the Lutheran believer had also to cultivate a certain "distance from the world" and an introspection (*Innerlichkeit*); indeed, even a latent mysticism is found in Lutheranism.[8]

Diligent work habits, for the ascetic Protestant, were not simply a matter of religious duty that served as a supplement to faith, as for the Lutheran; rather, they constituted the pathway to the acquisition of that elusive sense of inner certainty of being among the saved (Weber 1930, 98–128). Among the ethical salvation religions, only the vocational ethic of ascetic Protestantism succeeded, in a principled manner, in systematically unifying an inner-worldly calling with an acquisition of the *certitudo salutis*. Worldly work in a vocation was awarded with the potential to serve as the appropriate means for believers to convince themselves of their grace and to ameliorate their religious anxiety (Weber 1968, 587–588). Moreover, the Calvinist concept of a *calling* explicitly recognized legal profit from capitalist enterprises as justified and, as Calvinist doctrine developed, "such profit and the rational means of its realization received an ever more positive evaluation" (Weber 1968, 1199). To Weber, the awarding of religious "psychological premiums" of the highest intensity to economic activity in a vocation meant that the Calvinist's search for profit had to be clearly distinguished from mere business astuteness (*Geschäftsklugheit*), or the clever making of an individual's way in the world (*Lebenstechnik*), both of which lacked an infusion of values and were comprised primarily of means-end rational action alone.

Because it involved a rigid patterning of action on behalf of purely religious goals, asceticism comprehensively uprooted the devout from the *status naturalis*. This uprooting meant an emancipation from the random flux of daily life and the replacement of action oriented to the world's given morality by the Calvinist ethic of conviction (*Gesinnungsethik*), in which ethical action rationally integrated with respect to "meaning, end, and means . . . governed by principles and rules" (Weber 1968, 549) predominated. Weber notes that, because a psychological certainty of salvation could be found only in such a *surpassing* of everyday routines and not merely in intellectual consistency, "a more intensive form of the religious valuation of ethical *action* than that which Calvinism produced in its followers has perhaps never existed" (Weber 1930, 115–116, translation altered, original italics; see also 118, 121, 1968, 498, 619). In a radical manner, the entire existence of the devout became penetrated by religious values, and a " 'meaningful' total relationship of the pattern of life to the goal of religious salvation" took place (Weber 1968, 578, see also 424, 1951, 247–248, 1946, 357). Thus, the labor demanded by God of the Calvinist devout—disciplined, methodical work in a calling—existed only as an expression of his or her desire for otherworldly salvation and did not originate out of a striving for terrestrial success. On the contrary, systematic labor was viewed as the single means to prove membership among the predestined elect. This fact alone endowed the Calvinist's work ethic with its internalized and obligatory—or *ethical*—quality. To Weber, the methodical rational way of life of the inner-worldly ascetic was centrally determined "from the inside" (*von innen heraus*) by deeply internalized religious values (see Weber 1951, 243–244).

The Lutheran attitude toward work, like the medieval Catholic, provided the basis for a less hectic and more comfortable, or *gemütlich*, style of life. The ascetic component, above all, infused ascetic Protestantism with its unusually strong capacity to defend ethical action against all heretical challenges and to transform difficulty and extreme stress into virtues. Although German Lutheranism and Catholicism also firmly upheld action in reference to ethical values, no inner-worldly asceticism existed in these religions. Believers here were provided with institution-alized means of redeeming themselves from sin: the exercise of faith for the Lutheran and good works and the confession for the Catholic. Such modes of acknowledging creaturely weakness were not offered to Cal-vinists; they stood alone before their God and without the help of a church, priests, or the sacraments to intercede for them. Moreover, Lutheranism's traditional economic ethic prevented it from attempting to dominate or transform the world, as did Calvinism, in the name of comprehensive ethical goals. Even though the Protestantism of Luther represented a distinct break from medieval Catholicism, it failed to introduce asceticism. Even though it cultivated a craftsmanship ideal and understood methodical labor as a religious duty, it never managed to sever traditional economic dualism (Weber 1930, 79–92).

Thus, with respect to both the *content* of religious values and the *intensity* of religious belief as they relate to attitudes and motives regard-ing work, Catholicism and Lutheranism significantly differ from ascetic Protestantism. The doctrines of Lutheranism and ascetic Protestantism, in particular, articulated clear, though *varying*, values with respect to work. Despite secularization in both Germany and the United States, each religion left distinct legacies. These legacies in Germany, anchored in strong churches and sect carriers, interacted with prominent status groups in the nineteenth century: the civil service stratum (*Beamten-tum*) and the intellectuals (*Bildungsbürgertum*).

The Stratification and Cultural Configuration: The Be-amtentum *and* Bildungsbürgertum *as Prominent Carriers in Nineteenth-Century Germany.* The French Enlightenment and classical liberalism, which were embraced unequivocably on American soil and provided very optimistic assessments of individuals as strong and as capable of shaping (in reference to worldly activity) their own destinies, met with ambivalence and reaction in nineteenth-century Germany (Mosse 1964, 148; Löwenthal 1970, 14–22). It was widely believed, particularly among the German romantics and the cultivated intellectuals of the *Bildungsbürgertum,* that both of these schools of thought conceived the individual as too isolated, too detached from the *Gemeinschaft,* and too separated from social ties. Moreover, because German liberalism lacked a carrier bourgeoisie strong enough to stand effectively against the social privileges and particularism of the feudal aristocracy and the *Beamtentum* caste of state civil servants, it remained weak. As a consequence, the state, to avoid a position of extreme inferiority vis-à-vis the Anglo-Saxon powers, became an unusually consistent and powerful advocate of industrialization. This took place to such an extent that the German bourgeoisie, far from asserting its independence from the Prussian state and opposing it, adapted broadly to its bureaucratic and military hierarchical structures (Bendix 1978, 378–430; Veblen 1966; Dahrendorf 1967, 3–206; Bussman 1958; Mann 1975, 193–233).

The weakness of the German bourgeoisie and its failure to develop an independent posture hindered the development, as Germany industrialized, of a legitimizing ideology of equal opportunity and a "rags-to-riches" optimism that praised unabashedly a steady ascendance to the peaks of wealth and success. This vacuum allowed romanticism, in various forms, to flourish. Unusually strong variants permeated nineteenth-century Germany and established, on the one hand, a strong anticapitalism and antimodernity tradition and, on the other hand, a protective boundary around the private sphere. This firm boundary served to insulate the family and the socialization of children from the corrupting influence of industrialization (see Craig 1982; Walker 1971; Brunschwig 1975; Kalberg 1987a). Nor could Germans, hampered by their elaborate apprenticeship system and the enduring strength of the old feudal craftsmanship ideal, easily become upwardly mobile. On the contrary, a traditionalist economic ethic prevailed that viewed a change of occupation as suspect, especially in light of a prominent legacy left by Luther—his enduring admonition to the believer to "stay in your vocation."

Given this particular stratification and cultural configuration, the aggrandizement of authoritarian state power throughout the latter half of the nineteenth century had fateful consequences, not least for work motivations and occupational life in general in Germany. A cohesive and powerful civil service stratum became the predominant status group, and its status ethic—duty, service, obedience, loyalty to the state, reliability, objectivity, and discipline—reinvigorated the fading legacy of the Lutheran economic ethic and notion of *Beruf*. Its values, consequently, acquired a new viability and retarded its routinization to means-end rational action. Moreover, a *Bildungsbürgertum* of cultivated literati set the standards of the idealized German *Kulturnation* until the

1930s. This stratum, as well as the *Beamtentum*, stigmatized rugged competition and upward mobility in general. As Germany industrialized, the attainment of the lifelong security offered by the civil service position prevailed as an ideal among members of its central social strata, the *Bildungsbürgertum* and the *Beamtentum*, rather than risk taking on behalf of a hope for wealth (Ringer 1969; Conze and Kocka 1985; Engelhardt 1986; Kocka 1981).

Thus, work motivation in Germany remained, in the nineteenth century, clearly infused with values. However, unlike the individualism of extreme self-reliance that arose from the ascetic Protestant sects and churches and the "small state" tradition in America, these values did not place high premiums upon a *heroic* notion of work; they did not view work as the single means toward world mastery and the shaping of individual destinies. Nor were they located within a stratification and cultural context that viewed upward mobility without ambivalence. Americans were better able to see social mobility as wholly positive.

Lacking the enduring tradition of romanticism that emphasized the organicism of the *Gemeinschaft* and the integration of the individual into an organic *Volk*[9] and embracing modern capitalism as promising emancipation from the past and even rags-to-riches success, Americans placed work on a pedestal. Americans in the nineteenth century, as had their Calvinist ancestors, widely viewed work as the single means to attain "the good life" and allowed an aggrandizing, all-consuming, and heroic notion of it to penetrate even into the family's socialization practices. By the turn of the century, a social Darwinism of "opportunity" and "survival of the fittest," carried by a powerful bourgeoisie, had crystallized as a legitimizing ideology (Sumner 1906; Hofstadter 1944; Konwitz and Kennedy 1960).

Because opportunities in the industrializing United States to acquire riches were now pronounced as available to all and individuals were believed to be strong and capable of mastering worldly adversity and shaping their own destinies, hard work alone separated the poor from the wealthy. Concomitantly, the old Calvinist stigmatization of the poor was revived; the impoverished were believed to be not only lazy but also of poor moral character. Moreover, those who labored intensely were promised not only material gain and high social status but access to political power as well, for no cohesive upper class or caste of civil servants existed to block the route toward political office and power. In the American stratification and cultural context, a pragmatic, *world-oriented* notion of work had become again imbued in a manifold manner with values, indeed values inseparable from an American understanding of itself as the "land of opportunity." Once again, methodical work had been awarded a special place: endowed earlier with a central role in one's salvation, work, as well as entrepreneurial activity and upward mobility, became infused with a wide array of secular values. This occurred just when the possibility loomed that the prevalent American work motivation might become routinized back to purely utilitarian and means-end rational action.

The strong emphasis in the particular American stratification and cultural configuration upon world mastery through entrepreneurial activity tended to overwhelm all countervailing forces. The juxtaposition of an ascetic Protestant heritage with a strong bourgeoisie, a Horatio Alger and social Darwinist ideology, a prevalent conception of modern capitalism as offering opportunities, and a weak state bestowed—especially in a comparative perspective—an unusually high social status upon particular strata: businessmen and entrepreneurs.[10]

The German stratification and cultural configuration not only implied far greater ambivalence in regard to the capitalist entrepreneur but also articulated competing prestigious strata: the *Bildungsbürgertum* and the *Beamtentum*. After the middle of the nineteenth century, the Bismarckian state tradition itself tended to bestow unusually high social status upon the civil servant. While the functionary generally, in the name of a larger aim of securing German state power, supported the economic ends of the capitalist class and its preference for a cartellization of German industry, this fact, as well as Germany's rapid industrialization, failed to endow entrepreneurs with a social standing equal to that of the *Beamtentum* (Conze and Kocka 1985; Engelhardt 1986; Kocka 1981). The traditions of this status group and a reverence for its institution, the state, were too firmly established for this to occur. Furthermore, the other great pillar of high prestige in German society, the literati *Bildungsbürgertum*, placed German *Kultur* on a pedestal and expressed scorn for capitalist activity as well as, very frequently, modernity, Anglo-Saxon *Zivilisation*, and the "mass society" in general (Ringer 1969; Stern 1965; Elias 1969; Epstein 1977; Kalberg 1987a).

Thus, at the turn of the century, a tripartite occupational prestige structure could be found in German society, one characterized by competition between state civil servants, professors and academics, and capitalists. The bourgeoisie constituted clearly the weaker link in this structure. Moreover, the more prestigious groups—the *Bildungsbürgertum* and the *Beamtentum*—idealized contemplative values, learning, job security, and the dutiful execution of tasks, rather than risk taking and the activity-oriented heroic individualism of the "self-made man." The prevalence of such ideals, as well as an image of systematic work in the world as the means to shape personal destiny and to acquire the fruits offered by a "land of opportunity," confronted in the United States no countervailing force capable of moderating the prestige of entrepreneurial activity. Least of all, neither American academics, who confronted widespread populism, nor civil servants, who stood within a small state tradition, could challenge the high social status of the entrepreneur.

Another social domain arose to prominence in the nineteenth century in Germany, indeed one that, as a powerful social carrier, tended further to institutionalize legacies of the classical Lutheran notion of work in German society: the state. Again, comparisons to the United States will facilitate isolation of the distinct contours of the German development.

The Strong State. In the United States, political freedoms and personal liberties have always been understood as involving freedom *from* state interference. Early on, the strong Enlightenment, liberal, and ascetic Protestant traditions effectively opposed the development of a strong state. Moreover, given the widespread ascetic Protestant and Jeffersonian populist trust in the common man—his virtuousness, good character, self-reliance, independence, and capacity to use wisely his political freedom—and, as Tocqueville emphasized, the ubiquitous presence of civil associations and churches, no necessity arose for protective and strong government. As a result of this unique configuration of factors, and in addition to the historical fact that the original immigrants arrived on American shores with hopes of exercising their rights to religious expression free from arbitrary state intervention, the state became viewed as a danger to all individual freedom and as correctly empowered to exercise only minimal functions. Furthermore, the firm embrace of capitalism and entrepreneurship, which was rooted deeply in the dominant religious tradition, assisted the development of a powerful bourgeoisie. This class then directly opposed the aggrandizement of state power, articulated an ideology that emphasized the beneficent side of capitalism, and perceived a compatibility between this economic system and justice and democracy.

There prevailed in Germany, not a small-state tradition, but, as noted, a view of the state as correctly playing a powerful advocacy role in behalf of industrialization. The uniquely German configuration—a powerful state and civil servant stratum, a comparatively weak bourgeoisie and civil society, a bestowing of high social prestige upon a literati status group, and a skepticism regarding the individual's capacity, as espoused by liberalism and the Enlightenment, to transform worldly evils—not only restricted the power of capitalism to stand against the state but also oriented Germans directly to the state. They viewed the state and its civil servants as responsible for employment and as "protectors" of the public's welfare against an economic system widely perceived as disruptive of the *Gemeinschaft* and inherently unjust and exploitative. By 1889, this *Vaterstaat* offered an array of measures to insulate its citizens against the burdens imposed by urbanization and industrialization, such as unemployment insurance, health insurance, accident insurance, and social security (Born 1975, 149).

The crystallization in the latter half of the nineteenth century of these differing views of the state and the proper role it should play in respect to the capitalist economy and the welfare of citizens strengthened and institutionalized core values in the respective German and American religious traditions and cultural and stratification configurations, thereby ensuring their continued capacity to orient action. Thus, for example, unemployment in the United States was understood as an individual concern and explained in terms of personality traits (laziness, lack of initiative, poor moral character, and so on). As a consequence of the American tradition of heroic individualism founded in ascetic Protestantism and reinforced throughout the nineteenth century, a proclivity to oppose all structural views of unemployment was set into motion.[11] The German industrializing experience in this respect stood at nearly the opposite end of the spectrum. The state, not the individual, was generally held responsible for unemployment, and capitalism was widely assumed to be a flawed economic system that inherently required, for the maintenance of economic stability, the regular interference by and assistance of the state (Plessner 1974). Thus, not exhortation to greater effort, more initiative taking by individuals, or upward mobility, but an alteration of state economic policy in behalf of a more effective protection of the population against capitalism, was deemed appropriate whenever economic problems persisted. These different views of the proper role of the state regarding unemployment had congealed clearly by the end of the nineteenth century.

In playing a paternal role, the strong German state sought to insulate its citizens against not only the irregular swings of the modernizing capitalist economy but also the disorder brought about by rapid urbanization and the new civil society. The bestowing of high prestige upon the German state and its *Beamtentum* and a strong protective function allowed the legal regulation, in behalf of order and social harmony, of the many institutions of this society (Kocka 1981; Kocka and Ritter 1974; Craig 1978). These institutions, such as the schools, the universities, and the economy, were viewed in the United States as fundamentally belonging to the private sphere and beyond the legitimate grasp of centralized state control.

Perhaps the argument could be made that the *locus* of work in the contemporary FRG must be understood in reference to a putative general ambivalence toward work among the Germans. This ambivalence could be surmised to result, most importantly, from the strong social welfare state tradition, the comparative weakness of the German bourgeoisie and its failure to articulate a rags-to-riches legitimating ideology of opportunity, the strength of German romanticism's introspection and antimodernism, and the awarding of paramount social status to two strata, each of which articulated quasicontemplative status ethics: the *Bildungsbürgertum* and *Beamtentum*. Such a conclusion, however, would be premature.[12] Only a more *configurational* analysis, one that acknowledges the *interaction* of the past with the present, will enable an accurate location of work and occupational life in the FRG.

The particular turn-of-the-century dynamic that resulted from the German juxtaposition of a strong state and civil servant stratum with a weak civil society and parliamentary democracy must be first examined. While reinvigorating further the values of the Lutheran notion of *Beruf,* this dynamic, because it called forth a revival of German romanticism, *also* sustained the private sphere. This development became manifest among some social groups in the form of a withdrawal from occupational life and an alienation from modern office and factory work as such. The unique *locus* of work in contemporary Western Germany cannot be established without noting the strong legacies left by this configuration.

PAST AND PRESENT I:
THE TURN-OF-THE-CENTURY
CONFIGURATION IN GERMANY AND THE
ESTABLISHMENT OF PUBLIC TRUST

An array of values that strongly legitimated parliamentary democracy failed to permeate the developing civil society of nineteenth-century Germany. This fact, however, neither implied the hegemony of means-end rational calculations and power in the civic realm nor led to societal breakdown and chaos. Rather, public trust, carried by the *Beamtentum* and the state, crystallized. While the status ethic of this stratum and the constellation of values that justified the strong state provided neither a firm foundation for the unfolding of democratic political institutions nor social egalitarianism, they did strongly uphold and nourish the values of the Lutheran notion of *Beruf.* A clear definition of the German "strong state-weak civil society" configuration and an assessment of its consequences with respect to the locus of occupational life can be best undertaken after another brief comparison to the United States.

The Contrast Case: The Establishment of Public Trust through a Strong Civil Society in the United States. Americans believe strongly that the common good is best served whenever individuals are left free from state interference to pursue their self-interests. Formulated most succinctly by Adam Smith in *The Wealth of Nations* as well as by English utilitarianism and liberalism, this notion has always appeared unrealistic and even dangerous to German philosophers and social thinkers. It became, however, broadly based in nineteenth-century American society. More than any other nation, the United States accepted the French Enlightenment's optimism regarding the capacity of individuals to shape their own destinies and its conception of the "common man" as inherently virtuous. It also embraced wholeheartedly the social Darwinist belief, as formulated by Spencer and Sumner, in the inevitability of evolutionary progress. An indigenous social carrier of the trust of others that permeated American public life, however, also existed in early American history: the inner-worldly asceticism of the Protestant sects and churches.

Membership alone in a sect or church established the ascetic Protestant's reputation as an honest merchant who offered a just price in all business transactions. Indeed, because believers' reputation for fair play and truthfulness in all financial matters was widespread, even nonbelievers preferred to conduct business with them. With the Protestant sects and churches as its carrier, trust extended beyond the intimate bonds of the family and became awarded to others—as long as they were members of a Protestant sect or church (Weber 1930, 98–128, 155–185, 1946, 302–322).

Although great differences existed by region, Protestant asceticism's successful introduction of trust into economic relationships carried over into the domain of politics and formulated a strong national *ideal* of truthfulness, good will, and fair play for public life. These religious values resonated well with the optimistic views of the individual as virtuous that were prevalent in both English liberalism and the French Enlightenment and facilitated their broad reception. In addition, this American religious tradition tended to support social egalitarianism and democratic self-rule. Uncontested by a feudal tradition of hierarchical social relations and authoritarian rulership, these values could spread relatively easily in America. The ascetic Protestant believed that the earthly ruler, like all men, was obligated to uphold God's commandments. As his servant and as merely an instrument for the realization of his Divine Plan, the earthly ruler stood "below" his divinity. Should the ruler act otherwise, believers were dutifully bound to rebel against the kingdom. Thus, through their religious beliefs, subjects were endowed with both the *right to judge* the acts of rulers and the *obligation* to overthrow all who failed to follow God's laws (Hill 1964; Miller 1961; Herr 1981; Weber 1930, 98–128).

These values of social egalitarianism and an optimism regarding the capacities of individuals not only established a firm foundation for public trust but also legitimated a constellation of values antagonistic to all "strong" government. This brief overview provides a comparative case in reference to which the mode of establishing trust in German civil society can be isolated.

Germany: The Dominance of the Beamtentum *and Strong State, the Weakness of Civil Society, and the Withdrawal into the Private Sphere.* Lutheranism failed to sever the traditional economic dualism: trust toward blood relations and distrust of others (Weber 1930, 79–92; Dillenberger 1961; Troeltsch 1931). Thus, a generalization of trust beyond the family and sibling group and into business transactions could not take place, with this religion as its carrier, as industrialization proceeded in the nineteenth century. As with medieval Catholic entrepreneurs, financial dealings with Lutherans occurred in reference to the old motto—*caveat emptor*—rather than to the ascetic Protestant axiom of trust and fair play. Furthermore, because it was not a strong class in Germany and it lacked a firm sense of itself as independent, the bourgeoisie, like Lutheranism, was unable to carry effectively a notion of social trust that embraced functional relationships in the rapidly expanding economic sphere. Nor was the bourgeoisie a strong carrier of legal equality and an effective opponent, as it had been in Holland, England, and France, of the social privileges and particularism of the feudal aristocracy (Veblen 1966; Dahrendorf 1967, 3–206; Bussman 1958; Mann 1975, 193–233; Kocka and Ritter 1974; Walker 1971).

Moreover, no strong religious organization served as a carrier of parliamentary democracy and social egalitarianism in Germany. Lutheranism, in denying the right of believers to revolt against the prince and in rejecting the position that rulers could be held accountable before God by their subjects, failed to challenge a rigid class structure and authoritarian divisions between rulers and ruled. The impulse toward social egalitarianism introduced by ascetic Protestantism was lacking in Luther's teachings. For him, no equality before God reigned; rather, even if rulers were exploitative and in violation of God's commandments, religious duty required obedience to the state (Dillenberger 1961, 363–402; Troeltsch 1931). Furthermore, feudal rulership, which remained widespread until the mid-nineteenth century, constituted direct domination. Finally, the French Enlightenment, an ideology of equality and open opportunity, met with a strong German reaction and also failed to legitimize a civil society of egalitarianism (Mosse 1964, 13–148; Löwenthal 1970, 14–22; Brunschwig 1975).

Thus, not a trust in the virtue and good judgment of the "common man" and a belief in social egalitarianism, but a widespread suspicion of democracy, political parties, and modernity, particularly among members of the *Bildungsbürgertum* and the *Beamtentum,* permeated the political arena in late nineteenth-century Germany. Yet, although it lacked strong carriers of egalitarianism and democracy, public trust was not absent; rather, it was carried by the *Beamtentum* and the state. A Lutheran respect for and obedience to the state and its laws established public trust in German civil society, as did the values of the *Beamtentum:* duty, service, obedience, order, loyalty to the state, and discipline in the performance of tasks.[13]

In confirming Lutheran and Prussian legacies, which viewed the state as possessing an inherent dignity as well as a legitimacy above and beyond its citizens' wishes, these accomplishments enhanced the power and prestige of the state and its civil servants. In the process, public trust became tied even more closely to the values of this stratum and this institution. The old Lutheran notion of *Beruf* thus acquired a new and more widespread viability, to the extent that the values carried by civil servants and the state expanded *beyond* their respective boundaries (Elias

1989). The weakness of parliamentary democracy and social egalitarianism created a vacuum that allowed this development, yet it was carried by an entrenched institution, one that conveyed and cultivated the Lutheran values of *Beruf*: the elaborate and state-supported apprenticeship system of training workers. The values associated with the status ethic of civil servants and the authority of the state, rather than social egalitarianism, populism, and individual liberties on the one hand or avarice, wealth, and ostentatious consumption on the other, became the dominant value constellation in German civil society (Rosenberg 1931, 1–33; Sell 1953; Holborn 1981, 227–407; Greiffenhagen 1981, 54–129; Kocka 1981; Weber 1968, 1381–1469).

Thus, as industrialization and urbanization proceeded rapidly, individuals became linked with occupational life and the German nation not simply through means-end rational action in behalf of economic survival and the desire to accumulate wealth, or only through an emotional attachment to the munificent social welfare state, but *also* as a consequence of an array of values that bestowed trust upon the expanding civil society. Although these Lutheran values found major social carriers in the *Beamtentum* and the Prussian state, they constituted at the turn of the century, as a result of the high prestige and vast power of this stratum and the state, values respected across broad sectors of German society. These values were challenged repeatedly by the aspirations of the working class for social egalitarianism, viable parliamentary democracy, and economic justice, as well as by sheer means-end rational action in behalf of survival. Nonetheless, the apprenticeship system, the Lutheran churches, and the paternal ethos of the manifold and powerful German social welfare state carried the values of the *Beamtentum* and the Prussian state far and wide throughout German society.

While the Lutheran notion of *Beruf* and a high respect for the authority of the state left very strong legacies, a particular *consequence* of the German mode of formulating public trust became, for an establishment of the *locus* of work, just as important. Because the values dominant in German civil society—duty, obedience, respect for authority, order, and so on—were widely perceived as antagonistic to the *person-oriented* values of compassion indigenous to the family, they failed to foster a bridging and thorough intertwining of the two domains as took place in Colonial America and the United States. Instead, these civil values set into motion a dynamic that articulated and then solidified a severe division between all "public sphere" social relationships outside the home and the private sphere of family and *Freunde*.[14] How did this occur?

The specific values carried by the German state and the status ethic of civil servants stood opposed to an array of modern values endowed with far greater *potential* to bridge public and private spheres: individual rights and personal freedoms, populism, and social egalitarianism. Moreover, and although in Germany widely deemed appropriate as well as indispensable to the stability of occupational and even political life, the values carried by the state and the *Beamtentum* stood severely in opposition to the private sphere of deep intimacy and compassion, all the more so because this domain had been distinctly strengthened first by the *Innerlichkeit* of Lutheranism and then by nineteenth-century romanticist movements.

Thus, the family stood in stark contrast to the "impersonal" values carried by the German state and the status ethic of its civil servants and to the purely conventional and functional (*sachlich*) relationships, power, and domination that characterized the occupational, political, and economic domains. This polarization became so severe by the early twentieth century that the formal and hierarchical character of social relationships in all public spheres called forth a reaccentuation of the private sphere. In the process, the old romanticism that idealized the values of intimacy and the organic harmony of the *Gemeinschaft* was further rejuvenated as was the latent mysticism and introspection in Lutheranism. Clear barriers arose against industrialized society's impersonal and merely functional relationships, which were characterized by great social distance. Germans cherished the private sphere's intimacy, defined it as at the foundation of "the good life," and elevated further their idealization of the family[15] and of the spiritual and emotional dimensions of the deep friendship, or *Freundschaft*, relationship. By the turn of the century, a deprecation of the *Gesellschaft* had become widespread and the family had become widely viewed as a refuge against the "anonymity" and "homogeneity" of the German civil society (Kalberg 1987a). This period constituted "the golden age of privacy" (Kruse 1980, 39): "There are epochs in which every conviction flees into the family. . . . Hearth and home is now and will remain the secure refuge of the sincere life, a general union of humanity" (Gutzkow 1963, 7).

To the extent that the private sphere stood effectively against the values of the *Beamtentum* and the state, the prestige of occupational life and its legitimating constellation of values declined. Wherever this occurred, a routinization of the civil servant's status ethic back to instrumental orientations in respect to work and to civil society in general threatened to become widespread. Moreover, a withdrawal and alienation from these domains spread more easily. Although this latter course of action was available only to a few, particularly youth and students (see Becker 1946), the instrumental view of occupational life increasingly challenged the Lutheran notion of *Beruf* and the values of the *Beamtentum*. To the same degree, work became understood as simply necessary for economic survival. It was also viewed, as urbanization and industrialization advanced, as an indispensable and purely functional means of integrating individuals socially and psychologically into the "impersonal" industrial society.[16]

This German configuration contrasts sharply with the American. The values of the American economic and political domains deeply permeated, virtually unobstructed, the private sphere. Social egalitarianism, individual liberties, and parliamentary democracy were evaluated extremely positively as were those legitimating values of a strong bourgeois class: competition, achievement, upward mobility, opportunity, and the striving for worldly abstract goals. Indeed, a consensus surrounded these values and, in combination, they reinvigorated social trust. They, moreover, were taught in the family as ideals, were reinforced in friendship relations, and, under the rubric of "good citizenship," became central in the curriculum of the public schools (Cleveland 1927). Securely anchored in American society by a singular configuration—a particular religious tradition, a strong bourgeoisie, and a weak state—these values remained favorably evaluated. Even as industrialization advanced, their thrust remained unchallenged by, for example, a strong romanticism that would extoll the organic harmony of the *Gemeinschaft* and would mistrust strong, activity-oriented individualism. Patterned action in reference to the values dominant in American civil society was believed to ensure progress on the path to worldly success and the good life, and thus a *maximum* penetration of the private realm by the public sphere could take place. In turn, socialization processes in the family reinforced the public sphere, indeed to such an extent that the boundary between these two domains became porous and difficult to define (Kalberg 1987a).[17]

In Germany, on the other hand, amid rapid structural change, the state and its legitimating ethos as well as the status ethic of the *Beamtentum* called forth social trust. The values of these social carriers, however, were not capable of supporting incipient movements toward social egalitarianism and parliamentary democracy coming from the left and left-center.

On the contrary, the impersonal and functional values prevalent in the occupational, economic, and political domains in Germany *facilitated* the unfolding of a severe polarization: the private life of the family was increasingly in opposition to the social conventions and social distance characteristic of the formalized and hierarchical relationships prevalent in German civil society.[18] A dynamic crystallized, one that would, in reaffirming the boundaries placed originally by Lutheranism around the private sphere, cast a long shadow into twentieth-century Germany. Just this division and the prominence it bestowed upon the private sphere resulted in a widespread ambivalence toward competition and functional relationships, the establishment of a delineated countervailing force in opposition to occupational life and its aggrandizement, and a high salience of private sphere relationships. Among some groups, withdrawal from modern occupational life seemed the only appropriate and honorable course.[19]

This configuration—a polarization of public and private spheres and the establishment of public trust by a strong stratum and institution that did not carry the values of parliamentary democracy or social egalitarianism—left prominent legacies. Tripartite orientations toward work resulted from it at the turn of the century: (1) a *predominant* orientation characterized by motivations in reference to the constellation of values implied by the status ethic of the *Beamtentum* and the Prussian state; (2) the means-end rational orientations of large segments of the new, urban working class that, despite the success of the apprenticeship system in institutionalizing central features of this status ethic and the Lutheran notion of *Beruf*, assessed work in terms of economic survival and as simply a means of securing a social and psychological integration into the "impersonal" industrial society; and (3) an alienation from the patterns of action expected in the workplace and a withdrawal from occupational life.

However deeply entrenched, this early twentieth-century *pluralism* of orientations to work did not simply endure unchanged to the present-day. Rather, significant historical events and developments called forth patterned action orientations in reference to new values, and these *interacted* dynamically with early twentieth-century legacies. As a consequence, the *weighting* of the factors in the turn-of-the-century tripartite pluralism became altered. Scrutiny of just this transformation constitutes the final stage in this Weberian configurational analysis of the locus of work in present-day Western Germany.

PAST AND PRESENT II:
THE DECLINE OF THE BEAMTENTUM
AND THE EQUAL COMPETITION
OF WORK MOTIVATIONS IN THE FRG

Whereas action orientations to the array of values associated with the status ethic of the civil servant stratum tended at the end of the nineteenth century in Germany to remain dominant over purely instrumental motivations and alienation and withdrawal from occupational life, a more open and *equal competition* between these orientations of action characterizes work motivations in the FRG. National Socialism and its legacies and the advent of affluence and a broad middle class in the 1960s were pivotal in bringing about this important shift. The resulting changes challenged the predominant orientation of work to the values of the status ethic of the *Beamtentum* and the Prussian state. How did this metamorphosis occur?

The concern to reconstruct a devastated economy united citizens of the young FRG in the immediate postwar years. Economic survival, for most, was the only issue. Later on, fueled by memories of the Weimar period and both wartime and immediate postwar chaos, an obsession with economic security took its place (Sontheimer 1971, 25–39). While reconstruction and the "economic miracle" in the fifties had given new sustenance to the disciplined performance of tasks and a dutiful execution of one's vocation, three developments in the sixties and seventies combined to call into question and even undermine the resurgence of these traditional values, particularly in the younger generation.

First, with the end of the economic reconstruction era, the growth of a large middle class, the advent of widespread affluence, and the establishment of a comprehensive social welfare state by the mid-sixties, direct necessity no longer served to strengthen the traditional notion of *Beruf* and the status ethic of the *Beamtentum*. As occurred in the United States in the late sixties, the entire work ethic was overtly challenged by values espoused by a younger generation. However, this work ethic had been carried in German history above all by a particular stratum: the civil servants. This status group became widely discredited because of its association with National Socialist authoritarianism and a posture of loyalty and subservience to the state.

The resulting decline in the prestige of the state and the *Beamtentum* was accelerated and intensified in the late seventies and early eighties by a second development. An investigation and acknowledgment of the horrors of the Holocaust could take place only at a distance. The second and even third generations, not the war generation, initiated the discussion (Herf 1980). As the questioning continued, the Lutheran and Prussian values of duty, order, obedience, and unquestioned allegiance to the state that were central to the status ethic of the *Beamtentum* and the authority of the state were further indicted among the younger generations. Now perceived as responsible for horrendous evils committed under National Socialism, these values became suspect.

Third, the decline of the prestige that had traditionally surrounded civil servants and the state was particularly marked in German society simply because of its customary mode of formulating social trust— through the values of just this stratum and a respect for the state. Now, in the sixties, trust could no longer be established in this manner. The resulting vacuum, however, did not prove irredeemable. Rather, postwar stability under a new form of government gradually called forth new values and these provided social trust—those values of the democratic political culture that were previously absent.

By the late seventies, a distinct trend away from the low levels of "civic competence" that traditionally characterized German political culture had been documented. Higher levels of social trust appeared and ideological differences and hostility between the major parties declined. More open elites now governed. Nonvoting participation and activism, from grass-roots initiatives (*Bürgerinitiativen*) to demonstrations, became common; they were, moreover, viewed as legitimate by a high percentage of the population. Loyalty and pride in their democratic form of government increased continuously among German citizens.[20] Concomitantly, cynicism toward political institutions and the percentage of individuals reporting a sense of powerlessness declined significantly. Support for the cornerstone values of representative democracy—freedom of expression, civil liberties, trust in government— increased. A politics devoid of broad economic and social policy shifts and rooted in a basic consensus came to dominate the FRG.[21]

In sum, a distinct and general democratization of German society and political culture occurred in the sixties and seventies. A social egalitarianism opposed to the authoritarian demeanor arose. No longer bound closely and exclusively to the state and the *Beamtentum* as its carrier, social trust in German society became increasingly anchored in a sense of pride in a stable political system and the values of parliamentary democracy (Schoonmaker 1989; Baldwin 1989).

As at the turn of the century, Germany's mode of anchoring public trust would have great consequences, not least of all in respect to work motivations and the locus of work. This time, however, the establishment of public trust was not linked closely to a constellation of values— the status ethic of the *Beamtentum*—that placed premiums directly upon disciplined, reliable, and systematic work in a vocation. Rather, while establishing social trust, the values of the FRG's democratic political institutions failed to reinvigorate and carry the old Lutheran notion of *Beruf;* on the contrary, these traditional values engendered suspicion and even disdain.

The American situation offers a distinct contrast in this regard. A *continuity* of development is characteristic, and, despite the turmoil of the sixties, the very array of values that define the American ideology— opportunity, individual achievement, social egalitarianism, upward mobility, individual liberties, freedom from government interference—were not discredited by their association with abhorrent events. American values not only continued to offer a foundation for a strong *ideal* of public trust but also continued to place work on a pedestal: hard work constituted the single most appropriate means for Americans to overcome obstacles and shape their own destinies. Thus, the workplace became bound intimately to America's view of itself. Wherever American ideals empirically infused occupational life, work motivations were sublimated away from mere means-end rational calculations.

No such constellation of values arose in the FRG to challenge and displace instrumental orientations toward work. No Horatio Alger rags-to-riches ideology of opportunity and upward mobility ethos underpins the view Germans hold of themselves (Craig 1982). On the contrary, all these factors—the advent of affluence, the association of the status ethic of civil servants with authoritarianism on the one hand and the Holocaust on the other, and the formation of public trust on the basis of a new, democratic political culture—pointed in the same direction: they opposed a bestowal of values explicitly upon work motivations. These factors tended to weaken the old notion of *Beruf,* the values associated with the status ethic of the *Beamtentum,* and the paternal ethos of the Prussian state, indeed to such an extent that these values increasingly lost their turn-of-the-century salience and capacity to legitimate action—that is, to sublimate action away from sheer means-end rational calculations—in the workplace. These values had become weakened and even discredited by the 1970s, especially among large segments of the younger generation. Thus, a clear impediment to the routinization of value-rational action in occupational life back to means-end rational action no longer existed. Self-interest and instrumental orientations of action toward personal advantage could more easily prevail. Work became viewed on the one hand as necessary for survival and economic security and, as German society became wealthier, as indispensable for the accumulation of consumer goods and the securing of high social status and on the other hand as an effective mode of integrating individuals socially and psychologically into the industrial society.

Now less thoroughly imbued with values, work motivations themselves failed to place strong obstacles to—and perhaps even facilitated—another development, one that would further oppose any attempts to endow occupational life with either an array of supportive values or an *elevated* status above other social domains: the *revival* in the seventies of the private sphere. This strong legacy was latent in the period of reconstruction in the fifties, and it could now, in a context of skepticism regarding the status ethic of civil servants and the authority of the state and catalyzed by a younger generation's disenchantment with the crass materialism of the consumer society and capitalism, become manifest. Moreover, even while providing a measure of social trust, the new political culture of democracy remained too underdeveloped to stand effectively against the reinvigoration of private life. Rooted deeply in Lutheran introspection and nineteenth-century German romanticism and accentuated at the end of the last century by the youth movement and antimodernism, this prominent orientation in German society did not simply fade away. As before, it carried a posture of distance and the withdrawal of emotional involvement from occupational life.

Another factor facilitated the revival of the private sphere in the seventies. The contemporary German social welfare state confirms—and in doing so, institutionalizes—a perpetual articulation of the boundaries between the private sphere and occupational life. The belief that the state should play a comprehensive role in guaranteeing the social welfare of all, in sponsoring cultural events, in organizing and financing higher education, and in maintaining the competitiveness of German industry, retains strong support. High legitimacy is granted to the German state to serve as a central mechanism to distribute resources, with the aim of ensuring the social welfare of all. In directly bolstering the integrity of the family through various explicit policies[22] and in fulfilling its designated task of "protecting" individuals against the rugged competition of modern capitalism and an intensification of the free market, the paternalistic German state *assists* the defense of the private sphere.

Whereas the accentuation of the private sphere at the turn of the century gave birth to social movements that espoused a return to the *Gemeinschaft*, this possibility, because of the advanced character of German industrialism and urbanism and the advent of widespread affluence in the post-1960 era, is no longer viable. Any thrust toward a cultivation of the family and personal relationships can become manifest only in a strengthened emphasis upon enduring and deep individual ties. The importance of private sphere concerns in Western Germany is visible in the resurgence of writing on private themes in the *neue Innerlichkeit* literary genre (see Struck 1986; Moser 1984; Muschg 1986); the flood of popular literature on the psychology of personal relationships (Richter 1976); the frequent choice by even professional women to interrupt their careers and spend up to five years as full-time mothers; and the unwillingness of the unemployed, even when offered a new position elsewhere, with a full moving subsidy, and a "transition allowance," to uproot themselves from family and friends.[23]

The new viability of private concerns further contests the weakened, though still enduring, values of the *Beamtentum*. As a withdrawal of emotional involvement from the workplace occurs, purely instrumental motivations move increasingly to the fore. Whereas the constellation of values linked to the status ethic of civil servants were dominant at the end of the last century, an *equal competition* of pluralistic work motives characterizes occupational life in the FRG: even while participating in the work force, some may be alienated from it; others may view work as a means to acquire material goods or to ensure social and psychological integration into their society; still others may continue to be motivated by the values that constitute the status ethic of the *Beamtentum*. The locus of work in the FRG can be established only by clear acknowledgment of this open and equal competition of action orientations in occupational life. This situation must be examined more closely.

THE LOCUS OF WORK IN THE FRG: THE OCCUPATIONAL, PRIVATE, AND LEISURE SPHERES

The precise locus of work in the contemporary FRG can now be identified. In comparison to other spheres of life, what is the relative *weight* of the occupational realm? Has it acquired an *elevated* status in Western German society in relation to other social domains?

The equal competition of diverse motives predominant in occupational life allows Germans to place clear boundaries around this sphere, far more so than would be the case if the value-rational action orientations dominant at the turn of the century that linked the realms of work and civil society continued to hold sway. Moreover, in recent years, a realm capable of erecting a clear resistance to occupational life has been revived and reaccentuated: the private sphere. More often than in the United States, which has not experienced such a reinvigoration of private life, personal well-being is viewed as dependent upon a concerted cultivation of intimate relationships. More time is allocated to the family and the cultivation of friendships. While important for the individual's sense of personal well-being, career goals and the occupational realm are kept separate from personal life, to such an extent that even German professionals can avoid immersion in vocational life. A firm boundary insulates and protects the private sphere of intimate relationships against an aggrandizement of occupational life far more effectively than in the United States. Indeed, this situation of viable competition between the occupational and private spheres creates a *dynamic* interaction that continuously articulates and reaffirms the boundaries of each sphere.

Widespread affluence and the social movements of the sixties failed in the United States, in spite of high inflation and unemployment in the seventies, to upset the hegemony of the occupational sphere. This sphere remains uncontested as the major realm within which men and women articulate personal identities. It is widely viewed as worthy of a high emotional investment and as the domain within which "self-realization" can take place, especially among middle-class professionals.[24] Moreover, rather than there being an overwhelming desire for lifelong economic security as the prevalent attitude in the middle class, as in the FRG, there is a high evaluation of the more risky path: occupational mobility and advancement.[25] Concomitantly, this unambivalent evaluation of the workplace renders unlikely a withdrawal from the occupational realm on a broad scale as well as a cultivation of private sphere relations and values,[26] particularly because no comprehensive social welfare state "protects" the private sphere in the United States. In addition, as noted previously, American romanticism was unable to establish itself as a strong cultural tradition, let alone to lend unequivocal support to the private sphere.

A simple polarization of the occupational and private realms fails, however, to portray adequately the locus of work in the FRG. The equal competition of pluralistic motives within the work sphere and its effective challenging by the private domain created a vacuum. In particular, as a consequence of affluence and the rise of a large middle class, further patterns of action formed to fill this vacuum and to create a distinct domain: the sphere of leisure.[27] A withdrawal from occupational life has involved not simply a retreat into the family, as often occurred at the beginning of the twentieth century, but also a cultivation of leisure pursuits. Indeed, hobbies and vacations now play a very pivotal part in daily life, far more than in the United States. The vacation, which is normally a legally mandated[28] five- or six-week period, is in many social circles the central subject of conversation. Because it weakens value-rational action in the occupational realm, the great emphasis now placed upon leisure challenges this realm directly, as does the high salience of the private sphere.

Whereas in the United States the occupational sphere clearly dominates the leisure and private spheres,[29] in the FRG these three domains compete equally. Characterized by a tempering of the hegemony of occupational life, a "decentralization" of social domains has taken place, even though the prestige of one's occupation still tends to determine social status. The locus of work in the FRG resides at the *intersection* of the private, leisure, and occupational realms.[30]

The data from the General Social Survey (*Allgemeine Bevölkerungsumfrage der Sozialwissenschaften*)[31] lend striking empirical support to this conclusion. These surveys indicate that Germans choose jobs with high security 52 percent more often than Americans, and 12 percent more Germans than Americans rate jobs highly that allow for extended periods of leisure time. Conversely, 32 percent more Americans than Germans choose jobs with good chances for advancement, and 25 percent more Americans than Germans rate highly jobs that are meaningful (Peterson 1985, questions 6B, 6D, 6E).

Conclusion

"The proper place of work" may differ in postindustrial societies. Using the firm theoretical framework and procedures of a Weberian configurational analysis, these differences can be isolated and defined clearly. The locus of work in the FRG was established in this study through a nonlinear analysis that, in focusing on dynamic interactions among various societal sectors and on the past and the present, ascertained the relative salience of occupational life vis-à-vis the private and leisure spheres. Underlying patterns of motivation toward work were first charted by reference to a *unique* configuration of past and present stratification and political and historical factors. Cultural forces—religion and the status ethics of carrier strata—were found to interweave perpetually throughout this configuration. Far from dying out amidst the massive structural transformations introduced by industrialization, action orientations to cultural forces cast strong legacies once they were anchored in powerful social carriers. As this investigation has sought to demonstrate, these cultural legacies even interacted with patterns of action orientations in the present and became manifest in sociologically significant ways in the FRG.

The Weberian mode of analysis used in this case study has sought to reveal the singular manner in which this transformation occurred. Indeed, the contemporary Western German configuration, because unique, should not lead policymakers and social scientists in the FRG to generalize their debates regarding de-coupling and to articulate them in reference to a putative "crisis of working society" as such.[32] Rather, the present "crisis" discussion must be acknowledged as rooted firmly within the constraints of the German cultural, political, and historical milieu.

Notes

1. I am using this term synonymously. It refers, of course, to the western sectors of the present-day united Germany.

2. The terms *place, location,* and *locus* are employed synonymously, as are *work* and *occupational life.*

3. This study complements my "The Origins and Expansion of *Kulturpessimismus*" (1987a). Weber's practiced configurational methodology as a whole has been reconstructed in my *Max Weber's Comparative Historical Sociology: A Comparison to Recent Schools* (1992b) in far more detail than is possible here.

4. Empirically, of course, all four flowed together. Weber does not treat these distinctions clearly. They have been, with the assistance of *Economy and Society* (Weber 1968), reconstructed.

5. Indeed, Weber states that society concerns, for him, the intermediate level only, namely "the general structures of human groups" (1968, 356). Terms

such as *society* or *system* are almost entirely avoided. (These terms appear in the translations, particularly those by Parsons, much more than in the original texts.)

6. For example, central values in Protestant asceticism—such as tithing to charities, the formation of impersonal and abstract goals, the orientation to the future and world mastery, and an optimism regarding the capacity to shape personal destinies—remain integral in American life despite the fact that many who uphold these values do not perceive them as religious virtues or as linked intimately to a religious heritage (Kalberg 1989).

7. Comparisons to countries "more similar" to Western Germany—that is, other European nations—would be necessary for a further refinement of this analysis. Such comparisons would allow a more precise identification of the major contours of German society. In this sense, this study must be viewed as a preliminary undertaking.

8. I am largely omitting a discussion of Catholicism. Earlier and more recent commentators agree on the "predominantly . . . Protestant cast" of German culture (Lowie 1945, 103). Two-thirds of all Germans in Imperial Germany were Lutherans, according to Lowie (102–104). Lidtke (1982, 23–24) and McLeod (1982) cite similar figures: in 1905, 62 percent of all Germans were Protestant and 36.5 percent were Catholic.

9. American romanticism, which persisted throughout the nineteenth and early twentieth centuries, tended to emphasize the purity of nature and to denounce the corrupting influences of urbanization and industrialization, as did German romanticism. Strong American, *world*-oriented individualism could coexist quite compatibly with this romanticism, yet not at all with a romanticism that emphasized also the subordination of the individual to the *Gemeinschaft*, as did the German. Nonetheless, and even while doing so, German romanticism tended to idealize a certain type of individualism, one that did not stand strongly against the *Gemeinschaft:* the inward-looking individualism of expressivity and artistic creation. To this day, German individualism retains a strongly introspective and even meditative aspect (see Mosse 1964, 13–148; Löwenthal 1970; Brunschwig 1975; Weiss 1986).

10. Whereas rugged frontier individuals who mastered nature were frequently cast as ideal figures during the middle decades of the nineteenth century, the acceleration of industrialization and the closing of the frontier in this century's latter decades saw more and more the casting of Herculean capitalist entrepreneurs as heroic figures.

11. Surveys undertaken even at the time of the Great Depression indicate that the unemployed tended to blame themselves, rather than their economic system, for their plight (see Lynd and Lynd 1937).

12. And, as well, burdened by too many American presuppositions.

13. Indeed, the successful guidance of the economy by the state in the latter half of the nineteenth century and its legitimating ethos of paternal "protection and care," which found concrete expression in manifold social welfare services, unemployment insurance, and social security programs, insulated large segments of the German population from the irregular swings of the capitalist economy.

14. Perhaps this term is best translated as "personal friend" or "intimate friend" (see Kalberg 1987b).

15. A series of family-oriented journals founded in the nineteenth century (for example, *Über Land und Meer, Gartenlaube* and *Daheim*) promoted a sentimental view of the family in which intimacy reigned and conflicts disappeared.

16. The German term *Arbeitsplatz* vividly captures just this integrating purpose of work. Work provides a *place* for individuals in society.

17. Lipset (1979) offers a summary of numerous comparative studies that lend empirical support to these statements. See also Bellah (1985) and Caplow et al. (1982).

18. Georg Simmel's microsociology documents this severe polarization in all its meandering ramifications. Conversely, the microsociology of Goffman is conceivable only against the backdrop of a comprehensive and distinctly American *intertwining* of public and private. The same must be said of American exchange theory. Similarly, this same backdrop provided the fundamental precondition for the birth and popularity of role theory in American sociology (as well as structural-functionalism in general). For a very German critique, see Tenbruck (1987); for a very German commentary, see Münch (1986).

19. This posture was particularly clear among followers of the Youth Movement (see Becker 1946).

20. An exception to this trend is found in the mid-seventies among highly educated younger people, undoubtedly as a consequence of the *Berufsverbot*.

21. These studies are summarized by Conradt (1980).

22. Such as monthly payments for each child until the completion of the child's education, maternity leave payments for twelve months, the legal right of mothers to return to their jobs up to three years after giving birth, and guarantees of and the financing of "rest and relaxation" vacations for mothers (*Muttergenesungswerk*).

23. To most Germans, the American practice of moving away from family, friends, and hometown to accept a new job or promotion remains incomprehensible (see Walker 1971; Hall and Hall 1983; Kalberg 1987a).

24. The notion of *self-realization* is itself a residual of American heroic individualism and the ideology of opportunity. The view that the individual can reorder his or her personality and life-chances through hard work or an act of will is viewed in those countries without traditions of Herculean, world-oriented individualism, and ascetic Protestantism, such as Germany, as exceedingly naive. Maslow's self-actualization theory (1962) is so rooted in and expressive of an American configuration that it should be transferred to other cultural contexts only with great caution. To the extent that a notion of self-realization does exist in Germany, it is not to be automatically assumed, given the particular locus of work in German society, that occupational life will be the major arena for its expression (the expectation that the workplace will provide a social and psychological integration of the individual seems far more widespread). In light of the introspective legacy, self-realization would more likely become manifest in artistic, creative, and even meditative pursuits (such as music or scholarship).

25. Whereas residuals of the German notion of *Beruf* and of the apprenticeship system even today oblige individuals in West Germany to labor regularly

and conscientiously in a familiar and stable setting, Americans feel compelled to experiment continuously with their capacities, qualifications, and interests in order to bring them more closely in line with workplace tasks and to increase material wealth and enhance social standing. Within Germany, such experimentation is viewed as a sign of immaturity.

26. An array of reports in the American media indicates that, far from passing on an attitude of skepticism toward the occupational sphere and its demands, the generation of the sixties appears to be instilling an achievement ethic in its children even more intense than the one it learned in the home.

27. Of course, the absence of a broad tradition of asceticism in German society—especially in regard to work—also played an important part.

28. Germans speak of a "right of vacation" (*Recht auf Urlaub*).

29. Not surprisingly, in view of this dominance, terms heretofore related exclusively to the sphere of work have invaded the leisure sphere. Common expressions that illustrate this penetration abound, such as "work on my tan," "work out," "work at winning," "work at my tennis," "working lunch," and "working vacation." Such a vocabulary has also permeated the domain of intimacy; we speak of "working at relationships" and "working at marriage." Conversely, an American may speak of "loving my work," while a demonstrated enthusiasm for work in Germany is very often suspect. Firmer boundaries between these three domains in the Federal Republic have prevented the free transfer of such expressions. Nor is it surprising that *Feierabend*—the "holiday evening" that begins punctually at five P.M.—cannot be translated literally into English.

30. The entire analysis here points also to the conclusion that the elevation of work and occupational life to a position of clear hegemony over other social domains does not constitute a precondition for the existence of a highly efficient work force.

31. These are the first standardized general social surveys of the United States and the Federal Republic (1982–1985); see Peterson (1985).

32. A long line of German "crisis" discussions (for example, of capitalism, authority, democracy, the *Industriestaat, Regierbarkeit,* modernity, the consumer society, the family, and legitimation) has fallen victim to just this error.

References

Almond, G. A., and J. S. Coleman, eds. 1960. *The Politics of Developing Areas.* Princeton: Princeton University Press.

Almond, G. A., and B. Powell, Jr. 1966. *Comparative Politics: A Developmental Approach.* Boston: Little, Brown.

Bahrdt, H. P. 1983. "Arbeit als Inhalt des Lebens." In *Krise der Arbeitsgesellschaft?*, edited by J. Matthes, 120–137. Frankfurt: Campus.

Baldwin, P. 1989. "Postwar Germany in the *Longue Durée.*" *German Politics and Society* 16 (1): 1–9.

Becker, H. 1946. *German Youth: Bond or Free.* London: K. Paul, Trench, Trubner and Co.

Bellah, R. et al. 1985. *Habits of the Heart.* Berkeley and Los Angeles: University of California Press.

Bendix, R. 1978. *Kings or Peoples.* Berkeley and Los Angeles: University of California Press.

Benseler, F. et al., eds. 1982. *Zukunft der Arbeit.* Hamburg: VSA.

Bonß, W., and R. G. Heinze, eds. 1984. *Arbeitslosigkeit in der Arbeitsgesellschaft.* Frankfurt: Suhrkamp.

Born, K. E. 1975. *Von der Reichsgründung bis zum Ersten Weltkrieg.* Munich: dtv.

Brunschwig, H. 1975. *Gesellschaft und Romantik in Preussen im 18. Jahrhundert.* Translated by M. Schultheis. Frankfurt: Ullstein.

Bussman, W. 1958. "Zur Geschichte des deutschen Liberalismus im 19. Jahrhundert." *Historische Zeitschrift* 186 (4): 527–557.

Caplow, T. et al. 1982. *Middletown Families.* Minneapolis: University of Minnesota Press.

Cleveland, F. A. 1927. *American Citizenship.* New York: Ronald Press.

Conradt, D. P. 1980. "Changing German Political Culture." In *The Civic Culture Revisited,* edited by G. A. Almond and S. Verba, 212–272. Boston: Little, Brown.

Conze, W., and J. Kocka, eds. 1985. *Bildungsbürgertum im 19. Jahrhundert.* Stuttgart: Klett-Cotta.

Craig, G. 1978. *Germany: 1866–1945.* New York: Oxford.

———. 1982. *The Germans.* New York: Putnam.

Dahrendorf, R. 1967. *Society and Democracy in Germany.* New York: Anchor.

———. 1980. "Im Entschwinden der Arbeitsgesellschaft." *Merkur* 34 (4): 749–760.

———. 1983. "Wenn der Arbeitsgesellschaft die Arbeit ausgeht." In *Krise der Arbeitsgesellschaft?,* edited by J. Matthes, 25–37. Frankfurt: Campus.

Dillenberger, J., ed. 1961. *Martin Luther: Selections from His Writings.* New York: Doubleday.

Elias, N. 1969. *Über den Prozess der Zivilisation.* Bern: Francke Verlag.

———. 1989. *Studien über die Deutschen.* Frankfurt: Suhrkamp.

Engelhardt, U. 1986. *Bildungsbürgertum.* Stuttgart: Klett-Cotta.

Epstein, K. 1977. *The Genesis of German Conservatism.* Princeton: Princeton University Press.

Greiffenhagen, M. 1981. *Die Aktualität Preussens.* Frankfurt: Fischer Verlag.

Guggenberger, B. 1982. "Am Ende der Arbeitsgesellschaft—Arbeitsgesellschaft ohne Ende?" In *Zukunft der Arbeit,* edited by F. Benseler, R. G. Heinze, and A. Klönne, 63–83. Hamburg: VSA.

Gutzkow, K. 1963. "Unterhaltungen am häuslichen Kamin." In *Facsimile. Querschnitt durch die Gartenlaube,* edited by H. D. Müller, 184–197. Munich: Scherz Verlag.

Hall, E. T., and M. R. Hall. 1983. *Hidden Differences.* Hamburg: Stern Verlag.

Herf, J. 1980. "The 'Holocaust' Reception in West Germany." *New German Critique* 22 (1): 30–52.

Herr, D. 1981. *Religion and Political Culture: Ascetic Rationalism and Political Modernization in the Thought of Max Weber.* Unpublished dissertation, New School for Social Research.

Hill, C. 1964. *Puritanism and Revolution.* New York: Schocken.

Hofstadter, R. 1955 [1944]. *Social Darwinism in American Thought.* Boston: Beacon.

Holborn, H. 1981. *Deutsche Geschichte in der Neuzeit.* Frankfurt: Fischer Verlag.

Kalberg, S. 1983. "Max Weber's Universal-Historical Architectonic of Economically Oriented Action: A Preliminary Reconstruction." In *Current Perspectives in Social Theory,* edited by S. G. McNall, 253–288. Greenwich, Conn.: JAI Press.

———. 1985. "The Role of Ideal Interests in Max Weber's Comparative Historical Sociology." In *A Marx-Weber Dialogue,* edited by R. J. Antonio and R. M. Glassman, 46–67. Lawrence: University Press of Kansas.

———. 1987a. "The Origin and Expansion of *Kulturpessimismus:* The Relationship between Public and Private Spheres in Early Twentieth-Century Germany." *Sociological Theory* 5 (2): 150–164.

———. 1987b. "West German and American Interaction Forms: One Level of Structured Misunderstanding." *Theory, Culture and Society* 4 (3): 603–618.

———. 1989. "Max Webers historisch-vergleichende Untersuchungen und das 'Webersche Bild der Neuzeit': eine Gegenüberstellung." In *Max Weber heute,* edited by J. Weiss, 425–444. Frankfurt: Suhrkamp.

———. 1992. *Max Weber's Comparative Historical Sociology: A Comparison to Recent Schools.* London: Polity Press.

———. 1992a. "Cultural Foundations of Modern Citizenship." In *The Nature of Citizenship: Theoretical Issues,* edited by B. S. Turner. London: Sage Publications.

Kocka, J. 1981. *Die Angestellten in der deutschen Geschichte. 1850–1980.* Göttingen: Vandenhöck & Ruprecht.

Kocka, J., and G. Ritter, eds. 1974. *Deutsche Sozialgeschichte.* Vol. 2. Munich: Verlag C. H. Beck.

Konwitz, M. R., and G. Kennedy. 1960. *The American Pragmatists.* Cleveland: World Publishing.

Kruse, L. 1980. *Privatheit als Problem und Gegenstand der Psychologie.* Frankfurt: Campus Verlag.

Lidtke, V. 1982. "Social Class and Secularization in Imperial Germany." *Yearbook of the Leo Baeck Institute* 25: 21–40.

Lipset, S. M. 1979 [1963]. *The First New Nation.* New York: W. W. Norton.

Löwenthal, R. 1970. *Der romantische Rückfall.* Stuttgart: Kohlhammer.

Lowie, R. H. 1945. *The German People: A Social Portrait to 1914.* New York: Farrar & Rinehart.

Lynd, R. S., and H. M. Lynd. 1937. *Middletown in Transition.* New York: Harcourt, Brace, and World.

Mann, G. 1975. *Deutsche Geschichte des 19. und 20. Jahrhunderts.* Frankfurt: Fischer Verlag.

Maslow, A. 1962. *Toward a Psychology of Being.* Princeton: Von Nostrand.

Matthes, J., ed. 1983. *Krise der Arbeitsgesellschaft?* Frankfurt: Campus.

McLeod, H. 1982. "Protestantism and the Working Class in Imperial Germany." *European Studies Review* 12 (3): 323–344.

Miller, P. 1961. *The New England Mind.* Boston: Beacon Press.

Moore, B. 1966. *The Social Origins of Dictatorship and Democracy.* Boston: Beacon.

Moser, T. 1984. *Lehrjahre auf der Couch.* Frankfurt: Insel.

Mosse, G. 1964. *The Crisis of German Ideology.* New York: Grosset & Dunlap.

Münch, R. 1986. "The American Creed in Sociological Theory: Exchange, Negotiated Order, Accommodated Individualism, and Contingency." *Sociological Theory* 4 (1): 41–60.

Muschg, A. 1986. *Literatur als Therapie?* Neuwied: Luchterhand.

Offe, C. 1984. *"Arbeitsgesellschaft." Strukturprobleme und Zukunftsperspektiven.* Frankfurt: Campus.

Peterson, B. L. 1985. *Codebook for the Combined 1982 General Social Survey and Allgemeine Bevölkerungsumfrage der Sozialwissenschaften (ALLBUS).* Chicago: NORC.

Plessner, H. 1974. *Die verspätete Nation.* Frankfurt: Suhrkamp.

Richter, H. 1976. *Flüchten oder Standhalten.* Reinbek bei Hamburg: Rowohlt.

Ringer, F. 1969. *The Decline of the German Mandarins.* Cambridge: Harvard University Press.

Rosenberg, A. 1931. *Imperial Germany.* New York: Oxford University Press.

Schoonmaker, D. 1989. "The Second Bonn Republic at Forty Years." *German Politics and Society* 16 (1): 10–21.

Sell, F. 1953. *Die Tragödie des deutschen Liberalismus.* Stuttgart: Deutsche Verlags-Anstalt.

Skocpol, T. 1979. *States and Social Revolutions.* New York: Cambridge University Press.

Sontheimer, K. 1971. *Grundzüge des politischen Systems der Bundesrepublik Deutschland.* Munich: Piper Verlag.

Stern, F. 1965. *The Politics of Cultural Despair.* New York: Anchor Books.

Struck, K. 1986. *Klassenliebe.* Frankfurt: Suhrkamp.

Sumner, G. 1906. *Folkways.* Boston: Ginn.

Tenbruck, F. H. 1987. "On the German Reception of Role Theory." In *Modern German Sociology,* edited by V. Meja and N. Stehr and translated by S. Kalberg and C. Wies-Kalberg, 410–445. New York: Columbia University Press.

Troeltsch, E. 1931 [1911]. *The Social Teachings of the Christian Churches.* 2 vols. New York: Harper Torchbook.

Veblen, T. 1966. *Imperial Germany and the Industrial Revolution.* Ann Arbor: University of Michigan Press.

Walker, M. 1971. *German Home Towns.* Ithaca: Cornell University Press.

Weber, M. 1930 [1958]. *The Protestant Ethic and the Spirit of Capitalism.* Translated by T. Parsons. New York: Charles Scribner's Sons.

———. 1946. *From Max Weber.* Edited and translated by H. H. Gerth and C. W. Mills. New York: Oxford University Press.

———. 1951. *The Religion of China.* Edited and translated by H. H. Gerth. New York: Free Press.

———. 1958. *The Religion of India.* Edited and translated by H. H. Gerth and D. Martindale. New York: Free Press.

———. 1968. *Economy and Society.* Edited by G. Roth and C. Wittich. New York: Bedminster Press.

———. 1972. *Die protestantische Ethik: Kritiken und Antikritiken.* Edited by J. Winckelmann. Hamburg: Siebenstern.

———. 1976. *The Agrarian Sociology of Ancient Civilizations.* Translated by R. I. Frank. London: New Left Books.

———. 1978. *Weber: Selections in Translation.* Edited by W. G. Runciman and translated by E. Matthews. Cambridge: Cambridge University Press.

Weiss, J. 1986. "Wiederverzauberung der Welt? Bemerkungen zur Widerkehr der Romantik in der gegenwärtigen Kulturkritik." In *Kultur und Gesellschaft,* edited by F. Neidhardt, M. R. Lepsius, and J. Weiss, 286–301. Opladen: Westdeutscher Verlag.

13

Culture and Crisis
Making Sense of the Crisis of the Work Society
Klaus Eder

Social Analysis beyond Cultural Pessimism

Whether there is a crisis in advanced industrial societies is open to debate. But there is undeniably a discourse on crisis. It focuses politically on the crisis of the welfare state, economically on the ecological limits of growth, and culturally on the loss of meaning in modern life. Even the social sciences, whose job it is to identify and monitor such discourses, are sometimes thought to be affected. Whether or not the crisis exists, there is a strong cultural pessimism in intellectual and everyday life that fuels the discourse. But there is no consensus as to its extent or its character, nor even a consensus as to what is meant by *a crisis*. This lack of consensus makes it difficult to transcend cultural pessimism and to turn to social analysis, to an "objectifying" account of the supposed crisis.

We will try to clarify the notion of crisis using the German discussion of the *Krise der Arbeitsgesellschaft* or "crisis of the work society" (Matthes 1983). This social science discourse on crisis, we claim, is a new version of the never-ending discourse on crisis in modern society. It puts crisis into perspective as the result of an accumulation of either changes in the objective structural conditions of work (for example, the labor market) or changes in the cultural conditions of work (for example, the work ethic). But these changes are not sufficient in themselves to explain the supposed crisis. We need an additional argument that distinguishes between situations of crisis and noncrisis. Crisis, we suggest, ensues when social changes lead to a block in the capacity of society to control its course and direction of change.

This analysis of crisis must take into account two elements: the cultural orientation of social actors and the objective location of social actors within a social structure that determines the relations between them. To determine the capacity of society to reproduce its structure and culture, we have to analyze the social usage of culture by groups within the system of social relations that define the place and status of these groups (Bourdieu 1984). We have to consider the socially stratified adoption of cultural traditions as the mediating process between culture and social structure in order to analyze how culture influences the course of the social development of a concrete society within the constraints set by social structure. The mediating concept is that of social groups (or classes) defined by their capacity to act upon society. The hypothesis is as follows: The conditions for the cultural effectiveness of social groups in a social structure change to the degree that their place and status change.[1] When, however, social groups within a specific societal context develop competing and even irreconcilable cultural models of society, we are faced with what we can call a "crisis of society."

An emphasis upon *agency* offers a new look at the role that culture plays in the reproduction of advanced industrial societies. One example is in the sphere of work. In accordance with their social placement and replacement in recent social developments, social groups have redefined the *modern work ethic* (once thought to be identical with the Protestant ethic) to produce competing versions of it. The outcome is what German sociologists have called the *Krise der Arbeitsgesellschaft*,[2] a crisis that cannot be understood adequately as either a structural or a cultural crisis (but certainly has to do with problems of the structural and cultural reproduction of work). We will examine the two processes that are used here as empirical proof of a crisis of work society: in structural terms, the de-coupling of work from status and, in cultural terms, the de-coupling of work from self-realization. To understand how both processes interact we will analyze class-specific work cultures that enable or prevent social groups from acting upon the structural changes of the work they experience. The hypothesis advanced is as follows: The crisis of the work society is, in the last instance, the crisis of the working class. The main idea that has provoked this discourse is that the work culture of the working class has lost its determining influence upon society. The working class has lost the capacity to determine how the work society will act upon itself and direct its development,[3] as the analysis of the processes of structural and cultural change in the sphere of work and their interaction will make clear. We are at present observing the rise of new social groups and of ultimately one new social class that will defend a different type of work culture. The frame of reference within which structural and cultural changes are perceived and interpreted changes— and with it what we experience as crisis. We have to find out, not whether there really is a crisis, but what are the frames of reference within which society interprets its own structural and cultural change as crisis. And the frame *work society* is only one among others, itself tied to a specific social class and a specific sociocultural environment.

Accounting for the Crisis of the Work Society

THE WORK SOCIETY IN CRISIS?

The German discussion about the crisis of the work society is a good example of the specific effects of culture on the constitution of a crisis. The crisis of the work society has become jargon in the program statements of political parties, especially the Social Democrats, which can be taken as an indicator of the relevance of this concept for public communication. This way of communicating a problem has been fostered, if not generated, by the sociological discourse that invented this jargon. It carries with it a cultural model oriented toward a specific type of collective action.

The concept suggests social processes that go beyond the emergence and relief of structural strains. They implicate a cultural evolution within the development of industrial society. The concept of *industry* in "industrial society" (Offe 1983) has lost the connotation of *industriousness*. It has been replaced by the value-laden concept of *work* in "work society." This substitution points to the fact that not only the systemic reproduction of society but also its cultural basis are now in fact vulnerable.

Thus the theory of the crisis of the work society has two complementary aspects. The first deals with changes in the labor market and in the relation between education and occupation (the system of status distribution). Different theories of postindustrial society from Bell to Touraine, industrial sociology research and stratification research, provide arguments to describe the crisis of the work society.[4] The second aspect of the theory is subsumed under the decline of the Protestant work ethic. This description has led to several misleading explanations, especially within the research on value change.[5] They have been misleading, first, because what we call *Protestant ethic* is itself a combination of different cultural elements that emerged at the beginning of capitalism and, second, because the Protestant ethic is only one among other cultural traditions that can generate possible orientations toward work in modern society.

These two parts of the theory of a crisis of the work society, the structuralist and the culturalist, are in themselves insufficient to explain the crisis. Even an attempt to use them thus would be an odd undertaking because the two contradict each other. The structural part claims that the labor market has become significantly more competitive (if unevenly so), that status no longer guarantees work, and that work is being de-coupled from status. It even claims that work has become scarce and the object of intensifying struggles between status groups. The cultural part says that there is a de-coupling of work from self-realization and that people are retreating from work. Thus the crisis of the work society is seen to result from work's increasing importance on the structural level and from its decreasing importance on the cultural level. Such a contradictory relationship cannot be reduced to a structural and a cultural crisis. I will argue that the crisis of the work society consists precisely in this contradictory relationship, a relationship that could not be understood if we did not account for the specific contributions of structure and culture.

In developing the argument let us first look briefly at the developmental processes in the social organization of work that are held to be responsible for changes in the work ethic. These explanations are shown to be short circuits because they assume deterministic relationships between structure and culture (mostly in the direction of culture). Second, we will see how changes in the modern work ethic open new possibilities for social actors to invent and defend specific versions and adaptations. The emergence of antagonistic groups defined in terms of structural location and cultural orientation points to a social crisis that will have far-reaching effects upon the course and intensity of structural and cultural changes that accompany the transformation of advanced modern societies into postindustrial societies.

STRUCTURAL CHANGES OF WORK:
THE DE-COUPLING OF WORK FROM STATUS

From a structural perspective, we must examine some assumptions and research findings about changes in the sphere of work that are supposed, in turn, to be changing how work is experienced and perceived. Four of the main ones are as follows: (1) the emergence of new forms of nonmanual labor (*Kopfarbeit*), (2) the reduction of working time and its implications for the lives of workers, (3) the division of the labor market into well-alimented and poorly alimented sectors, and (4) the de-coupling of work from status and their resulting realignment.

The Emergence of Nonmanual Labor. The hypothesis of an increase in and a structural dominance by nonmanual labor lies at the bases of the different theories about the course of postindustrial society.[6] These theories start with the assumption that organization and information technologies have led to the primacy of cognitive (nonmanual) work over productive (manual) work. Cognitively skilled work (*Kopfarbeit*) defines the postindustrial paradigm of work. Knowledge becomes the central means for the economic reproduction of society.

The usual conclusion, from the point of view of industrial society, is that this development is a liberation of labor. But one important implication is normally overlooked: the control of the new workers by the information technologies themselves. A more adequate conclusion, then, is that the substitution of nonmanual for manual work implies a further increase in the social control of work. Thus, although relief from work as toil is experienced as "liberation," workers are also placed in an increasingly instrumental relation to work that leads to a diminution of it as a central life interest.

The qualifications required for entry into the job market have also changed. The expansion of nonmanual work is accompanied simultaneously by an upgrading and a downgrading of skills. The significance of the expansion of nonmanual work, due mainly to the growth of the service sector, is therefore a subject of great controversy (Mutz 1987). The theory of *polarization* (Kern & Schumann 1984) suggested that this change leads to a minority of highly qualified workers and a majority of unqualified workers. But this polarization seems to have been a transitional phenomenon of the late 1960s and 1970s. Recent research shows that less qualified work is either eliminated or substituted for new forms of control. For those workers retained, the elimination of their competitors through unemployment is the structural solution.[7]

This new social differentiation of work is thought to be changing the distribution of cultural orientations across the working population. This hypothesis assumes that occupations within the service sector generate a different cultural orientation than that which is typical for occupations in the production sector. If this is true, the service occupations will dissolve traditional class cultures and give rise to cultural cleavages that could become the nucleus for new class formations.[8] The discussion about the emerging postindustrial society then can be transferred to more empirical levels: the levels of class differences and the related level of cultural differences. Empirical data on such cultural differences can be found in a new line of research on class: the research on differences in life-style. This research begins theoretically by taking a fresh look at Weber's famous distinction between status and class, with status as a cultural indicator of class (Bourdieu 1984). Within the emerging differences in life-style fostered by the expansion of nonmanual work, we may find some of the reasons that point to an end of the Protestant ethic.

This analysis is a first step toward a sociological theory of culture beyond culturalism. There is no change in class structure without parallel cultural changes. But such cultural changes open nothing more than an "objective possibility" for changes in the work culture. Whether the possibility has been or will be used remains to be seen.

The Shortening of Working Hours. Since 1960 the amount of time a worker works (wage labor) has steadily diminished—by any measure. A 1981 study by Emnid shows an average of 39.2 hours per worker per week. In the 1950s, the ratio of hours of work to hours of nonwork was 1 to 2.9; in 1980 it was 1 to 4.1 (Kern & Schumann 1983:355). The total period of life spent at work has also decreased.[9] From this overall shrinkage some have concluded that the relevance of work to life and the value attributed to it for a meaningful life have diminished.[10] Such a conclusion is unwarranted. For even if more time is spent outside work, we do not necessarily de-emphasize the value of work in our lives. We can conclude only that it has become *objectively* possible to change the relative meaning of work for life.

The theory of the devaluation of work and the corresponding theory of a rise in the valuation of nonwork, defined as *leisure,* has been defended in different studies using opinion polls. Such an inverse relationship is assumed, for example, by Noelle-Neumann (1980; Noelle-Neumann & Strümpel 1984) in survey data studies that interpret the ascending valuation of leisure over work as a sign of Germans' increasing laziness and antipathy to work.[11] The increasing number of people who no longer accept an eight-hour work day is taken as yet another sign. There are speculations that in the coming years an increasing portion of the working population in advanced industrial societies will have abandoned the regular full working day.

But to conclude that there is an increase in nonproductive activities such as laziness, sleeping, window shopping, and so on is unwarranted. Qualitative studies suggest instead that what we call *leisure time* is being used instead for another type of work. A substitution of do-it-yourself labor for wage labor can be observed. This type of work, hobby work, is holistic *bricolage* in Lévi-Strauss's sense. It is no longer *ponos*, but *ergon*. It is nonwage labor that—unlike much wage labor—offers intrinsic rewards to the worker.

If this observation is generally correct, then the reduction in time spent on wage labor has a quite different meaning: it points up the increasing relevance of nonwage labor. If this other form of work becomes the integrative experience of a population, it will foster a new work ethic, one beyond the Protestant work ethic. In that case, we would have to conclude that it is the type of work, whether wage labor or nonwage labor, that is decisive for people's cultural orientation to work. Instead of a devaluation, there is a revaluation of work going on in advanced industrial societies.[12] Thus the direction of cultural change in the sphere of work is an open question. If the data claiming a value change in the sphere of work allows for interpretations quite contrary to that of Noelle-Neumann, then we need even more data about the actors.

The New Polarization between Work and Nonwork. The new valuation of nonwage labor gains yet another meaning when nonwork and leisure are involuntary because of, for example, forced early retirement, forced periods in the educational system, or the forced status of being officially unemployed. Such forced reductions of the wage labor pool have increased in recent years because of pressures from the labor market. Yet those who are excluded from the labor market do not escape being forced to define their lives in terms of wage labor.[13]

The consequence of this shrinking labor market is a new form of polarization of work into stable wage labor (most of it highly qualified) and wage labor with a high risk of unemployment. Brandt (1981) has called this the "extended polarization of work." The structural implication of this polarization is a dual economy, separating a saturated formal economy from an informal economy. This structural separation will certainly change how the world of work is perceived and experienced. Thus a polarization of the work culture is also to be expected. Qualitative research on evaluative and cognitive attitudes toward work has detected new types of orientations toward work (Giegel et al. 1988). But whether the "reflexive," the "hedonistic," or the "traditional" type will predominate in shaping the work culture remains an open question. What we can observe is a differentiation of work-related (sub)cultures.

The De-coupling of Work from Status and Their Realignment. That the relationship between work and status has never corresponded to the ideal of "everyone according to his achievement" has often been analyzed and discussed in sociological literature. One of the reasons for this is the politics of income distribution. Redistribution by the modern welfare state has led to a relative de-coupling of work from status without destroying most people's belief in a relationship between the two. On the contrary, the educational revolution, striving to guarantee an equality of opportunity, has confirmed anew (at least for some time) a positive relationship between achievement and status and has thus strengthened this ideology.[14]

The realization of this ideal relationship is however again being frustrated because an increasing number of highly educated young people cannot be processed into employment. Employment opportunities do not correspond to the supply of qualified would-be workers. Bourdieu speaks of a "cheated generation" (Bourdieu 1984), whose aspirations to a social status corresponding to its qualifications have to be (and have been) disappointed. An educational status no longer guarantees a corresponding social status in the labor market.[15]

This phenomenon is reinforced by unemployment policies. In order to decrease unemployment figures, the unemployed are placed in programs for further education financed by state institutions. This tactic raises their educational status even further without expanding the labor market, although their competitive chances to get one of the scarce jobs are redistributed. These contradictory processes necessarily produce cognitive dissonances. How these dissonances are resolved (whether they lead to a distancing from the culture of work or to an even more rigid adherence to it) is an empirical question.

It has been claimed that such de-coupling undermines the desire for and the belief in achievement in such a way that this motivator, one of the basic engines of the modern work ethic, will vanish. But this is not a necessary consequence. The opposite can sometimes occur (a phenomenon that is related to the unpleasant experience of unemployment). Thus, in regard to the achievement principle, we are again forced to look more closely for the meaning and direction given by different social groups and social actors.

The de-coupling debate is interesting in itself as a description of structural strains within the system of status allocation. It shows that the relation of work and social status is mediated by social processes that leave it in a constant flux. There is no one legitimate relationship; the shape of the relationship is itself the outcome of social struggles. Such strains can potentially change the work culture. But not necessarily. Thus we are again left with the need to look at the changes on the cultural level and at the de-coupling on this cultural level.[16]

CULTURAL CHANGES OF WORK: THE DE-COUPLING OF WORK FROM SELF-REALIZATION

The sociostructural changes described so far have already altered work as a collective experience for nearly all groups engaged in wage labor. This is connected with a value change social scientists believe to have occurred in advanced industrial societies since World War II. The empirically based discussion concerning the relevance of competing interpretations of the crisis of the work culture has revolved around the decline of the work ethic in Germany (Noelle-Neumann & Strümpel 1984; Pawlowsky & Strümpel 1986; Reuband 1985, 1987) and the decline of the German virtues of achievement and diligence. This cultural explanation of the crisis of the *Arbeitsgesellschaft* is ultimately based on a deep feeling that the morality implicitly expected of even a modern work ethic is beyond recall.[17]

The message of this discourse on the decline of the work ethic is that, in comparison to the Japanese (a comparison made repeatedly, for example, in the influential liberal weekly journal *Die Zeit*), the Germans have become lazy people. This explanation is shortsighted and overlooks the following: (1) the emergence of new and more demanding orientations toward work, (2) changing relationships between work and leisure, (3) a new polarization of work-related life-styles due to the experience of a continuous or discontinuous biography, and (4) a de-coupling of work from self-realization.

New Demands upon Work. Research shows that the Protestant ethic is not dead yet. But new values for and demands on work seem to be gaining importance. Beyond the classic puritan virtues and the secondary ones as codified, for example, by Benjamin Franklin (Maccoby & Terzi 1981:22f.), new virtues have emerged. Flexibility, communicative competence, open-mindedness, humor, and related qualities are treated as "communicative virtues," as opposed to the classic Prussian virtues (Schmidtchen 1984b). Some researchers perceive the new virtues to be most widespread among the young and those of higher status, whereas others point to the service sector as the principal locus.

These new virtues are tied to new expectations of what work should be like. Work should above all contribute more to self-realization. But these new expectations are—as Strümpel argues—frustrated by a lag in structural changes in the workplace (Noelle-Neumann & Strümpel 1984). Because there is actually no chance for their realization in the workplace, a new type of work dissatisfaction emerges. Survey data show that satisfaction with work has declined, but not because work has been devalued. On the contrary, aspirations associated with work have increased; the decline in satisfaction is related to the fact that rising aspirations cannot be met given the social organization of work. Thus the rise in work dissatisfaction does not necessarily imply a decline in the relevance of work, but can result from the contrary.[18]

Work, Leisure, and Achievement Orientation. Another change in the work ethic is the supposed decline of the centrality of work. It has become a secondary life interest. Survey research does show a change in the centrality of work, but its meaning is quite controversial. Against the claim that leisure has been substituted for work, some argue that investments in work, family, and leisure have all become stronger (Hondrich et al. 1988). Thus there is no substitution effect.

For many people, though, the significance of work has changed in comparison to other life interests. We know of the "instrumentalism" of the workers in the Goldthorpe/Lockwood studies on the affluent worker and of the rise of leisure as a central life interest. But this instrumentalism seems to be part of a more complex attitude toward work. Work is seen less as a means to gaining income than as a means to investing in leisure. The Protestant work ethic seems to have spread from wage labor to other areas of modern life, to those areas we describe as part of a life-world, that is, public and private life. Working hard to organize and spend leisure time has become a virtue, as has working hard on a political engagement.[19]

Thus we cannot accept the proposition, offered in the literature on value change in the sphere of work, that hedonism is growing.[20] An achievement orientation still exists, and it is becoming generalized, no longer restricted to the sphere of work.

The New Polarization of Work-related Life-styles. Within the cultural background generally associated with the Protestant ethic several changes must be distinguished. One can be described as a movement toward an ethicization of work and the other toward a de-ethicization of work. The tendency toward ethicization is not uniform. It can lead toward a traditionalist emphasis on material values deriving from work or toward a postmaterialistic emphasis upon values of self-realization either in or outside work. The tendency toward de-ethicization can also follow contradictory paths, leading either toward a cynical distancing from work or to an instrumental attitude toward work (work conceived as mere *ponos*). These contradictory and crosscutting developments force us to relinquish the idea of a monolithic culture of work (assumed in much reasoning and research that uses the Protestant ethic as a theoretical reference point). Instead we have to deal wtih many different and even contradictory cultures. On the empirical level we are confronted with different work ethics at variance or even in direct conflict.[21] The common lament over the end of the Protestant work ethic thus is not empirically justified by survey data.

The weakness in this conclusion will become more apparent when we disaggregate the data. Analysis on the aggregate level is not thwarted by findings of contradictory processes of change in the work ethic. Initial sampling has been taken to differentiate among generations (Meulemann 1987). One of the surprising results of a long and controversial discussion among German social scientists is that the assumed secular value change toward a decline of the Protestant ethic is bound to one specific generation. In younger generations the achievement orientation is again on the rise.[22]

The most important differentiating factor is social class. We still lack studies that disaggregate with regard to class differences. That is not surprising because social differentiations presuppose theoretical ideas about new class lines between groups of social actors. And such differentiations force us to retreat from the idea of an autonomous cultural change (as analyzed in the sequence of generational differences) to a structural change: to the idea of changes in the class structures that provoke the differentiating usage of this culture and its elements. This implies connections between culture and structure within, not outside, the social space. And it opens alternatives to the prevalent developmental views on changes in the work ethic.[23]

The De-coupling of Work from Self-realization. The de-coupling of work from self-realization seems to be the most radical hypothesis within the discussion of changes in the modern work ethic (Illich 1978, 1979). If it occurs, meaning will increasingly be found outside the sphere of work, and work will become a sphere of life empty of any ethical content. This outcome could even be interpreted as confirming Max Weber's speculation that work in formally rationalized contexts would no longer need any ethical motivation.

The possibility of de-coupling work from self-realization engages a hypothesis advanced by Weber and radicalized by Habermas: that work is becoming something that will be done beyond any motivational demand. Weber (1956) is clear about this: To be a *Berufsmensch* (someone whose identity is rooted in work) means to act according to the constraints of the formal rationality of the economy and ultimately leads one into an "iron cage." Habermas, distinguishing between work and interaction, claims that the economy (taken as the social field of work) has become part of the systemic world. Work is instrumental action and as such opposed to communicative action constitutive for the life-world (Habermas 1984, 1987). For both, the idea of a morally grounded work culture must appear as a transitory problem or even as a regression.

But we could also, unlike Weber and Habermas, conclude that this discussion of de-coupling is evidence of a return of the life-world into work. The sphere of work turns out to be much more a part of the life-world than the postindustrial utopians thought. Even Marx can be seen as a contributor to such an idea. By reintroducing culture into the world of work we gain a more adequate understanding of what is going on in modern society. It helps us to narrow down what the crisis of the work society is all about. The crisis of the work society is simultaneously the result of changes in the objective structures that organize work in different dimensions. This crisis is also a result of new cultural patterns changing the motivations of those engaged in wage labor. But the two perspectives cannot be related to each other in a satisfactory way. We can state some plausible relationships between structural and cultural processes (Furnham 1982; Prescott-Clarke 1982; Krappmann 1983). We lack, however, the data on how these cultural processes affect in turn the sphere of work and thus lend a meaning to structural changes that engages social groups and social actors.

To understand these effects we will start with the assumption that the structural changes in the sphere of work have produced a cultural evolution in it. The interpretative scheme of the Protestant ethic will be reconstructed and extended so that we can discuss social groups that set the Protestant ethic in action. We can thus specify the carriers of the crisis of the work society. Ultimately we will see that this crisis is the crisis of the traditional working class.

The Protestant Ethic in Action

THE CULTURAL MODEL OF THE PROTESTANT WORK ETHIC

The Three Sources of the Modern Work Ethic. To reinterpret the supposed decline of the work ethic as a change in the Protestant ethic, we first have to reconstruct the basic assumptions of this model, tailoring them to our analysis of the crisis of the work society. The standard model of the Protestant ethic consists of a series of values and the motivational forces that compel adherence to these values. This has been called the *Calvinist model* and contains values such as achievement for its own sake, the virtue of work over nonwork, and the quest for excellence. Its motivational forces are even more important. The belief in the culture of possessive individualism (the secular version of not being sure about one's own election by God) and the related permanent proof of one's own competitiveness in the market (the secular version of finding evidence of one's own election by God) are the motivational forces that have together so advanced the capitalist spirit that it has become (at least ideologically) the dominant (and dominating) model of the modern work ethic.

Within the German tradition another work ethic model can be identified, namely *Lutheranism*.[24] This ethic can be seen as the inner-worldly variant of the Protestant ethic. It radicalizes the permanent self-observation necessary to decipher God's will. One has to examine one's day-to-day conduct to see whether one has really established a personal relation to God. The dread of failure becomes the motivational engine of one's life. Such a person is no longer part of a collectivity that gives security and warmth but is a highly individualized self-observing and self-controlling social being. In family life a system emerges in which the persons living together observe themselves and each other. The family becomes a community of disciplined persons, a disciplining institution. Concentrating on the self makes work a secondary, devaluated concern. The primary concern is one's inner life, one's motives and intentions. This predominance of the inner-worldly forced Luther to distinguish sharply between the sphere of work and the sphere of inner conviction. Self-realization through struggling with one's own self is life's main activity. The outer world is nothing but a necessary background to this drama.

This explanation clarifies the difference between Calvinism and Lutheranism. A Calvinist cultivates success in the outside world as evidence of being elected by God. A Lutheran looks within at his or her faith to discover God's will and intentions. The Calvinists therefore have become virtuosi of outer-worldly activity; the Lutherans have become virtuosi of self-observation and self-interpretation. Both patterns have contributed to the modern work ethic. The first produced the work ethic based on rational motivation. The second produced a mere instrumentalist work ethic, in which work is treated as a sphere of mere necessity to which we are subject. Work is amoral. This demoralized work ethic, resting upon the acceptance of social necessities, is not an adequate means to self-realization. As soon as the religious foundations of inner-worldly orientation are eroded any motivation can enter. Such a substitution took place in the rise of the Prussian work ethic. The Prussian functionary works as hard as the world demands and seeks self-realization by identifying, not with God, but with the state. Historically this substitution allowed for the rationalization of the state. Thus within the German tradition both traditions contribute to the rationalization of modern society. The work ethic of the capitalist entrepreneurs is no different from that of their Calvinist counterparts. And the work ethic of the state officials representing the Prussian virtues is characteristic of modern German work culture as such.

The values that lie at the heart of an emerging work culture today point simultaneously to the possible end and the possible revival of the Protestant ethic. They signal the end of the Calvinist heritage and the renaissance of the Lutheran heritage. The new values, emphasizing self-realization outside work, can be traced to the corresponding Lutheran conception of work. This historical conjuncture might explain the German bias and intensity of the discussion about the change in modern work culture.

But there remains a problem generally overlooked in the discussion of the Protestant ethic. Neither variant of the Protestant work ethic has ever become part of the work culture of plebeian and rural groups. Where then does their work ethic come from? What distinguishes it from the Protestant ethic that led highly motivated individuals to practice rational economic conduct? The answer lies in the general "Catholic" tradition that is oriented toward the collectivity, as opposed to the individual orientation of the Protestant tradition. This Catholic tradition, first embodied in the discipline of monastic life, is important in the development of a modern work ethic. Its specificity is found in a collectivistic ethic applied from the outset to productive manual labor. It has helped to "civilize" and "rationalize" the traditional "moral economy" of the lower classes. The collectivist model of disciplined labor characteristic of the monastery allowed for the inculcation of a disciplined work ethic into those groups forced into wage labor (Treiber & Steinert 1980). The rational timing of the working day and the rational control of bodily movements in modern industrial work emulates the model established in the monastery and then generalized in institutions such as hospitals, jails, and asylums.

We have identified at least three different traditions that have influenced and shaped the modern work ethic. Now we must differentiate between the contradictory elements contained in the model of the Protestant ethic and take the Catholic element into account. Then we must identify the groups that are carriers of these elements. While some groups may be acting out a disaffection with their Calvinist roots, other occupational groups might be acting out an intensification of the Calvinist element of the Protestant ethic. The same duality holds for the Lutheran version of the Protestant ethic.

We are still unable to interpret the aggregate data of survey research analyzing changes in attitudes toward work. Survey data show only the net result of contradictory changes of the work ethic in different social groups. We have to consider that the average net result may mask a trend toward wide social and cultural differentiation and even stratification. Without a precise idea of the differentiation and stratification of the work conditions and the work ethic, we risk producing nothing but fantasies.

From the Model Work Ethic to Its Practical Use. Weber himself is ambivalent about the general validity of the Protestant ethic.[25] On one hand he thinks that this ethic will be generalized throughout modern society. The Puritan, he says, wanted to be *Berufs-*

mensch, and we have to be *Berufsmenschen* (Weber 1965:188). On the other hand Weber states that the Protestant ethic has become part of the bourgeois life-style. This implies a different social interpretation of the modern work ethic. It assumes that it can be seen as an exclusive work ethic, typical only for some strata or classes in modern society. One can even claim that this work ethic establishes a cultural distinction between the ascetic elites and the joyous masses. From this perspective the work ethic symbolizes the cultural authority of one class over others. *We* who have to be *Berufsmenschen,* according to Weber, are not the people. *We* in fact are a specific social group, contrary to the supposed universalism of the *Berufsmenschen.*

On the theoretical level the difference between the two interpretations can be resolved by distinguishing between a model and its social usage. The Calvinist variant of the Protestant ethic is a model of a modern work ethic that has been adapted by specific social groups. But we have to go further because the Calvinist tradition can also be blended with other traditions. The blend of the Catholic ethic with Lutheranism, of a collectivist ethos of discipline with the Lutheran ethos of self-realization in and by work, the work ethic is sometimes said to constitute a specifically German work ethic. But this supposed ethic is—as we shall see—the work ethic of the skilled worker (the *Facharbeiterethos*), developed by a very specific group of workers in nineteenth-century Germany. Because the practices using and reproducing these different models are ongoing, the work culture of a society is necessarily in flux. Thus our theoretical application of the model of the Protestant ethic has to take into account changes in its usage to keep the model theoretically useful.

On the empirical level I would like to suggest that there is a close relationship between the pure model of Calvinism and its social use by the dominant class in modern societies. The class of capitalist entrepreneurs and managers is a social group that uses the Calvinist model of the Protestant ethic to reproduce its symbolic power over other social classes. The symbolic power built into this ethic is based on the fact that it serves as a touchstone to higher positions. It becomes cultural capital in the hands of these social groups inasmuch as it becomes the selective mechanism in all those social institutions that regulate access to social status and power. Research analyzing the "informal" criteria of access to higher educational institutions and to employment in better jobs shows that this work ethic is the touchstone conferring better chances (Windolf 1984; Windolf & Hohn 1984). But this selective mechanism works differentially in different sectors of the economy: banking, the steel industry, or different hierarchical levels in these branches. Informal qualifications that indicate a "Protestant" life-style (for example, dress and choice of discipline) have also become increasingly instrumental in the selection for higher social status in the sphere of work.

There have been some attempts at classifying class-specific adaptations of the Protestant ethic. Hinrichs and Wiesenthal (1982) distinguish among several groups: (1) workers with a traditional consciousness based upon an unquestioned achievement orientation, (2) overall maximizers (those in privileged positions who push the achievement principle), (3) opportunistic hedonists who work only as much as necessary to live a joyous life, and (4) those who abandon totally or partially the normal working day in order to organize their life-world in another form. Another classification by Kern and Schumann (1984:157) distinguishes among the following: (1) winners of rationalization, (2) losers of rationalization, (3) workers in unstable branches, and (4) the unemployed. These classifications differ in the perspective they adopt to grasp the increasing differentiation of work culture. The former takes the perspective of the middle classes, the latter that of the working classes. They do have one element in common: they point to a differentiation of work cultures that cuts across traditional class differences.

THE MODEL IN ACTION I:
THE WORKING CLASS

Such a cultural analysis can be applied to fractions of the working class in advanced modern societies. We can contrast two distinct types of the social usage of culture in the working class by using their specific work ethic as the central parameter. The empirical references are taken from survey research on value orientations toward work and from qualitative research on work culture.

The Skilled Worker. Industrial workers—in spite of their spending substantially more time outside work—are not impressed or influenced by what we call *value change* toward postmaterialism. They continue to see the workplace as the central life experience and still adhere to the traditional industrial culture. They are proud of their skills and invest their social energy in work. These skilled workers derive their self-image from traditional craftsmanship and thus manifest a specific version of the Protestant ethic. Although they accept the inner-worldly

(Lutheran) principle of achievement through hard work, they do not follow the ascetic practice, characteristic of the capitalist entrepreneur, of saving the money they earn. Members of this social class combine an ethic of hard work with a consumer attitude; they do not wait for future remuneration, they spend immediately. In this respect they maintain, alongside their Lutheranism, the strong Catholic tradition of identifying with the collectivity of the consumer.

The more the present developments in the sphere of work foster cognitive skills, the more the traditional ethic of the skilled worker is revitalized. The so-called *Arbeiterstolz* (being proud of being a worker) is extended to a *Technikerstolz* (being proud of manipulating new work technologies). Both are based on special experiences and qualifications accumulated in daily practice at the workplace (Rammert & Wehrsig 1988). But this type of the social usage of the Lutheran ethic is characteristic only for those who, thanks to their social location, can afford to defend this classical form of worker pride inherent in the German model of *Facharbeit* (skilled work) (Härtel, Matthiesen & Neuendorff 1985, 1986). They can be considered the beneficiaries of rationalization in the sphere of work. They have never de-coupled work from self-realization.

The Unskilled Worker. Unskilled or semi-skilled workers, on the contrary, adapt to the work situation without referring to either the Calvinist or the Lutheran aspect of the Protestant ethic. Their sociostructural location makes them the losers of the game. They know that they have to work where others can choose not to. They are forced into a type of work without motivation as such. The social groups making up this class include marginal industrial workers as well as workers in the low service jobs typically held by women. Even housework can be subsumed under this heading. What these "bad jobs" have in common is that they produce fatigue (Clausen 1981:27f.). This experience of work produces a work ethic that tries to avoid any moral significance. The Protestant ethic is not rejected as such but simply not accepted for the type of work that has to be done. The social usage of the Protestant ethic here is an attempt to neutralize its implications in the workplace.

These social groups are forced to instrumentalize work. Work becomes the means to another end, to a culture of consumption that emulates the principles of the Catholic ethic. Consumption becomes a collective activity that substitutes for the experience of a religious community. Work is seen as means to consumption, this heaven on earth.

Inasmuch as low income forces these groups to engage in intensive consumption work (looking for the cheapest goods, intensifying the do-it-yourself orientation), they are part of the "achieving society." But the achievement-oriented activities in the sphere of consumption remain separate from the sphere of work. These groups have succeeded not only in separating work from self-realization but also in ignoring the aspect of self-realization. The Protestant ethic has no relevance whatsoever. But this situation is not culture-free, as the instrumentalism hypothesis would imply. It is simply another culture derived from the Catholic tradition, that is used to give meaning to work. There is no need within this tradition for individual motivation like the achievement motivation in the sphere of work. Being part of a collectivity of workers suffices to produce the minimum of motivation. The strength of control, but not the internalized motivation, can change the investment in work.

An especially revealing group to observe within this subclass is the unemployed. In order to get state subsidies, these workers, excluded from work, are classified as "seeking work." This definition produces the image of somebody who upholds a normal work ethic. Such classification practices underscore the problem connected with living up to the Protestant ethic. The "Protestantism" of the unemployed is reduced to the proper bureaucratic behavior of showing up at administrative institutions that register those without work. The Protestant ethic is converted into rigid adherence to the requirements of state institutions. Here, enforced Protestantism loses all meaning, becoming a borrowed ethic that acts against all the life experiences of this group. The problems produced by this situation of having to simulate an occupational career and construct a consistent occupational biography are enormous.[26]

These examples show again that the effects of the Protestant ethic do not necessarily conform rigidly to the pure model. The specific adaptations have to be explained sociologically. And only these practical adaptations can explain which cultural effects a given system of social classes is mediating.

THE MODEL IN ACTION II:
THE MIDDLE CLASS

The different fractions of the middle class have generally been considered the best representatives of the Protestant work ethic. This view is only partially correct. The reasons are found both in the historical roots of the middle-class work ethic and in the internal differences within the middle class. The changes in the class structure of advanced modern societies will make the middle class and the cultural struggles within it the keys to an explanation of the crisis of modern work society and to an understanding of possible solutions.

The Old Middle Class. The old middle class, comprising small craftsmen and small shopkeepers (Haupt 1985), has become the symbol of a rigid and ascetic work ethic. The groups within this culture are viewed as representing the virtues of industry and parsimony par excellence. Their work ethic is considered an expression of a petit-bourgeois mentality.

This mentality can be seen as a specific adaptation of the Protestant ethic, sharing its emphasis on ascetic virtues. It differs with respect to the substantive values tied to this ethic. For it lacks the specific rationalization that distances these virtues from their religious background and remains instead bound to a substantive religious feeling. The old petit bourgeois still works out of a belief in God, whereas the modern work ethic motivates work without recourse to God. The petit bourgeoisie still needs God, is conservative, and retains the old virtues. This gives to their work ethic the social rigidity typical of traditional life-forms and life-styles. The traditional petit bourgeoisie leads an ambivalent life, with an outlook both materialistic and moralistic. Not having really internalized the Protestant ethic, they are prone to a moral crusade; they think that others should behave as they do. Their work ethic thus constitutes a culture that adapts the model of the Protestant ethic to the life experiences of petit-bourgeois existence (Münch 1984).

The central social experience of this old middle class was being threatened by industrialization and capitalist development. Unable to compete with big industry, yet dependent upon big money, craftsmen and shopkeepers were in permanent danger of slipping into the proletariat class. Fear might explain why they preferred to defend the old world, for it guaranteed their social (and emotional) security. They were for the state as long as it defended them against big industry and big money (as the fascists promised them after a decade of turmoil in the early twentieth century).

The petit bourgeoisie is not dying out. On the contrary, it is coming to life in those economies that have encountered problems with big industry and large labor forces. Recourse to the old virtues increases as such problems pervade advanced industrial societies. Independence has become fashionable. New craftspeople and new shopkeepers have emerged to join the ranks of the old ones. To what extent these new groups will change the outlook of the classic groups making up the old middle class is an open question. These new groups combine the idea of independence with a rigid ideology concerning the type of work that can satisfy strong moral standards. The "alternative" entrepreneurs (Vonderach 1980)—most of them small shopkeepers or craftspeople—seem unable to escape the structural constraints typical of this social location. They tend to become a new petit bourgeoisie living at the edge of the formal economy (Schlegelmilch 1983). Some even say that they are the constitutive part of an informal economy. This claim can be misunderstood because the new small entrepreneurs have to behave as members, though minor ones, of the formal economy if they want to survive (Tacke 1988). What distinguishes them from the traditional petit bourgeois, the old small entrepreneur, is their moral style. They are postmaterialists looking for psychological well-being. But this may be a minor difference, compared to the similarities in structural location and moral rigidity. Both invest in use-value, as against exchange-value, and this common interest is the decisive marker of their work culture (Eder 1989a, 1989c).

The New Middle Class. A new type of middle class has also emerged since the beginning of the century (Kocka 1981a, 1989b). This class comprises the new white-collar workers required by the expansion of the service sector. Their increase during the 1960s, especially in social service occupations (teachers, journalists, medical professionals, etc.) was fostered by an expansion of the public sector (Gershuny 1983). The members of the new middle class are not independent. On the contrary, they are often state functionaries (*Staatsbeamter*).

This class embodies the Lutheran version of the Protestant ethic par excellence. The social usage of this ethic emphasizes an individual's concern with the world and translates it into a social concern. For members of this class no problem exists that cannot be psychologized. Psychological work even becomes the organizational principle of the work ethic. "Working on myself" is the key—and this seems very close to the logic of the Lutheran variant of the Protestant work ethic. The concern with self constitutes a new form of the social usage of this Lutheran tradition. The concern with self is transformed—contrary to the logic of the Calvinist model ethic—into the duty to work upon oneself. At the same time this new class integrates into its work ethic an element formerly alien to it. An internalized duty to work is accompanied by an internalized duty to enjoy it (Bourdieu 1984). The upshot is a hedonistic attitude toward work.

The members of this class therefore become prone to conspicuous consumption as a means of realizing their individuality—that is, becoming socially distinct from their fellows—and this is precisely what cultural industry needs to expand and boom. An unstable work history among these groups reinforces this self-tinkering. It generates a work ethic of contingency that could produce the strongest obstacles in further accommodating the Lutheran (although less the Calvinist!) element of the Protestant ethic to its existence as a class. Whether the model itself will be queried is open to doubt.

The new middle class seems increasingly to dominate the cultural mood of advanced industrial societies. Its relative distance from the Protestant ethic, as it is customarily understood, makes it a possible carrier for changes in the work ethic, an agent for the construction of a new work culture. The structural change favoring the emergence of new groups (the extension of the service sector) has probably ended. But the continuing effect of this change will act as a starting point for cultural struggles. The new middle class is probably at the center of the cultural struggles that we are facing today. Its evolution will decisively shape the outcome of the crisis of the work society.

Conclusions

CULTURE IN ACTION: A BRIDGE TO SOCIAL STRUCTURE

The distinction between model and practice allows for a more complete answer to the question: What are the effects of the modern work ethic that is modeled on the Protestant ethic upon structural change in the work society? The answer: It depends on the social usage that social groups, or classes of social groups, make of this model.

This leads us to a genuinely sociological conception of culture. The analysis of the effects of culture on structure in modern work society accounts for the cultural practices of social groups that are explained by the model they refer to. But to analyze the social effects of culture we must also analyze the sociostructural location of a social group and how this location structures the social usage of culture. The analysis of the Protestant ethic in action helps us abandon the reification of Weber's model of a Protestant ethic as applied to the crisis of work society (a reification Weber himself provoked). It helps us to understand better the possible cultural effects upon those people whose life-worlds extend beyond the private and public spheres, that is, family or political life, into the sphere of work. And these people seem increasingly to be reintroducing the idea of self-realization into the sphere of work. The Protestant ethic, whose Calvinist element was dissolved in the process of formal rationalization (as Weber rightly saw it), still contains the Lutheran element. What we need to determine is how the distance between work and self-realization will be bridged, how Lutheranism will be acted out. There is no a priori reason to believe that it will be either all good or all bad.

A preliminary theoretical conclusion can be drawn. The Protestant ethic is a theoretical construction. It describes a model culture, not a real one. What is real is the social usage of this model—and the usages have changed and increasingly produced conflicting (and even confusing) versions of this model culture. To show this culture in action, we have analyzed its social usages. Such social usages are themselves an effect of structural developments that shape and reshape the perception and experience of social groups, thus producing cultural effects beyond changes in social structure. Thus, we have done the groundwork for a constructivist notion of the crisis of the work society.

THE CRISIS OF THE WORK SOCIETY
AS A SOCIAL CONSTRUCT

We began with the intention of taking the phenomenon of structural and cultural change seriously. Research on changes in the work ethic, we argued, must be tied more closely to research on structural developments in society, above all to changes in the class structure. The effects of culture are always mediated by social groups and therefore by a given social structure. But we should not reduce the explanation of change to sociostructural effects. For these changes take effect only because they have found some carrier in society. To really measure the effects of cultural change, we have to analyze the symbolic struggles between social groups that will generate the new cultural orientation of society. The German example of cultural change in the sphere of work, discussed above, was thought to provide a general pattern of how this could be done.

But we have seen that the objectivist idea of a structural or a cultural crisis is misleading. Both the structural strains and the restrictive cultural heritage can be and have been overcome by adaptation and differentiation. The crisis of modern work society is due neither to the iron laws of a structural crisis endemic to capitalism or welfare nor to an exhaustion of symbolic resources. There is, we know, an "ecological crisis" that provokes political, social, and even cultural conflicts. But its intensity depends on the capacity of social actors to work on ecological problems. There is a "cultural crisis" in the sense that a fashionable ideological system, postmodernism, has questioned the very basis of modernity. But this phenomenon is itself merely proof of the capacity of culture to produce images of crises these fashionable ideas claim to have discovered.

But where is the real crisis? It is ultimately the crisis of the working class, the class that defines the dominant model of the work culture and is located at the center of the present processes of structural adaptation. The crisis of the work society is the crisis of the working class. Work has been reorganized to such an extent that the type of work represented by the working class has lost its critical place. The withholding of this type of work no longer shatters modern society. The strikes that really matter today are organized by middle-class groups, by those regulating the administration of social life, its traffic, its financial processes, its educational reproduction. The work ethic that has started to predominate in modern life is also shaped to an increasing extent by middle-class groups. The decline of the Protestant ethic as embodied in the biography of the traditional skilled worker is part of the decline of this class and its work culture. Thus the crisis of the working society is the crisis of a class that has lost its function and role as a historical actor. And it is with the crisis of the working class that the crisis of its opponent, the bourgeois class, is inextricably connected.

Notes

1. I have developed this theoretical approach at length in a work on the evolution of political culture in nineteenth-century Germany (Eder 1985). The

idea of social groups that select for competing cultural ideas and images thus goes beyond both the classic approach of a mere history of political ideas and the theory of modernization.

2. For a parallel account of this discussion refer to Stephen Kalberg in this volume. Kalberg takes the most popular lines of this discussion and accounts for them by adopting a sociology of knowledge approach. That such arguments should arise within the German discussion might be due to the specific German cultural tradition. But this tradition is, typically, less monolithic and more open to discussion than many cultural sociologists (especially the Weberian ones) assume. Maybe Kalberg's perspective in this discussion should be incorporated in a sociology of knowledge analysis of specifically American ways of seeing German culture. Nonetheless, Kahlberg's contribution is important as an instance of self-reflection of sociological analyses and explanations. These become more important as more fields of analysis are ideologically and culturally at stake. For the German discussion of the *Krise der Arbeitsgesellschaft* see the collection of papers presented at the Meeting of the German Sociological Association 1982 in Bamberg (Matthes 1983). One of the organizers, Claus Offe, in fact argues against this notion.

3. This theoretical proposition draws on the actionalist sociology of Touraine (1977, 1985a, 1985b). The capacity for historical action is the key idea in his approach. It is used here as the starting point for reconstructing a sociological theory of crisis.

4. One of the appealing aspects of this specifically German discussion is the opportunity it provides to develop a new theoretical perspective on different strands of sociological theory and research within the fields of industrial relations and class analysis. For an overview of the broad range of discussions in this field see Pahl (1988). The German discussion also overcomes some other more nominalistic discussions about a postindustrial society and the new and fashionable discussion about postmodernity where nominalism seems to reemerge.

5. By treating the idea of a Protestant ethic as a model and distinguishing between it and the social practices that use it as a reference, I have sidestepped the discussion about the historical adequacy of Weber's theory. We can bypass any historical claim and simply start with the assumption that there is something called the *Protestant ethic*. To find out whether or not the elements attributed to it are there we have to look at group-specific practices in the work sphere. Which aspects of this ethic are found among business executives or workers is an empirical question.

6. Bell's (1973) and Touraine's (1969) earlier conception of a postindustrial society starts by assuming the increasing primacy of scientific work over industrial productive work. The changes we can observe are merely exaggerated generalizations (Bühl 1984). For a reorientation of this discussion see Braverman (1974), Brandt (1981), Gershuny (1983), Benseler et al. (1982), Gorz (1983), and Bonß and Heinze (1984).

7. See Mickler (1981) and Kern and Schumann (1984). For an extensive account of the new type of dependent, but highly skilled, work see Hermann and Teschner (1980), Teschner and Hermann (1981), or Baethge (1983). These studies contradict the well-known analysis of modern work by Braver-

man (1974), who defends the theory of a continual downgrading of qualified work.

8. It is important to notice that this type of structural differentiation alters the traditional class structure of industrial societies. But instead of proclaiming the end of class society, I prefer the research strategy of looking for the class structure that has replaced the old one. There are enough indicators of social differences on the level of culture, as well as on the level of work, to justify such research. Bourdieu has been the foremost theoretician to follow this line of reasoning. For a discussion of his views and its implications for class theory and class structure see my contributions to a volume on Bourdieu's theory of class (Eder 1989a, 1989b).

9. See data comparing the 1980s with the 1950s: people start their occupational careers two years later (at age seventeen); they retire three years earlier (at fifty-eight). Given the condition of scarce work (Dahrendorf 1983), the politics of working time takes on a new importance beyond the function of psychic and physical relief for the workers. See also Offe et al. (1982).

10. The relationship between biography and time spent working has been examined by Brose (1983, 1984). The type of worker who works irregularly (Gelegenheitsarbeiter) seems to have become a possible model, especially among adolescents (Pialoux 1979). But the conclusion that the value attributed to work will therefore diminish has so far found neither a logical nor an empirical basis.

11. These survey data relate to the question of whether work is still a central life interest. For a classic statement of this type of research see Dubin (1955). In recent research, the increase in the number of people who respond negatively and are undecided is interpreted as a decline in work-related values, for example, achievement orientation. Because of the semantic instability of such questions over time and because of changes in income that have also made consumption a central life interest, this proposition was attacked with fatal consequences to the scientific reputation of its authors. It did not, by the way, hinder its success in public discourse! A good critique is to be found in Vollmer (1986).

12. This is not apparent as long as all work outside wage labor is ideologically interpreted as leisure ("Frei"-zeit), as nonwork. But this ideology is effective, as seen in the demand for more leisure time. What really happens is a revaluation of work outside wage labor. See Rosenmayr and Kolland (1988).

13. Chronic unemployment disproves some of the central assumptions of theories on postindustrial society. The service sector—which was supposed to absorb a growing and highly skilled labor force—is no longer growing. The expansion of the service sector had already reached its limits before we even entered postindustrial society. Thus unemployment is a structural feature of both postindustrial society and industrial society. For this discussion see Mutz (1987).

14. This hypothesis has been taken by Kalberg (in this volume) as the central discussion point within the German crisis of the Arbeitsgesellschaft.

15. This relationship has been confirmed several times. See, in addition to Bourdieu (1984), the empirical research by Blossfeld (1983, 1985a, 1985b) and Windolf (1984).

16. For a general discussion of the de-coupling debate see Kalberg in this volume. It is important to distinguish between its structural and cultural aspects: the de-coupling of work from status and the de-coupling of work from self-realization. Only the latter process seems to be specifically German. For self-realization in work is something that is constitutive for the Lutheran work ethic.

17. In my discussion of cultural changes in the sphere of work, I refer to some of the research in the area of value change insofar as it is work related. I also rely upon unpublished qualitative research (including some of my own) concerning the cultural orientations of workers whose occupational careers have been interrupted by phases of unemployment. For the latter see also Brose (1986). For a more general discussion of work-related culture see Habermas (1968), Honneth (1982), Bahrdt (1983), Clausen (1981), Jahoda (1983), and Garfinkel (1986). For the empirical discussion see Cherns (1980), Hostede (1980), Hoffman-Nowotny and Gehrmann (1984), Klipstein and Strümpel (1985), Strümpel and Scholz-Ligma (1988), and Pawlowsky (1986). For critical accounts see Reuband (1985, 1989) and Gehrmann (1986). The research upon which Noelle-Neumann relies and which has fueled the German discussion is the comparative research on "Jobs in the 1980s and 1990s" (Yankelovich et al. 1985). See also, as a reference point for interpreting changes in the work ethic, the more recent research comparing value orientations with respect to work in Europe (Harding, Philips & Fogarty 1986:150ff.).

18. Some historical studies are pertinent to the specific German tradition of old and new virtues. See, as an example of classic secondary virtues (secondary to the principles of an abstract morality or ethic), the work of Münch (1984). See also the section on Lutheranism in Kalberg (in this volume). Also relevant in this context is the discussion about the new "reflexive" identity formations that foster a kind of rational planning of the meaning of one's life by permanent rational reflection of one's biography. This new "habitus" is widespread among the new middle classes, as Bourdieu argues using French data. Qualitative analyses of such identity formations in Germany point in the same direction. See among others Oevermann (1985, 1988).

19. This discussion has received renewed attention in recent research. See above all Rosenmayr and Kolland (1988). For a critical discussion of supposed instrumentalism see Knapp (1981), and for the famous hypothesis of the dual relationship of workers to work, that there is simultaneously an instrumental and a substantive relation to wage labor, see Kern and Schumann (1980).

20. Hedonism applied to the work culture is one of the favorite targets of cultural pessimists. Hedonism is an instrumentalist work ethic that has spread from the proletariat to the middle classes. At least this is the interpretation offered by Noelle-Neumann (1980).

21. The literature taking up this discussion is increasing. Most interesting is the redirection from mere quantitative reasoning to qualitative analyses of the work ethic. Researchers are apparently trying to escape from the sterility and futility of those quantitatively oriented discussions where the data are not adequate to the questions. An important alternative, or complement, has become

the "biographical" approach to the culture of work. See, among many others, the volume edited by Brose (1986) that contains empirical as well as methodological and theoretical contributions to this critical turn in the analysis of work culture.

22. The relation between youth and change in the work culture is one of the most interesting contemporary research areas. Recent studies show that differences correlate strongly with gender. Another important variable is the development of a youth culture with value orientations not related to work. Whether a delayed socialization into a work culture hinders the adoption of a work ethic is not clear, although research shows it probably does not. For a recent critical discussion of the available longitudinal data see Brock and Otto-Brock (1988).

23. Such an alternative is, for example, the "cyclical theory of value change." For this new approach in the interpretation of value change see Namenwirth and Weber (1987) and further research by Bürklin (1988).

24. For an excellent discussion of the genesis of an inner-worldly work ethic within Protestantism, see Soeffner (1988). He makes it clear that the Lutheran (as well as the Calvinist) ethic is intended to control the work force rather than intrinsically to motivate workers. A possible conclusion is that the Lutheran and the Calvinist variants point to national differences that have influenced the social use of the Protestant ethic. This conclusion allows us to address the question of the specificity of the German debate of the *Arbeitsgesellschaft* within the modern work culture, and it relates to Kalberg's argument (in this volume), which tries to relativize its relevance.

25. I will not go into the validity of Weber's theory that the spirit of capitalism has something to do with Calvinism. For a recent discussion of the historical relevance of Weber's hypothesis, see Pellicani (1988), who concludes that the historical origins of what we call the *Protestant ethic* have nothing to do with Calvinism. But I do accept Weber's analysis of the Protestant ethic as the reconstruction of the model of a work ethic that has been constitutive for the development of capitalism. The model is based on the assumption of a highly internalized ascetic attitude toward work—on the acceptance of work without external force. There may have been social groups that were close to this model, but such a relationship is already socially specific and has to be explained by specifying the social position of the group in question.

26. In qualitative interviews (conducted in a research project by the Münchner Projektgruppe), these problems manifest themselves as the dominant ones, contrary to the evidence of those who look for the psychic stress of unemployment. This psychological approach blocks recognition of the implicit cultural codes that demand and structure the formulation of a consistent work biography even under stress. Unemployment creates an ambivalent experience for those who still rely upon the Catholic ethic. For it destroys access to the collectivist alternative characteristic of the Catholic work ethic; or rather, it individualizes it. Those who still adhere to some Calvinist element in their work ethic can therefore cope with unemployment more easily. This alternative is structurally open to the skilled workers, less so to the unskilled and semiskilled.

References

Baethge, M. 1983. Wandel betrieblicher Strukturen von Angestelltentätig-keiten. In *Krise der Arbeitsgesellschaft?*, edited by J. Matthes, 175–188. Frankfurt: Campus.

Bahrdt, H. P. 1983. Arbeit als Inhalt des Lebens. In *Krise der Arbeitsgesell-schaft?*, edited by J. Matthes, 120–137. Frankfurt: Campus.

Bell, D. 1973. *The Coming of Postindustrial Society.* New York: Basic Books.

Benseler, F., R. G. Heinze, & A. Klönne, eds. 1982. *Die Zukunft der Arbeit.* Hamburg: VSA Verlag.

Blossfeld, H. P. 1983. Höherqualifizierung und Verdrängung. In *Beschäftigungssystem im gesellschaftlichen Wandel*, edited by M. Haller & W. Müller, 284ff. Frankfurt: Campus.

Blossfeld, H. P. 1985a. Berufseintritt und Berufsverlauf. *MittAB* 18: 177–197.

Blossfeld, H. P. 1985b. *Bildungsexpansion und Berufschancen. Empirische Analysen zur Lage der Berufsanfänger in der Bundesrepublik.* Frankfurt: Campus.

Bonß, W., & R. Heinze. 1984. Arbeit, Lohnarbeit, ohne Arbeit. Zur Soziologie der Arbeitslosigkeit. In *Arbeitslosigkeit in der Arbeitsgesellschaft*, edited by W. Bonß & R. Heinze. Frankfurt: Suhrkamp.

Bonß, W., & R. G. Heinze, eds. 1984. *Arbeitslosigkeit in der Arbeitsgesell-schaft.* Frankfurt: Suhrkamp.

Bourdieu, P. 1984. *The Distinction: A Social Critique of the Judgment of Taste.* Cambridge: Harvard University Press.

Brandt, G. 1981. Die Zukunft der Arbeit in der "nachindustriellen" Gesellschaft. *IHS-Journal* 5:109–123.

Braverman, H. 1974. *Labor and Monopoly Capital: The Degradation of Work on the Twentieth Century.* London: Monthly Review Press.

Brock, D., & E. Otto-Brock. 1988. Hat sich die Einstellung der Jugendlichen zu Beruf und Arbeit verändert? *Zeitschrift für Soziologie* 17:436–450.

Brose, H. G. 1983. *Die Erfahrung der Arbeit.* Opladen: Westdeutscher Verlag.

Brose, H. G. 1984. Arbeit auf Zeit—Biographie auf Zeit? In *Biographie und soziale Wirklichkeit*, edited by M. Kohli & G. Robert, 48–69. Stuttgart: Metzler.

Brose, H. G., ed. 1986. *Berufsbiographien im Wandel.* Opladen: West-deutscher Verlag.

Bühl, W. L. 1984. Gibt es eine soziale Evolution? *Zeitschrift für Politik* 31:302–331.

Bürklin, W. P. 1988. Wertwandel oder zyklische Wertaktualisierung? In *Wertwandel—Faktum oder Fiktion? Bestandsaufnahmen und Diagnosen aus kultursoziologischer Sicht*, edited by H. O. Luthe & H. Meulemann, 193–216. Frankfurt: Campus.

Cherns, A. 1980. Works and Values: Shifting Patterns in Industrial Society. *International Social Science Journal* 32:427–441.

Clausen, L. 1981. Die Wiederkehr der Arbeit. In *Ankunft bei Tönnies,* edited by L. Clausen & F. U. Pappi, 17–30. Kiel: Mühlau.

Dahrendorf, R. 1983. Wenn der Arbeitsgesellschaft die Arbeit ausgeht. In *Krise der Arbeitsgesellschaft?,* edited by J. Matthes, 25–37. Frankfurt: Campus.

Dubin, R. 1955. Industrial Worker's Worlds: A Study of the "Central Life Interests" of Industrial Workers. *Social Problems* 3:131–141.

Eder, K. 1985. *Geschichte als Lernprozeß? Zur Pathogenese politischer Modernität in Deutschland.* Frankfurt: Suhrkamp.

Eder, K. 1989a. Jenseits der nivellierten Mittelstandsgesellschaft. Das Kleinbürgertum als Schlüssel zu einer Klassenanalyse fortgeschrittener Industriegesellschaften. In *Klassenlage, Lebensstil und kulturelle Praxis,* edited by K. Eder, 341–393. Frankfurt: Suhrkamp.

Eder, K., ed. 1989b. *Klassenlage, Lebensstil und kulturelle Praxis.* Frankfurt: Suhrkamp.

Eder, K. 1989c. Social Inequality and the Discourse on Equality: The Cultural Foundations of Modern Class Society. In *Culture and Social Structure,* edited by H. Haferkamp, 83–100. Berlin: de Gruyter.

Furnham, A. 1982. The Protestant Work Ethic and Attitudes towards Unemployment. *Journal of Occupational Psychology* 55:277ff.

Garfinkel, H., ed. 1986. *Ethnomethodological Studies of Work.* London: Routledge.

Gehrmann, F., ed. 1986. *Arbeitsmoral und Technikerfeindlichkeit: Über demoskopische Fehlschlüsse.* Frankfurt: Campus.

Gershuny, J. I. 1983. Goods, Services and the Future of Work. In *Krise der Arbeitsgesellschaft?,* edited by J. Matthes, 82–94. Frankfurt: Campus.

Giegel, H. J., G. Frank, & U. Billerbeck. 1988. *Industriearbeit und Selbstbehauptung. Berufsbiographische Orientierung und Gesundheitsverhalten in gefährdeten Lebensverhältnissen.* Opladen: Leske & Budrich.

Gorz, A. 1983. *Wege ins Paradies.* Berlin: Rotbuch.

Habermas, J. 1968. Arbeit und Interaktion. In *Technik und Wissenschaft als "Ideologie,"* edited by J. Habermas, 9–47. Frankfurt: Suhrkamp.

Habermas, J. 1984. *The Theory of Communicative Action: Reason and the Rationalization of Society.* Vol. 1. Boston: Beacon Press.

Habermas, J. 1987. *The Theory of Communicative Action: Lifeworld and System. A Critique of Functionalist Reason.* Vol. 2. Boston: Beacon Press.

Harding, S., D. Philips, & M. Fogarty. 1986. *Contrasting Values in Western Europe.* London: Macmillan.

Härtel, U., U. Matthiesen, & H. Neuendorff. 1985. *Kontrastierende Fallanalysen zum Wandel von arbeitsbezogenen Deutungsmustern und Lebensentwürfen in einer Stahlstadt.* Manuskript Universität Dortmund.

Härtel, U., U. Matthiesen, & H. Neuendorff. 1986. Kontinuität und Wandel arbeitsbezogener Deutungsmuster und Lebensentwürfe—Überlegungen zum Programm einer kultursoziologischen Analyse von Berufsbiographien. In *Berufsbiographien im Wandel,* edited by H. G. Brose, 264–290. Opladen: Westdeutscher Verlag.

Haupt, H. G., ed. 1985. *Die radikale Mitte. Lebensweise und Politik von Handwerkern und Kleinhändlern in Deutschland seit 1848.* München: Deutscher Taschenbuchverlag.

Hermann, K., & E. Teschner. 1980. Taylorisierung geistiger Arbeit? Entwicklungstendenzen der Arbeits—und Berufssituation der Angestellten in der Industrie. In *Bildungsexpansion und betriebliche Beschäftigungspolitik,* edited by U. Beck, K. H. Hörning, & W. Thomssen, 202–209. Frankfurt: Campus.

Hinrichs, K., & H. Wiesenthal. 1982. Arbeitswerte und Arbeitszeit. Zur Pluralisierung von Wertemustern und Zeitverwendungswünschen in der modernen Industriegesellschaft. In *Arbeitszeitpolitik. Formen und Folgen einer Neuverteilung der Arbeit,* edited by C. Offe, K. Hinrichs, & H. Wiesenthal, 116–136. Frankfurt: Campus.

Hoffmann-Nowotny, H. J., & F. Gehrmann, eds. 1984. *Ansprüche an die Arbeit. Soziale Indikatoren 11.* Frankfurt: Campus.

Hondrich, K. O., J. Schumacher, K. Arzberger, F. Schlie, & C. Stegbauer. 1988. *Krise der Leistungsgesellschaft? Empirische Analysen zum Engagement in Arbeit, Familie und Politik.* Opladen: Westdeutscher Verlag.

Honneth, A. 1982. Work and Instrumental Action. *New German Critique* 26:31–54.

Hostede, G. 1980. *Culture's Consequences: International Differences in Work-Related Values.* Beverly Hills: Sage.

Illich, I. 1978. *Fortschrittsmythen. Schöpferische Arbeitslosigkeit oder Die Grenzen der Vermarktung.* Reinbek: Rowohlt.

Illich, I. 1979. Das Recht auf schöpferische Arbeitslosigkeit. In *Anders arbeiten—anders wirtschaften,* edited by J. Huber, 79–81. Frankfurt: Fischer.

Jahoda, M. 1983. *Wieviel Arbeit braucht der Mensch? Arbeit und Arbeitslosigkeit im 20. Jahrhundert.* Basel: Beltz.

Kern, H., & M. Schumann. 1980. *Industriearbeit und Arbeiterbewußtsein.* Frankfurt: Suhrkamp.

Kern, H., & M. Schumann. 1983. Arbeit und Sozialcharakter: Alte und neue Konturen. In *Krise der Arbeitsgesellschaft?,* edited by J. Matthes, 353–365. Frankfurt: Suhrkamp.

Kern, H., & M. Schumann. 1984. *Das Ende der Arbeitsteilung. Rationalisierung in der industriellen Produktion.* München: Beck.

Klipstein, M. von, & B. Strümpel, eds. 1985. *Gewandelte Werte—Erstarrte Strukturen. Wie die Bürger Wirtschaft und Arbeit erleben.* Bonn: Verlag Neue Gesellschaft.

Knapp, G. A. 1981. *Industriearbeit und Instrumentalismus. Zur Geschichte eines Vor-Urteils.* Bonn: Verlag Neue Gesellschaft.

Kocka, J., ed. 1981a. *Angestellte im europäischen Vergleich. Die Herausbildung angestellter Mittelschichten seit dem späten 19. Jahrhundert.* Göttingen: Vandenhoeck & Ruprecht.

Kocka, J. 1981b. *Die Angestellten in der deutschen Geschichte 1850–1980.* Göttingen: Vandenhoeck & Ruprecht.

Krappmann, L. 1983. Identität in diskontinuierlichen Berufslaufbahnen. *BeitrAB* 77:179–187.

Maccoby, M., & K. A. Terzi. 1981. What Happened to the Work Ethic? In *The Work Ethic in Business*, edited by W. M. Hoffman & T. J. Wyly, 19–58. Cambridge, Mass.: Oelgeschlager, Gunn & Hain.

Matthes, J., ed. 1983. *Krise der Arbeitsgesellschaft? Verhandlungen des 21. Deutschen Soziologentages in Bamberg 1982.* Frankfurt: Campus.

Meulemann, H. 1987. Bildung, Generationen und die Konjunktur des Wertes Leistung. *Zeitschrift für Soziologie* 16:272–287.

Mickler, O. 1981. *Facharbeit im Wandel. Rationalisierung im industriellen Produktionsprozeß.* Frankfurt: Campus.

Münch, P., ed. 1984. *Ordnung, Fleiß und Sparsamkeit. Texte und Dokumente zur Entstehung der "bürgerlichen Tugenden."* München: Deutscher Taschenbuch Verlag.

Mutz, G. 1987. Arbeitslosigkeit in der Dienstleistungsgesellschaft. *Soziale Welt* 3:255–281.

Namenwirth, Z. J., & R. P. Weber. 1987. *Dynamics of Culture.* Winchester, Mass.: Allen & Unwin.

Noelle-Neumann, E. 1980. *Werden wir alle Proletarier?* Zürich: Edition Interfrom.

Noelle-Neumann, E., & B. Strümpel. 1984. *Macht Arbeit krank? Macht Arbeit glücklich? Eine aktuelle Kontroverse.* München: Piper.

Oevermann, U. 1985. Versozialwissenschaftlichung der Identitätsformation und Verweigerung der Lebenspraxis. Eine aktuelle Variante der Dialektik der Aufklärung. In *Soziologie und gesellschaftliche Entwicklung. 22. Deutscher Soziologentag in Dortmund,* edited by B. Lutz, 463–475. Frankfurt: Campus.

Oevermann, U. 1988. Eine exemplarische Fallanalyse zum Typus versozialwissenschaftlichter Identitätsformation. In *Vom Ende des Individuums zur Individualität ohne Ende,* edited by H. G. Brose & B. Hildenbrand, 243–286. Opladen: Leske & Budrich.

Offe, C. 1983. Arbeit als soziologische Schlüsselkategorie? In *Krise der Arbeitsgesellschaft?,* edited by J. Matthes, 38–65. Frankfurt: Campus.

Offe, C., K. Hinrichs, & H. Wiesenthal, eds. 1982. *Arbeitszeitpolitik: Formen und Folgen einer Neuverteilung der Arbeitszeit.* Frankfurt: Campus.

Pahl, R. E. 1988. *On Work: Historical, Comparative and Theoretical Perspectives.* Oxford: Blackwell.

Pawlowsky, P. 1986. *Arbeitseinstellungen im Wandel. Zur theoretischen Grundlage und empirischen Analyse subjektiver Indikatoren der Arbeitswelt.* München: Minerva Publikation.

Pawlowsky, P., & B. Strümpel. 1986. Arbeit und Wertewandel: Replik. *Kölner Zeitschrift für Soziologie und Sozialpsychologie* 38:772–784.

Pellicani, L. 1988. Weber and the Myth of Calvinism. *Telos* 75:57–85.

Pialoux, M. 1979. Jeunes sans avenir et travail interimaire. *Actes de la recherche en sciences sociales* 5:19–48.

Prescott-Clarke, P. 1982. *Public Attitudes towards Industrial, Work-related and Other Risks.* London: Social and Community Planning Research.

Rammert, W., & C. Wehrsig. 1988. Neue Technologien im Betrieb: Politiken und Strategien betrieblicher Akteure. In *Regulierung—*

Deregulierung. Steuerungsprobleme der Arbeitsgesellschaft, edited by
J. Feldhoff, G. Kühlewind, C. Wehrsig, & H. Wiesenthal, 301–330.
Nürnberg: Institut für Arbeitsmarkt- und Berufsforschung.

Reuband, K. H. 1985. Arbeit und Wertewandel—Mehr Mythos als Realität?
Von sinkender Arbeitszufriedenheit, schwindender Arbeitsethik und
"vergiftetem" Arbeitsleben. *Kölner Zeitschrift für Soziologie und
Sozialpsychologie* 37:723–746.

Reuband, K. H. 1987. Die Arbeitsmoral der Arbeitslosen. Fragwürdige
Deutungen einer empirischen Studie. *Kölner Zeitschrift für Soziologie und
Sozialpsychologie* 39:550–559.

Rosenmayr, L., & F. Kolland, eds. 1988. *Arbeit—Freizeit—Lebenszeit.
Grundlagenforschungen zu Übergängen im Lebenszyklus.* Opladen:
Westdeutscher Verlag.

Schlegelmilch, C. 1983. Arbeitsorientierungen und Lebensperspektiven in
der Grauzone. In *Krise der Arbeitsgesellschaft?*, edited by J. Matthes, 385–
392. Frankfurt: Campus.

Schmidtchen, G. 1984a. *Neue Technik, Neue Arbeitsmoral. Eine sozialpsychologische Untersuchung über die Motivation in der Metallindustrie.* Köln:
Deutscher Instituts-Verlag.

Schmidtchen, G. 1984b. Vorhof zur Hölle? Die Deutschen haben immer
noch Lust zur Arbeit. *Die Zeit,* 23 November 1984, 39.

Soeffner, H. G. 1988. Luther—Der Weg von der Kollektivität des Glaubens
zu einem lutherisch-protestantischen Individualitätstypus. In *Vom Ende
des Individuums zur Individualität ohne Ende,* edited by H. G. Brose &
B. Hildenbrand, 107–149. Opladen: Leske & Budrich.

Strümpel, B., & J. Scholz-Ligma. 1988. Bewußtseins—und sozialer Wandel.
Wie erleben die Menschen die Wirtschaft. In *Wertwandel—Faktum oder
Fiktion?*, edited by H.O. Luthe & H. Meulemann, 21–48. Frankfurt:
Campus.

Tacke, A. 1988. Erwerbswirtschaftliche Alternativen zur Lohnarbeit. In
Regulierung—Deregulierung. Steuerungsprobleme der Arbeitsgesellschaft, edited by J. Feldhoff, G. Kühlewind, C. Wehrsig, & H. Wiesenthal, 245–
260. Nürnberg: Institut für Arbeitsmarkt und Berufsforschung.

Teschner, E., & K. Hermann. 1981. Zur Taylorisierung technischgeistiger
Arbeit. Gesellschaftliche Arbeit und Rationalisierung. *Leviathan-Sonderheft*
4:118–135.

Touraine, A. 1969. *La société postindustrielle.* Paris: Denoël.

Touraine, A. 1977. *The Self-Production of Society.* Chicago: University of Chicago Press.

Touraine, A. 1985a. An Introduction to the Study of Social Movements.
Social Research 52:749–788.

Touraine, A. 1985b. Klassen, soziale Bewegungen und soziale Schichtung in
einer nachindustriellen Gesellschaft. In *Die Analyse sozialer Ungleichheit,*
edited by H. Strasser & J. H. Goldthorpe, 324–338. Opladen:
Westdeutscher Verlag.

Treiber, H., & H. Steinert. 1980. *Die Fabrikation des zuverlässigen Menschen.*

Über die "Wahlverwandtschaft" von Kloster- und Fabrikdisziplin. München: Moos.

Vollmer, R. 1986. *Die Entmythologisierung der Berufsarbeit. Über den sozialen Wandel von Arbeit, Beruf und Freizeit.* Opladen: Westdeutscher Verlag.

Vonderach, G. 1980. Die "neuen Selbständigen." *MittAB* 13:153–169.

Weber, M. 1956. *Wirtschaft und Gesellschaft.* Tübingen: Mohr.

Weber, M. 1965. *Die protestantische Ethik.* Neudruck München: Siebenstern.

Windolf, P. 1984. Formale Bildungsabschlüsse als Selektionskriterium am Arbeitsmarkt. Eine vergleichende Analyse zwischen Frankreich, BRD und Großbritannien. *Kölner Zeitschrift für Soziologie und Sozialpsychologie* 36: 75–106.

Windolf, P., & H. W. Hohn. 1984. *Arbeitsmarktchancen in der Krise. Betriebliche Rekrutierung und soziale Schließung.* Frankfurt: Campus.

Yankelovich, D., H. Zetterberg, B. Strümpel, M. Shanks, J. Immerwahr, & E. Noelle-Neumann. 1985. *The World at Work—An International Report on Jobs Productivity and Human Values.* New York: The Public Agenda Foundation.

Index

Wahlke, J., 222
Wallerstein, I., 208–9
The Wealth of Nations (Smith), 344
Weber, Max: on charismatic personalities, 126–27, 141n.6; comparative historical sociology of, 329–33, 358–59n.5, 359n.6; on cultural coherence, 12; on Protestant ethic, 336, 380–81, 393n.25; rationalization of, 48–49, 265, 293, 294, 296, 301, 377; religion theory of, 298–99, 305–7, 318n.13, 334; on work motives, 326–28, 358n.4
Weiss, Johannes, xi
Weltgeschichtliche Betrachtungen (Burckhardt), 122, 123
Western societies; cultural representation in, 128–29, 130–31, 132–33; "self" as social unit of, 134, 141n.9; symbolism of goods in, 272–73
West Germany. *See* FRG (Federal Republic of Germany)
Whiting, J. W. M., 11
Wiesenthal, H., 382
Wilkins, A. L., 222
Williams, Raymond, 14, 43, 146, 148
Work; and "crisis of work society," 366–68, 390n.2; cultural changes in, 374–78; de-coupled from self-realization, 367, 368–69, 374–75, 377–78, 392nn.17,18; de-coupled from status, 324–25, 348–49, 367, 368, 369, 373–74, 392n.16; dominant in United States, 356, 357, 360n.24, 360–61n.25, 361n.26; ethicization of, 376–77; expanding cognitive, 370–71, 372, 390n.6; instrumentalism of, 375, 383–84, 392nn.19,20; locus for, 324, 325, 343, 347; polarized with nonwork, 372–73, 391n.13; private sphere separate from, 338, 354–55, 356, 357; structural changes in, 369–74, 376–77, 391nn.8–12, 392–93n.21, 393n.22; Max Weber's motives for, 326–28, 358n.4; withdrawal from, 350, 360n.19
Work ethic; Calvinist, 335, 336, 339; Catholic, 380; challenges to, 351–55; Lutheran, 334–35, 346–47, 354, 378–79, 393n.24; new virtues for, 374–75; Protestant, 368–69, 372, 376, 378–85, 390n.5; Prussian, 379; redefined by new social class, 367, 368, 369, 372, 374–75, 376, 385–86, 387, 389–90n.1; Max Weber on, 326–28
Working class; crisis for, 367–68, 389, 390n.3; cultural changes for, 370–71, 372; skilled, 382–83; unskilled, 383–84
Wuthnow, Robert, x, xi

Compositor: Huron Valley Graphics
Text: 10/13 Galliard
Display: Galliard
Printer and Binder: BookCrafters, Inc.